# Monetary Policies and Independence of the Central Banks in E7 Countries

Hasan Dinçer
*İstanbul Medipol University, Turkey*

Serhat Yüksel
*İstanbul Medipol University, Turkey*

A volume in the Advances in Finance, Accounting, and Economics (AFAE) Book Series

IGI Global
DISSEMINATOR OF KNOWLEDGE

Published in the United States of America by
IGI Global
Business Science Reference (an imprint of IGI Global)
701 E. Chocolate Avenue
Hershey PA, USA 17033
Tel: 717-533-8845
Fax: 717-533-8661
E-mail: cust@igi-global.com
Web site: http://www.igi-global.com



Library of Congress Cataloging-in-Publication Data

Names: Dinçer, Hasan, 1982- author. | Yuksel, Serhat, 1983- author.
Title: Monetary policies and independence of the central banks in E7 countries / by Hasan Dinçer and Serhat Yüksel.
Description: Hershey, PA : Business Science Reference, [2020] | Includes bibliographical references and index. | Summary: ""This book examines the effectiveness of the monetary policies and the independence of the central banks in 7 emerging economies"--Provided by publisher"-- Provided by publisher.
Identifiers: LCCN 2019031661 (print) | LCCN 2019031662 (ebook) | ISBN 9781799816430 (hardcover) | ISBN 9781799816447 (paperback) | ISBN 9781799816454 (ebook)
Subjects: LCSH: Monetary policy--Developing countries. | Banks and banking, Central--Developing countries.
Classification: LCC HG1496 .D56 2020 (print) | LCC HG1496 (ebook) | DDC 339.5/3091724--dc23
LC record available at https://lccn.loc.gov/2019031661
LC ebook record available at https://lccn.loc.gov/2019031662

This book is published in the IGI Global book series Advances in Finance, Accounting, and Economics (AFAE) (ISSN: 2327-5677; eISSN: 2327-5685)

British Cataloguing in Publication Data
A Cataloguing in Publication record for this book is available from the British Library.

All work contributed to this book is new, previously-unpublished material.
The views expressed in this book are those of the authors, but not necessarily of the publisher.

For electronic access to this publication, please contact: eresources@igi-global.com.

# Advances in Finance, Accounting, and Economics (AFAE) Book Series

Ahmed Driouchi
Al Akhawayn University, Morocco

ISSN:2327-5677
EISSN:2327-5685

**MISSION**

In our changing economic and business environment, it is important to consider the financial changes occurring internationally as well as within individual organizations and business environments. Understanding these changes as well as the factors that influence them is crucial in preparing for our financial future and ensuring economic sustainability and growth.

The **Advances in Finance, Accounting, and Economics (AFAE)** book series aims to publish comprehensive and informative titles in all areas of economics and economic theory, finance, and accounting to assist in advancing the available knowledge and providing for further research development in these dynamic fields.

**COVERAGE**

- Wages and Employment
- Interest Rates and Annuities
- Auditing
- Comparative Accounting Systems
- Evidence-Based Studies
- Economics of Natural and Environmental Resources
- Economics of Migration and Spatial Mobility
- Development Economics
- Behavioral Economics
- Environmental and Social Accounting

IGI Global is currently accepting manuscripts for publication within this series. To submit a proposal for a volume in this series, please contact our Acquisition Editors at Acquisitions@igi-global.com or visit: http://www.igi-global.com/publish/.

The Advances in Finance, Accounting, and Economics (AFAE) Book Series (ISSN 2327-5677) is published by IGI Global, 701 E. Chocolate Avenue, Hershey, PA 17033-1240, USA, www.igi-global.com. This series is composed of titles available for purchase individually; each title is edited to be contextually exclusive from any other title within the series. For pricing and ordering information please visit http://www.igi-global.com/book-series/advances-finance-accounting-economics/73685. Postmaster: Send all address changes to above address. 

## Titles in this Series

*For a list of additional titles in this series, please visit:*
*https://www.igi-global.com/book-series/advances-finance-accounting-economics/73685*

***Advanced Integrated Approaches to Environmental Economics and Policy Emerging Research and Opportunities***
Sebastiano Patti (University of Catania, Italy) and Giampiero Trizzino (Regional Council of Environment and Territory, Italy)
Business Science Reference • © 2020 • 218pp • H/C (ISBN: 9781522595625) • US $195.00 (our price)

***Networked Business Models in the Circular Economy***
Bogdan Nogalski (WSB University in Gdańsk, Poland) Agnieszka Anna Szpitter (University of Gdańsk, Poland) Adam Jabłoński (WSB University in Poznań, Poland) and Marek Jabłoński (WSB University in Poznań, Poland)
Business Science Reference • © 2020 • 302pp • H/C (ISBN: 9781522578505) • US $205.00 (our price)

***Impact of Financial Technology (FinTech) on Islamic Finance and Financial Stability***
Nader Naifar (Imam Mohammad Ibn Saud Islamic University, Saudi Arabia & University of Sfax, Tunisia)
Business Science Reference • © 2020 • 312pp • H/C (ISBN: 9781799800392) • US $215.00 (our price)

***Transforming Businesses With Bitcoin Mining and Blockchain Applications***
Dharmendra Singh Rajput (VIT University, India) Ramjeevan Singh Thakur (Maulana Azad National Institute of Technology Bhopal, India) and Syed Muzamil Basha (Sri Krishna College of Engineering and Technology, India)
Business Science Reference • © 2020 • 282pp • H/C (ISBN: 9781799801863) • US $215.00 (our price)

***Sharing Economy and the Impact of Collaborative Consumption***
Iviane Ramos de Luna (Open University of Catalonia, Spain) Àngels Fitó-Bertran (Open University of Catalonia, Spain) Josep Lladós-Masllorens (Open University of Catalonia, Spain) and Francisco Liébana-Cabanillas (University of Granada, Spain)
Business Science Reference • © 2020 • 323pp • H/C (ISBN: 9781522599289) • US $245.00 (our price)

IGI Global
DISSEMINATOR OF KNOWLEDGE

701 East Chocolate Avenue, Hershey, PA 17033, USA
Tel: 717-533-8845 x100 • Fax: 717-533-8661
E-Mail: cust@igi-global.com • www.igi-global.com

# Table of Contents

# Preface

There are eight different chapters in this book. In the first chapter, the mechanism of the financial system is defined. Within this scope, fund demanders, fund suppliers and financial instruments are defined. In the second chapter, financial intermediaries are identified. In this framework, necessary information is given related to the banks and nonbanking financial institutions.

In the third chapter, the role of the central banks in the financial system is discussed. In this framework, necessary information is given related to the need for the central bank, the subject of central bank independence and analytical balance sheet of the central bank. On the other hand, the fourth chapter includes monetary policy operations of the central banks. In this context, first of all, monetary policy instruments of the central banks are defined that are required reserve ratio, rediscount rate, open market operations, standing facilities and asset purchase program. In addition to them, monetary policies of E7 economies are also identified. For this purpose, some macroeconomic information of these countries is also shared.

In the fifth chapter, data and methodology are defined. In this framework, methodological information for fuzzy DEMATEL, fuzzy TOPSIS, fuzzy VIKOR, Kao panel cointegration, Pedroni panel cointegration and Dumitrescu Hurlin panel causality analyses is given. In addition to them, the sixth chapter includes the application related to the effectiveness of the central bank policies is measured with the help of fuzzy logic. In this context, five different monetary policy instruments are defined as the criteria. In addition to them, E7 countries are selected as the alternatives. Fuzzy DEMATEL methodology is taken into consideration to weight the criteria according to their importance. Furthermore, fuzzy TOPSIS and fuzzy VIKOR approaches are used in order to rank the alternatives related to the monetary policy effectiveness.

In the sixth chapter, it is aimed to understand whether central banks of E7 economies implement effective monetary policies or not. The main difference of this study in comparison with the previous one is that Kao panel cointegration, Pedroni panel cointegration and Dumitrescu Hurlin panel causality analyses are considered in the analysis process. Two different variables are selected for this purpose. Central bank interest rates represent the monetary policies whereas inflation rate gives information about the purpose of these central banks.

In the last chapter, independence of the central banks in E7 countries is evaluated. In this framework, 5 different criteria are defined for the independence of the central banks with the help of detailed literature review. In addition to this issue, E7 countries are chosen as the alternatives. These criteria are weighted with the help of fuzzy DEMATEL approach. On the other side, fuzzy TOPSIS and fuzzy VIKOR methods are taken into consideration so as to rank E7 countries. By using two different methodology for this purpose, it is aimed to make a comparative analysis.

This book has some significant novelties in comparison with similar books. Most of the books related to the central bank application do not have an analysis part. However, in this book three different analyses are performed in addition to the theoretical information. Another important novelty is that two analyses are made by using fuzzy logic and one analysis is performed with econometric models. Therefore, it shows that analyses are made by considering both expert opinions and quantitative information. Additionally, effectiveness of the monetary policies and independence of the E7 economies are firstly discusses by using fuzzy logic and econometric methods in this book.

In addition to these items, in this book, some important analysis results and recommendations are presented. It is believed that they are very helpful for academicians and practitioners in the market. By considering these results and recommendations, significant strategies can be developed to have more effective central bank and financial system. Therefore, it can be possible improve macroeconomic conditions of these countries. Hence, it is thought that this book makes important contribution to the literature.

Target Audience and potential users of this book are defined below.

- Researchers
- Academicians
- Policy Makers
- Government Officials
- Upright Students in the concerned fields
- Members of Chambers of Commerce and Industry
- Top managers of the companies

*Hasan Dinçer*
*Istanbul Medipol University, Turkey*

*Serhat Yüksel*
*Istanbul Medipol University, Turkey*

# Acknowledgment

The authors would like to acknowledge the help and patience of their families in this book process. Without their support, this book would not have become a reality.

Second, the authors wish to acknowledge the valuable contributions of the reviewers regarding the improvement of quality, coherence, and content presentation of chapters.

*Hasan Dinçer*
*Istanbul Medipol University, Turkey*

*Serhat Yüksel*
*Istanbul Medipol University, Turkey*

# Introduction

The main purpose of all countries is to reach economic development. With the help of this situation, it can be possible to provide high living standards for their citizens. Therefore, many different actions are taken by the governments so as to reach this objective. In this framework, increasing the effectiveness in the financial system can be very helpful to contribute economic development of the countries.

There are many different players in the financial system, such as fund demanders, fund suppliers, financial intermediaries, financial instruments, financial authorities. Hence, in order to provide an effective financial system, all these players should work successfully to perform the financial functions in an effective way. Thus, economic development of the countries can be provided much easier.

Globalization causes many different risks for both companies and countries. In the first aspect, higher international trade volume has an increasing effect on the volatility in the currency exchange rates. This situation creates a significant risk for the countries in case of having foreign debt. It shows that there is a strong need for a governmental authority that can control this process. With the help of this institution, a destructive financial crisis can be prevented.

Central bank is the financial authority in the globalized financial system that can play a very key role to increase investment amount in the country by controlling inflation and interest rates. Furthermore, some actions can also be taken by the central bank to decrease the currency exchange rate volatility. These strategies can be very helpful to prevent bankruptcies of the companies and financial crisis in the country.

Central banks are the main authority to define interest rates and the amount of the money in the financial system. Moreover, assisting the development of the financial system is another responsibility of the central banks. This situation increases the power of the central banks because the actions of central banks have been a guide for other players on the market. However, central banks have been open to interventions by political authorities in carrying out these important tasks.

In order to work effectively, central banks should be independent. With the help of this issue, it is possible to prevent the populist practices of political power. Hence, central bank independence is a crucial factor for the sustainable economic development of the countries. This independence should be occurred with respect to the purpose and instrument, economic and political.

With respect to the purpose and instrument independence, central banks should be independent in the selection of the main objectives or targets taken as basis in the policies. On the other side, regarding economic independence, there should not be any relationship between central bank and government with respect to the economic issues. Similarly, as for political independence, top management level of central banks can be independent from the government. Thus, selection of top managers should be outside of the government interventions.

In addition to the independence, monetary policies play a very significant role for the success of the central banks. Monetary policy usually deals with interest rates and control of money supply. Therefore, in this framework, central banks aim to take some actions to reach their objectives by changing interest rates or the amount of money in the market. Within this context, there are mainly five different monetary policy tools which are required reserve ratio, rediscount rate, open market operations, standing facilities and asset purchase program.

Parallel to the aspects emphasized above, in this study, it is aimed to evaluate the effectiveness of the monetary policies and the independence of the central banks. Within this scope, emerging 7 economies (E7) are taken into consideration which are Brazil, China, India, Indonesia, Mexico, Russia and Turkey. In the implementation process, three different analysis are performed. In this circumstance, fuzzy DEMATEL, fuzzy TOPSIS, fuzzy VIKOR, Kao panel cointegration, Pedroni panel cointegration and Dumitrescu Hurlin panel causality analyses are considered.

*Hasan Dinçer*
*Istanbul Medipol University, Turkey*

*Serhat Yüksel*
*Istanbul Medipol University, Turkey*

# Introduction

This book aims to evaluate the effectiveness of the monetary policies and the independence of the central banks. For this purpose, emerging 7 economies (Brazil, China, India, Indonesia, Mexico, Russia and Turkey) are taken into consideration. Three different analyses are performed in this book to reach this objective. In these analyses, six different methodologies are used that are fuzzy DEMATEL, fuzzy TOPSIS, fuzzy VIKOR, Kao panel cointegration, Pedroni panel cointegration and Dumitrescu Hurlin panel causality analyses.

Hence, this book includes four different sections. The first section is related to the definition of the mechanism of the financial system. Fund demanders, fund suppliers, financial instruments, financial intermediaries, and nonbanking financial institutions are explained in this section. On the other side, the role of the central banks in the financial system is discussed in the second section. Additionally, the third part includes monetary policy operations of the central banks and the details of the monetary policies in E7 economies.

The final part is related to the applications on the central banking in E7 economies. In this context, three different analyses are performed in this book. In the first analysis, effectiveness of the central bank policies is measured with the help of fuzzy logic (fuzzy DEMATEL, fuzzy TOPSIS, fuzzy VIKOR). Another analysis for this framework is also made by using econometric models (Kao panel cointegration, Pedroni panel cointegration and Dumitrescu Hurlin panel causality analyses) in the second analysis. In the third analysis, independence of the central banks in E7 countries is evaluated under the fuzzy environment.

This book has some significant novelties in comparison with similar books. Most of the books related to the central bank application do not have an analysis part. However, in this book three different analyses are performed in addition to the theoretical information. Another important novelty is that two analyses are made by using fuzzy logic and one analysis is performed with econometric models. Therefore, it shows that analyses are made by considering both expert opinions and quantitative information. Additionally, effectiveness of the monetary policies and independence of the E7 economies are firstly discusses by using fuzzy logic and econometric methods in this book.

The analysis results of this book give very important information for the central banks. These results show the possible ways to have more effective central bank and financial system. In addition to this situation, some significant recommendations are provided according to these analysis results. Therefore, it is believed that they are very helpful for academicians and practitioners in the market. Thus, it is thought that this book makes important contribution to the literature.

*Hasan Dinçer*
*Istanbul Medipol University, Turkey*

*Serhat Yüksel*
*Istanbul Medipol University, Turkey*

# Chapter 1
# The Mechanism of Financial System


## ABSTRACT

*Financial systems bring fund demanders and fund suppliers together. Therefore, with the help of these systems, fund suppliers can earn interest income by using their savings. On the other hand, fund demanders can find money they need so that they can make their investments more easily. Since the investment increase leads to higher GDP, it can be said that effective financial systems make an important contribution to the economic improvement of the countries. Therefore, to provide recommendations to have more effective financial systems, the mechanism of the financial system should be understood appropriately. Hence, in this chapter, firstly, general information about the financial system is given. After that, different fund demanders and suppliers are explained. In the final part, financial instruments are identified.*


## GENERAL INFORMATION ABOUT FINANCIAL SYSTEM

Each country aims to reach economic improvement. The main reason behind this condition is that with the developed economy, countries can provide high living standards for their citizens. Owing to this situation, countries try to take many different actions in order to achieve this objective (Yüksel, Dincer, & Hacioglu, 2015). For example, giving incentives, such as decreasing tax is an example action for this aspect. In addition to the incentives, countries should also increase the effectiveness in the financial system to contribute economic development (Nica and Potcovaru, 2015).

DOI: 10.4018/978-1-7998-1643-0.ch001

In the countries, there are some parties that have some savings and they aim to earn some money with these savings. At the same time, there are also some other parties that need the money and their main objective is to satisfy this need easily. As it can be seen, it is very difficult for these parties to reach others. Therefore, it is obvious that there should be a mechanism that brings these two different parties together. Owing to this issue, it has a contributing effect on the improvement of the economy (Komal and Abbas, 2015).

Financial system refers to this mechanism that plays a key role to bring the parties who have saving and need money together. It is defined that there are many different players in the financial system, such as fund demanders, fund suppliers, financial intermediaries, financial instruments, financial authorities (Galaz et al., 2015; Ersin and Eti, 2017). Therefore, financial system can also be defined as the framework that includes all these players to perform the financial functions in an effective way. For example, financial intermediaries should work effectively to provide fund flow and regulations should be designed to prevent any problems in this system (Valickova et al., 2015).

While considering the aspects emphasized above, it can be understood that effective financial system has a significant role in the development of the economy. The main factor is that with the effective financial system, parties can earn money by using their savings (Dincer, Hacioglu, & Yuksel, 2016a,b). At the same time, companies can increase their investment with the fund provided from fund suppliers. Owing to the new investment, they can employ new people in the countries which has a decreasing effect on unemployment (Kumar, 2017; Eti, 2019).

## FUND DEMANDERS

Fund demanders refers to the parties that have some purposes, but they do not have enough money in order to achieve this objective (Wang and Yang, 2016). Therefore, they demand money from the outside for this purpose. As it can be understood fund demanders play a significant role in the financial system. When their needs can be satisfied in this market, it contributes the development of the economy in the country. In other words, if the funds can be allocated to the fund demanders effectively, it has an increasing effect on the investment amount. Thus, this situation leads to lower unemployment rate in the countries. Fund demanders can be individuals, companies or government and they are explained detailed in the following subtitles.

## Individuals

Individuals can be fund demanders in many different ways. First of all, they aim to start a new business. In other words, they think that they can earn a significant amount of income with their entrepreneurial spirit. However, they may not have enough money in order to reach this objective. In this circumstance, they demand money from third parties. Hence, it is obvious that by having an effective working financial system, the individuals, who aim to start business, can reach the money easily and it has a contributing factor on investment in the countries (Naczyk and Hassel, 2019).

In addition to the individuals who aim to start a new business, there may also some individuals that need money to satisfy their personal needs. For example, some individuals aim to become the owner of a house, but they may not have enough money for this purpose. Moreover, some other individuals may want to purchase new furniture. As it can be seen they demand this money from the financial intermediaries. In this case, the funds coming from fund suppliers can satisfy the needs of these individuals (Muda, 2017; Li et al., 2019).

## Companies

All companies need money due to some different reasons. First of all, they need money in order to satisfy their operational needs, such as paying the salaries of the employees, rent and the bills. In addition to these factors, companies also need money so as to increase their liquidity powers. Liquidity risk gives information about the situation in which the companies do not have enough liquid assets when it is necessary (Zengin and Yüksel, 2016; Yüksel, 2016). In this case, the companies cannot pay their debts and this condition may result in the bankruptcy of these companies. Therefore, all companies prefer to have some liquid assets in order to prevent this kind of problem.

In addition to these aspects, companies need money to increase their investment amount. The main purpose of all companies is to increase their profitability. For this purpose, companies try to take actions, such as decreasing cost or increasing revenues (Maskell et al., 2016). Therefore, it can be seen that companies want to make new investments so as to increase the sales revenue. This condition has a contributing effect on the profitability of the companies by increasing the sales amount. By considering the issues emphasized above, it can be seen that investment purpose is the main factor of the companies to need money. In other saying, with the purpose of increasing investments, the companies can be significant fund demanders (He, 2017; Rodriguez-Fernandez, 2016).

## Government

The main role of the governments is to save independence of the countries against the third parties. In addition to this issue, governments should make some investment so as to increase the living standards of the citizens. For example, making bridge, building a metro line are the services of the governments with the aim of increasing the comfort of the people who live in the country. Thus, it is seen that governments should also take role in the subject of the economy (Berger et al., 2019).

The main income of the governments is the tax collected from the citizens of the country. On the other hand, governments have also some expenses, such as salaries of the civil servants. Moreover, there are also some operational expenses of governmental institutions like electricity and water bills. Furthermore, there can also be government expenditures, such as building bridges and metro lines. Hence, it is defined that governments should give importance to making budget (Nahar et al., 2018).

Within this scope, if the income of the governments is lower than the expenses, it means that governments need money. For this purpose, governments can take some actions. For instance, governments issue a bond in order to reach the money they need. Investors in the market prefer to purchase this bond in order to earn interest income. Because of this process, governments can collect money from them. As it can be seen, government can be a very important fund demander in the market (Jianjun and Xun, 2016; Dobuzinskis, 2019).

# FUND SUPPLIERS

Fund suppliers refer to the parties that have some savings in the country. These parties mainly aim to earn some income by using this money. The main reason behind this situation is that without making an investment, the saving amount will lose its value because of the inflation problem which is defined as the increase in the level of the prices of the goods and services.

Because inflation problem is occurred almost all of the countries in the world, people who have savings seek the alternatives to save the value of their savings (Adhikary and Kutsuna, 2016; Liu, 2019).

There are many different ways of using these savings. First of all, people can start a new business with this saving. However, this situation contains many different risks. For example, there may be credit risk that means that the counterparty may not pay its debt to the company. In addition to the credit risk, while starting a new business, the company can be subject to liquidity risk which refers that the company cannot have enough liquid items when it is necessary. Furthermore, the company can have operational risk because of natural disasters or problems caused by employees (Zengin and Yüksel, 2016; Dinçer, Hacıoğlu, & Yüksel, 2017; Manova, 2015).

Because of these conditions, some people may be reluctant to open a new business and seek for other opportunities to reach this objective. As an example, these parties can prefer to make investment in financial instruments by using these savings (Hou et al., 2018; Holland, 2019). The main reason is that financial investment is thought to be less risky in comparison with starting a new business. Hence, the parties can purchase marketable securities, such as government bonds and stocks. In other words, these parties can play a fund supplier role in the financial system (Block et al., 2017).

As it is emphasized before, there are fund demanders in the financial market who have some purpose, but they do not have enough money to achieve their aims. Because they demand this money from the financial market, this situation gives a chance to the fund suppliers to earn income. Within this framework, fund suppliers can have interest or dividend income according to the type of the financial instruments they made investment (Xu et al., 2019). These fund suppliers can be individuals, companies and government which are detailed in the following subtitles.

## Individuals

In the previous part, it is underlined that individuals can be fund demanders due to many different reasons, such as starting a new business or satisfying their personal needs. In addition to this aspect, individuals in the country may be also fund suppliers. When individuals have some savings, they aim to assess this amount in order to increase their wealth. For example, they may start a new business in order to achieve this objective. However, starting a new business contains many different risks and it is a process that requires specialization in some subjects. Due to this condition, some individuals do not prefer to start a new business (Hosseini and Owlia, 2016).

On the other side, the individuals, who do not want to start a new business, can assess their savings in the financial market. As an example, they may purchase government bonds or put this money to the banks as deposits in order to earn interest income (Yüksel, Dinçer and Emir, 2017). Moreover, these individuals may also prefer to make investment in company stocks so that they can get a chance to have dividend income. As it can be understood from these examples, there is an alternative for individuals to make investment in financial instruments. In this circumstance, these individuals are named as fund suppliers.

## Companies

Companies can have some savings and make investment in the financial instruments. There are many different reasons for the companies to prefer financial investments instead of the investment in their core operations. First of all, they may decide to wait for the correct time to make investment in their core operations. In this process, the main factor may be the expectations about the market. For example, if the companies expect that there will be high inflation rate, they may be anxious to increase their investment. Hence, their saving amount increases, and they prefer to investment in financial instruments

Another important reason for the companies to make financial investment is that they opt for having higher liquidity power. Since the liquidity risk is very dangerous for the companies and may cause bankruptcy if it cannot be managed effectively, companies can sometimes aim to increase liquid assets. Financial instruments refer to the assets that can be converted into the liquid in a very short time. Hence, it can be seen that financial instruments are appropriate alternatives for the companies to use their savings (Haslem, 2015).

As it can be understood, companies can be fund suppliers in the financial system due to the reasons underlined above. When they prefer to make investment in the financial instruments, it means that the fund amount for fund demander increases. In other words, it is identified that companies play a significant role in the effectiveness of the financial system because they have a contributing effect on the increase in the liquidity level in the financial market.

## Government

As it is stated before, taxes collected from the citizens are named as income of the government whereas government expenditures, such as building a bridge and salaries of civil servants refer to the expenses. If taxes are lower than the expenses, it means that this government has budget deficit. On the other side, in case of the situation in which incomes exceed the expenses, it identifies that government has budget surplus. This condition gives information that government has some savings (Yüksel and Özsarı, 2017). Therefore, it is obvious that government should assess this money so as to increase efficiency. In other words, governments can become fund suppliers in the financial system when they have budget surplus (Block et al., 2017).

# FINANCIAL INSTRUMENTS

Financial instruments refer to the assets that can be traded in the financial system. It can be understood from this definition is that financial instruments have an important contribution on fund flow in this system. In other words, with the help of these instruments, it can be possible to reach the savings of fund suppliers to the fund demanders. Owing to this condition, it is obvious that they should be developed according to the needs and expectations of fund demanders and fund suppliers (Linnerooth-Bayer and Hochrainer-Stigler, 2015).

Financial instruments have many important benefits for the effectiveness of the financial system. Firstly, they increase the liquidity amount in the market. With the help of financial instruments, it can be much easier to provide fund flow. In addition to this issue, financial instruments have a positive influence on the effectiveness of the players in the financial market. they are the assets that can be converted into the cash easily. Due to this aspect, it is seen that financial instruments also increase the liquidity power of the individuals and companies.

Financial instruments can be classifier into different categories with respect to some aspects. For example, they can be named as money market instruments or capital market instruments according to the maturity. For instance, if the maturity of a financial asset is lower than 1 year, it is named as money market instrument. On the other side, in case of the maturity that exceeds one-year, financial instruments are called as capital market instruments. In the following subtitles, different types of the financial instruments are explained.

## Time Deposit

Fund suppliers can prefer to give their saving to the banks. This money is named as deposits. If fund suppliers do not give any promise to the banks about holding time of the money about bank accounts, it is called as normal deposit. Fund suppliers can withdraw this money any time, but there is no interest income for these deposits. As it can be seen that this type of deposit is 100% cash for the fund suppliers (Ismail et al., 2016).

On the other hand, fund suppliers can make a contract with the banks and promise that they will not withdraw their money until maturity defined between fund suppliers and the banks. This type of deposit is called as time deposit. By using time deposit, fund suppliers can get a chance to earn interest income. Moreover, fund suppliers can also withdraw their money before the maturity date. However, in this circumstance, they cannot get interest payment from the banks because of not fulfilling their promises (Dinçer and Yüksel, 2018; Yüksel et al., 2018).

## T-bills and Bonds

When government have budget deficits, they should take an action to find necessary money. One significant way to reach this objective is to issue Treasury bills which are also named as T-bills. The significant difference of T-bills is that they have a maturity lower than 1 year. In this process, the governments issue these bills and fund supplier prefer to purchase them. By making these operations, governments can reach their objectives. On the other side, the main benefit of the fund suppliers is getting coupon payment on specific dates (Fontana and Scheicher, 2016).

In addition to T-bills, government can also issue government bonds that have the maturity more than 1 year. Hence, it is a long-term financial instrument in comparison with T-bills. Therefore, if the fund suppliers aim to make long term investment, they will prefer to get government bond instead of T-bills. Because governments issue T-bills and government bonds, these financial instruments are accepted as risk free investments. In other words, it is thought that they provide lower income, but they contain lower risks.

Furthermore, companies may also need some money in addition to the governments due to many different reasons, such as paying debt or salaries of the employees. Issuing bonds can be the significant alternative for these companies in order to achieve this objective. In other words, companies can sell their bonds and have necessary money. Although the situation is very similar with government bonds, in this case, it is named as company bonds because of the issuing parties. Therefore, company bonds should provide higher income because they contain greater risks in comparison with the government bonds.

## Stocks

In addition to the company bonds, selling the stocks is another alternative for the companies to reach the money necessary for them. In this process, they sell some portion of their equity to the investors. In this case, investors can have a chance to earn dividend income at the end of the year if the companies have profit. In other words, the companies share some portion of their profit to the stock owners according to the stock ratio of the investors. Another important benefit for this situation to the investors is that they can decrease their financial risks by purchasing various stocks of the companies from different sectors (Revelli and Viviani, 2015).

Stocks have many differences in comparison with the other financial instruments. For instance, investors do not have any guarantee to have income when they purchase stocks. They can get dividend income if the companies declare profit. This means that in case of any loss situation of the companies, investors cannot earn any dividend income. At the same time, the value of these stocks may decrease due to the financial problems of the companies. However, when investors prefer to purchase bonds, it is known that they can get coupon payment on certain periods.

Another important difference of the stocks by comparing with other financial instruments is that they give ownership right to the investors. In other words, investors become the owner of the companies according to the ratio of their stocks. Owing to these aspects, investors can vote and take a please in management of the companies. Nevertheless, while purchasing company bonds, investors cannot have any rights regarding the ownership, such as voting power.

## Loans

Loans are also accepted as the significant financial instruments in the financial system. They refer to the money given by the banks to the companies or individuals as a debt. In some periods defined by customers and the banks, customers have to make some payments (Dinçer et al., 2019). As it is emphasized before in this study, there can be different types of the loans, such as installment loans and non-cash loans (Yüksel, 2017a,b; Tunay and Yüksel, 2017). With respect to the installment loans, banks can get a chance to earn interest income. Moreover, banks can also earn commission income in case of giving non-cash loans. As it can be understood that loans play a crucial role in the financial system regarding the effectiveness of the fund flow (Rostamkalaei and Freel, 2016; Yüksel and Zengin, 2016).

## Foreign Exchanges

Foreign exchanges are also the financial instruments that can be preferred by many different players in the financial system. Especially after the globalization, it can be said that financial borders among the countries almost disappeared. This situation has an increasing effect on international trade. Although this condition has many different advantages for the parties, it leads to higher currency risk for them. For example, investors can have a loss when they make investment on the domestic currencies because of losing value in comparison with the foreign currencies.

In spite of the advantages, making investment on foreign exchanges also include some risks for the parties. Because of the changes in the market conditions, there may be radical increase or decrease in currency exchange rates. This situation may lead to significant amount of loss for the players in the financial market. For example, if fund demanders have a debt in foreign currency, it may cause important financial problems for them in case of depreciation. On the other hand, fund suppliers, who invested in foreign exchanges, may be in a loss situation when there is a decrease in the value of them (Salisu and Ayinde, 2016).

## Repurchase Agreements

Repurchase agreements are also called as "REPO". It is a type of financial product that has a contract in which a security is sold, but it will be repurchased again in a future date. In other words, although a party sells this security, it will be repurchased by this party again according to the terms in the contract. As it can be understood that the main reason of the repurchase agreement is to provide short term fund to the parties which have securities (McVea, 2017).

When people or companies need money in a very short term, they do not have many opportunities to satisfy their needs. If they apply the banks, the process may not be finished in a short time because of the procedures in the bank. In such a situation, if they have securities, these parties can have chance to find this money without getting loan from the banks. These parties can get some debt from some others by selling the securities. However, they do not want to lose the interest income which will be earned at the maturity date of the securities.

In this circumstance, they can make an agreement with counterparties about this debt process. According to this agreement, these people will sell the securities and they will repurchase in a future day again. This situation is called as repurchase agreement. With the help of this financial product, these people can find money immediately. The counterparties also have a chance to earn interest because they give debt. Another important advantage of repurchase agreement is that the counterparties have securities as a guarantee until taking their money back. If the parties cannot pay their debt amount, the counterparties can eliminate the loss by converting the marketable securities into cash.

## Derivatives

As it is stated in the previous titles, there is an important increase in the financial risk for the parties especially after the globalization, such as interest rate risk, liquidity risk and currency risk. It is also seen that these risks can cause crucial problems for these parties when they cannot be managed effectively. For example, in the last 20 years, there were many different financial crises all over the world. Another important issue is that these crises were occurred not only in developing economies but also in developed countries (Yüksel and Zengin, 2016a,b; Oktar and Yüksel, 2015; Oktar and Yüksel, 2016; Dinçer, Yüksel, & Şenel, 2018). Because they have an important influence on other countries, it can be said that some actions should be taken in order to prevent these financial crises, such as managing the risks (Blanco and Wehrheim, 2017).

Derivatives are the financial instruments that can be used in order to manage risks. They refer to the financial assets in which a good or cash flow is bought for a future date with a pre-determined price and amount. In other words, with respect to the derivatives, two different parties make a contract about purchasing an asset in a future date. However, the price, amount and maturity are defined at the contract date. With the help of derivatives, parties can get a chance to fix the prices of an asset. Therefore, these parties can protect themselves against any increase in the prices of the goods.

There are three main reasons of using derivatives. As it can be understood from the previous explanations, hedging is the most preferred reason of derivatives. It means that parties mainly use derivatives to manage the risks, such as currency risk, liquidity risk and interest rate risk. In addition to the hedging, derivatives can also be used for the speculative purposes. Within this framework, parties prefer to use derivatives in order to get income from the changes in the price of the product. The final reason of using derivatives is the arbitrage. In other words, by using derivatives with arbitrage purpose, parties aim to purchase an asset at a lower price in a market and sell this asset with a higher price in different markets (Donohoe, 2015).

While considering these aspects, it can be understood that derivatives have an important contribution on the improvement of the financial system. For example, parties in the financial system can manage their risks more effectively by using these instruments. Thus, their default risks can be minimized, and this situation increases the profitability of these parties. Another important contribution of the derivatives to the financial system is that it has an increasing effect on the liquidity in the financial system. The main reason behind this situation is that while generating derivatives, alternative financial instruments in the market for the investors increase. This situation has a significant contribution on the liquidity amount in the financial system which plays a key role for the improvement of the economy.

In spite of the advantages, it is accepted that derivative products contain important risks for both investors and the effectiveness of the financial system. Because derivatives are complex financial instruments, parties may have difficulties to understand the meaning behind them. Therefore, these products, which are not clearly understood by some investors, can be used with strategies that are not suitable for their purposes. This situation may cause high amount of losses for these parties. In addition to this issue, it is thought that derivative usage with speculative purposes can cause losses for the investors if they take high amount of risks in this process. This condition has a negative impact on the effectiveness of the financial system. There are four different types of the derivatives which are forward, future, swap and options which are explained in the following subtitles.

## Forward

Forward contracts are transactions where the price and amount of a good are determined today. However, this good is foreseen to be delivered to the buyer at a later date which is called as maturity date. There is no standard in forward contracts. In other words, the parties signing the contract are free to determine the terms of the contract, such as price, quantity and maturity. Another important point is that forward contracts are made at over-the-counter markets. Because of this situation, it can be said that there is no guarantee of a third party or institution in these contracts (Yılmaz and Aslan, 2016).

There are three different types of forward contracts: foreign exchange, interest and commodity forward contracts. A foreign exchange forward contract refers to the foreign exchange purchase or sale agreement in which the exchange of foreign and domestic currency will be occurred at a future date with a specified exchange rate (Dinçer, Hacıoğlu and Yüksel, 2018). It is obvious that parties can get a chance to manage volatility in the foreign exchange rates. In addition to the foreign exchange forward contract, interest forward contracts are contracts to make a payment on a certain date in the future with a predetermined principal and interest rate. Moreover, in the commodity forward contracts, the price and quantity of a commodity is determined from today. However, the exchange of the money and the commodity will be made in a future date according to the conditions defined today. Hence, the investors can hedge the risk caused by the price increase in this commodity.

## Future

Future contracts are standard contracts that express the obligation to purchase or sell at a future date with a fixed price and quantity of a good. While considering this definition, it can be understood that forward and future contracts are very similar to each other. The main difference of future contract is that future contracts are bought and sold on organized market which is called as stock exchange. Also, in future contracts, every detail, such as maturity, price and quantity are defined by stock exchange. Therefore, it can be said that there is no flexibility in these contracts (Marthinsen, 2018).

Because stock exchange gives guarantee if one of the parties does not follow the rules, it implements some strategies in order not to have loss. For example, each party gives some amount of money to the stock exchange as collateral at the beginning which is named as initial margin. In addition to this condition, stock exchange also follows the position of the parties every day so as to understand the amount of profit or loss for these parties. This following process is called as mark to market (MTM).

In this analysis, if it is realized that the loss amount of one of these parties exceed a level, the stock exchange wants this party to increase collateral amount. The process of demanding extra collateral is called as margin call and this extra collateral amount is also named as maintenance margin. If the party does not fulfill this request, the forward contract is stopped, and the loss amount is given to the other party by using the initial margin. As it can be seen that stock exchange always keep itself in a secured position with the initial and maintenance margin. Similar to the forward contract, future contracts can be formed in different ways, such as foreign exchange, interest and commodity future contracts (Miron et al., 2016).

## Swap

Swap transactions are the process of exchanging cash flows of financial assets between two parties in a future date under predetermined conditions (Oktar and Yüksel, 2016). It means that in swap contracts, debts belonging to different parties are exchanged. Swap contracts are generally traded on over-the-counter markets. However, in recent years there have been swap contracts that are also traded on organized markets. The main requirement of the swap contract is that parties should have different type of the debts (Kahalé, 2017).

There are different types of the swap contracts, such as foreign exchange, interest rate and cross currency swaps. With respect to the foreign exchange swap contracts (FX Swap), two different sides are obliged to change their debts in different types of foreign exchange at the moment of the contract and to return them back in a future date. In other words, one party is afraid of increase in currency exchange rate because he has a debt in this currency. However, other party does not have any worries of this situation. Therefore, they make an FX swap contract in order to decrease their risk according to their expectations (Fries and Kohl-Landgraf, 2018).

On the other hand, regarding interest rate swap contracts (IRS), the two sides mutually exchange interest payments or revenues. As it can be understood from this definition that two parties have different interest payments, such as fixed and variable. The party, which has variable interest payment, is worried that interest rate can go up because their debt will increase in such a situation. Nonetheless, the counterparty does not have this kind of expectations. Consequently, these parties make IRS in order to satisfy their needs. In addition to them, there is also cross currency swap contracts (CCS) which is the combination of foreign currency and interest rate swaps.

### Options

Option contracts are contracts that give the contract purchaser the right to purchase or sell a financial asset in the future with a predetermined price and at a predetermined date. The main difference of the option contracts from the other derivatives is that they give usage right to the parties that have the option. As it can be seen that there are two different parties in the option contract, which are buyers and sellers. Buyers are the parties that purchase the option form the seller. In this process, buyers make a payment to the sellers for this option which is called as option premium. Therefore, by having the option, the buyers have the right to use the option or not at the maturity. On the other side, the sellers of the option have to comply with the decisions of the buyers (Hudson, 2017).

The buyers of the option cannot take the option premium back even they do not use the option. Therefore, the maximum amount of the loss for the buyers in the option contract can be option premium. On the other side, the maximum loss of the option sellers in unlimited. Parallel to the issue mentioned above, the maximum profit of the buyers of the option is unlimited. However, the maximum profit for the sellers is limited to the option premium. Option contracts can be processed at the organized markets or over-the-counter markets (Shcherbakov & Larsson, 2016).

There are different types of the option contracts. In European type options, the party that bought the option can only use the right at the due date. On the other side, the buyers can use the option right any time until the maturity in American options. Also, in Asian options, option price is not certain until the maturity date. It is calculated as the average of all prices in this period.

## CONCLUSION

In this chapter, it is aimed to explain the mechanism of the financial system. In this framework, firstly, we gave the definition of the finance. Additionally, the importance of the financial system was also underlined. In addition to them, the role of different players in the financial system was also identified. On the other side, necessary information was given with respect to the financial instruments. It is concluded that there is a strong need for an institution that controls monetary policy of the country so that it can be more possible to reach more effective financial system.

## REFERENCES

Adhikary, B., & Kutsuna, K. (2016). Small Business Finance in Bangladesh: Can'Crowdfunding'Be an Alternative? *Review of Integrative Business and Economics Research*, *4*, 1–21.

Berger, A. N., Roman, R. A., & Sedunov, J. (2019). Did TARP reduce or increase systemic risk? The effects of government aid on financial system stability. *Journal of Financial Intermediation*, 100810. doi:10.1016/j.jfi.2019.01.002

Blanco, I., & Wehrheim, D. (2017). The bright side of financial derivatives: Options trading and firm innovation. *Journal of Financial Economics*, *125*(1), 99–119. doi:10.1016/j.jfineco.2017.04.004

Block, J. H., Cumming, D. J., & Vismara, S. (2017). International perspectives on venture capital and bank finance for entrepreneurial firms. *Economia e Politica Industriale*, *44*(1), 3–22. doi:10.100740812-017-0069-6

Dincer, H., Hacioglu, U., & Yuksel, S. (2016a). Balanced scorecard-based performance assessment of Turkish banking sector with analytic network process. *International Journal of Decision Sciences & Applications-IJDSA*, *1*(1), 1–21.

Dincer, H., Hacioglu, U., & Yuksel, S. (2016b). Performance assessment of deposit banks with CAMELS analysis using fuzzy ANP-moora approaches and an application on Turkish banking sector. *Asian Journal of Research in Business Economics and Management*, *6*(2), 32–56. doi:10.5958/2249-7307.2016.00009.8

Dinçer, H., Hacıoğlu, Ü., & Yüksel, S. (2017). A Strategic Approach to Global Financial Crisis in Banking Sector: A Critical Appraisal of Banking Strategies Using Fuzzy ANP and Fuzzy Topsis Methods. *International Journal of Sustainable Economies Management*, *6*(1), 1–21. doi:10.4018/ijsem.2017010101

Dinçer, H., Hacıoğlu, Ü., & Yüksel, S. (2018). Determining Influencing Factors of Currency Exchange Rate for Decision Making in Global Economy Using MARS Method. In *Geopolitics and Strategic Management in the Global Economy* (pp. 261–273). IGI Global. doi:10.4018/978-1-5225-2673-5.ch013

Dinçer, H., & Yüksel, S. (2018). Comparative Evaluation of BSC-Based New Service Development Competencies in Turkish Banking Sector with the Integrated Fuzzy Hybrid MCDM Using Content Analysis. *International Journal of Fuzzy Systems, 20*(8), 2497–2516. doi:10.100740815-018-0519-y

Dinçer, H., Yüksel, S., Pınarbaşı, F., & Çetiner, İ. T. (2019). Measurement of Economic and Banking Stability in Emerging Markets by Considering Income Inequality and Nonperforming Loans. In *Maintaining Financial Stability in Times of Risk and Uncertainty* (pp. 49–68). IGI Global. doi:10.4018/978-1-5225-7208-4.ch003

Dinçer, H., Yüksel, S., & Şenel, S. (2018). Analyzing the global risks for the financial crisis after the great depression using comparative hybrid hesitant fuzzy decision-making models: Policy recommendations for sustainable economic growth. *Sustainability, 10*(9), 3126. doi:10.3390u10093126

Dobuzinskis, L. (2019). Financial Regulation and Monetary Policy: The Spectre of Government Failure. In *The Failure of Financial Regulation* (pp. 37–69). Cham: Palgrave Macmillan. doi:10.1007/978-3-030-05680-3_2

Donohoe, M. P. (2015). The economic effects of financial derivatives on corporate tax avoidance. *Journal of Accounting and Economics, 59*(1), 1–24. doi:10.1016/j.jacceco.2014.11.001

Ersin, İ., & Eti, S. (2017). Measuring the Waste-Conscious and Saving Habits of the Youth in Turkey: The Sample of Istanbul Medipol University. *International Journal of Islamic Economics and Finance Studies, 3*(3).

Eti, S. (2019). The Use of Quantitative Methods in Investment Decisions: A Literature Review. In *Handbook of Research on Global Issues in Financial Communication and Investment Decision Making* (pp. 256–275). IGI Global. doi:10.4018/978-1-5225-9265-5.ch013

Fontana, A., & Scheicher, M. (2016). An analysis of euro area sovereign CDS and their relation with government bonds. *Journal of Banking & Finance, 62*, 126–140. doi:10.1016/j.jbankfin.2015.10.010

Fries, C. P., & Kohl-Landgraf, P. (2018). *Smart Derivative Contracts (Detaching Transactions from Counterparty Credit Risk: Specification, Parametrisation, Valuation).* Available at SSRN 3163074

Galaz, V., Gars, J., Moberg, F., Nykvist, B., & Repinski, C. (2015). Why ecologists should care about financial markets. *Trends in Ecology & Evolution, 30*(10), 571–580. doi:10.1016/j.tree.2015.06.015 PMID:26411614

Haslem, J. A. (2015). Mutual fund heterogeneity and fee dispersion. *The Journal of Wealth Management, 18*(1), 41–48. doi:10.3905/jwm.2015.18.1.041

He, R. (2017). The Study on the Problem of the Relationship between the "Heterogeneity" of the Neighbor Enterprise and the Financing Efficiency of SMEs in China—Empirical Data from China Industrial Enterprises Database. *Open Journal of Applied Sciences, 7*(04), 171–183. doi:10.4236/ojapps.2017.74015

Holland, J. (2019). A new approach to research and theory development for financial firms-building a "house with windows". *Journal of Financial Regulation and Compliance.*

Hosseini, M., & Owlia, M. S. (2016). Designing a model for measuring and analyzing the relational capital using factor analysis: Case study, Ansar bank. *Journal of Intellectual Capital, 17*(4), 734–757. doi:10.1108/JIC-04-2016-0042

Hou, X., Li, S., & Wang, Q. (2018). Financial structure and income inequality: Evidence from China. *Emerging Markets Finance & Trade, 54*(2), 359–376. doi:10.1080/1540496X.2017.1347780

Hudson, A. (2017). *The law on financial derivatives (No. 6).* Sweet and Maxwell Ltd.

Ismail, A. G., Nik Abdul Ghani, N. A. R., & Mat Zain, M. N. (2016). Tawarruq time deposit with wakalah principle: An option that triggers new issues. *International Journal of Islamic and Middle Eastern Finance and Management, 9*(3), 388–396. doi:10.1108/IMEFM-05-2014-0048

Jianjun, L., & Xun, H. (2016). The Macroeconomic Effect of Shadow Credit Market Financing. *Applied Economics and Finance, 3*(3), 158–171. doi:10.11114/aef.v3i3.1587

Kahalé, N. (2017). Superreplication of financial derivatives via convex programming. *Management Science*, *63*(7), 2323–2339. doi:10.1287/mnsc.2017.2786

Komal, R., & Abbas, F. (2015). Linking financial development, economic growth and energy consumption in Pakistan. *Renewable & Sustainable Energy Reviews*, *44*, 211–220. doi:10.1016/j.rser.2014.12.015

Kumar, N. R. (2017). Intelligenece Report for Female Players & Non Players. *Indian Journal of Forensic Medicine & Toxicology*, *11*(2), 387–389. doi:10.5958/0973-9130.2017.00150.5

Li, Y., Chiu, Y. H., Lin, T. Y., & Huang, Y. Y. (2019). Market share and performance in Taiwanese banks: Min/max SBM DEA. *Top (Madrid)*, 1–20.

Linnerooth-Bayer, J., & Hochrainer-Stigler, S. (2015). Financial instruments for disaster risk management and climate change adaptation. *Climatic Change*, *133*(1), 85–100. doi:10.100710584-013-1035-6

Liu, C. (2019). FinTech and Its Disruption to Financial Institutions. In *Organizational Transformation and Managing Innovation in the Fourth Industrial Revolution* (pp. 104–124). IGI Global. doi:10.4018/978-1-5225-7074-5.ch006

Manova, K. (2015). *Global value chains and multinational activity with financial frictions. The Age of Global Value Chains: Maps and Policy Issues* (pp. 187–200). London: CEPR.

Marthinsen, J. E. (2018). *Risk takers: uses and abuses of financial derivatives*. Walter de Gruyter GmbH & Co KG. doi:10.1515/9781547400034

Maskell, B. H., Baggaley, B., & Grasso, L. (2016). *Practical lean accounting: a proven system for measuring and managing the lean enterprise*. Productivity Press. doi:10.1201/b11454

McVea, H. (2017). Central counterparties and sale and repurchase agreements: Regulating financial markets in the light of yet another false dawn. *Journal of Corporate Law Studies*, *17*(1), 111–135. doi:10.1080/14735970.2016.1254451

Miron, R. J., Sculean, A., Cochran, D. L., Froum, S., Zucchelli, G., Nemcovsky, C., ... Stavropoulos, A. (2016). Twenty years of enamel matrix derivative: The past, the present and the future. *Journal of Clinical Periodontology*, *43*(8), 668–683. doi:10.1111/jcpe.12546 PMID:26987551

Muda, I. (2017). User Impact of Literacy on Treatment Outcomes Quality Regional Financial Information System. *Management Dynamics in the Knowledge Economy*, *5*(2), 307–326. doi:10.25019/MDKE/5.2.08

Naczyk, M., & Hassel, A. (2019). Insuring individuals… and politicians: Financial services providers, stock market risk and the politics of private pension guarantees in Germany. *Journal of European Public Policy*, 1–20.

Nahar, A., Subadriyah, S., & Sofwan, A. (2018). The Analysis of Human Resources Policies and Regional Financial Accounting System on Regional Government Financial Statements' Quality. *Srıwıjaya Internatıonal Journal Of Dynamıc Economıcs And Busıness*, *1*(4), 387–404. doi:10.29259ijdeb.v1i4.387-404

Nica, E., & Potcovaru, A. M. (2015). Effective m-government services and increased citizen participation: Flexible and personalized ways of interacting with public administrations. *Journal of Self-Governance and Management Economics*, *3*(2), 92–97.

Oktar, S., & Yüksel, S. (2015). 1998 Yılında Rusya'da Yaşanan Bankacılık Krizi Ve Öncü Göstergeleri. *Marmara University Journal of Economic & Administrative Sciences*, *37*(2).

Oktar, S., & Yüksel, S. (2015). *Bankacılık krizlerinin erken uyarı sinyalleri: Türkiye üzerine bir uygulama*. Academic Press.

Oktar, S., & Yüksel, S. (2016). Bankalarin Türev Ürün Kullanimini Etkileyen Faktörler: Mars Yöntemi ile Bir Inceleme/Determinants of the Use Derivatives in Banking: An Analysis with MARS Model. *Finans Politik & Ekonomik Yorumlar*, *53*(620), 31.

Revelli, C., & Viviani, J. L. (2015). Financial performance of socially responsible investing (SRI): What have we learned? A meta-analysis. *Business Ethics (Oxford, England)*, *24*(2), 158–185. doi:10.1111/beer.12076

Rodriguez-Fernandez, M. (2016). Social responsibility and financial performance: The role of good corporate governance. *BRQ Business Research Quarterly*, *19*(2), 137–151. doi:10.1016/j.brq.2015.08.001

Rostamkalaei, A., & Freel, M. (2016). The cost of growth: Small firms and the pricing of bank loans. *Small Business Economics*, *46*(2), 255–272. doi:10.100711187-015-9681-x

Salisu, A. A., & Ayinde, T. O. (2016). Testing the martingale difference hypothesis (MDH) with structural breaks: Evidence from foreign exchanges of Nigeria and South Africa. *Journal of African Business*, *17*(3), 342–359. doi:10.1080/15228916.2016.1183274

Shcherbakov, V., & Larsson, E. (2016). Radial basis function partition of unity methods for pricing vanilla basket options. *Computers & Mathematics with Applications (Oxford, England)*, *71*(1), 185–200. doi:10.1016/j.camwa.2015.11.007

Tunay, K. B., & Yüksel, S. (2017). The relationship between corporate governance and foreign ownership of the banks in developing countries. *Contaduría y Administración*, *62*(5), 1627–1642. doi:10.1016/j.cya.2017.05.007

Valickova, P., Havranek, T., & Horvath, R. (2015). Financial development and economic growth: A meta-analysis. *Journal of Economic Surveys*, *29*(3), 506–526. doi:10.1111/joes.12068

Wang, J. G., & Yang, J. (2016). Enjoy "Free Rides" with the "Core Firms"—Supply Chain Financing. In *Financing without Bank Loans* (pp. 85–95). Singapore: Springer. doi:10.1007/978-981-10-0901-3_7

Xu, D., Tang, S., & Guttman, D. (2019). China's campaign-style Internet finance governance: Causes, effects, and lessons learned for new information-based approaches to governance. *Computer Law & Security Review*, *35*(1), 3–14. doi:10.1016/j.clsr.2018.11.002

Yılmaz, E., & Aslan, T. (2016). Usage Derivatives In Management Financial Risks: A Study On Firms In Borsa Istanbul (Bist) 100 Stock Index. *Journal of Business Research*, *8*(1), 663–678.

Yüksel, S. (2016). Bankaların Takipteki Krediler Oranını Belirleyen Faktörler: Türkiye İçin Bir Model Önerisi. *Bankacılar Dergisi*, *98*, 41–56.

Yüksel, S. (2016). Türkiye'de Cari İşlemler Açığının Belirleyicileri: Mars Yöntemi ile Bir İnceleme. *Bankacılar Dergisi*, *96*(27), 102–121.

Yüksel, S. (2017). Determinants of the credit risk in developing countries after economic crisis: A case of Turkish banking sector. In *Global financial crisis and its ramifications on capital markets* (pp. 401–415). Cham: Springer. doi:10.1007/978-3-319-47021-4_28

Yüksel, S. (2017). Strategies Out of Global Recession in Emerging Markets: An Application for 2008 Global Crisis. In *Global Business Strategies in Crisis* (pp. 57–75). Cham: Springer. doi:10.1007/978-3-319-44591-5_5

Yüksel, S. (2017). The impacts of research and development expenses on export and economic growth. *International Business and Accounting Research Journal*, *1*(1), 1–8. doi:10.15294/ibarj.v1i1.1

Yüksel, S., Dinçer, H., & Emir, Ş. (2017). Comparing the performance of Turkish deposit banks by using DEMATEL, Grey Relational Analysis (GRA) and MOORA approaches. *World Journal of Applied Economics*, *3*(2), 26–47. doi:10.22440/wjae.3.2.2

Yüksel, S., Dincer, H., & Hacioglu, U. (2015). CAMELS-based Determinants for the Credit Rating of Turkish Deposit Banks. *International Journal of Finance & Banking Studies*, *4*(4), 1.

Yüksel, S., Mukhtarov, S., Mammadov, E., & Özsarı, M. (2018). Determinants of Profitability in the Banking Sector: An Analysis of Post-Soviet Countries. *Economies*, *6*(3), 41. doi:10.3390/economies6030041

Yüksel, S., & Özsarı, M. (2017). Türkiye'nin Kredi Notunu Etkileyen Faktörlerin MARS Yöntemi İle Belirlenmesi. *Politik Ekonomik Kuram*, *1*(2), 16–31. doi:10.30586/pek.356929

Yüksel, S., & Zengin, S. (2016a). leading indicators of 2008 global crisis: An analysis with logit and mars methods. *Finansal Araştırmalar ve Çalışmalar Dergisi*, *8*(15), 495–518.

Yüksel, S., & Zengin, S. (2016b). *Causality relationship between import, export and growth rate in developing countries*. Academic Press.

Yuksel, S., & Zengin, S. (2017). Influencing factors of net interest margin in Turkish banking sector. *International Journal of Economics and Financial Issues*, *7*(1).

Zengin, S., & Yüksel, S. (2016). A comparison of the views of internal controllers/auditors and branch/call center personnel of the banks for operational risk: A case for Turkish banking sector. *International Journal of Finance & Banking Studies*, *5*(4), 10.

Zengin, S., & Yüksel, S. (2016). *Likidite riskini etkileyen faktörler: Türk bankacılık sektörü üzerine bir inceleme*. Academic Press.

# Chapter 2
# Financial Intermediaries

## ABSTRACT

*Effective financial systems provide significant benefits for the sustainable development of the countries. Therefore, most governments aim to take some actions to increase the effectiveness of the financial system. In this framework, financial intermediaries play a crucial role for this purpose. Financial intermediaries can be mainly classified into two different categories: banks and nonbanking organizations. In this chapter, the responsibilities of the financial intermediaries are explained. Within this context, first of all, the different types of the banks are identified. In addition, nonbanking organizations are defined. It is concluded that financial intermediaries should work effectively to increase the performance of the financial system. This situation has a positive influence on the economic growth of the countries.*

## GENERAL INFORMATION ABOUT FINANCIAL INTERMEDIARIES

Financial intermediaries mean the institutions, such as banks, leasing or insurance company that bring fund suppliers and fund demanders together. Hence, it is obvious that they play a crucial role in the effectiveness of the financial system by making connection between these two different parties. Owing to this condition, it is possible to talk about many different advantages of the financial intermediaries for both the performance of the financial system and the development of the economies (McLeod et al., 2018; Piskorski et al., 2015).

DOI: 10.4018/978-1-7998-1643-0.ch002

Firstly, financial intermediaries lead to have easy and fast exchange of the funds among the parties. For instance, there may be an individual or a company that needs money in the north of a country. In addition to this situation, assume that there is also an individual or a company who has some savings, but he lives in the south of the country. In this circumstance, it can be seen that it is very difficult for these parties to bring together without a financial intermediary (Alberici & Querci, 2016; Dinçer, Yüksel and Adalı, 2018). With the help of a financial intermediary, these parties can reach to each other and fund demanders can have the funds easily. On the other hand, fund suppliers can get a chance to earn income by using their savings (Tagoe, 2016).

Another important benefit of the financial intermediaries is that it has a role to provide the convenience of the amount. For example, there can be an individual or a company who needs $500,000 for his needs. However, there may be 2 different fund suppliers who have the saving amount of $400,000 and $100,000. If there is no financial intermediary in the country, none of the fund suppliers can satisfy the needs of the fund demander by himself. Therefore, owing to the financial intermediaries, these parties can become together, and the convenience of the amount is provided (Chen et al., 2017; Dinçer et al., 2019).

Furthermore, financial intermediaries play also a significant role in order to decrease the risk in this transaction. Although there are lots of different risks, such as liquidity risk, market risk, currency risk, the most outstanding risk for the fund suppliers is accepted as the credit risk which means the possibility that fund demanders cannot pay the debt (Brogi & Lagasio, 2018). When there is no financial intermediary, fund suppliers do not have a chance to analyze the financial performance of the fund demander in a detailed aspect. However, financial institutions have qualified personnel and necessary technological background to make this kind of analysis (Tunay et al., 2019; Yüksel, 2017). Hence, it shows that financial intermediaries have a contributing effect to decrease the credit risk.

While considering the information emphasized above, the effectiveness of the financial intermediaries is very important in the performance of the financial system. When these institutions do not perform effectively, it will cause significant problems in this system, such as bankruptcy. Similar to this issue, this condition has also negative influence on the improvement of the economy of the country. The most popular financial intermediary is accepted as the banks (Atanasov et al., 2015). However, there are also non-banking financial institutions in the market, such as leasing, factoring companies. The details of these institutions are given on the following subtitles.

## BANKS

A bank is a financial institution that collects money from the fund suppliers and allocate these funds to the fund demanders. In this case, the money collected from the fund suppliers is called as deposit whereas the money given to the fund demanders is named as the credit. Therefore, it can be said that banks have a significant influence on the investment amount of the country. This situation leads to also many different benefits (Dinçer, Hacıoğlu and Yüksel, 2017). For example, when a company makes new investment, it means that this company employs new people. This condition contributes to decrease unemployment rate (Alberici & Querci, 2016; Yüksel and Adalı, 2017). Moreover, increasing investment has a positive influence on the economic growth (Yüksel, 2016; Gallemore et al., 2019).

Furthermore, banks have also advantages for the fund suppliers. Firstly, these parties get a chance to earn income with the help of the banks. In other words, fund supplier can earn interest income at the maturity for the money given to the banks as deposit. In addition to this aspect, banks have qualified personnel and effective technological investment (Setyawati et al., 2017). Thus, the banks can manage the risks better than the fund suppliers. Within this context, banks can be selective to give loans to the fund demanders by making detailed financial analysis for these parties. In this case, if there is a risk for a fund demander about paying the debt, banks can decide not to give the loan to this party. It is obvious that a fund supplier cannot make this kind of analysis without the help of the banks (Mukhtarov, Yüksel & Mammadov, 2018).

Banks can give different type of the loans to the individuals or companies. First of all, bank can provide loans for only individuals (Mirzaei & Moore, 2016). For example, the banks can give auto loan for the individuals who aim to purchase automobile. In addition to the auto loan, a mortgage loans can be presented to the individuals who want to purchase a house. Moreover, there can be consumer loans for the individuals to satisfy their personnel needs, such as purchasing new furniture or marriage expenses (Yüksel, Zengin and Kartal, 2016).

Moreover, banks can provide commercial loans to the companies according to their needs. For instance, there may be a specific loan for the companies, such as loan for purchasing a vehicle. The companies can purchase the vehicles they need with the commercial loan taken from the banks and pay the amount to the banks easily with the installments. Also, banks can give loans to the companies without installment. In this circumstance, there will be a limit for the companies (Chou & Buchdadi, 2016; Yüksel & Özsarı, 2016). Within the maturity date, the companies can use the amount of the loans when they need, but this amount cannot exceed the limit of the companies. In certain periods, the company pay the interest amount to the banks according to the amount of the loans used. Additionally, at the maturity date, the companies have to pay whole debt to the banks (Dinçer, Hacıoğlu & Yüksel, 2016).

Furthermore, banks can also provide some non-cash loans for the companies. For example, the banks can give a letter of credit to the companies who are the buyers in the trade. Because the seller company has doubts about the payments of the buyer company. In this case, the seller company requests a letter of credit by the banks which gives assurance about the payment conditions. In other words, if buyer company does not pay the amount, the banks will pay this amount to the seller company. For this guarantee, the buyer company gives a commission to the banks according to the amount of the guarantee (Yüksel and Özsarı, 2017a,b).

In addition to these issues, banks also provide some other financial services, such as money transferring and safe deposit boxes. People can use safe deposit boxes in the banks and put special belongings to these boxes. For this service, they pay a commission to the banks. Moreover, individuals or the companies sometimes need to transfer some amount of money to other parties. In order to achieve this objective, they can use the channels of the banks by paying a commission (Anginer et al., 2018).

As it can be seen that banks can give different services to their customers. However, some banks may not prefer to give some services. Additionally, it may also be prohibited for some banks provide some services in the legal regulations. Owing to this aspect, banks are classified into the different groups. The details of these bank types are explained in the following subtitles.

## Deposit Banks

Deposit banks refer to the banks which have the right to collect deposit from the individuals or companies according to the legal rules. By looking at this explanation, it is understood that some types of the banks cannot collect money from these parties. The main reason behind this situation is that collecting money is a very significant aspect because banks get responsibility about the savings of the parties by collecting their money (Brahmana et al., 2018). If there is a problem for the bank, such as bankruptcy, there can be a problem for the individuals or the customers to reach their money. Hence, it can be said that money collection right should not be given to each bank (Dinçer, Yüksel and Çetiner, 2019).

The deposit banks can also be divided into 3 different groups which are named as state, private and foreign banks. State banks refer to the banks which are owned by the government. On the other side, with respect to the private banks, domestic investors are the owners. However, the owner cannot be the government in this type of the banks. In addition to them, foreign banks express the banks which are owned by foreign companies.

## Investment Banks

Investment banks give support to the companies in many different ways. For instance, companies need expert opinions in the process of merger and acquisition. The main reason is that it is a very complicated process. It depends on the legal regulations of the countries where these companies locate in. Therefore, since investment banks have expert personnel in this subject, they can give support to these companies in this process. In addition to the merger and acquisition, some companies aim to issue bonds to the public in order to collect money. However, there are many different complex situations for these companies to consider in this process. In this circumstance, investment banks can manage this process on behalf of these companies. As it can be understood that investment banks do not have the right to collect money from the individuals or companies. Their revenues include the commission amount collected from the individuals and companies for these services (Zengin, Yüksel and Kartal, 2018; Corwin et al., 2017).

## Development Banks

Similar to the investment banks, development banks refer to the banks that do not have the right to collect money from the individuals and companies. The main purpose of the development banks is to provide loans with the aim of economic development of the countries. In other words, while giving loans, development banks give priority to the sectors that have a significant influence on the economic improvement of the countries, such as railway transportation and dam building (Wijesiri et al., 2019; Dinçer et al., 2019; Lazzarini et al., 2015)

The important point in this situation is that deposit banks can also provide these loans. However, because the amount of these kinds of loans is very high, the development banks are reluctant to give them. The main reason is that there are significant risks in these loans due to the high amount. For example, if counterparty cannot pay its debt to the banks, it will cause high amount of losses for the banks. Additionally, the maturity of the loans given by development banks is generally very long. Therefore, deposit banks do not prefer to provide these loans due to this aspect (Desai et al., 2016).

Although development banks cannot collect money from the public directly, they can issue bonds in order to achieve this objective. While selling these bonds, they can collect the money from the investors and make interest payments on certain times to them. On the other side, there may be government support for these banks in order to have money. As an example, governments can give incentives to the development banks with the aim of economic development of the countries (Haryanto, 2016).

## Islamic Banks

Islamic banks refer to the types of the banks that make operations according to Islam. In Islam religion, interest is strongly prohibited because it is thought that it increases income inequality among individuals. Therefore, there is a need of new banking type which satisfies the expectations of the people who give importance to this religion. Otherwise, it will be impossible to attract the attention of these people (Wanke et al., 2016; Yüksel and Canöz, 2017).

In Islamic banking, there is no interest payment. Instead of this situation, there is profit or loss sharing. In other words, fund demanders give their saving to the Islamic banks and wait for the maturity to understand whether they will get profit or loss (Ersin and Duran, 2017). At maturity date, if Islamic banks have profit, they will distribute the profit according to the amount of the deposits of the fund demanders. It is understood that the rate of the profit sharing is not certain at the beginning. Additionally, if Islamic banks have loss, the principle amount of the fund demanders will go down because the banks will also share the loss according to the regulations (Hussein, 2016; Yüksel, Canöz and Özsarı, 2017).

In addition to the interest, Islamic banks do not also give services which are not appropriate in Islamic religion. For example, these banks do not give loans to the companies which sell alcoholic drinks since these products are prohibited in Islam. Moreover, these banks do not present a service which is not approved by Sharia board that consists of the experts about the rules of Islamic religion. Otherwise, the image of these banks may be tarnished on the eyes of the customers (Ab-Rahim & Chiang, 2016).

Islamic banks became so popular especially in the last years. Malaysia and Saudi Arabia are the most outstanding countries with respect to the Islamic banking. Nevertheless, it can be identified that not only Muslim countries focus on this banking type. For instance, some non-Muslim countries, such as United States and United Kingdom also give importance to Islamic banking system. The main reason behind this condition is that these countries aim to attract the attention of investors who are sensitive to Islamic rules. Therefore, they can have a chance to increase the liquidity amount in the market so that it has a contribution factor to the development of the economy.

## NON-BANKING FINANCIAL INSTITUTIONS

Banks are accepted as the most significant financial institutions in the financial system. Hence, it can be seen that banks have the highest percentage in comparison with other financial institutions for most of the countries in the world. However, non-banking financial institutions also play an important role in this system, such as leasing, factoring, portfolio management companies and investment companies. These institutions are detailed in the following subtitles.

### Leasing Companies

The term leasing comes from the word of "lease" and it means that the companies hire the machinery or equipment from the leasing companies instead of purchasing them. It provides an alternative opportunity to the companies. At the end of the maturity, this process gives an opportunity to the lessee to purchase this machinery or equipment. The purchasing price is generally very low. With the help of the leasing process, the companies can get a chance to have a machinery without using their liquid money (Andaleeb et al., 2018).

There are usually three different parties in the leasing process, which are lessor, lessee and the seller of the machinery. The lessor refers to the party who purchases machinery from the seller and rents it to the lessee. Hence, it is obvious that the lessor is leasing company. On the other side, the lessee is the party who hires this machinery from the lessor. In addition to them, the seller of the machinery is the first owner and he sells this product to the leasing company.

There are mainly two different types of the leasing which are operating leasing and financial leasing. With respect to the operating leasing, the ownership of the machinery transfers to the lessee for the shorter time of economic life of this machinery. This type of leasing is mainly preferred for the situation in which the lessee need this equipment only for a project that has a specific time. On the other hand, in the financial leasing, the time is longer than the operational leasing. In other words, the leasing period generally contains the significant percentage of the economic life of the equipment.

There are some important points for the leasing process according to the regulations. First of all, there should be a written leasing contract between the parties, and it should be signed by both parties. In this contract, all significant aspects, such as the amount and the maturity should be detailed. In addition to this issue, in some countries, there is a requirement that the lessee should insure the machinery that is the subject of the leasing. Moreover, in some regulations about the leasing, there is a necessity that the ownership of the machinery should be transferred to the lessee at the end of the maturity.

The properties which are subject to the leasing process are generally used by the companies in their operations. For example, hospitals prefer leasing especially for tomography and construction companies make leasing contract in order for lifting crane. These companies can get loan from the banks so as to have this equipment. However, these are the products that requires expertise in the loan process, so the loan process may take longer time in the banks. Another important benefit of the leasing in comparison with bank loans is that companies can get finance 100% of the machinery. However, banks generally give loans about 75% of the amount of the equipment.

While considering the information above, it can be said that the leasing companies have great importance in the financial system. With the help of leasing companies, especially new companies can get a chance to obtain equipment because banks do not prefer give loans these new companies. As it is underlined before, the time of the process is very shorter in leasing in comparison with bank loans. Because of this condition, many companies may prefer leasing in their operations. Therefore, it is obvious that the leasing companies have significant contribution to the financial system.

## Factoring Companies

Factoring refers to the process in which the receivables can be converted into the cash before their maturities. As it can be understood from this definition, in order to make a factoring operation, there should be a receivable with a maturity. In this process, the right of the receivables is transferred to the factoring companies. In other words, factoring companies purchase this receivable with a lower amount of the original one. This difference constitutes the profit of the factoring companies (Kaur and Dhaliwal, 2016).

It can be identified that there are three different parties in the factoring operations which are factor, debtor and seller. Within this framework, the debtor is the party who has the liability. On the other side, the seller is the party who has the receivables. In the process of the factoring, the seller does not want to wait to have cash money until the maturity of this receivable. Therefore, this seller prefers to sell this receivable to the factoring company which is also named as factor.

There are some advantages of factoring transaction for the different parties. First of all, the seller can get a chance to have liquid money before the maturity of the receivable. Owing to this aspect, this company can increase its power in order to manage liquidity risk. For example, it can pay its short-term debts or it can prefer to make new investment. On the other hand, factoring company can catch the opportunity to increase its income by purchasing the receivable with a lower amount than the original one.

In spite of the advantages, it can be said that factoring operation also contains some risks for these parties. Firstly, while purchasing the receivables, factoring companies undertake all risks caused by these receivables. As an example, if the debtors cannot pay this amount at the maturity, the factoring companies may have high amount of loss. On the other side, the sellers may also have some loss due to this factoring operation. For instance, if they do not assess the amount on the market efficiently, it means the difference between the original amount of the receivable and the factoring amount will be the loss for these companies.

While considering these aspects, the price of the factoring operation plays a very key role in this process. Hence, it can be said that factoring companies have significant responsibilities with respect to the identification of the price. For this purpose, financial analysis of the debtors should be performed effectively. Within this scope, the balanced sheet, income statement and market intelligence for these companies should be examined in a very detailed way. As a result of this analysis, a unique price can be determined for this receivable.

With the help of factoring companies, companies can get the right to reach liquid money earlier than the maturity. Because these companies collect the receivables, they can have the opportunity to increase their efficiency by using this liquid money. This situation has a positive influence on the stability of the financial market. Additionally, these companies can also make new investment by using this money. Therefore, it can be said that factoring companies also make a contribution to economic development of the countries.

## Portfolio Management and Investment Companies

Portfolio management refers to the process of decision making about making investment in financial instruments. As it can be understood rom this definition, investors can have a chance to invest in different instruments at the same time. The main reason behind this situation it that these investors prefer to spread the risks. For example, if the investors make all their investments to the government bond, they may get high amount of loss in case of increase in market interest rate. This situation shows that by making investment only one type of financial instrument has an increasing effect on the portfolio risk (Ahmad et al., 2017).

Owing to these aspects, it can be seen that investors prefer to make investments in different financial instruments. For example, they can make investment on government bonds by using some parts of their savings and they can also purchase stocks of some companies with the other remaining amount. In this case, it is very difficult to understand what portion of the savings should be transferred to which financial instruments. In addition to this issue, it is also very complex to define which companies' stocks should be purchased.

In order to solve this problems, portfolio management and investment companies play an important role in the financial system. Portfolio management companies, also called as asset management companies, make investment on behalf of the fund suppliers. In other words, the companies or individuals who have savings give usage right of these saving to the portfolio management companies. Hence, these portfolio management companies make asset allocation for these investors.

By looking at this information, it can be understood that portfolio management companies have important benefits for the financial system. Firstly, portfolio management companies can manage the risks better than the individuals and companies because they have qualified personnel for this subject. With the help of these personnel, portfolio management companies can make appropriate investments so that the profitability of the fund suppliers can go up. This situation leads to more effective financial investment in the system (Yüksel, Mukhtarov & Mammadov, 2016).

In addition to the portfolio management companies, investment companies also play a significant role in the financial system. Investment companies aim to direct investors for making decision among alternatives. The main difference of investment companies from portfolio management companies is that investment companies can only give their ideas about the investment, but they cannot make investment by using the savings of the fund suppliers. While considering these issues, it is obvious that both portfolio management companies and investment companies have a significant contribution on the process of transferring funds from fund suppliers to the fund demanders.

## FINANCIAL AUTHORITIES AND LEGAL REGULATIONS

In the financial market, there are lots of risks for different parties. For instance, the most significant risk for fund suppliers is the credit risk. It refers to the possibility that fund demanders cannot pay back the debt to the fund demanders. In this case, fund suppliers cannot earn interest or dividend income and at the same time they cannot get the principal amount which is given. As it is underlined in the previous titles, financial intermediaries have a decreasing effect on the risk of the transactions. With the help of the financial intermediaries, funds can be allocated to the fund demanders more carefully. The main reason is that these institutions can be more selective by making detailed analysis about the financial performance of the fund demanders.

Although there is a decrease in the risk owing to the financial intermediaries, it is impossible to prevent all risk in these transactions. For example, in spite of making detailed analysis about the financial performance, there is still a risk for fund demanders not to perform their obligations. This situation negatively affects the financial performance of the intermediary institutions. In case of lower profitability or having loss, financial intermediaries will not be willing to make operation in the market. This condition leads to decrease the fund transaction and it will decrease the effectiveness of the financial system.

Another important problem may be occurred because financial intermediaries take too much risk in their operations. In other words, these institutions prefer to take higher risk with the aim of increasing profitability. As an example, they may not be selective for the fund demanders to allocate the funds. In this situation, because fund demanders with lower credibility can also reach the funds, it is obvious that there will be problems in the future about the payment performance of the debts. This issue causes significant problems for the financial intermediaries. When the impact of these problems goes up, it can lead to bankruptcy for these institutions. Similarly, it means that fund suppliers will be affected from this situation in a negative aspect.

In addition to the problems stated above, there may also be problem related to negative expectations of the parties in the financial market. For instance, investors become anxious about the negative financial performance of one significant company or whole system. If there is no authority to give confidence about this negative expectation, the fund suppliers will be reluctant to give their savings. Parallel to this aspect, intermediary institutions may not prefer to give funds to the fund demanders. This situation has a negative influence on the effectiveness of the financial system.

By considering the aspects underlined in previous paragraphs, it can be said that there is a crucial need for financial authorities and legal regulations (Kenward, 2016). Financial authorities have an auditing role for the parties in the financial system (Yüksel, Zengin and Kartal, 2016). Therefore, they give confidence about the performance of the companies and the financial system. In addition to the financial authorities, legal regulations are also necessary so as to increase the effectiveness of the financial system.

With the help of these regulations, the responsibilities of all parties can be identified. Thus, this situation has a controlling effect on the players in the financial system. The regulations and financial authorities can be classified in two different areas, such as "money market authorities and regulations" and "capital market authorities and regulations". The details of these issues are defined in the following subtitles.

## CONCLUSION

This chapter aims to examine the responsibilities of the financial intermediaries. In the first issue, the responsibilities of the banks were identified. In this circumstance, necessary information was given about the responsibilities of the different bank types. After that, nonbanking institutions were defined which are leasing, factoring and portfolio management companies. It is determined that financial intermediaries play a significant role for the effectiveness of the financial system. Another important conclusion is that there is a need for a regulatory institution which can control these financial intermediaries. With the help of this issue, financial market can be more effective.

## REFERENCES

Ab-Rahim, R., & Chiang, S. N. (2016). Market structure and performance of Malaysian banking industry. *Journal of Financial Reporting and Accounting*, *14*(2), 158–177. doi:10.1108/JFRA-11-2014-0086

Ahmad, M. O., Lwakatare, L. E., Kuvaja, P., Oivo, M., & Markkula, J. (2017). An empirical study of portfolio management and Kanban in agile and lean software companies. *Journal of Software: Evolution and Process*, *29*(6), e1834.

Alberici, A., & Querci, F. (2016). The quality of disclosures on environmental policy: The profile of financial intermediaries. *Corporate Social Responsibility and Environmental Management*, *23*(5), 283–296. doi:10.1002/csr.1375

Alberici, A., & Querci, F. (2016). The quality of disclosures on environmental policy: The profile of financial intermediaries. *Corporate Social Responsibility and Environmental Management*, *23*(5), 283–296. doi:10.1002/csr.1375

Andaleeb, S., Abbasi, M. A., Naqvi, S. I. H., & Ali, S. (2018). Determinants Of Capital Structure Of Leasing Companies In Pakistan. *Archives of Business Research*, *6*(3). doi:10.14738/abr.63.4145

Anginer, D., Demirguc-Kunt, A., Huizinga, H., & Ma, K. (2018). Corporate governance of banks and financial stability. *Journal of Financial Economics*, *130*(2), 327–346. doi:10.1016/j.jfineco.2018.06.011

Atanasov, V., Davies, R. J., & Merrick, J. J. Jr. (2015). Financial intermediaries in the midst of market manipulation: Did they protect the fool or help the knave? *Journal of Corporate Finance*, *34*, 210–234. doi:10.1016/j.jcorpfin.2015.07.011

Brahmana, R., Kontesa, M., & Gilbert, R. E. (2018). Income diversification and bank performance: Evidence from malaysian banks. *Economic Bulletin*, *38*(2), 799–809.

Brogi, M., & Lagasio, V. (2018). Environmental, social, and governance and company profitability: Are financial intermediaries different? *Corporate Social Responsibility and Environmental Management*.

Chen, D., Guan, Y., Zhang, T., & Zhao, G. (2017). Political connection of financial intermediaries: Evidence from China's IPO market. *Journal of Banking & Finance*, *76*, 15–31. doi:10.1016/j.jbankfin.2016.11.023

Chou, T. K., & Buchdadi, A. D. (2016). Bank performance and its underlying factors: A study of rural banks in Indonesia. *Accounting and Finance Research*, *5*(3), 55–63. doi:10.5430/afr.v5n3p55

Corwin, S. A., Larocque, S. A., & Stegemoller, M. A. (2017). Investment banking relationships and analyst affiliation bias: The impact of the global settlement on sanctioned and non-sanctioned banks. *Journal of Financial Economics*, *124*(3), 614–631. doi:10.1016/j.jfineco.2017.03.005

Desai, H., Rajgopal, S., & Yu, J. J. (2016). Were information intermediaries sensitive to the financial statement-based leading indicators of bank distress prior to the financial crisis? *Contemporary Accounting Research*, *33*(2), 576–606. doi:10.1111/1911-3846.12161

Dinçer, H., Hacıoğlu, Ü., & Yüksel, S. (2016). Managerial and Market-Based Appraisal of Agriculture Banking Using ANP and ELECTRE Method. *Management & Organizational Studies*, *3*(3), 29–40. doi:10.5430/mos.v3n3p29

Dinçer, H., Hacıoğlu, Ü., & Yüksel, S. (2017). A Strategic Approach to Global Financial Crisis in Banking Sector: A Critical Appraisal of Banking Strategies Using Fuzzy ANP and Fuzzy Topsis Methods. *International Journal of Sustainable Economies Management*, *6*(1), 1–21. doi:10.4018/ijsem.2017010101

Dinçer, H., Yuksel, S., & Adalı, Z. (2018). Relationship Between Non-Performing Loans, Industry, and Economic Growth of the African Economies and Policy Recommendations for Global Growth. In *Globalization and Trade Integration in Developing Countries* (pp. 203–228). IGI Global. doi:10.4018/978-1-5225-4032-8.ch009

Dinçer, H., Yüksel, S., Adalı, Z., & Aydın, R. (2019). Evaluating the Role of Research and Development and Technology Investments on Economic Development of E7 Countries. In Organizational Transformation and Managing Innovation in the Fourth Industrial Revolution (pp. 245-263). IGI Global.

Dinçer, H., Yüksel, S., & Çetiner, İ. T. (2019). Strategy Selection for Organizational Performance of Turkish Banking Sector With the Integrated Multi-Dimensional Decision-Making Approach. In *Handbook of Research on Contemporary Approaches in Management and Organizational Strategy* (pp. 273–291). IGI Global. doi:10.4018/978-1-5225-6301-3.ch014

Dinçer, H., Yüksel, S., Eti, S., & Tula, A. (2019). Effects of Demographic Characteristics on Business Success: An Evidence From Turkish Banking Sector. In *Handbook of Research on Business Models in Modern Competitive Scenarios* (pp. 304–324). IGI Global. doi:10.4018/978-1-5225-7265-7.ch016

Ersin, İ., & Duran, S. (2017). Faizsiz Finans Döngüsünü Oluşturma Açisindan Adil Ekonomik Düzen Söyleminin Kredileşme İlkeleri Ve Uygulanabilirliğinin Değerlendirilmesi. *Electronic Turkish Studies*, *12*(8).

Gallemore, J., Gipper, B., & Maydew, E. (2019). Banks as tax planning intermediaries. *Journal of Accounting Research.*

Haryanto, S. (2016). Profitability Identification of National Banking through Credit, Capital, Capital Structure, Efficiency, and Risk Level. *Jurnal Dinamika Manajemen*, *7*(1), 11–21. doi:10.15294/jdm.v7i1.5749

Hussein, K. (2016). Bank-Level Stability Factors and Consumer Confidence—A Comparative Study of Islamic and Conventional Banks' Product Mix. In *Islamic Finance* (pp. 86–104). Cham: Palgrave Macmillan. doi:10.1007/978-3-319-30918-7_6

Kaur, H., & Dhaliwal, N. K. (2016). Operational performance of factoring companies in India: A study of SBI Global factors and Canbank factors. *Abhigyan*, *33*(4), 12–23.

Kenward, L. R. (2016). The Macro Forecasting Record of the Indonesian Financial Authorities, 2004–15. *Bulletin of Indonesian Economic Studies*, *52*(3), 321–342. doi:10.1080/00074918.2016.1198466

Lazzarini, S. G., Musacchio, A., Bandeira-de-Mello, R., & Marcon, R. (2015). What do state-owned development banks do? Evidence from BNDES, 2002–09. *World Development*, *66*, 237–253. doi:10.1016/j.worlddev.2014.08.016

McLeod, M. S., Moore, C. B., Payne, G. T., Sexton, J. C., & Evert, R. E. (2018). Organizational virtue and stakeholder interdependence: An empirical examination of financial intermediaries and IPO firms. *Journal of Business Ethics*, *149*(4), 785–798. doi:10.100710551-016-3021-1

Mirzaei, A., & Moore, T. (2016). Banking performance and industry growth in an oil-rich economy: Evidence from Qatar. *The Quarterly Review of Economics and Finance*, *60*, 58–69. doi:10.1016/j.qref.2015.06.001

Mukhtarov, S., Yüksel, S., & Mammadov, E. (2018). *Factors that increase credit risk of Azerbaijani banks*. Academic Press.

Piskorski, T., Seru, A., & Witkin, J. (2015). Asset quality misrepresentation by financial intermediaries: Evidence from the RMBS market. *The Journal of Finance*, *70*(6), 2635–2678. doi:10.1111/jofi.12271

Setyawati, I., Suroso, S., Suryanto, T., & Nurjannah, D. S. (2017). Does financial performance of Islamic banking is better? Panel Data Estimation. *European Research Studies*, *20*(2), 592.

Tagoe, N. A. (2016). The Emerging Role of Financial Intermediaries in the Financial Market of Ghana. *Bus Eco J*, *7*(253), 2.

Tunay, N., Yüksel, S., & Tunay, K. B. (2019). The Effects of Technology on Bank Performance in Advanced and Emerging Economies: An Empirical Analysis. In *Handbook of Research on Managerial Thinking in Global Business Economics* (pp. 263–280). IGI Global. doi:10.4018/978-1-5225-7180-3.ch015

Wanke, P., Azad, M. A. K., Barros, C. P., & Hassan, M. K. (2016). Predicting efficiency in Islamic banks: An integrated multicriteria decision making (MCDM) approach. *Journal of International Financial Markets, Institutions and Money*, *45*, 126–141. doi:10.1016/j.intfin.2016.07.004

Wijesiri, M., Martínez-Campillo, A., & Wanke, P. (2019). Is there a trade-off between social and financial performance of public commercial banks in India? A multi-activity DEA model with shared inputs and undesirable outputs. *Review of Managerial Science*, *13*(2), 417–442. doi:10.100711846-017-0255-y

Yüksel, S. (2016). Rusya Ekonomisinde Büyüme, Issizlik ve Enflasyon Arasindaki Nedensellik Iliskileri/The Causality Relationship Between Growth, Unemployment and Inflation in Russian Economy. *Finans Politik & Ekonomik Yorumlar*, *53*(614), 43.

Yüksel, S. (2017). The impacts of research and development expenses on export and economic growth. *International Business and Accounting Research Journal*, *1*(1), 1–8. doi:10.15294/ibarj.v1i1.1

Yüksel, S., & Adalı, Z. (2017). *Determining influencing factors of unemployment in Turkey with MARS method.* Academic Press.

Yüksel, S., & Canöz, İ. (2017). Does Islamic Banking Contribute to Economic Growth and Industrial Development in Turkey. *Ikonomika, 2*(1), 93–102. doi:10.24042/febi.v2i1.945

Yüksel, S., Canöz, İ., & Özsarı, M. (2017). Causality relationship between interest rate of deposit banks and profit share rate of islamic banks in turkey. *IKONOMIKA, 2*(2), 131–148. doi:10.24042/febi.v2i2.1894

Yüksel, S., Mukhtarov, S., & Mammadov, E. (2016). Comparing the efficiency of Turkish and Azerbaijani banks: An application with data envelopment analysis. *International Journal of Economics and Financial Issues, 6*(3).

Yüksel, S., & Özsarı, M. (2016). *Türkiye'deki Bireysel Krediler ile Enflasyon ve Cari İşlemler Açığı Arasındaki Nedensellik İlişkisinin İncelenmesi.* Roma: Econworld Konferansı.

Yüksel, S., & Özsari, M. (2017a). Türkiye Cumhuriyet Merkez Bankası'nın Döviz Rezervlerine Etki Eden Makroekonomik Faktörlerin Belirlenmesi. *Finans Politik & Ekonomik Yorumlar, 54*(631), 41–53.

Yüksel, S., & Özsari, M. (2017b). Identifying the Factors Influence Turkish Deposit Banks to Join Corporate Social Responsibility Activities by Using Panel Probit Method. *International Journal of Finance & Banking Studies, 6*(1), 39.

Yüksel, S., Zengin, S., & Kartal, M. T. (2016). Banka Personelinin Teftiş Kuruluna Bakış Açısının Değerlendirilmesi [An Evaluation of the Perspectives of Bank Personnel Regarding Internal Audit Department]. *Finans Politik & Ekonomik Yorumlar, 53*(622).

Yüksel, S., Zengin, S., & Kartal, M. T. (2016). Identifying the macroeconomic factors influencing credit card usage in Turkey by using MARS method. *China-USA Business Review, 15*(12), 611–615.

Zengin, S., Yüksel, S., & Kartal, M. T. (2018). Understanding the Factors that aFFect Foreign direct investment in Turkey by Using mars method. *Finansal Araştırmalar ve Çalışmalar Dergisi, 10*(18), 1309–1123.

# Chapter 3
# Understanding the Role of Central Banks in the Financial System


## ABSTRACT

*The main responsibility of the central banks is to implement monetary policies. In this framework, they define interest rates and the amount of the money in the financial system. Hence, it can be said that central banks have the critical role in the development of the financial system. Because of this situation, it is obvious that central banks should satisfy some requirements, such as independence, in order to contribute to the effectiveness of the financial systems. Parallel to this aspect, this chapter aims to understand the role of the central banks in the financial system. In this context, the purpose and historical background of the central banking are explained. In addition to this situation, the subject of the central bank independence is identified as well. In the final aspect, important accounts in the analytical balance sheet of the central bank are defined.*


## THE NEEDS FOR CENTRAL BANK IN THE GLOBALIZED FINANCIAL SYSTEM

Especially after the globalization, economic borders between the countries are disappeared. This situation creates many different advantages for the economies. First of all, companies get an opportunity to enter new countries. In other words, they can reach new markets. This situation has an increasing

DOI: 10.4018/978-1-7998-1643-0.ch003

effect on the trade volume of these countries. Parallel to this aspect, it also makes contribution to the economic development of these countries (Claessens & Van Horen, 2015; Duarte et al., 2016).

In addition to this factor, new companies, which entered to the countries, increased the competition in these markets. In such a competitive environment, these companies have to take some actions in order to deal with their competitors. Otherwise, it becomes very difficult for these companies to survive in this competition. Within this framework, these companies can prefer to decrease the price of the goods. This situation brings an advantage for the consumers in this country (Nica et al., 2016; Greer and Hauptmeier, 2016).

Another important strategy, which can be implemented by the companies in such a competitive market, is to increase the quality of the goods. By developing more quality goods, these companies can be preferred more by the consumers. It can be seen that this competition provides a chance for the people to consume quality items. Moreover, innovation is an essential issue for the companies to compete with their competitors. That is to say, by creating innovative products and services, these companies can get competitive advantage. This issue also increases the quality of the products and services in this country (Kimatu, 2016).

In spite of these advantages, globalization causes many different risks for both companies and countries. Firstly, because there is an increase in international trade volume, the volatility in the currency exchange rates goes up as well (Figueiredo & Parhizgari, 2017). This situation creates a significant risk when the countries have foreign debt. Therefore, it is obvious that there is a strong need for a governmental authority which controls this situation. With the help of this institution, a destructive financial crisis can be prevented. Thus, it can be possible to take measures to prevent bankruptcy (Walter, 2017).

Another important risk caused by globalization is the volatility in interest rates. Interest rates play a very key role in the economic performance of the countries (Babajide et al., 2016; Nikolova et al., 2017). The main reason is that when interest rates are too high, the companies become very reluctant to make investments because their costs increase in an important manner. Hence, it is understood that high interest rate is not a preferred situation for the economic improvement of the countries. In this framework, it is obvious that there is a need for an authority to control interest rate volatility in the country.

Furthermore, globalization also caused an inflation problem for the countries (Alikar et al., 2017). When there is high inflation in the country, investors become reluctant to make investment since they are uncertain about the future prices of the raw materials. This situation decreases investment amount in the country which affects economic growth negatively. This condition explains that there is an important need for a governmental institution which can take some actions to control inflation rates (Bianchi & Civelli, 2015; Fiedler et al., 2016).

The conditions emphasized above show that there is a strong need for a central bank in the globalized financial system (Coombs, 2017; Yüksel & Adalı, 2017). This central bank can play a very key role to increase investment amount in the country by controlling inflation and interest rates. In addition to them, this central bank can also take some actions to decrease the currency exchange rate when it is necessary. Hence, these strategies can be very helpful to prevent bankruptcies of the companies and financial crisis in the country (Kartal et al., 2017; Yüksel, Canöz & Adalı, 2017).

As it can be understood central banks play a crucial role in the financial system. In this section, the importance of the central bank is explained in a detailed manner. In this context, first of all, some necessary information regarding the concept of the central bank is presented. In addition to this issue, the historical background of the central banking is explained as well. In the final sub section, the purpose of the central banks is identified.

## The Concept of Central Banking

In the general sense, central banks are independent non-profit organizations which are responsible for the implementation of monetary policy and printing the money in the name of their country. In this circumstance, printing money process is also called as emission. As it can be seen that central banks have the great importance in the financial system and macroeconomic stability of the countries (Dinçer, Hacıoğlu & Yüksel, 2016). They mainly determine the amount of money in the financial system. This situation has a significant influence on the inflation rates of the countries. On the other side, it is regarded as a symbol of the independence and power of the state (Hall & Reis, 2015).

In addition to the price stability, central banks can also affect the financial stability in the country. There is no consensus on the definition of the financial stability in the literature. The most important reason for this is that financial stability is based on many different risk types and there is no single model covering these risk factors (Zengin and Yüksel, 2016). In other words, no criteria have been developed by everyone about how to measure the financial risk. While some experts define other financial stability, some others define financial instability first and indirectly achieve financial stability (Reis, 2016; Adler et al., 2016; Dinçer, Hacıoğlu, & Yüksel, 2018).

As a general definition, financial stability represents the resilience of financial markets against shocks. In order to achieve stability in financial markets, it is necessary to efficiently allocate resources in the economy and to manage the risks in the economy appropriately. In order to manage the risks in the economy successfully, the risks must be appropriately distributed. According to another definition, financial stability means the functioning of financial institutions and the environment in which they operate. In other words, it is very important that there is no turmoil in the market in order to achieve financial stability.

Central banks have focused on price stability for years. However, the crises have shown that it is very important to consider financial stability in addition to price stability. Therefore, central banks have started to attach importance to financial stability as well as price stability (Henning, 2015; Dinçer, Yüksel and Kartal, 2016). While the central banks pursue financial stability, they try to determine the risks that threaten the market and try to take necessary measures in order to prevent these risks. Achieving financial stability is also very important for ensuring price stability. If these conditions are not met, financial instability will occur in the market. Financial instability is associated with financial crises in the literature. Because if an economy is experiencing a crisis, financial stability in that economy is disrupted (Conti-Brown, 2018; Hansen and McMahon, 2016).

## The Historical Background of Central Banking

Duties, authorities and responsibilities of central banks in accordance with the requirements of the age has undergone a change. In the first, the central banks were established to provide loans for the development targets of the government. The main reason behind this situation is that governments have many different purposes. In addition to this issue, these governments need some money so as to achieve their purposes (Levieuge et al., 2018).

In this circumstance, an important problem for the governments is to find the funds. In this situation governments had an opportunity to satisfy their needs with the help of the central banks. In other words, central banks printed money and gave this money to the governments. However, this situation caused many different problems for the stability of the economy. Mainly, this situation led to inflation problems in the country. Since the inflation increases the uncertainty in the economy, it causes investments to go down.

The history of the central banks operating today as the most important monetary body dates back to the last two centuries. However, especially with the effects of the globalization, there was a significant change in the functions of the money. This situation increased the importance of the central banks. The main reason is that globalization caused many different financial crises. This condition led to many people lose their jobs and lots of the companies went bankrupt (Dempster, 2018).

It can be seen that the most important crises were occurred after the globalization process. In these crises, one of the most significant problem was the volatility in the exchange rates. Because the countries have high amount of foreign debts, any increase in the currency exchange rates caused them to go bankrupt. In addition to this aspect, sudden fall in the stock market index also led to the financial crisis in many countries (Lentner et al., 2017; Yüksel, Özsarı & Canöz, 2016).

These issues showed that there should be a mechanism to control the risks in the market mainly caused after the globalization. There is a significant increase in the effect of the central banks on the economy as the effect of money on life is very high. After this period, central banks have begun to give significant direction to the economies of the country. In this case, the central banks have become the most important institution in the economy due to these aspects (Emir et al., 2016).

Because of the problems emphasized above, it was understood that printing money function of the central banks should be used more carefully. For this purpose, it was accepted that it is very dangerous for the central banks to give loans to the government by printing money. Therefore, in many different countries, it was prohibited for the governments to take loans from the central banks. That is to say, it is underlined that central banks should be independent from the government intervention (Corsetti et al., 2018).

## The Purpose of Central Banking

The concept of central bank is known as the bank of banks. Additionally, it is possible to talk about different functions of the central banks. First of all, central banks have activities such as implementing monetary policy. That is to say, central banks are the main authority to define interest rates and the amount of the money in the financial system (Dinçer, Yüksel & Martínez, 2019). Moreover, assisting the development of the financial system is another responsibility of the central banks. It explains that central banks should implement policies which make contribution to the financial stability of the countries (Luburić, 2017; Dincer, Uzunkaya & Yüksel, 2019). In this circumstance, the important point is that the first duty of the central bank is price stability whereas financial stability is the second purpose (Dowd, 2015).

In addition to them, another important purpose of the central banks is providing currency exchange stability in the countries. If country has foreign debts, any increase in the currency exchange rates will cause high amount of losses. This situation is similar for the companies as well. In case of high foreign debts of the companies, there is a high risk of bankruptcy when currency exchange rate goes up. Therefore, central banks should take some actions in order to minimize the volatility in the currency exchange rates (Dincer and Yuksel, 2019; Braun, 2015). Within this framework, purchasing or selling foreign currency is the main policy of the central banks. However, the central banks can maintain this application as long as they have foreign reserves.

Another important activity of the central banks is funding the government. In this scope, central banks print money and give it to the governments with the name of the loan. As it was emphasized before, in this circumstance, there is a significant risk that government can use this issue for their own interests. However, the interest of the governments cannot be appropriate with the benefits of the financial and economic system. Due to this condition, funding government can cause high inflation in the countries. Hence, in the last years, this application of the central banks is not used because of this problem.

## THE SUBJECT OF CENTRAL BANK INDEPENDENCE

As it was emphasized before, the central banks became the most significant institutions in the economic system. The main reason is that it determines the amount of the money in the system. This situation increases the power of the central banks because the actions of central banks have been a guide for other players on the market. However, central banks have been open to interventions by political authorities in carrying out these important tasks (Garriga, 2016).

Governments may choose to implement policies that are not appropriate to national economies in order to maintain political stability. In this circumstance, these governments prefer that central bank policies become similar to their purposes. Because of this condition, in the past, central banks had the creditor role to the governments. In other words, central banks printed Money and gave it to the governments as a loan. With the help of this fund, governments got an opportunity to satisfy their purposes.

Nevertheless, when these government policies are not logical, this role of the central banks created many problems for the economies of the countries. Printing too much Money by the central banks caused inflation problems in these countries. Inflation is an important for the economies which increased uncertainties. In case of uncertain environment, investors become unwilling to make new investments. This situation has a negative effect on the economic development of the countries.

Especially in the financial crises, central banks were criticized very much by both researchers and academicians. For example, in Asian crisis occurred in 1998, countries suffered from significant losses because of exchange rate volatility. In this process, central banks of these countries did not implement appropriate strategies according to many researchers. Because of this condition, the importance of central bank independence increased very much (Bodea & Hicks, 2015).

Consequently, it was understood that central banks should be independent. With the help of this issue, it is possible to prevent the populist practices of political power. In addition to this situation, potential investors also give importance to this issue. The main reason is that they prefer to make investment to the countries where central banks can take their actions independent from the government. As a result, central bank independence is a crucial factor for the sustainable economic development of the countries. This independence should be occurred with respect to the purpose and instrument, economic and political (Doumpos et al., 2015). These items are explained in the following subtitles.

## Purpose and Instrument Independence

In the first instance, central banks should have purpose and instrument independence. With respect to the purpose independence, central banks should be independent in the selection of the main objectives or targets taken as basis in the policies. Another important aspect is that this situation should be clearly stated in the laws. On the other hand, regarding instrument independence, central banks should be independent from the government to select monetary policy tools. For example, if central banks give decisions to decrease the interest rates, any other authority should not intervene. Similar to this issue, central banks should also have a right to select any tool they prefer (Dinçer, Yüksel & Kartal, 2019; de Haan et al., 2018).

## Economic Independence

Economic independence is an important factor of central bank independence. It refers that there is no relationship between central bank and government with respect to the economic issues. In other words, central banks should not give loans to the government in order to have economic independence. Otherwise, this situation can lead to high inflation problems in the country (Berggren et al., 2016; Yüksel and Kavak, 2019). In the past, it was seen that in most of the countries, which suffer from high inflation, central banks provided loans to the government (Blancheton, 2016).

It is obvious that governments desire to win the following elections. Therefore, they prefer to implement policies which make citizens more satisfied. That is to say, governments demand central banks to implement expansionary monetary policies because this policy has an increasing effect on the volume of the money in the market. This situation leads to a further revival of the economy. However, this policy may not be appropriate for each condition.

Furthermore, another significant issue is that this situation should be stated in the law. In other words, it should be prohibited to give loans by central banks with the law. If the central bank's funding of the government is not restricted by law, governments can insist on this issue when they need money. Therefore, legal issue is an essential aspect to have economic independence.

## Political Independence

One of the most significant factors regarding central bank independence is political independence. In this circumstance, an essential aspect is the appointment of central bank managers. Therefore, top management level of central banks can be independent from the government. Thus, selection of top managers should be outside of the government interventions.

Within this context, it is possible to see many different opportunities. First of all, the head of the central bank can be selected by the central bank top management personnel. With such an implementation, it is obvious that government does not have any role in this process. Hence, it has a very positive effect on the political independence of the central bank. However, if the central bank personnel give subjective and inappropriate decision, the performance of the central banks is affected negatively (Goodhart and Lastra, 2018).

Another important way in this purpose is that the top management personnel of central bank can be selected by both government and opposition parties. In other words, each party has a right to select central bank top management personnel according to their voting power. This situation has a positive contribution on the political independence on the central banks because all parties from different views have a right in this process. However, there is also risk in such an implementation. For instance, both government and opposition parties can select the central bank personnel for their future purposes. In such a condition, if they do not give importance to the qualification of the personnel and only political views of these personnel are considered, this issue affects the performance of the central bank in a negative manner.

Moreover, the head of central bank can be selected by the president of the country. It can be seen that according to this condition, president is the only power on the selection central bank personnel. Thus, it is thought that it is very difficult to have political independence of the central banks. However, it is the most commonly used method nowadays by the countries as for the selection of the head of the central bank (Martin, 2015).

Since this implementation creates problems for the independence of the central banks, these countries give importance to the tenure of the central bank governor. In most of the applications, president of the country assigns the central bank governor, but nobody can remove this governor on his/her duty time. It is obvious that this situation makes an important contribution to the central bank independence. Otherwise, if the governor of the central bank can be removed any time by the government, it is impossible to have political independence.

Nonetheless, this situation does not mean that central bank governor can have a right to do everything. If the president of the central bank has an unlawful activity, it is possible to be dismissed by court decision. In addition to this situation, if the central bank governor cannot continue to work due to health problems, another person may be appointed. In this process, it is not necessary to wait for the presidency of the chairman. As a result, in the case of only compulsory conditions the head of the central bank may be removed from office.

On the other side, it is also important to identify the length of tenure for the central bank governor. If this time is very short, it means that there is a problem regarding the independence of the central bank. The main reason is that central bank governor cannot give independent decision in such a situation. Similar to this issue, the longer tenure of the central bank governor, the more independent the decision will be possible.

In addition to these factors, legal power of the central bank plays a crucial role with respect to the political independence. Within this context, the duties of the central bank must be clearly stated in the laws. For instance, it should be emphasized in the relevant laws that the central bank is responsible for price stability and can give decisions independently from the government intervention. In such a situation, government cannot force central bank to implement a policy because it takes its power from the law.

Another significant factor of the political independence is that monetary policy programs should be defined only by the central banks. That is to say, governments should not be included in this process. In this scope, inflation targets should be determined without the intervention of the government. This situation gives information about the political independence of the central banks.

## ANALYTICAL BALANCE SHEET OF CENTRAL BANK

Balance sheet is a financial table which gives information about what a company has and how it is obtained. In other words, the balance sheet is a financial statement showing the assets of the entity at a certain date and the sources where these assets are provided (Del Negro and Sims, 2015). The balance sheet is highly beneficial for the enterprises because of many different reasons. First of all, it gives information about the investor profile of the company. In addition to this aspect, the proportion of debt and equity can be evaluated with the help of the balance sheet. Moreover, it is also possible to understand whether this company has liquidity risk or not by comparing short term assets and liabilities. Furthermore, the performance of collecting receivables and selling the items under the inventor. Balance sheet is one of the most important tables of the accounting system. Parallel to this situation, central banks also have balance sheet that is called as analytical balance sheet. To make a good and accurate analysis of the balance sheet of the central bank makes it easier to be informed about the market. Similar to the companies, the balance sheet of the central bank has mainly two different components that are assets and liabilities. In spite of this situation, the detailed items under the balance sheet of the central banks look very different from the companies. The details of the main items are emphasized below.

## Assets

Regarding the definition, asset means something a company has. In other words, it represents the tangible and intangible properties that the entity owns. It can be seen that these materials should have economic importance for the companies (Sunder et al., 2018). There may be different types of the assets for the companies. First of all, the companies have liquid assets which can be converted into the cash in a short period. Cash, checks, government bonds, stocks, short term accounts receivables and inventories can be categorized in these assets. The companies mainly hold these assets in order to satisfy their short-term needs, such as personnel wages, short term debts, payment of the bills.

In addition to them, companies also have fixed assets. The main purpose of these assets is to increase investment of the companies. In other words, companies hold fixed assets without the aim of converting into the cash. Lands, buildings, machinery and equipment can be given as an example of tangible fixed assets. Similarly, intangible fixed assets include patent, goodwill, computer programs. All fixed assets are related to the companies' core operation. It shows that increasing fixed assets gives information that the companies make investment.

This situation is quite similar for the analytical balance sheet of central bank. There are also assets on the left side of this balance sheet. These assets show the properties central bank has. The central bank uses these assets while trying to adjust the liquidity of the financial market. These assets can be divided into two different categories that are foreign assets and domestic assets. The accounts are explained in the following subtitles.

## Foreign Assets

Foreign assets mainly refer to the gold and foreign currency assets and receivables. The Central Bank's gold reserves consist of gold held in its own banks or in foreign banks. The main reason of holding gold in foreign banks is that it becomes easier to make financial investment by using this gold. For example, some central banks prefer to hold their golds in Central Bank of

England because they can make financial investment much easier in such a way. Gold is preferred by many central banks because it is a type of reserve that is always valid and has international standards. Therefore, even if there is a financial crisis, central banks can make payments by using these golds. However, in case of a global financial crisis, foreign currencies may not be used because of the devaluation (Dinçer et al., 2019; Rule, 2015).

In addition, central banks can have foreign currencies. These currencies consist of the important percentage of the central bank reserves. Similar to the gold, foreign currencies of the central banks can be placed on both in its own banks or in foreign banks. These currencies play a very significant role in the actions of the central banks. In this framework, in order to prevent high increase in currency exchange rate, central banks sell some currencies to the market by using their reserves. Central banks mainly prefer to have foreign currencies which are valid in the world, such as dollar and euro.

While considering the factors emphasized above, it is understood that having high amount of foreign currencies has an increasing effect on the power of the central banks. Therefore, most of the central banks prefer to have foreign currencies. However, it is obvious that central banks' intervention in the market is also limited by the amount of reserves it has. Thus, any sudden decrease in the market is accepted as the indicator of the financial crisis. For example, in the financial crisis of Turkey occurred in 2001, the central bank reserves decreased at a very small amount.

## Domestic Assets

With respect to the domestic assets, marketable securities play a very key role for the central banks. In this framework, central banks prefer to purchase government bonds. Governments issue the bonds when they need money. Taxes comprise the main component of the government income. On the other side, salaries of the civil servants and bills of the governmental institutions are the essential parts of the government expenses. If this income is lower than the expenses, it means that there is a budget deficit for this government. In this circumstance, governments need money and issuing government bond is the main factor to satisfy this need (Arce et al., 2017).

While issuing a bond, governments borrow some money from the investors. Additionally, government pays this amount with an additional interest at the maturity date. Thus, with the help of this process, investors get an opportunity to gain interest income and at the same time, governments can find the funds very easily. It can be understood that government bonds are crucial elements for the effectiveness and the sustainability of the financial system.

Central banks also prefer to have government bonds in their assets. The main reason is that while purchasing or selling governments bonds, central banks can influence the markets very easily. For example, if the central banks aim to implement expansionary monetary policy, they will purchase government bonds so that the liquidity amount in the market goes up. On the other hand, in order to implement contractionary monetary policy, in this case, the central banks should sell the governments bonds to decrease the liquidity in the market.

In addition to them, company bonds and stocks can also be preferred by the central banks for the same purpose. Central banks want to intervene the market in sometimes according to their purposes. In this circumstance, marketable securities can be very helpful to reach this objective. In other words, if the bond market is improved in the country, it means that central banks can implement their policies much easier by purchasing or selling these bonds.

Moreover, the amount of the loans given to the banks by central bank is classified under the domestic assets. One of the most important roles of the central bank is that it is the bank of other banks. It means that when other banks need funds, they can satisfy these needs by borrowing money from the central bank. At the maturity date, these banks pay interest to the central bank. Because the central bank makes a loan to the other banks, this loan is stated under the assets.

Furthermore, central banks can also have some fixed assets. They are acquired to use in operating activities for a period of more than one year. The aim is not to convert them into the cash in a short period. In addition to this issue, they are not considered to be consumed as well. Building, land, machinery and equipment can be given as examples for the fixed assets. As a result, these kind of properties of the central banks can be defined under the fixed assets of the balance sheet.

## Liabilities

As it is defined in the previous section, assets give information about the properties a company has. On the other hand, the liabilities explain the ways how these assets are obtained. There are mainly two different items under the liabilities which are debt and equity (Hulagu and Yalcin, 2016). Debt refers to the payables taken from the third parties. Most likely, company has to pay interest for this debt. On the other side, capital can be defined in different ways. First of all, the company can find a new partner who provides money for the purposes. In addition to this situation, special wealth of the current owners can be considered for the company purposes. Similar to the companies, the central bank can also have liabilities, such as foreign exchange liabilities and central bank money. These liabilities are identified in the following titles.

## Foreign Exchange Liabilities

Foreign exchange liabilities denote the foreign debts of the central bank within and outside the country. Within this framework, the foreign deposits held by the government can be the first example. Governments can have foreign deposits and prefer to hold this deposit on the central bank accounts. In this circumstance, this deposit shows the debt of the central banks to the government. Therefore, this account is stated on the liability part of central bank balance sheet. Additionally, the deposit of the public sector in foreign currency is also classified under the foreign exchange liabilities. Similar to these issues, the foreign currency deposits of the banks refer to the foreign exchange liabilities for the central bank. Parallel to the government deposit, both public and bank deposits give information about the debt of the central banks to these parties (Nagahisarchoghaei et al., 2018).

## Central Bank Money

The second part of the liabilities in central bank balance sheet is the central bank money. In the first section of this part, there are emission, banks' reserve requirements and banks deposits. Emission refers to the money on the circulation. With the help of this money, central banks can control the volume of money in the market. However, if central banks print too much money without an effective control, this situation leads to high inflation. It is obvious that this condition increases uncertainty in the country which makes investors unwilling to make investment (Bech and Garratt, 2017).

In most of the countries, banks have to hold a portion of their deposits on the central bank account as a reserve. In other words, in any negative environment, central banks can have a chance to use these reserves in order to minimize the problem. Therefore, it can be said that this money has an insurance role in any crisis period. Although this money is stated on the central bank accounts, the real owners of this money are the banks. Because of this situation, it can be said that this money defines the liabilities of the central banks. In addition to them, there can also be bank deposits in the central bank money account of the balance sheet. Different from the reserves, central banks can also prefer to hold some of their money on the central bank accounts (Braun, 2016).

Moreover, there is also "open market operation" account in the liability side of the central bank balance sheet. When central banks sell marketable securities to the markets, they mainly aim to decrease the liquidity amount in the financial market. In this circumstance, the liquidity amount taken form the market is stated under the open market operation account. Because central banks have to pay this amount to the counterparties, they are classified in the liability part of the central bank balance sheet (Thornton, 2019).

## LITERATURE REVIEW ON INDEPENDENCE AND BALANCE SHEET OF CENTRAL BANKS

The subjects of central bank independence and the balance sheet of the central banks attracted the attentions of many different researchers in the literature. In this section, these studies are classified into two different categories. The details of some selected studies are given on the following subtitles.

### Literature Review on Central Bank Independence

Sims (2016) made a study about the importance of the central bank independence. In this study, it is underlined that politicians prefer to take loans from the central banks. The main reason is that when there is increase in the liquidity in the market, it can provide a chance for the governments to gain votes from the citizens because of the successful macroeconomic figures. However, this situation causes an inflation problem in the long run. Thus, central banks should have political independence. In this scope, it is underlined that taking loans from the central banks should be strongly prohibited.

There are also similar studies in the literature which gave importance to the political independence of the central banks. For instance, Goodhart and Lastra (2018), Martin (2015), Blancheton (2016), Lastra (2018), Selim et al. (2018) and Hayo & Neumeier (2018) also emphasized the importance of the political independence in their studies. In addition to them, Kern et al.

(2019), Demiralp and Demiralp (2019), Doumpos et al. (2015), Haga (2015), Fernández-Albertos (2015), Garriga (2016), Bodea and Hicks (2015) and Masciandaro and Romelli (2019) also other studies which identified that central banks should have political independence in order to operate more effectively.

On the other side, Jordan and Luther (2019) made a study about the independence of the central banks. In this study, Federal Reserve's new operating regime is taken into consideration. It is concluded that central banks should have economic independence. In this context, central banks should give economic decisions independently, such as increasing or decreasing interest rate. Otherwise, it is obvious that there will be important decrease in the performance of the central banks.

Parallel to this study, the importance of economic independence of the central banks was also identified in some different studies. For example, Kern et al. (2019), Agur (2019), Nicolay and de Oliveira (2019), Wyplosz (2019), Lord (2019) and Garcia Osma et al. (2019) also reached the similar conclusion in their studies. In addition to these studies, Law et al. (2019), Jitmaneeroj et al. (2019), Conrad and Hartmann (2019), Jasmine et al. (2019), Goncharov et al. (2019), Khadan and Ruprah (2019) and Taylor et al. (2019) also underlined the economic independence of the central banks in their studies.

## Literature Review on Central Bank Balance Sheet

Central bank balance sheet was also evaluated by many different researchers in the literature. As an example, Arce et al. (2019) made a study related to the central bank balance sheet. In this study, it is defined that the size of the central bank balance sheet gives information about the quantitative easing policies of the banks. Similarly, Titzck and van den End (2019) identified that the size of the central bank balance sheet has an effect on the success of the inflation targeting program. Additionally, Cúrdia and Woodford (2011), Shiratsuka (2010), Jeanne and Svensson (2007), Berriel and Bhattarai (2009), Iwata and Takagi (2012) and Adler et al. (2016) also focused on the importance of the central bank balance sheet in many different ways.

## CONCLUSION

Globalization causes many different risks for both companies and countries, such the volatility in the currency exchange rates. This condition leads to significant losses for the companies in case of having foreign debt. Another important risk caused by globalization is the volatility in interest rates. Furthermore, globalization also caused an inflation problem for the countries. This kind of problems show that there is a strong need for a governmental authority which controls the volatility in the market. Effective management of this system can have a positive influence on preventing bankruptcy of the companies and the financial crisis. This central bank can play a very key role to increase investment amount in the country by controlling inflation and interest rates (Dinçer Yüksel & Adalı, 2019).

Within this framework, this chapter aimed to identify the role of central banks in the financial system. For this purpose, firstly, historical background and the main purpose of the central banking were discussed. In the next part, the subject of central bank independence was defined. In this scope, purpose and instrument independence, economic independence and political independence were explained. In the final part, necessary information was given about the analytical balance sheet of the central banks. As a result, it is determined that central banks play a very crucial role in order to provide effectiveness in the financial system.

## REFERENCES

Adler, G., Castro, P., & Tovar, C. E. (2016). Does central bank capital matter for monetary policy? *Open Economies Review*, *27*(1), 183–205. doi:10.100711079-015-9360-1

Agur, I. (2019). Revisiting the institutional determinants of central bank independence. *Applied Economics Letters*, 1–6.

Alikar, N., Mousavi, S. M., Ghazilla, R. A. R., Tavana, M., & Olugu, E. U. (2017). A bi-objective multi-period series-parallel inventory-redundancy allocation problem with time value of money and inflation considerations. *Computers & Industrial Engineering*, *104*, 51–67. doi:10.1016/j.cie.2016.12.006

Arce, Ó., Nuño, G., & Thomas, C. (2019). *A large central bank balance sheet? Floor vs corridor systems in a new Keynesian environment*. Academic Press.

Babajide, A., Isola, L., & Somoye, R. O. (2016). Stock market response to economic growth and interest rate volatility: Evidence from Nigeria. *International Journal of Economics and Financial Issues*, *6*(1), 354–360.

Bech, M. L., & Garratt, R. (2017, September). *Central bank cryptocurrencies. BIS Quarterly Review*.

Berggren, N., Daunfeldt, S. O., & Hellström, J. (2016). Does social trust speed up reforms? The case of central-bank independence. *Journal of Institutional Economics*, *12*(2), 395–415. doi:10.1017/S1744137415000284

Berriel, T. C., & Bhattarai, S. (2009). Monetary policy and central bank balance sheet concerns. *The B.E. Journal of Macroeconomics*, *9*(1). doi:10.2202/1935-1690.1770

Bianchi, F., & Civelli, A. (2015). Globalization and inflation: Evidence from a time-varying VAR. *Review of Economic Dynamics*, *18*(2), 406–433. doi:10.1016/j.red.2014.07.004

Blancheton, B. (2016). Central bank independence in a historical perspective. Myth, lessons and a new model. *Economic Modelling*, *52*, 101–107. doi:10.1016/j.econmod.2015.02.027

Bodea, C., & Hicks, R. (2015). Price stability and central bank independence: Discipline, credibility, and democratic institutions. *International Organization*, *69*(1), 35–61. doi:10.1017/S0020818314000277

Braun, B. (2015). Governing the future: The European Central Bank's expectation management during the Great Moderation. *Economy and Society*, *44*(3), 367–391. doi:10.1080/03085147.2015.1049447

Braun, B. (2016). Speaking to the people? Money, trust, and central bank legitimacy in the age of quantitative easing. *Review of International Political Economy*, *23*(6), 1064–1092. doi:10.1080/09692290.2016.1252415

Claessens, S., & Van Horen, N. (2015). The impact of the global financial crisis on banking globalization. *IMF Economic Review*, *63*(4), 868–918. doi:10.1057/imfer.2015.38

Conrad, C., & Hartmann, M. (2019). On the determinants of long-run inflation uncertainty: Evidence from a panel of 17 developed economies. *European Journal of Political Economy*, *56*, 233–250. doi:10.1016/j.ejpoleco.2018.09.002

Conti-Brown, P. (2018). Central banking and institutional change in the United States: punctuated equilibrium in the development of money, finance and banking. *Research Handbook on Central Banking*, 6.

Coombs, N. (2017). Macroprudential versus monetary blueprints for financial reform. *Journal of Cultural Economics, 10*(2), 207–216. doi:10.1080/17530350.2016.1234404

Corsetti, G., Dedola, L., Jarociński, M., Maćkowiak, B., & Schmidt, S. (2018). Macroeconomic stabilization, monetary-fiscal interactions, and Europe's monetary union. *European Journal of Political Economy*.

Cúrdia, V., & Woodford, M. (2011). The central-bank balance sheet as an instrument of monetarypolicy. *Journal of Monetary Economics, 58*(1), 54–79. doi:10.1016/j.jmoneco.2010.09.011

de Haan, J., Bodea, C., Hicks, R., & Eijffinger, S. C. (2018). Central bank independence before and after the crisis. *Comparative Economic Studies, 60*(2), 183–202. doi:10.105741294-017-0050-4

Del Negro, M., & Sims, C. A. (2015). When does a central bank' s balance sheet require fiscal support? *Journal of Monetary Economics, 73*, 1–19. doi:10.1016/j.jmoneco.2015.05.001

Demiralp, S., & Demiralp, S. (2019). Erosion of Central Bank independence in Turkey. *Turkish Studies, 20*(1), 49–68. doi:10.1080/14683849.2018.1505512

Dempster, M. (2018). *The End of Alchemy: Money*. Banking and the Future of the Global Economy.

Dinçer, H., Hacıoğlu, Ü., & Yüksel, S. (2016). The Impacts of Financial Variables on Employment Planning in Turkish Banking Sector. *International Journal of Sustainable Entrepreneurship and Corporate Social Responsibility, 1*(2), 1–20. doi:10.4018/IJSECSR.2016070101

Dinçer, H., Hacıoğlu, Ü., & Yüksel, S. (2018). Evaluating the Effects of Economic Imbalances on Gold Price in Turkey With MARS Method and Discussions on Microfinance. In Microfinance and Its Impact on Entrepreneurial Development, Sustainability, and Inclusive Growth (pp. 115-137). IGI Global.

Dincer, H., Uzunkaya, S. S., & Yüksel, S. (2019). An IT2-Based Hybrid Decision-Making Model Using Hesitant Fuzzy Linguistic Term Sets for Selecting the Development Plan of Financial Economics. *International Journal of Computational Intelligence Systems, 12*(2), 460–473. doi:10.2991/ijcis.d.190312.001

Dincer, H., & Yuksel, S. (2019). IT2-Based Fuzzy Hybrid Decision Making Approach to Soft Computing. *IEEE Access: Practical Innovations, Open Solutions, 7*, 15932–15944. doi:10.1109/ACCESS.2019.2895359

Dinçer, H., Yüksel, S., & Adalı, Z. (2019). Economic Effects in Islamic Stock Development of the European Countries: Policy Recommendations for Ethical Behaviors. In Handbook of Research on Managerial Thinking in Global Business Economics (pp. 58-78). IGI Global.

Dinçer, H., Yüksel, S., & Kartal, M. T. (2016). Evaluating the Corporate Governance Based Performance of Participation Banks in Turkey with the House of Quality Using an Integrated Hesitant Fuzzy MCDM [Türkiye'de Katılım Bankalarının Kurumsal Yönetiminin Çok Değişkenli Entegre Bulanık Karar Verme Yaklaşımı Kullanılarak Kalite Evi ile Değerlendirilmesi]. *BDDK Bankacılık ve Finansal Piyasalar Dergisi, 10*(1).

Dinçer, H., Yüksel, S., & Kartal, M. T. (2019). The Role of Bank Interest Rate in the Competitive Emerging Markets to Provide Financial and Economic Stability. *Ekonomi, İşletme ve Maliye Araştırmaları Dergisi, 1*(2).

Dinçer, H., Yüksel, S., & Martínez, L. (2019). Interval type 2-based hybrid fuzzy evaluation of financial services in E7 economies with DEMATEL-ANP and MOORA methods. *Applied Soft Computing*.

Dinçer, H., Yüksel, S., Yazici, M., & Pınarbaşı, F. (2019). Assessing Corporate Social Responsibilities in the Banking Sector: As a Tool of Strategic Communication During the Global Financial Crisis. In Handbook of Research on Global Issues in Financial Communication and Investment Decision Making (pp. 1-27). IGI Global.

Doumpos, M., Gaganis, C., & Pasiouras, F. (2015). Central bank independence, financial supervision structure and bank soundness: An empirical analysis around the crisis. *Journal of Banking & Finance, 61*, S69–S83. doi:10.1016/j.jbankfin.2015.04.017

Dowd, K. (2015). Central bank stress tests: Mad, bad, and dangerous. *The Cato Journal, 35*, 507.

Duarte, R., Pinilla, V., & Serrano, A. (2016). Globalization and natural resources: The expansion of the Spanish agrifood trade and its impact on water consumption, 1965–2010. *Regional Environmental Change, 16*(1), 259–272. doi:10.100710113-014-0752-3

Emir, S., Dincer, H., Hacioglu, U., & Yuksel, S. (2015). Comparative Study of Outlier Detection Algorithms via Fundamental Analysis Variables. *International Journal of Research in Business and Social Science, 4*(4), 45-60.

Fernández-Albertos, J. (2015). The politics of central bank independence. *Annual Review of Political Science, 18*(1), 217–237. doi:10.1146/annurev-polisci-071112-221121

Fiedler, S., Jannsen, N., Reitz, S., & Wolters, M. (2016). Is Globalization Reducing the Ability of Central Banks to Control Inflation? A Literature Review with an Application to the Euro Area. *Review of Economics, 67*(3), 231–253. doi:10.1515/roe-2016-0007

Figueiredo, A., & Parhizgari, A. M. (2017). Currency volatility and bid-ask spreads of ADRs and local shares. *Global Finance Journal, 34*, 54–71. doi:10.1016/j.gfj.2016.07.002

Garcia Osma, B., Mora, A., & Porcuna-Enguix, L. (2019). *Prudential Supervisors' Independence and Income Smoothing in European Banks.* Available at SSRN 3172753

Garriga, A. C. (2016). Central bank independence in the world: A new data set. *International Interactions, 42*(5), 849–868. doi:10.1080/03050629.2016.1188813

Goncharov, I., Novotny-Farkas, Z., & Wu, X. (2019). *Disclosure Choice When Market-Wide Externalities Matter: Evidence from IFRS Adoptions by Central Banks.* Available at SSRN 3330830

Goodhart, C., & Lastra, R. (2018). Populism and central bank independence. *Open Economies Review, 29*(1), 49–68. doi:10.100711079-017-9447-y

Greer, I., & Hauptmeier, M. (2016). Management whipsawing: The staging of labor competition under globalization. *Industrial & Labor Relations Review, 69*(1), 29–52. doi:10.1177/0019793915602254

Haga, M. (2015). On central bank independence and political cycles. *Journal of Applied Econometrics, 18*(2), 267–295.

Hall, R. E., & Reis, R. (2015). *Maintaining central-bank financial stability under new-style central banking (No. w21173)*. National Bureau of Economic Research. doi:10.3386/w21173

Hansen, S., & McMahon, M. (2016). Shocking language: Understanding the macroeconomic effects of central bank communication. *Journal of International Economics*, *99*, S114–S133. doi:10.1016/j.jinteco.2015.12.008

Hayo, B., & Neumeier, F. (2018). *Central Bank Independence in New Zealand: Public Knowledge About and Attitude Towards the Policy Target Agreement*. Available at SSRN 3318545

Henning, C. R. (2015). The ECB as a strategic actor: Central banking in a politically fragmented monetary union. In J. A. Caporaso & M. Rhodes (Eds.), *The ECB as a Strategic Actor: Central Banking in a Politically Fragmented Monetary Union*. New York: Oxford University Press.

Hulagu, T., & Yalcin, C. (2016). Micro evidence on foreign exchange liabilities and the exchange rate risk in non-financial firms in Turkey: a descriptive analysis. *IFC Bulletin*, (41).

Iwata, K., & Takagi, S. (2012). Central bank balance sheet expansion: Japan's experience. *BIS Paper*, (66g).

Jasmine, M. F., Mona, E. F., & Talla, A. E. H. (2019). A New Insight into the Measurement of Central Bank Independence. *Journal of Central Banking Theory and Practice*, *8*(1), 67–96. doi:10.2478/jcbtp-2019-0004

Jeanne, O., & Svensson, L. E. (2007). Credible commitment to optimal escape from a liquidity trap: The role of the balance sheet of an independent central bank. *The American Economic Review*, *97*(1), 474–490. doi:10.1257/aer.97.1.474

Jitmaneeroj, B., Lamla, M. J., & Wood, A. (2019). The implications of central bank transparency for uncertainty and disagreement. *Journal of International Money and Finance*, *90*, 222–240. doi:10.1016/j.jimonfin.2018.10.002

Jordan, J. L., & Luther, W. J. (2019). *Central Bank Independence and the Federal Reserve's New Operating Regime*. Available at SSRN 3313068

Kartal, M. T., Yüksel, S., & Zengin, S. (2017). Türk Bankacılık Sektöründeki Kar Dağıtım Kısıtlamalarının Yatırımcıların Kararları Üzerindeki Etkileri. *Bankacılık ve Sermaye Piyasası Araştırmaları Dergisi*, *1*(1), 38–51.

Kern, A., Rau-Göhring, M., & Reinsberg, B. (2019). IMF conditionality and central bank independence. *European Journal of Political Economy, 59*, 212–229. doi:10.1016/j.ejpoleco.2019.03.002

Khadan, J., & Ruprah, I. J. (2019). The Economic and Political Costs of Diversification as a Way Out of a Recession: The Case of Trinidad and Tobago. In *Development, Political, and Economic Difficulties in the Caribbean* (pp. 117–148). Cham: Palgrave Macmillan. doi:10.1007/978-3-030-02994-4_7

Kimatu, J. N. (2016). Evolution of strategic interactions from the triple to quad helix innovation models for sustainable development in the era of globalization. *Journal of Innovation and Entrepreneurship, 5*(1), 16. doi:10.118613731-016-0044-x

Lastra, R. M. (2018). 15. The institutional path of central bank independence. *Research Handbook on Central Banking*, 296.

Law, C. H., Tee, C. L., & Lau, W. T. (2019). The Impacts of Financial Integration on the Linkages Between Monetary Independence and Foreign Exchange Reserves. *International Economic Journal*, 1–24.

Lentner, C., Szegedi, K., & Tatay, T. (2017). Social Responsibility in the Operation of Central Banks. *Financial and Economic Review, 16*(2), 64–85.

Levieuge, G., Lucotte, Y., & Ringuedé, S. (2018). Central bank credibility and the expectations channel: Evidence based on a new credibility index. *Review of World Economics, 154*(3), 493–535. doi:10.100710290-018-0308-6

Lord, C. (2019). No epistocracy without representation? The case of the European Central Bank. *European Political Science, 20*(1), 1–15.

Luburić, R. (2017). Strengthening the Three Lines of Defence in Terms of More Efficient Operational Risk Management in Central Banks. *Journal of Central Banking Theory and Practice, 6*(1), 29–53. doi:10.1515/jcbtp-2017-0003

Martin, F. M. (2015). Debt, inflation and central bank independence. *European Economic Review, 79*, 129–150. doi:10.1016/j.euroecorev.2015.07.009

Masciandaro, D., & Romelli, D. (2019). *Peaks and troughs: Economics and political economy of central bank independence cycles*. Academic Press.

Nagahisarchoghaei, M., Nagahi, M., & Soleimani, N. (2018). Impact of Exchange Rate Movements on Indian Firm Performance. *International Journal of Finance and Accounting, 7*(4), 108–121.

Nica, E., Manole, C., & Potcovaru, A. M. (2016). Competition in the worldwide workplace: Economic globalization and labor rights. *Journal of Self-Governance and Management Economics*, *4*(3), 73. doi:10.22381/JSME4320165

Nicolay, R., & de Oliveira, A. J. (2019). Inflation volatility, monetary policy signaling and clarity of the central bank communication: Evidence from an inflation targeting emerging economy. *Journal of Economic Studies*. (accepted for publication)

Nikolova, L. V., Rodionov, D. G., & Afanasyeva, N. V. (2017). Impact of globalization on innovation project risks estimation. *European Research Studies*, *20*(2), 396.

Reis, J. (2016). The Emergence of Central Banks and Banking Supervision in Comparative Perspective. In *State and Financial Systems in Europe and the USA* (pp. 139–154). Routledge. doi:10.4324/9781315610603

Rule, G. (2015). *Understanding the central bank balance sheet*. Handbooks.

Selim, H., Galal, A., Elbadawi, I., & Nugent, J. (2018, September). Does Central Bank Independence Matter in Arab Oil Exporters. *Economic Research Forum Working Papers* (No. 1223).

Shiratsuka, S. (2010). Size and composition of the central bank balance sheet: Revisiting Japan's experience of the quantitative easing policy. *Monetary and Economic Studies*, *28*(3), 79–105.

Sims, C. A. (2016, August). Fiscal policy, monetary policy and central bank independence. *Kansas Citi Fed Jackson Hole Conference*.

Sunder, J., Sunder, S. V., & Zhang, J. (2018). Balance sheet conservatism and debt contracting. *Contemporary Accounting Research*, *35*(1), 494–524. doi:10.1111/1911-3846.12356

Taylor, M. W., Arner, D. W., & Gibson, E. C. (2019). Central Banks' New Macroprudential Consensus. The Oxford Handbook of the Economics of Central Banking, 482.

Thornton, D. L. (2019). The Fed and Short-Term Rates: Is It Open Market Operations, Open Mouth Operations or Interest Rate Smoothing? *Federal Reserve Bank of St. Louis Working Paper Series*, (1999-022).

Titzck, S., & van den End, J. W. (2019). *The impact of size, composition and duration of the central bank balance sheet on inflation expectations and market prices*. Academic Press.

Walter, S. (2017). Globalization and the demand-side of politics: How globalization shapes labor market risk perceptions and policy preferences. *Political Science Research and Methods*, *5*(1), 55–80. doi:10.1017/psrm.2015.64

Wyplosz, C. (2019). Limits to the independence of the ECB. *Review of World Economics*, 1–7.

Yüksel, S., & Adalı, Z. (2017). Farklı kredi türleri ve ekonomik büyüme arasındaki nedensellik ilişkisinin belirlenmesi: Türkiye üzerine bir uygulama. *Politik Ekonomik Kuram*, *1*(1), 1–21. doi:10.30586/pek.319282

Yüksel, S., Canöz, İ., & Adalı, Z. (2017). Türkiye'deki Mevduat Bankalarının Fiyat-Kazanç Oranını Etkileyen Değişkenlerin Mars Yöntemi İle Belirlenmesi. *Fiscaoeconomia*, (3).

Yüksel, S., & Kavak, P. T. (2019). Do Financial Investment Decisions Affect Economic Development?: An Analysis on Mortgage Loans in Turkey. In Handbook of Research on Global Issues in Financial Communication and Investment Decision Making (pp. 168-191). IGI Global.

Yüksel, S., Özsarı, M., & Canöz, İ. (2016). *Influencing factors of currency risk of deposit banks in Turkey by using probit method*. Academic Press.

Zengin, S., & Yüksel, S. (2016). A comparison of the views of internal controllers/auditors and branch/call center personnel of the banks for operational risk: A case for Turkish banking sector. *International Journal of Finance & Banking Studies*, *5*(4), 10.

# Chapter 4
# Monetary Policy Operations of Central Banks in the E7 Economies


## ABSTRACT

*Both monetary and fiscal policies have a crucial role in the financial markets of the countries. In this framework, policies can be used for mainly two different purposes, which are contractionary and expansionary policies. Hence, it can be said that monetary policies play a key role especially for the emerging economies. The main reason is that these are the economies that aim to be a developed economy. In order to reach this objective, they aim to make investment to obtain sustainable economic growth. Similar to this aspect, this chapter aims to identify different monetary policy operations of the central banks. Thus, various monetary policy instruments are explained. After this issue, necessary information is given related to the central banking operations of E7 economies. As a result, it is defined that central banks of these countries play an active role especially during the recession period.*


## GENERAL INFORMATION ABOUT MONETARY POLICIES

Monetary policy and fiscal policy are two important tools used to regulate a country's economic activities. Monetary policy usually deals with interest rates and control of money supply (Wu and Xia, 2016). That is to say, by changing interest rates or the amount of money in the market, central banks

DOI: 10.4018/978-1-7998-1643-0.ch004

aim to take some actions to reach their objectives. Another important point in this circumstance is that the central bank is the only authority in the country that can implement monetary policies. The main reason behind this issue is to provide independence of the central banks (Bruno & Shin, 2015; Gali, 2015).

On the other side, fiscal policy is a general name given to government regulations on tax and government expenditures. In other words, governments can increase or decrease the tax ratio in order to reach their purposes (Gertler & Karadi, 2015). Similar to the tax ratio, expenditures made by the governments have an important influence on the financial market and economic development of the country as well. As it can be understood from this definition that fiscal policies are implemented by the governments (Bergsten, 2017; Rendahl, 2016).

In summary both monetary and fiscal policies have a crucial role in the financial markets of the countries. In this framework, policies can be used for mainly two different purposes which are contractionary and expansionary policies. The aim of the contractionary monetary policy is to reduce the money supply in the market. Hence, it is obvious that this kind of policy is usually applied to reduce inflation in the country. In this context, it is aimed to reduce consumer demand by reducing money supply (Nelson et al., 2018).

In addition to them, central banks aim to increase the money supply in the market through expansionary monetary policy. The important point in this circumstance is that central banks implement these policies when there is no inflation problem in the country. Because of this situation, central banks aim to obtain financial stability. Thus, the actions are taken mainly to increase investment amounts. With the help of these policies, unemployment can be decreased in the country as well (Neely, 2015; Coibion et al., 2017).

On the other hand, if a government does not think there is enough economic activity in the country, it aims to implement expansionary fiscal policies. Within this framework, it is possible to improve the economy by increasing government expenditures. In addition to this policy, the government can also reach this objective by changing tax rates. When the tax rates are decreased in the country, this situation has an increasing effect on the investment amount (Fratzscher et al., 2016; Rey, 2016). Therefore, it plays a very important role to increase economic activity. Similarly, these policies can be implemented on the opposite way. It means that the government can implement contractionary fiscal policy by increasing tax rates and reducing government expenditures (Dellepiane-Avellaneda, 2015).

Monetary policies play a very key role especially for the emerging economies. The main reason is that these are the economies that aim to be a developed economy. In order to reach this objective, they aim to make investment to obtain sustainable economic growth. However, if this strategy is implemented with an uncontrolled manner, there may be some problems in the economy, such as inflation. Therefore, it is obvious that central banks of these countries have a great importance for this situation (Angrist et al., 2018; Obstfeld & Duval, 2018).

Parallel to the issues emphasized above, in this section, first of all, monetary policy instruments of the central banks are explained. In this scope, necessary information is given related to the required reserve ratio, rediscount rate, open market operations, standing facilities and asset purchase program. After this topic, central banking in the major seven emerging economies (E7) is identified.

## MONETARY POLICY INSTRUMENTS OF CENTRAL BANKS

The policies implemented by central banks to achieve price stability, employment growth and economic growth in a country are called monetary policies. In order to reach this objective, central banks can change interest rates and money supply in the financial market with respect to the monetary policies. The basis of the monetary policy is to influence the consumption and investment expenditures in the country by changing the interest rates. The only authorized institution in the implementation of monetary policy is the central bank. For this purpose, central banks can implement different monetary policy instruments, such as required reserve ratio, rediscount rate, open market operations, standing facilities and asset purchase program. These instruments are explained in the following subtitles.

### Required Reserve Ratio

Banks are the institutions which give loans to the people and companies for their purposes. It means that banks need some amount of funds to reach this objective. Thus, the main source of this fund is the deposit collected from the fund savers. In other words, banks give loans to the parties mainly by using the money collected from the fund savers with the name of the deposits. However, there is an important rule specific for this condition. The banks should allocate a portion of these deposits on the central bank accounts as a reserve (Li et al., 2017; Rockoff, 2018).

This situation explains that banks cannot use all deposit amount as loans. The amount transferred on the central bank account is called as required reserves. In this circumstance, the important point is to decide the percentage of the deposit which is transferred to the central bank account as required reserves. The name of the percentage is required reserve ratio and the central bank is the only authority to decide this ratio (Omer, 2016; Tallman & White, 2017).

By using required reserve ratio, central banks can intervene the financial market. In this scope, if there is high inflation in the economy, central banks aim to implement contractionary monetary policy. For this purpose, they increase the required reserve ratio to decrease the amount of liquidity. It means that banks can give lower amount of the credit to the market because they have to keep higher reserves on the central bank accounts (Park and Van Horn, 2015; Hammad, 2019).

On the other side, central banks aim to use expansionary monetary policy when there is no inflation problem. In order to reach this objective, central banks can decrease required reserve ratio. Lower required reserve ration means that banks can give higher amount of credit to the people and companies than in the past. It is obvious that this condition increases the liquidity amount in the market (Salahesh et al., 2017; Yimer, 2018).

## Rediscount Rate

Central bank is accepted as the "bank of other banks". Therefore, when banks need money, they can borrow this money from the central bank. Additionally, banks pay interest rate for the debt taken by the central bank. This interest rate is defined by the central bank and it is named as "rediscount rate". In the past, many different banks benefit from this opportunity in order to manage their liquidity levels (Amiri & Gong, 2018; Chong and Liu, 2017).

Rediscount rate can be used as a monetary policy tool by the central banks. In this context, if central banks aim to implement contractionary monetary policy, they can increase rediscount rates. In other words, these rates should be increased in case of high inflation. The main reason is that when these rates are high, banks become reluctant to take loans form the central banks. Therefore, liquidity amount in the market can be decreased by increasing rediscount ratio (Udude & Nwachukwu, 2016; Kamińska et al., 2018).

On the other side, rediscount rate can also be used by the central banks to implement expansionary monetary policies. That is to say, if central banks decide to decrease rediscount rate, bank take an opportunity to find fund much easily. Therefore, the amount of the liquidity in the market goes up. While considering these issues, it is understood that decreasing rediscount rate can be implemented when there is not an inflation problem in the country. However, it can be seen that rediscount rate is not an active monetary policy tool of the central banks. The main reason is that bank can find money from other sources of the central bank. Hence, increasing rediscount rate does not mean that the liquidity in the market will decrease immediately (Nwandu, 2016; Agbo & Nwankwo, 2018).

## Open Market Operations

Open market operations are the most important monetary policy tool. In this process, central banks purchase or sale government bonds in the market. With the help of these operations, they aim to increase or decrease liquidity amount in the market. Open market operations are the most active monetary policy tool. The main reason is that by selling or purchasing bonds, central banks can directly influence the market (Carlson & Lackman, 2018; Eggertsson and Proulx, 2016).

Similar to the previous monetary policy tools, open market operations can also be used for both expansionary and contractionary monetary policies. In this scope, if there is an inflation problem in the country, central banks aim to decrease the liquidity level in the market. For this purpose, they sell government bonds to the market. In this circumstance, it means that they collect money from the market (Eggertsson & Proulx, 2016; Nishiyama, 2017).

On the other side, open market operations can also be used with the aim of expansionary policies. In other words, central banks can purchase government bonds from the market. With the help of this action, liquidity amount in the market can be increased. However, for such a policy, the main requirement is that there should not be any inflation problem in the country. Another important point is that there should be a developed bond market in the country in order for open market operations to operate effectively (McRae et al., 2017; Ross et al., 2015).

## Standing Facilities

Standing facilities can also be used by the central banks to control liquidity in the market. With these facilities, it can be possible to provide and absorb liquidity. In this policy, central banks can provide loans to the financial institutions. With the help of them, financial institutions can minimize the liquidity risk. Within this framework, there may be intraday liquidity facility and late liquidity window facility (Näther, 2018; Vollmer and Wiese, 2016).

### Asset Purchase Programs

Asset purchase programs mainly aim to purchase long-term bonds, which were released to be borrowed by the Treasury or the institutions. In other words, it can be defined as purchasing money market instruments, such as commercial papers and government bonds within the framework. In such a program, it is intended to increase the liquidity amount in the market. In other words, by paying the price and giving money to the market, central banks try to implement expansionary monetary policy (Gibson et al., 2016; Sahuc, 2016; Wang, 2018).

## CENTRAL BANKING IN E7 ECONOMIES

E7 countries consist of Brazil, China, India, Indonesia, Mexico, Russia and Turkey. The term "E7" comes from the expression of "emerging 7". It is thought that these countries have a significant potential to be a developed economy. The details of central bank policies of these countries are demonstrated on the following subtitles.

### Brazil

Brazil is an important emerging economy in the world. Some information related to Brazil is given on Table 1.

Table 1 shows that there is an increase in the percentage of the central government debt over the years. Another important point is that Brazil started to have current account deficit after 2008. Additionally, in the last years, there is a problem related to the economic growth. Although inflation increase from 4.89% to 9.03%, it has a decreasing trend in the last two years. Moreover, the population of the Brazil increases, and unemployment rate exceeded 10% after 2016.

Brazil had significant economic growth after 1994. In this period, Brazilian currency, Real, was fixed to US dollar and this situation is named as "Real Plan". However, 1997 Asian crises had very negative effects on Brazilian

*Table 1. General information about Brazil*

| Year | Central Government Debt, Total (% of GDP) | Current Account Balance (% of GDP) | GDP Growth (annual %) | GINI Index (World Bank estimate) | Inflation, consumer prices (annual %) | Population, total | Unemployment, Total (% of total labor force) (national estimate) |
|---|---|---|---|---|---|---|---|
| 2005 | 65.45 | 1.57 | 3.20 | 56.30 | 6.87 | 186,917,361 | 9.31 |
| 2006 | 63.95 | 1.23 | 3.96 | 55.60 | 4.18 | 189,012,412 | 8.39 |
| 2007 | 62.45 | 0.11 | 6.06 | 54.90 | 3.64 | 191,026,637 | 8.09 |
| 2008 | 60.66 | -1.66 | 5.09 | 54.00 | 5.68 | 192,979,029 | 7.63 |
| 2009 | 63.81 | -1.46 | -0.13 | 53.70 | 4.89 | 194,895,996 | 8.28 |
| 2010 | 61.32 | -3.43 | 7.54 | - | 5.04 | 196,796,269 | 7.26 |
| 2011 | 59.34 | -2.94 | 3.99 | 52.90 | 6.64 | 198,686,688 | 6.69 |
| 2012 | 59.85 | -3.00 | 1.93 | 52.60 | 5.40 | 200,560,983 | 7.19 |
| 2013 | 57.23 | -3.03 | 3.01 | 52.80 | 6.20 | 202,408,632 | 6.99 |
| 2014 | 58.46 | -4.24 | 0.51 | 51.50 | 6.33 | 204,213,133 | 6.67 |
| 2015 | 67.54 | -3.30 | -3.55 | 51.30 | 9.03 | 205,962,108 | 8.44 |
| 2016 | 73.54 | -1.32 | -3.47 | - | 8.74 | 207,652,865 | 11.61 |
| 2017 | 79.54 | -0.48 | 0.98 | - | 3.45 | 209,288,278 | 13.32 |

Source: World Bank

economy (Kalkavan and Ersin, 2019). In this circumstance, stock prices experienced extraordinary decreases. On the other side, Brazil started to have current account deficit. This situation increased the vulnerability of the Brazilian economy. As a result, Brazil had to devaluate its currency. After that, it was declared that central bank of Brazil does not intervene to the market in order to control currency exchange rate. With this strategy, it is aimed to provide trust for the foreign investors.

After this stabilization process, central bank of Brazil also gave information that the country will adopt inflation targeting program. It is understood that expect the years between 2001 and 2003, central bank of Brazil was successful to achieve the inflation targets (Afonso et al., 2016). The overnight rate of central Bank of Brazil is called as SELIC rate. The main purpose of this rate is to make open market operations with the aim of intervening the market. This ratio decreased to 6.75% in order to boost the market. However, because of the expected inflation, central bank of Brazil planned to increase it more than 7.5%.

In summary, Brazil experiences an important financial crisis in 1998. It is accepted that the main reason of this crisis is the fixed exchange rate regime used in Brazil (de Medeiros et al., 2016; Perissinotto et al., 2017). In this crisis process, central Bank of Brazil played an active role by implementing floating exchange rate regime. In addition to this aspect, it also did not intervene to the market to control the currency exchange rate in this process. With the help of these successful strategies and achieving inflation targets, Brazilian economy started to have economic stability (Codato et al., 2016; Azevedo and Pereira, 2018; de Vilaca Burgos et al., 2017).

## China

Similar to Brazil, China also plays a key role for the economy of the world. Some information related to China is given on Table 2.

It is seen that China always has current account surplus. Another significant point is that there is also economic growth in all years between 2005 and 2017. On the other hand, there is low inflation in China. It is also understood that China has the biggest population in the world. In spite of this huge population, there is not high unemployment rate in China.

Central Bank of China is the central bank that has the highest amount of US dollar reserves (McCauley & Ma, 2015; Hess, 2017). The monetary

*Table 2. General information about China*

| Year | Current Account Balance (% of GDP) | GDP Growth (annual %) | Inflation, Consumer Prices (annual %) | Population, Total | Unemployment, Total (% of total labor force) (national estimate) |
|---|---|---|---|---|---|
| 2005 | 5.79 | 11.40 | 1.78 | 1,303,720,000 | 4.14 |
| 2006 | 8.42 | 12.72 | 1.65 | 1,311,020,000 | 4.00 |
| 2007 | 9.94 | 14.23 | 4.82 | 1,317,885,000 | 3.76 |
| 2008 | 9.15 | 9.65 | 5.93 | 1,324,655,000 | 4.36 |
| 2009 | 4.76 | 9.40 | -0.73 | 1,331,260,000 | 4.29 |
| 2010 | 3.90 | 10.64 | 3.18 | 1,337,705,000 | 4.20 |
| 2011 | 1.80 | 9.54 | 5.55 | 1,344,130,000 | 4.34 |
| 2012 | 2.52 | 7.86 | 2.62 | 1,350,695,000 | 4.47 |
| 2013 | 1.54 | 7.76 | 2.62 | 1,357,380,000 | 4.54 |
| 2014 | 2.25 | 7.30 | 1.92 | 1,364,270,000 | 4.59 |
| 2015 | 2.75 | 6.90 | 1.44 | 1,371,220,000 | 4.61 |
| 2016 | 1.81 | 6.70 | 2.00 | 1,378,665,000 | 4.65 |
| 2017 | 1.35 | 6.90 | 1.59 | 1,386,395,000 | 4.68 |

Source: World Bank

policy of Chinese Central Bank can be defined as prudently and neutrally. It has highlighted its monetary policy stance in order to counter the systemic risks in the economy and underlined that they will maintain their liquidity conditions in a stable manner (Han, 2015; Hu et al., 2015).

In addition to this aspect, it is also seen that central bank of China actively intervened to the market in order to control high inflation rate. For example, when the inflation was negative in 2009, central bank of China also decreased interest rate in order to boost the economy. On the other side, it decided to decrease interest rate in 2011 in order to decrease inflation rate (Suzuki and Miah, 2017; Wildau, 2017).

## India

India is the third emerging country in our analysis. Some information related to India is given on Table 3.

Table 3 indicates that India has current account deficit in all years. On the other side, there is economic growth in India. Although inflation exceeded 10% in some years, it has a decreasing trend especially in the last years.

*Table 3. General information about India*

| Year | Current Account Balance (% of GDP) | GDP Growth (annual %) | Inflation, Consumer Prices (annual %) | Population, Total | Unemployment, Total (% of total labor force) (national estimate) |
|---|---|---|---|---|---|
| 2005 | -1.27 | 9.28 | 4.25 | 1,144,118,674 | 4.40 |
| 2006 | -1.01 | 9.26 | 6.15 | 1,161,977,719 | 4.24 |
| 2007 | -0.67 | 9.80 | 6.37 | 1,179,681,239 | 4.06 |
| 2008 | -2.61 | 3.89 | 8.35 | 1,197,146,906 | 4.12 |
| 2009 | -1.98 | 8.48 | 10.88 | 1,214,270,132 | 3.75 |
| 2010 | -3.29 | 10.26 | 11.99 | 1,230,980,691 | 3.54 |
| 2011 | -3.43 | 6.64 | 8.86 | 1,247,236,029 | 3.53 |
| 2012 | -5.00 | 5.46 | 9.31 | 1,263,065,852 | 3.62 |
| 2013 | -2.65 | 6.39 | 10.91 | 1,278,562,207 | 3.46 |
| 2014 | -1.34 | 7.41 | 6.66 | 1,293,859,294 | 3.41 |
| 2015 | -1.07 | 8.15 | 4.91 | 1,309,053,980 | 3.49 |
| 2016 | -0.53 | 7.11 | 4.95 | 1,324,171,354 | 3.51 |
| 2017 | -1.47 | 6.68 | 3.33 | 1,339,180,127 | 3.52 |

Source: World Bank

The population of India is very near to China. Moreover, there is no high unemployment rate in this country.

It can be understood that central bank of India plays an active role in the market. Before the period of 2008 global mortgage crisis, Indian economy had significant economic growth. In this period, central bank of India took actions to control this extraordinary growth. In other words, it implemented contractionary monetary policy to have stable economic growth. Within this framework, it increased interest rate with the aim of decreasing liquidity in the market (Sharma, 2016; Gupta & Kaur, 2015).

On the other side, after 2009, it is seen that central bank of India decided to decrease interest rate. The main purpose of implementing this expansionary monetary policy is to increase the liquidity amount in the market. Therefore, it can be possible to boost the economy. As a result, with the help of making new investment, Indian economy experienced significant economic growth (Trivedi & Srinivasan, 2016; Lakshmi and Reddy, 2017).

## Indonesia

Indonesia is another emerging country which takes a place in E7 econmies. Some information related to Indonesia is presented on Table 4.

Table 4 indicates that Indonesia started to have current account deficit after 2012. However, there is economic growth in all years. Inflation rate and population have a decreasing trend in Indonesia. On the other side, unemployment rate decreased to 4.18% whereas it was 8.06% in 2007.

Central Bank of Indonesia adopted inflation targeting system after 2005. Therefore, it implemented monetary policies in order to achieve these targets. It can be seen that these monetary policies were very successful in this framework (Edward, 2017; Juhro, 2015; Williams, 2018). For instance, inflation rate exceeded 10% after 2008 mainly due to the negative effects of global mortgage crisis. In this period, central bank of Indonesia decided to increase interest rate to control this inflation (Lan & Nugroho, 2019; Chou and Buchdadi, 2016; Wuryandani & Mardiani, 2015).

## Mexico

Mexico is the fifth emerging country in the analysis process. Some information related to Mexico is presented on Table 5.

*Table 4. General information about Indonesia*

| Year | Current Account Balance (% of GDP) | GDP Growth (annual %) | Inflation, Consumer Prices (annual %) | Population, Total | Unemployment, Total (% of total labor force) (national estimate) |
|---|---|---|---|---|---|
| 2005 | 0.10 | 5.69 | 10.45 | 226,712,730 | 7.71 |
| 2006 | 2.98 | 5.50 | 13.11 | 229,838,202 | 7.55 |
| 2007 | 2.43 | 6.35 | 6.41 | 232,989,141 | 8.06 |
| 2008 | 0.02 | 6.01 | 10.23 | 236,159,276 | 7.21 |
| 2009 | 1.97 | 4.63 | 4.39 | 239,340,478 | 6.11 |
| 2010 | 0.68 | 6.22 | 5.13 | 242,524,123 | 5.61 |
| 2011 | 0.19 | 6.17 | 5.36 | 245,707,511 | 5.15 |
| 2012 | -2.66 | 6.03 | 4.28 | 248,883,232 | 4.47 |
| 2013 | -3.19 | 5.56 | 6.41 | 252,032,263 | 4.34 |
| 2014 | -3.09 | 5.01 | 6.39 | 255,131,116 | 4.05 |
| 2015 | -2.04 | 4.88 | 6.36 | 258,162,113 | 4.51 |
| 2016 | -1.82 | 5.03 | 3.53 | 261,115,456 | 4.12 |
| 2017 | -1.71 | 5.07 | 3.81 | 263,991,379 | 4.18 |

Source: World Bank

*Table 5. General information about Mexico*

| Year | Current Account Balance (% of GDP) | GDP Growth (annual %) | Inflation, Consumer Prices (annual %) | Population, Total | Unemployment, Total (% of total labor force) (national estimate) |
|---|---|---|---|---|---|
| 2005 | -1.03 | 2.31 | 3.99 | 108,472,228 | 3.56 |
| 2006 | -0.38 | 4.50 | 3.63 | 110,092,378 | 3.57 |
| 2007 | -0.96 | 2.29 | 3.97 | 111,836,346 | 3.65 |
| 2008 | -1.53 | 1.14 | 5.12 | 113,661,809 | 3.90 |
| 2009 | -0.88 | -5.29 | 5.30 | 115,505,228 | 5.38 |
| 2010 | -0.50 | 5.12 | 4.16 | 117,318,941 | 5.33 |
| 2011 | -1.06 | 3.66 | 3.41 | 119,090,017 | 5.19 |
| 2012 | -1.56 | 3.64 | 4.11 | 120,828,307 | 4.92 |
| 2013 | -2.45 | 1.35 | 3.81 | 122,535,969 | 4.94 |
| 2014 | -1.87 | 2.80 | 4.02 | 124,221,600 | 4.83 |
| 2015 | -2.59 | 3.29 | 2.72 | 125,890,949 | 4.34 |
| 2016 | -2.22 | 2.90 | 2.82 | 127,540,423 | 3.88 |
| 2017 | -1.69 | 2.04 | 6.04 | 129,163,276 | 3.42 |

Source: World Bank

Table 5 shows that Mexico always has current account deficit. However, the rate of this deficit is lower than 3%. Although there is economic shrinkage in 2009 mainly because of the global mortgage crisis, Mexico always have economic growth. Despite the fact that there is not high inflation rate between the years 2005 and 2016, it exceeded 6% in 2017. Similar to the other emerging economies, there is an increase in the population of Mexico. Finally, it is also seen that unemployment has a decreasing trend.

After the oil crisis in Mexico in 1974, the country experienced high inflation. Moreover, the crisis has caused economic recession in the country. The mentioned problems caused a severe recession in the Mexican economy. In order to prevent these problems, the new economy program started to be implemented in 1988.

It is seen that the program yielded very positive results in the first years. However, when we look at the results of the said program, it is understood that the country's foreign trade figures are uneven. In this period, Mexico has significant amount of current account deficit. The main reason behind the problem is that the domestic currency of the country is indexed to the dollar. In this process, the highly valued Mexican peso has made import goods more attractive. On the other hand, the demand for export goods decreased as the country's export goods became more expensive. As a result, increasing imports and declining export figures led to the country's current account deficit.

In order to prevent these problems, Mexico started to have floating exchange rate regime. With the abandonment of the fixed exchange rate system, there has been a significant increase in interest rates and inflation. After the crisis, some measures were taken by the Mexican government (López-Balderas et al., 2019). In the first stage, reforms and regulations were made in the banking sector and measures were taken. In this context, audits on banks were increased. On the other hand, tight monetary and fiscal policies have been implemented in order to prevent the effects of the crisis (Guerra, 2017; Kollmann, 2016).

## Russia

Russia is another significant emerging country in the analysis process. Some information related to Russia is shown on Table 6.

Table 6 explains that Russia has always current account surplus. Another significant issue is that Russia has economic growth in many years between 2005 and 2017. However, there is economic recession in 2009 mainly because

*Table 6. General information about Russia*

| Year | Current Account Balance (% of GDP) | GDP Growth (annual %) | Inflation, Consumer Prices (annual %) | Population, Total | Unemployment, Total (% of total labor force) (national estimate) |
|---|---|---|---|---|---|
| 2005 | 11.05 | 6.38 | 12.69 | 143,518,523 | 7.17 |
| 2006 | 9.33 | 8.15 | 9.67 | 143,049,528 | 7.16 |
| 2007 | 5.55 | 8.54 | 9.01 | 142,805,088 | 6.10 |
| 2008 | 6.26 | 5.25 | 14.11 | 142,742,350 | 6.32 |
| 2009 | 4.12 | -7.82 | 11.65 | 142,785,342 | 8.42 |
| 2010 | 4.42 | 4.50 | 6.85 | 142,849,449 | 7.37 |
| 2011 | 4.74 | 5.28 | 8.44 | 142,960,868 | 6.54 |
| 2012 | 3.23 | 3.66 | 5.07 | 143,201,676 | 5.44 |
| 2013 | 1.46 | 1.79 | 6.75 | 143,506,911 | 5.46 |
| 2014 | 2.79 | 0.74 | 7.82 | 143,819,666 | 5.16 |
| 2015 | 4.95 | -2.83 | 15.53 | 144,096,870 | 5.57 |
| 2016 | 1.91 | -0.22 | 7.04 | 144,342,396 | 5.54 |
| 2017 | 2.11 | 1.55 | 3.68 | 144,495,044 | 5.20 |

Source: World Bank

of the global mortgage crisis. Similarly, Russia also has economic recession in 2015 and 2016. The main reason behind this situation is the political problems with US. Furthermore, inflation has a decreasing trend especially in the last years. Population goes up in this period whereas there is decreasing in unemployment rate.

In the early 1990s, Russia experienced an economic transformation. In this period, Russia, which has entered a free market economy, has made the local currency Ruble a transactionable process in the international market. Especially as a result of the decrease in oil prices, a significant decrease has occurred in the foreign exchange revenues of Russia. As a result of this situation, Russia has begun to pay its short-term debts. As a result of the mentioned problems, uneasiness began in the Russian markets (Sapova et al., 2018; Everett, 2017; Surovneva & Sukhorukova, 2017).

Russia experienced a very terrible economic crisis in 1998. It caused important decrease in economic growth. In addition to this aspect, it also led to increase in unemployment rates. In order to solve these problems, central bank of Russia had an active role in the market (Kononenko et al., 2018; Oktar and Yüksel, 2015). It can be seen that after this crisis period,

*Table 7. Details of the monetary policies of Central Bank of Russia*

| Type of Operations | Purpose | Instrument | Term | Frequency |
|---|---|---|---|---|
| Main auction-based operations | Steering money market rates | REPO auctions / deposit auctions | 1 week | weekly |
| Overnight standing facilities | Restricting the fluctuation range of money market rates with the borders of the interest rate corridor | Overnight loans; FX swaps; Lombard loans; REPOs; loans secured by non-marketable assets; deposit operations | 1 day | daily |
| Fine-tuning operations | Preventing excessive fluctuations of money market rates within the interest rate corridor | REPO and FX swap auctions / deposit auctions | from 1 to 6 days1 | occasionally |
| Long-term auctions | Improving conditions for conducting main operations: | Auctions to provide loans secured by non-marketable assets | 3 months | monthly |
| | absorbing medium-term liquidity surplus | Issuance of Bank of Russia bonds | 3,6, 12 months | occasionally |
| | compensating medium-term liquidity needs | Auctions to provide loans secured by non-marketable assets | 3 months | |
| Standing facilities | Improving conditions for conducting main operations, restricting the impact of structural liquidity deficit on maturity of credit institutions' liabilities | Loans secured by non-marketable assets | from 2 to 549 days | daily |

**Source:** Bank of Russia, Monetary Policy Framework, https://www.cbr.ru/eng/DKP/about_monetary_policy/monetary_policy_framework/

Russian economy had better macroeconomic conditions mainly with the help of successful monetary policies. Table 7 gives information about the details of the monetary policies of central bank of Russia.

## Turkey

Turkey is the final emerging country in the analysis process. Some information related to Turkey is indicated on Table 8.

Table 8 gives information that Turkey has an important current account deficit problem. For example, this ratio was greater than 8% in 2011. Except 2009, Turkey always has economic growth. Moreover, inflation rate exceeded

*Table 8. General information about Turkey*

| Year | Current Account Balance (% of GDP) | GDP Growth (annual %) | Inflation, Consumer Prices (annual %) | Population, Total | Unemployment, Total (% of total labor force) (national estimate) |
|---|---|---|---|---|---|
| 2005 | -4.18 | 9.01 | 8.18 | 67,903,406 | 10.64 |
| 2006 | -5.64 | 7.11 | 9.60 | 68,763,405 | 8.72 |
| 2007 | -5.47 | 5.03 | 8.76 | 69,597,281 | 8.87 |
| 2008 | -5.16 | 0.85 | 10.44 | 70,440,032 | 9.71 |
| 2009 | -1.76 | -4.70 | 6.25 | 71,339,185 | 12.55 |
| 2010 | -5.78 | 8.49 | 8.57 | 72,326,914 | 10.66 |
| 2011 | -8.94 | 11.11 | 6.47 | 73,409,455 | 8.80 |
| 2012 | -5.49 | 4.79 | 8.89 | 74,569,867 | 8.15 |
| 2013 | -6.70 | 8.49 | 7.49 | 75,787,333 | 8.73 |
| 2014 | -4.67 | 5.17 | 8.85 | 77,030,628 | 9.88 |
| 2015 | -3.73 | 6.09 | 7.67 | 78,271,472 | 10.24 |
| 2016 | -3.84 | 3.18 | 7.78 | 79,512,426 | 10.84 |
| 2017 | -5.56 | 7.44 | 11.14 | 80,745,020 | 11.26 |

Source: World Bank

10% in 2017. In addition to them, there is increase in the population. On the other hand, unemployment rate has an increasing trend after 2012.

Turkey suffered from two different economic crises in 2000 and 2001. The measures taken to repair the damage of the 1994 crisis were not fully effective. These damages have been effective in eliminating the damage caused by the crisis to the national economy. However, it has failed to completely eliminate the factors that have caused the crisis. In other words, the measures that were not taken after the 1994 crisis caused the 2000 and 2001 crises to occur (Yüksel, 2015; Görgen, 2018).

The central bank's stance during the crisis has made banks even more difficult. The banks, which could not find debt even from each other because of the environment of insecurity, became even more difficult when they could not get help from the central bank. This situation had affected Turkish banks negatively and some of them went bankrupt. Therefore, ineffective policies of the central bank caused the crisis to deepen (Erdoğdu, 2017; Aytaç et al., 2015).

After these crises, new economy program was announced. In this context, it was aimed to provide the independence of the central bank. While providing the independence, central bank of Turkey had a chance to implement more effective policies (Heinemann, 2016). With the help of these strategies, Turkey achieved sustainable economic growth in a very short time. In addition to them, it is also thought that central bank of Turkey has taken successful actions during global mortgage crisis.

Another important point is that central bank of Turkey implemented modern monetary policy tools. For example, it used "Interest Rate Corridor" which can be defined as the area between the Central Bank's overnight borrowing rate and lending rate. This situation increased the flexibility of central bank of Turkey. In addition to the interest rate corridor, central bank of Turkey also implemented reserve option mechanism. Reserve option mechanism can be defined as the process in which banks can keep a certain percentage of the required reserves as foreign currency denominated or gold. This situation has a positive contribution to the foreign currency reserves of the central bank. In addition to this situation, banks can also get an opportunity to minimize currency risk (Saraç and Zeren, 2015).

## LITERATURE REVIEW ON MONETARY POLICY INSTRUMENTS AND CENTRAL BANKING ACTIVITIES IN E7 ECONOMIES

In this section, the studies, which focused on monetary policy instruments and central banking activities in E7 economies, are taken into consideration. The details of these studies are given in the following subtitles.

### Literature Review on Central Bank Monetary Policy Instruments

There are lots of studies in the literature which analyzed the central bank policy instruments. For example, Alper et al. (2018), Chang et al. (2018), Xi et al. (2015), Liu and Spiegel (2017) and Hammad (2019) made a study about the importance of required reserve requirements. They mainly reached the conclusion that required reserves have an effect on the liquidity, velocity of the money and inflation rate. On the other hand, Rocheteau et al. (2018), Carlson and Lackman (2018), Cassola and Koulischer (2019), Nishiyama (2017), Toporowski (2019) and Hanes (2019) evaluated the importance of the open market operations.

## Literature Review on Central Banking Activities in E7 Economies

Central banking activities in E7 economies were also examined by many different researchers. In this framework, Chamon and Garcia (2016), Ponticelli and Alencar (2016), Upper et al. (2016) and Puffer et al. (2016) evaluated the operations of the central bank of Brazil. On the other side, Hess (2017) and Destais (2016) concluded that the operations of the central bank of China has a significant role of the financial development. Moreover, Ghate et al. (2017) and Shah and Bahri (2017) concluded that central bank of India is very successful to control high inflation.

In addition to these studies, Kisman (2017) and Setiawan et al. (2018) identified that central bank of Indonesia took certain actions in order to increase financial stability of the country. Moreover, Carriere-Swallow et al. (2016) and Alcaraz et al. (2018) focused on the operational activities of the central bank of Mexico. Furthermore, Everett (2017) and Johnson (2018) determined that central bank of Russia has taken very effective decisions to control the market. Finally, the performance of the central bank of Turkey was evaluated in some different studies (Iglesias et al., 2017; Eken et al., 2019; Aldan and Çulha, 2016).

## CONCLUSION

There are mainly two different tools of the country to regulate economic activities which are monetary and fiscal policies. With respect to the monetary policy, interest rates and money supply are controlled. On the other hand, fiscal policy is a general name given to government regulations on tax and government expenditures. In summary both monetary and fiscal policies have a crucial role in the financial markets of the countries. These policies can be considered by both contractionary and expansionary purposes.

The contractionary monetary policy aims to reduce the money supply in the market mainly with the aim of reducing inflation rates. Moreover, regarding the expansionary monetary policy, the amount of the money supply is aimed to be increased. In this circumstance, tax rate can be decreased, or government expenditure can be increased. For this purpose, central banks can implement different monetary policy instruments, such as required reserve ratio, rediscount rate, open market operations, standing facilities and asset purchase program.

This chapter aimed to analyze monetary policy operations of the central banks. Firstly, general information was given related to the monetary policies. In the next part, different monetary policy instruments of the central banks are identified. In the final aspect, central banking activities of E7 economies are explained. As a result, it is defined that central banks of these countries play an active role especially during the recession period.

## REFERENCES

Agbo, E. I., & Nwankwo, S. N. P. (2018). Effect of Financial Sector Development on Economic Growth: A Case of Nigeria. *Journal of Economics and Sustainable Development*, *9*(20), 80–91.

Alcaraz, C., Claessens, S., Cuadra, G., Marques-Ibanez, D., & Sapriza, H. (2018). *Whatever it takes. What's the impact of a major nonconventional monetary policy intervention?* Academic Press.

Aldan, A., & Çulha, O. Y. (2016). The role of the extensive margin in export of Turkey: A comparative analysis. *Central Bank Review*, *16*(2), 59–64. doi:10.1016/j.cbrev.2016.05.002

Alper, K., Binici, M., Demiralp, S., Kara, H., & Özlü, P. (2018). Reserve requirements, liquidity risk, and bank lending behavior. *Journal of Money, Credit and Banking*, *50*(4), 817–827. doi:10.1111/jmcb.12475

Amiri, A. J. G., & Gong, Z. (2018). The Impact of liquidity on Economic Growth in America's Economy Using a New Approach TVP-FAVAR. *Revista Publicando*, *5*(14), 370–385.

Angrist, J. D., Jordà, Ò., & Kuersteiner, G. M. (2018). Semiparametric estimates of monetary policy effects: String theory revisited. *Journal of Business & Economic Statistics*, *36*(3), 371–387. doi:10.1080/07350015.2016.1204919

Aytaç, I. A., Rankin, B. H., & İbikoğlu, A. (2015). The social impact of the 2008 global economic crisis on neighborhoods, households, and individuals in Turkey. *Social Indicators Research*, *124*(1), 1–19. doi:10.100711205-014-0769-5

Azevedo, L. F. P., & Pereira, P. L. V. (2018). *Effects of official and unofficial central bank communication on the Brazilian interest rate curve*. Academic Press.

Bergsten, C. F. (2017). *Dilemmas of the Dollar: Economics and Politics of United States International Monetary Policy: Economics and Politics of United States International Monetary Policy*. Routledge.

Bruno, V., & Shin, H. S. (2015). Capital flows and the risk-taking channel of monetary policy. *Journal of Monetary Economics*, *71*, 119–132. doi:10.1016/j.jmoneco.2014.11.011

Carlson, W. H., & Lackman, C. L. (2018). Raising Interest Rates: IOER vs. OMO: Interest on Excess Reserves vs Open Market Operations. *International Journal of Financial Research*, *9*(1), 142–146. doi:10.5430/ijfr.v9n1p142

Carlson, W. H., & Lackman, C. L. (2018). Raising Interest Rates: IOER vs. OMO: Interest on Excess Reserves vs Open Market Operations. *International Journal of Financial Research*, *9*(1), 142–146. doi:10.5430/ijfr.v9n1p142

Carriere-Swallow, M. Y., Faruqee, M. H., & Srinivasan, M. K. (2016). *Challenges for Central Banking: Perspectives from Latin America*. International Monetary Fund.

Cassola, N., & Koulischer, F. (2019). The collateral channel of open market operations. *Journal of Financial Stability*, *41*, 73–90. doi:10.1016/j.jfs.2019.03.002

Chamon, M., & Garcia, M. (2016). Capital controls in Brazil: Effective? *Journal of International Money and Finance*, *61*, 163–187. doi:10.1016/j.jimonfin.2015.08.008

Chang, C., Liu, Z., Spiegel, M. M., & Zhang, J. (2018). Reserve requirements and optimal chinese stabilization policy. *Journal of Monetary Economics*.

Chong, T. T. L., & Liu, W. (2017). The roadmap of interest rate liberalisation in China. *Economic and Political Studies*, *5*(4), 421–440. doi:10.1080/20954816.2017.1384614

Chou, T. K., & Buchdadi, A. D. (2016). Bank performance and its underlying factors: A study of rural banks in Indonesia. *Accounting and Finance Research*, *5*(3), 55–63. doi:10.5430/afr.v5n3p55

Codato, A., Cavalieri, M., Perissinotto, R., & Dantas, E. G. (2016). Economic mainstream and power: A profile analysis of Central Bank directors during PSDB and PT governments in Brazil. *Nova Economia*, *26*(3), 687–720. doi:10.1590/0103-6351/2845

Coibion, O., Gorodnichenko, Y., Kueng, L., & Silvia, J. (2017). Innocent Bystanders? Monetary policy and inequality. *Journal of Monetary Economics*, *88*, 70–89. doi:10.1016/j.jmoneco.2017.05.005

de Medeiros, G. B., Portugal, M. S., & Aragón, E. K. D. S. B. (2016). Robust monetary policy, structural breaks, and nonlinearities in the reaction function of the Central Bank of Brazil. *Economía*, *17*(1), 96–113. doi:10.1016/j.econ.2016.01.001

de Vilaca Burgos, A., de Oliveira Filho, J. D., Suares, M. V. C., & de Almeida, R. S. (2017). *Distributed ledger technical research in Central Bank of Brazil*. Working Paper.

Dellepiane-Avellaneda, S. (2015). The Political Power of Economic Ideas: The Case of 'Expansionary Fiscal Contractions'. *British Journal of Politics and International Relations*, *17*(3), 391–418. doi:10.1111/1467-856X.12038

Edward, N. (2017). *Corruption, Bank Access and Distribution of Social Benefits: The Case for Central Bank Digital Currency as an Alternative to Cash in Indonesia*. Available at SSRN 3095805

Eggertsson, G. B., & Proulx, K. (2016). *Bernanke's No-arbitrage Argument Revisited: Can Open Market Operations in Real Assets Eliminate the Liquidity Trap? (No. w22243)*. National Bureau of Economic Research.

Eken, A., Ozek, A., Cakmak, B., & Serdengecti, S. (2019). New electronic data delivery system of Central Bank of the Republic of Turkey. *IFC Bulletins Chapters, 49*.

Erdogdu, A. P. A. (2017). Functioning and Effectiveness of Monetary Transmission Mechanisms: Turkey Applications. *The Journal of Finance*, *5*(1), 29–41.

Everett, R. (2017). *Russia's Crisis Modernisation Fallacy: An analysis of the 1998 and 2008 economic crises and their effects on the development of the Central Bank of Russia* (Doctoral dissertation). University of Kent.

Fratzscher, M., Duca, M. L., & Straub, R. (2016). ECB unconventional monetary policy: Market impact and international spillovers. *IMF Economic Review*, *64*(1), 36–74. doi:10.1057/imfer.2016.5

Galí, J. (2015). *Monetary policy, inflation, and the business cycle: an introduction to the new Keynesian framework and its applications*. Princeton University Press.

Gertler, M., & Karadi, P. (2015). Monetary policy surprises, credit costs, and economic activity. *American Economic Journal. Macroeconomics*, *7*(1), 44–76. doi:10.1257/mac.20130329

Ghate, C., Gupta, S., & Mallick, D. (2017). The inflationary impact of the grain procurement policy in India. *International Growth Centre Blog*.

Gibson, H. D., Hall, S. G., & Tavlas, G. S. (2016). The effectiveness of the ECB's asset purchase programs of 2009 to 2012. *Journal of Macroeconomics*, *47*, 45–57. doi:10.1016/j.jmacro.2015.09.006

Görgen, H. İ. (2018). *Turkey and Argentina: a comparative study on industrial policies in the post–2001 financial crisis period* (Doctoral dissertation). Bilkent University.

Guerra, M. (2017). Monetary Policy and the Propagation of Shocks Under Imperfect Exchange-Rate Pass-Through. *Sobre México. Revista de Economía*, *3*(3), 46–65.

Gupta, P. K., & Kaur, S. (2015, October). Credit Rating Framework for Financing of SMEs in India and role of central bank. In *Proceedings of Business and Management Conferences* (No. 3005373). International Institute of Social and Economic Sciences.

Hammad, S. A. K. (2019). The size of the legal reserve and the stability of the rate of inflation: The case of Iraq study for the period 2004-2016. *Tikrit Journal Of Administrative and Economic Sciences*, *2*(42), 277.

Han, M. (2015). *A comparative study of central bank regulation and financial stability: lessons for the People's Republic of China* (Doctoral dissertation). Durham University.

Hanes, C. (2018). Explaining the appearance of open-mouth operations in the 1990s US. *The North American Journal of Economics and Finance*.

Heinemann, T. (2016). Relational geographies of emerging market finance: The rise of Turkey and the global financial crisis 2007. *European Urban and Regional Studies*, *23*(4), 645–661. doi:10.1177/0969776414531970

Hess, P. (2017). The Ongoing Evolution of Payment Instruments in China: A Case Study in Financial Innovation, and on the Role of the Central Bank. In *Cash in East Asia* (pp. 117–131). Cham: Springer. doi:10.1007/978-3-319-59846-8_8

Hu, R., Wei, Q., & Zhang, Q. (2015, February). The Timing of Central Bank Communication: Evidence from China. *Asian Finance Association (AsianFA) 2015 Conference Paper.*

Iglesias, J., Ortiz, A., & Rodrigo, T. (2017). *How do the EM Central Bank talk? A Big Data approach to the Central Bank of Turkey* (No. 17/24). Academic Press.

Johnson, J. (2018). The Bank of Russia: from central planning to inflation targeting. In Research Handbook on Central Banking. Edward Elgar Publishing. doi:10.4337/9781784719227.00012

Juhro, S. M. (2015). The role of the central bank in promoting sustainable growth: perspectives on the implementation of flexible ITF in Indonesia. *Afro Eurasian Studies Journal, 4*(1).

Kalkavan, H., & Ersin, I. (2019). Determination of Factors Affecting the South East Asian Crisis of 1997 Probit-Logit Panel Regression: The South East Asian Crisis. In Handbook of Research on Global Issues in Financial Communication and Investment Decision Making (pp. 148-167). IGI Global.

Kamińska, A., Parkitna, A., Rutkowska, M., Górski, A., & Wilimowska, Z. (2018, September). Economic Determinants of the Effectiveness of Polish Enterprises. In *International Conference on Information Systems Architecture and Technology* (pp. 36-48). Springer, Cham.

Kisman, Z. (2017). Model For Overcoming Decline in Credit Growth (Case Study of Indonesia with Time Series Data 2012M1-2016M12). *Journal of Internet Banking and Commerce*, *22*(3), 1–11.

Kollmann, R. (2016). Discussion of "Financial Intermediation in a Global Environment". *International Journal of Central Banking.*

Kononenko, O. V., & Chudinovskikh, M. V. (2018). Comparative Analysis of the Depositor Rights' Protection Systems in the Russian Federation and the Republic of Belarus. *Journal of the Ural State University of Economics*, *19*(5), 32–43. doi:10.29141/2073-1019-2018-19-5-3

Lakshmi, T. V., & Reddy, M. S. (2017). Impact of NPAs on Indian Schedule Commercial Banking Sector and Instruments Initiated by the Central Bank of India. *Asian Journal of Research in Banking and Finance*, *7*(3), 18–37. doi:10.5958/2249-7323.2017.00011.6

Lan, L. S., & Nugroho, J. L. E. (2019, March). Management commitment to service quality and service recovery performance of customer service officer at PT. Bank Central Asia, Tbk. Surabaya-Indonesia. In *16th International Symposium on Management (INSYMA 2019)*. Atlantis Press. 10.2991/insyma-19.2019.49

Li, B., Xiong, W., Chen, L., & Wang, Y. (2017). The impact of the liquidity coverage ratio on money creation: A stock-flow based dynamic approach. *Economic Modelling*, *67*, 193–202. doi:10.1016/j.econmod.2016.12.016

Liu, Z., & Spiegel, M. M. (2017). Reserve Requirements as a Chinese Macro Policy Tool. *FRBSF Economic Letter*, *2017*, 15.

López-Balderas, N., Hernández-Romano, J., Cámara-Contreras, M., Bravo-Sarmiento, E., & Hernández-Romano, P. A. (2019). Trends in prevalence of HIV and syphilis in a central blood bank of Veracruz, Mexico. *Transfusion and Apheresis Science*, *58*(1), 94–99. doi:10.1016/j.transci.2018.12.001 PMID:30554960

McCauley, R., & Ma, G. (2015). Transforming central bank liabilities into government debt: The case of China. *China & World Economy*, *23*(4), 1–18. doi:10.1111/cwe.12118

McRae, K., Durr, S., & Manzo, D. (2017). an initial assessment of changes to the Bank of canada's Framework for market Operations. *Bank of Canada Review*, *2017*(Autumn), 42–52.

Näther, M. (2018). The effect of the central bank's standing facilities on interbank lending and bank liquidity holding. *Economic Theory*, 1–41.

Neely, C. J. (2015). Unconventional monetary policy had large international effects. *Journal of Banking & Finance*, *52*, 101–111. doi:10.1016/j.jbankfin.2014.11.019

Nelson, B., Pinter, G., & Theodoridis, K. (2018). Do contractionary monetary policy shocks expand shadow banking? *Journal of Applied Econometrics*, *33*(2), 198–211. doi:10.1002/jae.2594

Nishiyama, Y. (2017). Open market operations and associated movements of the federal funds rate during the week prior to target changes. *Journal of Economics and Finance*, *41*(4), 806–828. doi:10.100712197-016-9380-8

Nwandu, E. (2016). Impact of Rising Interest Rate on the Performances of the Nigerian Manufacturing Sector. *European Journal of Business and Management.*

Obstfeld, M., & Duval, R. (2018). *Tight monetary policy is not the answer to weak productivity growth.* Retrieved from http://voxeu. org/article/tight-monetary-policy-not-answer-weak-productivity-growth

Oktar, S., & Yüksel, S. (2015). 1998 Yılında Rusya'da Yaşanan Bankacılık Krizi Ve Öncü Göstergeleri. *Marmara University Journal of Economic & Administrative Sciences, 37*(2).

Omer, M. (2016). *Should Central Bank Forget Reserve Requirements? Assessment of Reserve Requirements in Transmitting SBP's Policy Shocks to Retail Interest Rates and Exchange Rate (No. 81).* State Bank of Pakistan, Research Department.

Park, H., & Van Horn, P. (2015). Did the Reserve Requirement Increases of 1936–37 Reduce Bank Lending? Evidence from a Quasi-Experiment. *Journal of Money, Credit and Banking, 47*(5), 791–818. doi:10.1111/jmcb.12235

Perissinotto, R. M., Cavalieri, M. A. R., Dantas, E. G., & Dias, R. P. (2017). Social networks and the recruitment of directorates and presidents of the Central Bank of Brazil (1994-2016). *Tempo Social, 29*(3), 61–82. doi:10.11606/0103-2070.ts.2017.125881

Ponticelli, J., & Alencar, L. S. (2016). Court enforcement, bank loans, and firm investment: Evidence from a bankruptcy reform in Brazil. *The Quarterly Journal of Economics, 131*(3), 1365–1413. doi:10.1093/qje/qjw015

Puffer, S. M., McCarthy, D. J., & Jaeger, A. M. (2016). Institution building and institutional voids: Can Poland's experience inform Russia and Brazil? *International Journal of Emerging Markets, 11*(1), 18–41. doi:10.1108/IJoEM-02-2015-0027

Rey, H. (2016). International channels of transmission of monetary policy and the Mundellian trilemma. *IMF Economic Review, 64*(1), 6–35. doi:10.1057/imfer.2016.4

Rocheteau, G., Wright, R., & Xiao, S. X. (2018). Open market operations. *Journal of Monetary Economics, 98*, 114–128. doi:10.1016/j.jmoneco.2018.04.012

Rockoff, H. (2018). Milton Friedman and Anna J. Schwartz on the Inherent Instability of Fractional Reserve Banking. In *Coping with Financial Crises* (pp. 107–129). Singapore: Springer. doi:10.1007/978-981-10-6196-7_5

Ross, C., Wiggins, R., & Metrick, A. (2015). European Central Bank Tools and Policy Actions A: Open Market Operations, Collateral Expansion and Standing Facilities. *Yale Program on Financial Stability Case Study.*

Sahuc, J. G. (2016). The ECB's asset purchase programme: A model-based evaluation. *Economics Letters*, *145*, 136–140. doi:10.1016/j.econlet.2016.06.009

Salahesh, T., Kazerooni, A., & Asgharpur, H. (2017). The Role of Interest Coverage Ratio in Monetary Transmission Mechanism: Evidence from Iran. *Journal of Economic & Management Perspectives*, *11*(4), 409–420.

Sapova, A., Porshakov, A., Andreev, A., & Shatilo, E. (2018). *Review of Methodological Specifics of Consumer Price Index Seasonal Adjustment in the Bank of Russia Under the inflation targeting regime, the main goal of the Bank of Russia is to maintain price stability. In order to analyse the options that the central bank can use to implement its monetary policy aimed at bringing inflation down to sustainable low levels it is necessary to understand, considering the available short-term statistical data, the dynamics of consumer prices and individual components of ... (No. wps33).* Bank of Russia.

Saraç, M., & Zeren, F. (2015). The dependency of Islamic bank rates on conventional bank interest rates: Further evidence from Turkey. *Applied Economics*, *47*(7), 669–679. doi:10.1080/00036846.2014.978076

Setiawan, M. I., Surjokusumo, S., Ma'soem, D. M., Johan, J., Hasyim, C., Kurniasih, N., ... Nasihien, R. D. (2018, January). Business Centre Development Model of Airport Area in Supporting Airport Sustainability in Indonesia. *Journal of Physics: Conference Series*, *954*(1), 012024. doi:10.1088/1742-6596/954/1/012024

Shah, A., & Bahri, A. (2017). *Asymmetric and Symmetric Volatility Models for Exchange Rates in India–The Impact of the Net Purchase of US Dollars by the Central Bank and Net Inflows by Foreign Institutional Investors.* Academic Press.

Sharma, M. P. (2016). Comprehensive study of Kisan Credit Card at Central Bank of India-A useful credit tool for rural development. *IBMRD's Journal of Management Research*, *5*(1), 21–29.

Surovneva, K. A., & Sukhorukova, N. V. (2017). The role of the central bank of Russia in ensuring stability of the banking system. *Russian Journal of Agricultural and Socio-Economic Sciences*, *61*(1), 4–9. doi:10.18551/rjoas.2017-01.01

Suzuki, Y., & Miah, M. D. (2017). China's non-performing bank loan crisis: The role of economic rents 1. In *Banking and Economic Rent in Asia* (pp. 71–85). Routledge. doi:10.4324/9781315558677-6

Tallman, E., & White, E. N. (2017, May). Monetary Policy When One Size Does Not Fit All: the Federal Reserve Banks and the Recession of 1920–1921. *Workshop on Monetary and Financial History Federal Reserve Bank of Atlanta and Emory University.*

Toporowski, J. (2019). Open market operations. The Oxford Handbook of the Economics of Central Banking, 436.

Trivedi, S. R., & Srinivasan, B. (2016). Impact of Central Bank Intervention in the Foreign Exchange Market: Evidence from India Using an Event Study Approach. *Economic Papers: A Journal of Applied Economics and Policy, 35*(4), 389-402.

Udude, C. C., & Nwachukwu, U. G. (2016). An Empirical Study of the Relationship between Interest Rate and Investment in Nigeria (1980-2013). *NG-Journal of Social Development*, *417*(3948), 1–17.

Upper, C., Patel, N., Villar, A., Arslan, Y., Jašová, M., Takáts, E., ... Yetman, J. (2016). *Why is inflation so high and volatile in Brazil? A primer*. Academic Press.

Vollmer, U., & Wiese, H. (2016). Central bank standing facilities, counterparty risk, and OTC-interbank lending. *The North American Journal of Economics and Finance*, *36*, 101–122. doi:10.1016/j.najef.2015.12.003

Wang, L. (2018). Monetary-fiscal policy interactions under asset purchase programs: Some comparative evidence. *Economic Modelling*, *73*, 208–221. doi:10.1016/j.econmod.2018.03.019

Wildau, G. (2017). China Central Bank Chief Warns of 'Minsky Moment': Risk of Excessive Optimism as China Reports Strong Headline GDP Growth. *The Financial Times*.

Williams, J. C. (2018). *Moving toward'normal' US monetary policy: remarks at the Joint Bank Indonesia-Federal Reserve Bank of New York Central Banking Forum, Nusa Dua, Indonesia* (No. 296). Academic Press.

Wu, J. C., & Xia, F. D. (2016). Measuring the macroeconomic impact of monetary policy at the zero lower bound. *Journal of Money, Credit and Banking*, *48*(2-3), 253–291. doi:10.1111/jmcb.12300

Wuryandani, G., & Mardiani, I. (2015). Surveys as leading information to support central bank policy formulation: the case of Indonesia. *IFC Bulletins Chapters, 39*.

Xi, N., Ding, N., & Wang, Y. (2005). How required reserve ratio affects distribution and velocity of money. *Physica A*, *357*(3-4), 543–555. doi:10.1016/j.physa.2005.04.014

Yimer, M. M. (2018). Lending and Cash Required Reserve: Empirical Evidence from Ethiopian Commercial Bank. *European Scientific Journal, ESJ*, *14*(13), 179. doi:10.19044/esj.2018.v14n13p179

Yüksel, S. (2015). *Bankacılık krizlerinin erken uyarı sinyalleri: Türkiye üzerine bir uygulama*. Academic Press.

# Chapter 5
# Fuzzy Multicriteria Decision Making Methodologies Used in the Book


## ABSTRACT

*Using an appropriate methodology is crucial in the analysis. Therefore, the suitable model should be selected according to the type of the evaluation. Otherwise, there is a risk of having inappropriate results. Because of this situation, recommendations can be problematic. In this book, three different analyses are performed. In two of them, fuzzy DEMATEL, fuzzy TOPSIS, and fuzzy VIKOR approaches are taken into consideration. In this chapter, these three methods are explained. In this framework, some studies, which used these methods, are explained.*


## GENERAL INFORMATION ABOUT METHODOLOGIES

This study aims to analyze the effectiveness of the monetary policies and the independence of the central banks. Within this scope, emerging 7 economies (E7) are taken into consideration which are Brazil, China, India, Indonesia, Mexico, Russia and Turkey. In the implementation process, three different analysis are performed. In this circumstance, fuzzy DEMATEL, fuzzy TOPSIS, fuzzy VIKOR, Kao panel cointegration, Pedroni panel cointegration and Dumitrescu Hurlin panel causality analyses are considered. In this section, firstly, these different methodologies are explained. After that, three different analyses are shared.

DOI: 10.4018/978-1-7998-1643-0.ch005

In this study, it is aimed to make three different analyses related to the effectiveness of the monetary policies and the independence of the central banks in E7 economies. In order to reach this objective, 6 different methods are used in the analysis process. Fuzzy DEMATEL method is mainly used to weight the criteria. In addition to this approach, fuzzy TOPSIS and fuzzy VIKOR methods are considered to rank the central banks of E7 economies regarding the effectiveness of monetary policies and independence. On the other hand, Kao panel cointegration, Pedroni panel cointegration and Dumitrescu Hurlin panel causality analysis are used to understand whether monetary policies are effective for E7 countries. In this section, three different fuzzy methodologies are explained in detail in the following subsections.

## FUZZY DEMATEL

The word DEMATEL refers to the expression of "The Decision Making Trial and Evaluation Laboratory". As it can be understood from this expression, this method is mainly used to make decisions under the complex environment. This model was developed by Gabus and Fontela in Genova research center. Another important benefit of this method is that it can be considered in order to understand the causal relationship between the criteria (Vinodh et al., 2016; Dinçer, 2018). In addition to them, impact relationship analysis can be performed by using this model. This situation provides a significant benefit to DEMATEL approach in comparison with the similar models, such as AHP and ANP (Dinçer et al., 2018; Gorener et al., 2013; Dinçer and Gorener, 2011; Dinçer, 2015). In summary, complex problems can be solved much easier with the help of this methodology (Lin et al., 2018; Dinçer and Hacıoğlu, 2017). There are mainly six different steps in DEMATEL model. The details of these steps are given below.

In the first step, the main purpose is determined so as to solve the problem. Moreover, in the second step, different criteria are generated in order to make evaluation. Furthermore, fuzzy linguistic scale is defined. Therefore, it can be possible to solve problems in case of uncertainty because there is human assessment process. In the development process of this scale, five different aspects are taken into consideration which are "No", "Low", "Medium", "High", "Very High".

Additionally, the third step includes the calculation of the initial direct-relation fuzzy matrix. In order to reach this objective, the decision makers' evaluations are taken into consideration for each dimension and criterion. In addition to these issues, triangular fuzzy numbers are also considered for the development of this matrix. The calculation process of the initial direct-relation fuzzy matrix ($\tilde{Z}$) is demonstrated on the equations (1) and (2).

$$Z = \begin{bmatrix} 0 & \tilde{z}_{12} & \cdots & \cdots & \tilde{z}_{1n} \\ \tilde{z}_{21} & 0 & \cdots & \cdots & \tilde{z}_{2n} \\ \vdots & \vdots & \ddots & \cdots & \cdots \\ \vdots & \vdots & \vdots & \ddots & \vdots \\ \tilde{z}_{n1} & \tilde{z}_{n2} & \cdots & \cdots & 0 \end{bmatrix} \tag{1}$$

$$\tilde{Z} = \frac{\tilde{Z}^1 + \tilde{Z}^2 + \tilde{Z}^3 + \ldots \tilde{Z}^n}{n} \tag{2}$$

The direct effect matrix is normalized in the fourth step. In this process, equations (3)-(5) are taken into consideration.

$$\tilde{X} = \begin{bmatrix} \tilde{x}_{11} & \tilde{x}_{12} & \cdots & \cdots & \tilde{x}_{1n} \\ \tilde{x}_{21} & \tilde{x}_{22} & \cdots & \cdots & \tilde{x}_{2n} \\ \vdots & \vdots & \ddots & \cdots & \cdots \\ \vdots & \vdots & \vdots & \ddots & \vdots \\ \tilde{x}_{n1} & \tilde{x}_{n2} & \cdots & \cdots & \tilde{x}_{nn} \end{bmatrix} \tag{3}$$

$$\tilde{x}_{ij} = \frac{\tilde{z}_{ij}}{r} = \left( \frac{l_{ij}}{r}, \frac{m_{ij}}{r}, \frac{u_{ij}}{r} \right) \tag{4}$$

$$r = \max_{1 \le i \le n} \left( \sum_{j=1}^{n} u_{ij} \right) \tag{5}$$

On the other side, the fifth step includes the development of the total influence fuzzy matrix. In this process, the equations (6)-(12) are considered.

$$X_l = \begin{bmatrix} 0 & l'_{12} & \cdots & \cdots & l'_{1n} \\ l'_{21} & 0 & \cdots & \cdots & l'_{2n} \\ \vdots & \vdots & \ddots & \cdots & \cdots \\ \vdots & \vdots & \vdots & \ddots & \vdots \\ l'_{n1} & l'_{n2} & \cdots & \cdots & 0 \end{bmatrix}$$

$$X_m = \begin{bmatrix} 0 & m'_{12} & \cdots & \cdots & m'_{1n} \\ m'_{21} & 0 & \cdots & \cdots & m'_{2n} \\ \vdots & \vdots & \ddots & \cdots & \cdots \\ \vdots & \vdots & \vdots & \ddots & \vdots \\ m'_{n1} & m'_{n2} & \cdots & \cdots & 0 \end{bmatrix}$$

$$X_u = \begin{bmatrix} 0 & u'_{12} & \cdots & \cdots & u'_{1n} \\ u'_{21} & 0 & \cdots & \cdots & u'_{2n} \\ \vdots & \vdots & \ddots & \cdots & \cdots \\ \vdots & \vdots & \vdots & \ddots & \vdots \\ u'_{n1} & u'_{n2} & \cdots & \cdots & 0 \end{bmatrix} \quad (6)$$

$$\tilde{T} = \lim_{k \to \infty} \tilde{X} + \tilde{X}^2 + \ldots + \tilde{X}^k \quad (7)$$

$$\tilde{T} = \begin{bmatrix} \tilde{t}_{11} & \tilde{t}_{12} & \cdots & \cdots & \tilde{t}_{1n} \\ \tilde{t}_{21} & \tilde{t}_{22} & \cdots & \cdots & \tilde{t}_{2n} \\ \vdots & \vdots & \ddots & \cdots & \cdots \\ \vdots & \vdots & \vdots & \ddots & \vdots \\ \tilde{t}_{n1} & \tilde{t}_{n2} & \cdots & \cdots & \tilde{t}_{nn} \end{bmatrix} \quad (8)$$

$$\tilde{t}_{ij} = \left( l''_{ij}, m''_{ij}, u''_{ij} \right) \quad (9)$$

$$\left[l''_{ij}\right] = X_l \times \left(I - X_l\right)^{-1} \tag{10}$$

$$\left[m''_{ij}\right] = X_m \times \left(I - X_m\right)^{-1} \tag{11}$$

$$\left[u''_{ij}\right] = X_u \times \left(I - X_u\right)^{-1} \tag{12}$$

The final step gives information about the defuzzified total influence matrix. In this circumstance, $\tilde{R}_i^{def}$ represents the sum of all vector columns whereas $\tilde{D}_i^{def}$ indicates the sum of all vector rows. Therefore, $\left(\tilde{D}_i + \tilde{R}_i\right)^{def}$ indicates the total degree of the influence among criteria. It means that when this value is higher, the criterion becomes much closer to the central point. On the other hand, the value of $\left(\tilde{D}_i - \tilde{R}_i\right)^{def}$ explains the degree of causality between the criteria. Hence, when this value is positive, it means that the criterion is has an influence on the other criteria. However, this criterion is influenced by the others in case of negative value. In this calculation process, $\tilde{f}_{ij} = \left(l_{ij}, m_{ij}, u_{ij}\right)$ represents triangular fuzzy numbers. Additionally, equations (13)-(21) are used to achieve this objective.

$$u_i^{\max} = \max u_i, l_i^{\min} = \min_j l_i \tag{13}$$

$$\Delta_{\min}^{\max} = u_i^{\max} - l_i^{\min} \tag{14}$$

$$x_{lj} = \left(l_{ij} - l_i^{\min}\right) / \Delta_{\min}^{\max} \tag{15}$$

$$x_{mj} = \left(m_{ij} - l_i^{\min}\right) / \Delta_{\min}^{\max} \tag{16}$$

$$x_{uj} = \left(u_{ij} - l_i^{\min}\right) / \Delta_{\min}^{\max} \tag{17}$$

$$x_j^{ls} = x_{mj} / \left(1 + x_{mj} - x_{lj}\right) \tag{18}$$

$$x_j^{rs} = x_{uj} / \left(1 + x_{uj} - x_{mj}\right) \tag{19}$$

$$x_j^{crisp} = \left[x_j^{ls}\left(1 - x_j^{ls}\right) + x_j^{rs} x_j^{rs}\right] / \left[1 - x_j^{ls} + x_j^{rs}\right] \tag{20}$$

$$f_{ij} = l_i^{\min} + x_j^{crisp} \Delta_{\min}^{\max} \tag{21}$$

Fuzzy DEMATEL approach was considered in many different studies in the literature. Some of them are shown on Table 1.

*Table 1. Studies related to Fuzzy DEMATEL*

| Author | Subject |
|---|---|
| Liu, Deng & Chan (2018) | evidential supplier selection |
| Abdel-Basset et al. (2018) | developing supplier selection criteria |
| Lin et al. (2018) | sustainable supply chain management |
| Dinçer et al. (2019) | performance measurement of internationalized firms |
| Kaur et al. (2018) | investigating barriers in green supply chain management |
| Tsai (2018) | job satisfaction in china's cell industry |
| Bhatia & Srivastava (2018) | external barriers to remanufacturing |
| Dinçer, Yüksel & Pınarbaşı | evaluation of service quality of energy companies in Turkey |
| Chauhan, Singh & Jharkharia (2018) | analysis of barriers of waste recycling in India |
| Roy et al. (2018) | analyzing the key success factors of hospital service quality |
| Dinçer, Yuksel & Bozaykut-Buk (2018) | financial and economic effects on green supply chain management |
| Li & Mathiyazhagan (2018) | sustainable supply chain adoption in the manufacturing industry |
| Luthra et al. (2018) | sustainability initiatives in supply chains in India |
| Dinçer and Yüksel (2019) | soft computing |
| Yüksel et al. (2019) | financial analysis of international energy trade |
| Mousavizade, & Shakibazad (2019) | ranking urban water and sewage companies |
| Tian et al. (2019) | vehicle reverse logistics in china |
| Mangla et al. (2018) | benchmarking the logistics management implementation |
| Addae et al. (2019) | analyzing barriers in energy industry |
| Sennaroglu et al. (2018) | parking lots evaluation |
| Wang et al. (2019) | renewable energy investment |
| Sharma et al. (2018) | sustainable food supply chain management implementation |
| Si et al. (2018) | literature review |

*continues on following page*

*Table 1. Continued*

| Author | Subject |
|---|---|
| Mavi & Standing (2018) | sustainable project management in construction |
| Gopal et al. (2018) | evaluating knowledge transfer effectiveness |
| Yang, Lan & Tseng (2019) | development path of metropolitan logistics |
| Wang, Cao & Zhou (2018) | influencing factors in coal mine production safety |
| Liu et al. (2018) | selection of the transport service provider |
| Yadegaridehkordi et al. (2018) | manufacturing companies' performance |
| Chen et al. (2018) | influencing factors of museum visit |
| Dinçer et al. (2019) | the quality of the financial services |
| Kumar et al. (2018) | the role of social media in polio prevention in India |
| Kazancoglu, Kazancoglu & Sagnak (2018) | green supply chain management performance |
| Quezada et al. (2018) | causal relationships in strategy maps |
| Shi et al. (2019) | the performance of the universal health coverage |
| Kumar & Dixit (2018) | critical barriers to implementation of WEEE management |
| Kumar et al. (2018) | optimal supplier selection |
| Yüksel, Dinçer & Emir (2017) | the performance of Turkish deposit banks |
| Ilgin (2019) | disassembly line balancing |
| Ding & Liu (2018) | identifying critical success factors in emergency management |
| Rad et al. (2018) | assessment of ubiquitous cities |
| Zhou et al. (2018) | recycling partner selection |
| Ji (2018) | analysis of machine failure |
| Feng et al. (2018) | product optimization |
| Dinçer et al. (2019) | the evaluation of the brand equity |
| Gupta & Barua (2018) | modeling enablers of green innovation in manufacturing |
| Lin et al. (2018) | risk analysis of new energy power system in china |
| Gardas, Raut & Narkhede (2018) | critical causal factors for post-harvest losses in the fruit and vegetables supply chain |
| Cui et al. (2018) | critical factors of green business failure |
| Alzahrani et al. (2018) | design requirements for mobile environments |
| Atthirawong, Panprung & Leerojanaprapa (2018) | consumers' behaviors in buying green products |
| Bakir et al. (2018) | determinants of environmentally oriented public procurement |
| Yadav & Barve (2018) | critical success factors of humanitarian supply chains |
| Abdullah & Zulkifli (2018) | developing causal relationship of knowledge management criteria |
| Aviso et al. (2018) | key factors to learning process systems engineering |
| Ganji, Rassafi & Kordani (2018) | vehicle safety analysis |

*continues on following page*

*Table 1. Continued*

| Author | Subject |
|---|---|
| Acuña-Carvajal et al. (2019) | validate a business strategy |
| Leksono, Suparno & Vanany (2018) | healthcare supply chain performance measurement |
| Gardas, Raut & Narkhede (2018) | the challenges to sustainability in the textile industry |
| Goyal, Routroy & Singhal (2018) | analyzing environment sustainability enablers |
| Liu, Ming & Song (2019) | evaluation of co-creative value propositions |
| Costa et al. (2019) | improving the customer–supplier relationship |
| Shahi, Alavipoor & Karimi (2018) | the development of nuclear power plants |
| Azimifard, Moosavirad & Ariafar (2018) | designing steel supply chain |
| Sepehri-Rad, Sadjadi & Sadi-Nezhad (2019) | transaction authentication in online banking. |
| Ocampo, Tan & Sia (2018) | the causal relationships of the antecedents of organizational citizenship behavior |
| Ali et al. (2018) | evaluation for adoption of SCP practices in footwear industry |
| Dinçer, Hacıoğlu and Yüksel (2017) | performance measurement of European airline industry |
| Majumdar, Kapur & Khatri (2019) | software upgradation attributes and optimal release planning |
| Bhagawati et al. (2019) | key success factors of sustainability in supply chain management |
| Chang & Chen (2018) | critical factors for social games |
| Ma et al. (2019) | stakeholders' assessment of bike sharing service quality |
| Hatefi & Tamošaitienė (2019) | evaluating construction projects |
| Pourjavad & Shahin (2018) | performance evaluation of sustainable service and manufacturing supply chain management |

## FUZZY TOPSIS

The word TOPSIS represents "The Technique for Order of Preference by Similarity to Ideal Solution". This approach was developed by Hwang and Yoon (1981) with the aim of ranking different alternatives. As it can be identified from these explanations that it is an important type of multicriteria decision making methods. In this framework, the shortest and longest distance from the ideal solution are taken into consideration in order to rank the factors. There are mainly four different steps in the process of TOPSIS methodology (Şengül et al., 2015; Dinçer and Hacıoğlu, 2015).

In the first step, the fuzzy decision matrix is developed. For this purpose, the fuzzy weights are calculated. Equation (22) gives information about this process.

$$\tilde{X}_{ij} = \frac{1}{k}\left(\tilde{X}_{ij}^{1} + \tilde{X}_{ij}^{2} + \tilde{X}_{ij}^{3} + \ldots.. + \tilde{X}_{ij}^{k}\right) \tag{22}$$

In the second step, there is normalization of this fuzzy decision matrix. This process is calculated with the help of the equations (23) and (24).

$$\tilde{r}_{ij} = \left(\frac{a_{ij}}{c_{ij}^{*}}, \frac{b_{ij}}{c_{ij}^{*}}, \frac{c_{ij}}{c_{ij}^{*}}\right) \tag{23}$$

$$c_{ij}^{*} = \sqrt{\sum_{i=1}^{m} c_{ij}^{2}} \tag{24}$$

On the other side, the third step includes the identification of the fuzzy positive-ideal solution $A^+$ and the fuzzy negative-ideal solution $A^-$. In this process, equation (25) is taken into consideration.

$$A^{+} = \left(\tilde{v}_1^{*}, \tilde{v}_2^{*}, \tilde{v}_3^{*}, \ldots \tilde{v}_n^{*}\right) \text{ and } A^{-} = \left(\tilde{v}_1^{-}, \tilde{v}_2^{-}, \tilde{v}_3^{-}, \ldots \tilde{v}_n^{-}\right) \tag{25}$$

The distances of each alternative from the positive and negative-ideal solution can be computed with the help of the equations (26) and (27). In these equations $\tilde{v}_j^{*}$ is equal to (1,1,1) and $\tilde{v}_1^{-}$ represents (0,0,0).

$$D_i^{*} = \sum_{j=1}^{n} d\left(\tilde{v}_{ij}, \tilde{v}_j^{*}\right) \tag{26}$$

$$D_i^{-} = \sum_{j=1}^{n} d\left(\tilde{v}_{ij}, \tilde{v}_j^{-}\right) \tag{27}$$

On the other side, the final step includes the calculation of the closeness coefficient. In this process, the main purpose is to rank the alternatives. Within this framework, equation (28) is used.

$$CC_i = \frac{D_i^-}{D_i^+ + D_i^-} \tag{28}$$

Similar to fuzzy DEMATEL, fuzzy TOPSIS methodology also attracted the attention of the many researchers in the literature. Some recent studies in this context are given on Table 2.

*Table 2. Studies related to fuzzy TOPSIS*

| Author | Subject |
|---|---|
| Ervural et al. (2018) | SWOT analysis for Turkey's energy planning |
| Bian et al. (2018) | failure mode analysis |
| Kumar & Garg (2018) | connection number of set pair analysis |
| Amiri et al. (2019) | prioritization of flood inundation |
| Mohammed et al. (2018) | green and resilient supplier performance |
| Jain et al. (2018) | supplier selection |
| Chou et al. (2019) | human resource in science and technology |
| Bai & Sarkis (2018) | sustainability into supplier selection |
| Aloini et al. (2018) | technology assessment |
| Dinçer & Yüksel (2019) | evaluation of global investments on the renewable energy |
| Liang et al. (2018) | literature review |
| dos Santos et al. (2019) | performance evaluation of green suppliers |
| Rostamzadeh et al. (2018) | sustainable supply chain risk management |
| Cavallaro et al. (2019) | concentrated solar power technologies |
| Seyedmohammadi et al. (2018) | cultivation priority planning |
| Zhao & Gong (2018) | e-commerce application |
| Abdel-Basset et al. (2018) | supplier selection problems |
| Shen et al. (2018) | credit risk evaluation |
| Kwok & Lau (2019) | hotel selection |
| Hadi-Vencheh et al. (2018) | inventory classification |
| Dinçer, Yüksel & Martínez (2019) | European energy investment policies |
| Nazari et al. (2018) | solar farm site selection |
| Peng & Dai (2018) | new similarity measure with score function |
| Bianchini (2018) | 3pl provider selection |
| Abdel-Basset et al. (2019) | developing supplier selection |
| Indahingwati et al. (2018) | fertilizer selection |
| Tian et al. (2018) | green performance evaluation of design alternatives |

*continues on following page*

*Table 2. Continued*

| Author | Subject |
|---|---|
| Yazdi (2018) | risk assessment |
| Sasikumar & Vimal (2019) | selection of green suppliers |
| Rahim et al. (2018) | selecting best employees |
| Şen et al. (2018) | process management software |
| Rao et al. (2018) | experimental investigation |
| Wu et al. (2018) | social network information |
| Ameri et al. (2018) | erodibility prioritization of sub-watersheds |
| Sajjad Ali Khan et al. (2018) | literature review |
| Ouenniche et al. (2018) | bankruptcy prediction |
| Dinçer, Yüksel, & Çetiner (2019) | strategy selection for organizational performance |
| Mao et al. (2018) | optimization of residential air conditioning systems |
| Janaki et al. (2018) | supply chain performance in the oil products distribution company |
| Dinçer and Yüksel (2018) | financial sector-based analysis of the G20 economies |
| Dong & Bao (2018) | evaluation of some public service platform |
| Liu et al. (2019) | improving risk evaluation |
| Tang et al. (2019) | public blockchain evaluation |
| Ananthakumar et al. (2019) | optimization of multi-response characteristics in plasma arc cutting |
| Yurdakul & İç (2018) | performance measurement model for manufacturing companies |
| Abdel-Basset et al. (2019) | smart medical device selection |
| Han & Trimi (2018) | performance evaluation of reverse logistics in social commerce platforms |
| Liu & Wei (2018) | risk evaluation of electric vehicle charging |
| Ortega et al. (2018) | social-environmental prospective assessment of water quality management |
| Daneshvar Rouyendegh et al. (2018) | site selection of wind power plants |
| Dwivedi et al. (2018) | literature review |
| Yadav et al. (2018) | prioritizing solutions for lean six sigma adoption barriers |
| Koulinas et al. (2019) | risk assessment |
| Sun et al. (2018) | literature review |
| Ganesh Kumar et al. (2018) | optimum glazing material for solar thermal applications |
| Khedrigharibvand et al. (2018) | sustainable rangeland management |
| Yang et al. (2018) | flood vulnerability assessment approach |
| Taleai et al. (2019) | solar power plants |
| Azimifard et al. (2018) | sustainable supplier countries for iran's steel industry |
| Zareie et al. (2018) | maximization in social networks |
| Certa et al. (2018) | food safety risk analysis |
| Torğul & Paksoy (2019) | green supplier selection |

*continues on following page*

*Table 2. Continued*

| Author | Subject |
|---|---|
| Li et al. (2019) | sustainable supplier selection |
| Luan et al. (2019) | green stormwater infrastructure strategies efficiencies |
| Yildiz & Uğur (2018) | evaluation of 3d printers used in additive manufacturing |
| Araujo et al. (2018) | performance analysis of Brazilian public health |
| Nguyen et al. (2018) | optimization of process parameters |
| Chen et al. (2018) | economic transformation and upgrading of resource-based cities |

## FUZZY VIKOR

The word VIKOR comes from the expression of "Vlsekriterijumska Optimizacija I Kompromisno Resenje". It is an important multicriteria decision making methods under the complex environment. The main aim of this approach is to rank different alternatives according to their importance. This methodology can also be considered with fuzzy logic. There are five different steps in order to reach the conclusion with VIKOR approach (Rostamzadeh et al., 2015; Dinçer and Hacıoğlu, 2013; Dinçer et al., 2016).

The first step is related to the development of fuzzy decision matrix. In this situation, the decision makers' evaluations are obtained (Dinçer, Hacıoğlu and Yılmaz, 2013). In addition to this issue, linguistic evaluations are also provided. Within this framework, equation (29) is taken into consideration.

$$\tilde{x}_{ij} = \frac{1}{k}\left[\sum_{e=1}^{n}\tilde{x}_{ij}^{\ e}\right],\ i=1,2,3,\ldots,m \tag{29}$$

Moreover, the fuzzy best value $\tilde{f}_j^*$ and fuzzy worst value $\tilde{f}_j^-$ are calculated for all criterion in the second step. In this context, equation (30) is considered.

$$\tilde{f}_J^* = \max_i \tilde{x}_{ij} \quad \text{and} \quad \tilde{f}_j^- = \min_i \tilde{x}_{ij} \tag{30}$$

Thirdly, the mean group utility and maximal regret are also calculated with the help of equations (31) and (32).

$$\tilde{S}_i = \sum_{i=1}^{n} \tilde{w}_j \frac{\left(\left|\tilde{f}_j^* - \tilde{x}_{ij}\right|\right)}{\left(\left|\tilde{f}_j^* - \tilde{f}_j^-\right|\right)} \tag{31}$$

$$\tilde{R}_i = \max_j \left[\tilde{w}_j \frac{\left(\left|\tilde{f}_j^* - \tilde{x}_{ij}\right|\right)}{\left(\left|\tilde{f}_j^* - \tilde{f}_j^-\right|\right)}\right] \tag{32}$$

In these equations, $\tilde{w}_j$ represents the fuzzy weights of criteria. On the other side, the fourth step includes the calculation of the $\tilde{Q}_i$. Within this context, equation (33) is used.

$$\tilde{Q}_i = v\left(\tilde{S}_i - \tilde{S}^*\right) / \left(\tilde{S}^- - \tilde{S}^*\right) + \left(1 - v\right)\left(\tilde{R}_i - \tilde{R}^*\right) / \left(\tilde{R}^- - \tilde{R}^*\right) \tag{33}$$

In this equation, v gives information about the weight of the strategy of maximum group utility. On the other hand, 1 – v is the weight of the individual regret. In the final step, values of S, R and Q are sorted for different alternatives. In the literature, fuzzy VIKOR methodology was preferred by many researchers. Some recent studies in this context are shown on Table 3.

*Table 3. Studies related to fuzzy VIKOR*

| Author | Subject |
|---|---|
| Awasthi et al. (2018) | sustainable global supplier selection |
| Siregar et al. (2018) | literature review |
| Gupta (2018) | service quality of airline industry |
| Chen (2018) | remoteness index-based pythagorean |
| Sennaroglu & Celebi (2018) | military airport location selection |
| Hashemi et al. (2018) | contractor assessment problem |
| Uztürk et al. (2018) | green building certification selection |
| Shojaei et al. (2018) | airports evaluation and ranking model |
| Pramanik et al. (2018) | green supply chain management |
| Emeç & Akkaya (2018) | warehouse location selection problem |
| Hu et al. (2018) | new doctors ranking system |
| Wang et al. (2018) | risk evaluation of construction project |
| Pramanik & Mallick (2018) | green supply chain management |

*continues on following page*

*Table 3. Continued*

| Author | Subject |
|---|---|
| Liu et al. (2018) | sustainable supplier selection |
| Ceballos et al. (2018) | literature review |
| Tian et al. (2018) | integrated approach for failure mode |
| Shen & Wang (2018) | distance measure |
| Wang et al. (2019) | sustainable energy conversion technologies for agricultural residues |
| Abdel-Basset et al. (2018) | e-government website evaluation |
| Tavana et al. (2018) | decision maker's attitude towards risk |
| Büyüközkan et al. (2019) | selecting hazardous waste carriers |
| Yang et al. (2018) | literature review |
| Kim & Ahn (2019) | literature review |
| Simab et al. (2018) | pumped-hydro-thermal scheduling problem |
| Fei et al. (2018) | supplier selection |
| Wang et al. (2018) | literature review |
| Narayanamoorthy et al. (2019) | industrial robots selection |
| Wu et al. (2019) | possibility distributions |
| Kiani et al. (2018) | material selection for repair of structural concrete |
| Liu (2019) | literature review |
| Wu et al. (2018) | global productive efficiency of Chinese banks |
| Dalapati & Pramanik (2018) | neutrosophic cubic set environment |
| Wang et al. (2018) | failure mode and effects analysis |
| Dinçer and Yüksel (2018) | new service development competencies in Turkish banking sector |
| Liang et al. (2018) | performance assessment of circular economy |
| Dev et al. (2019) | material selection for automotive piston component |
| Çalı & Balaman (2019) | literature review |
| Rani et al. (2018) | correlative multi-criteria decision making problems |
| Rajesh (2018) | manufacturing supply chains |
| Chakraborty et al. (2019) | utilization potential of wave energy converter |
| Ture et al. (2018) | euro 2020 strategy |
| Liang et al. (2019) | internet banking website quality |
| Zhou et al. (2018) | mobile robot selection model for hospital pharmacy |
| Sianturi et al. (2018) | supplier selection |
| Beloševič et al. (2018) | evaluations of infrastructure projects |
| Cui et al. (2018) | optimal siting of electric vehicle charging stations |
| Ghadikolaei et al. (2018) | group decision making |
| Acuña-Soto et al. (2018) | the ranking of mathematical instructional videos |

*continues on following page*

*Table 3. Continued*

| Author | Subject |
|---|---|
| Zare et al. (2018) | computerized maintenance management system selection |
| Zhou et al. (2018) | land reclamation and utilization schemes |
| Titiyal et al. (2019) | distribution strategy selection for an e-tailer |
| Baccour (2018) | literature review |
| Devadoss et al. (2018) | ranking the factors |
| Bu et al. (2018) | optimization of enhanced geothermal system power |
| Khan et al. (2018) | multi-attribute decision-making |
| Zeng et al. (2019) | multi-attribute decision-making |
| Liu et al. (2018) | low-carbon energy planning |
| Umam et al. (2018) | supplier selection |
| Lee & Tseng (2018) | selecting qualified and stable employee |
| Sharma et al. (2019) | software vulnerability prioritization |
| Han et al. (2018) | identification for skeleton-network of power systems |
| Sutrikanti et al. (2018) | supplier selection |
| Suganthi (2018) | sectoral investments for sustainable development |
| Chen et al. (2018) | project evaluation of ambient intelligence product |
| Wu et al. (2018) | site selection decision |
| Wang et al. (2019) | distributed energy system for sustainability transition |

## CONCLUSION

This chapter aimed to explain fuzzy DEMATEL, fuzzy TOPSIS and fuzzy VIKOR approaches. These three methods are the examples of multicriteria decision making methodology. These are mainly used to make decisions under the complex environment. With respect to the fuzzy DEMATEL, it is possible to weight the criteria. In addition to this aspect, impact relation map can also be generated with this method. On the other side, fuzzy TOPSIS and fuzzy VIKOR approaches are used to rank the alternatives according to their significance.

## REFERENCES

Abdel-Basset, M., Manogaran, G., Gamal, A., & Smarandache, F. (2018). A hybrid approach of neutrosophic sets and DEMATEL method for developing supplier selection criteria. *Design Automation for Embedded Systems*, 1–22.

Abdel-Basset, M., Manogaran, G., Gamal, A., & Smarandache, F. (2019). A Group Decision Making Framework Based on Neutrosophic TOPSIS Approach for Smart Medical Device Selection. *Journal of Medical Systems*, *43*(2), 38. doi:10.100710916-019-1156-1 PMID:30627801

Abdel-Basset, M., Mohamed, M., & Smarandache, F. (2018). A hybrid neutrosophic group ANP-TOPSIS framework for supplier selection problems. *Symmetry*, *10*(6), 226. doi:10.3390ym10060226

Abdel-Basset, M., Saleh, M., Gamal, A., & Smarandache, F. (2019). An approach of TOPSIS technique for developing supplier selection with group decision making under type-2 neutrosophic number. *Applied Soft Computing*, *77*, 438–452. doi:10.1016/j.asoc.2019.01.035

Abdel-Basset, M., Zhou, Y., Mohamed, M., & Chang, V. (2018). A group decision making framework based on neutrosophic VIKOR approach for e-government website evaluation. *Journal of Intelligent & Fuzzy Systems*, *34*(6), 4213–4224. doi:10.3233/JIFS-171952

Abdullah, L., & Zulkifli, N. (2018). A new DEMATEL method based on interval type-2 fuzzy sets for developing causal relationship of knowledge management criteria. *Neural Computing & Applications*, 1–17.

Acuña-Carvajal, F., Pinto-Tarazona, L., López-Ospina, H., Barros-Castro, R., Quezada, L., & Palacio, K. (2019). An integrated method to plan, structure and validate a business strategy using fuzzy DEMATEL and the balanced scorecard. *Expert Systems with Applications*, *122*, 351–368. doi:10.1016/j.eswa.2019.01.030

Acuña-Soto, C. M., Liern, V., & Pérez-Gladish, B. (2018). A VIKOR-based approach for the ranking of mathematical instructional videos. *Management Decision*.

Addae, B. A., Zhang, L., Zhou, P., & Wang, F. (2019). Analyzing barriers of Smart Energy City in Accra with two-step fuzzy DEMATEL. *Cities (London, England)*, *89*, 218–227. doi:10.1016/j.cities.2019.01.043

Ali, K., Moktadir, M. A., Shaikh, A. A., Deb, A. K., & Rashed-Ul-Islam, M. (2018). Challenges Evaluation for Adoption of SCP Practices in Footwear Industry of Bangladesh: A DEMATEL Approach. *Journal of Operations and Strategic Planning*, *1*(2), 168–184. doi:10.1177/2516600X18812984

Aloini, D., Dulmin, R., Mininno, V., Pellegrini, L., & Farina, G. (2018). Technology assessment with IF-TOPSIS: An application in the advanced underwater system sector. *Technological Forecasting and Social Change*, *131*, 38–48. doi:10.1016/j.techfore.2017.07.010

Alzahrani, A. I., Al-Samarraie, H., Eldenfria, A., & Alalwan, N. (2018). A DEMATEL method in identifying design requirements for mobile environments: Students' perspectives. *Journal of Computing in Higher Education*, *30*(3), 466–488. doi:10.100712528-018-9176-2

Ameri, A. A., Pourghasemi, H. R., & Cerda, A. (2018). Erodibility prioritization of sub-watersheds using morphometric parameters analysis and its mapping: A comparison among TOPSIS, VIKOR, SAW, and CF multi-criteria decision making models. *The Science of the Total Environment*, *613*, 1385–1400. doi:10.1016/j.scitotenv.2017.09.210 PMID:29898506

Amiri, M., Pourghasemi, H. R., Arabameri, A., Vazirzadeh, A., Yousefi, H., & Kafaei, S. (2019). Prioritization of Flood Inundation of Maharloo Watershed in Iran Using Morphometric Parameters Analysis and TOPSIS MCDM Model. In *Spatial Modeling in GIS and R for Earth and Environmental Sciences* (pp. 371–390). Elsevier. doi:10.1016/B978-0-12-815226-3.00016-8

Ananthakumar, K., Rajamani, D., Balasubramanian, E., & Davim, J. P. (2019). Measurement and optimization of multi-response characteristics in plasma arc cutting of Monel 400™ using RSM and TOPSIS. *Measurement*, *135*, 725–737. doi:10.1016/j.measurement.2018.12.010

Araujo, C. A. S., Wanke, P., & Siqueira, M. M. (2018). A performance analysis of Brazilian public health: TOPSIS and neural networks application. *International Journal of Productivity and Performance Management*, *67*(9), 1526–1549. doi:10.1108/IJPPM-11-2017-0319

Atthirawong, W., Panprung, W., & Leerojanaprapa, K. (2018). Using DEMATEL To Explore The Relationship Of Factors Affecting Consumers' Behaviors In Buying Green Products. In ECMS (pp. 317-322). Academic Press.

Aviso, K. B., Lucas, R. I. G., Tapia, J. F. D., Promentilla, M. A. B., & Tan, R. R. (2018). Identifying Key Factors to Learning Process Systems Engineering and Process Integration through DEMATEL. *Chemical Engineering Transactions*, *70*, 265–270.

Awasthi, A., Govindan, K., & Gold, S. (2018). Multi-tier sustainable global supplier selection using a fuzzy AHP-VIKOR based approach. *International Journal of Production Economics*, *195*, 106–117. doi:10.1016/j.ijpe.2017.10.013

Azimifard, A., Moosavirad, S. H., & Ariafar, S. (2018). Designing steel supply chain and assessing the embedded CO2 emission based on the input-output table by using DEMATEL method. *Management Decision*, *56*(4), 757–776. doi:10.1108/MD-05-2017-0478

Azimifard, A., Moosavirad, S. H., & Ariafar, S. (2018). Selecting sustainable supplier countries for Iran's steel industry at three levels by using AHP and TOPSIS methods. *Resources Policy*, *57*, 30–44. doi:10.1016/j.resourpol.2018.01.002

Baccour, L. (2018). Amended fused TOPSIS-VIKOR for classification (ATOVIC) applied to some UCI data sets. *Expert Systems with Applications*, *99*, 115–125. doi:10.1016/j.eswa.2018.01.025

Bai, C., & Sarkis, J. (2018). Integrating sustainability into supplier selection: A grey-based TOPSIS analysis. *Technological and Economic Development of Economy*, *24*(6), 2202–2224. doi:10.3846/tede.2018.5582

Bakir, S., Khan, S., Ahsan, K., & Rahman, S. (2018). Exploring the critical determinants of environmentally oriented public procurement using the DEMATEL method. *Journal of Environmental Management*, *225*, 325–335. doi:10.1016/j.jenvman.2018.07.081 PMID:30099147

Belošević, I., Kosijer, M., Ivić, M., & Pavlović, N. (2018). Group decision making process for early stage evaluations of infrastructure projects using extended VIKOR method under fuzzy environment. *European Transport Research Review*, *10*(2), 43. doi:10.118612544-018-0318-4

Bhagawati, M. T., Manavalan, E., Jayakrishna, K., & Venkumar, P. (2019). Identifying Key Success Factors of Sustainability in Supply Chain Management for Industry 4.0 Using DEMATEL Method. In *Proceedings of International Conference on Intelligent Manufacturing and Automation* (pp. 583-591). Springer. 10.1007/978-981-13-2490-1_54

Bhatia, M. S., & Srivastava, R. K. (2018). Analysis of external barriers to remanufacturing using grey-DEMATEL approach: An Indian perspective. *Resources, Conservation and Recycling*, *136*, 79–87. doi:10.1016/j.resconrec.2018.03.021

Bian, T., Zheng, H., Yin, L., & Deng, Y. (2018). Failure mode and effects analysis based on D numbers and TOPSIS. *Quality and Reliability Engineering International*, *34*(4), 501–515. doi:10.1002/qre.2268

Bianchini, A. (2018). 3PL provider selection by AHP and TOPSIS methodology. *Benchmarking: An International Journal*, *25*(1), 235–252. doi:10.1108/BIJ-08-2016-0125

Bu, Y., Guo, M., & Cheng, P. (2018). Optimization of Enhanced Geothermal System Power Generation Investment Scheme Based on Fuzzy VIKOR Model. In *E3S Web of Conferences* (Vol. 57, p. 01001). EDP Sciences. doi:10.1051/e3sconf/20185701001

Büyüközkan, G., Göçer, F., & Karabulut, Y. (2019). A new group decision making approach with IF AHP and IF VIKOR for selecting hazardous waste carriers. *Measurement*, *134*, 66–82. doi:10.1016/j.measurement.2018.10.041

Çalı, S., & Balaman, Ş. Y. (2019). A novel outranking based multi criteria group decision making methodology integrating ELECTRE and VIKOR under intuitionistic fuzzy environment. *Expert Systems with Applications*, *119*, 36–50. doi:10.1016/j.eswa.2018.10.039

Cavallaro, F., Zavadskas, E. K., Streimikiene, D., & Mardani, A. (2019). Assessment of concentrated solar power (CSP) technologies based on a modified intuitionistic fuzzy topsis and trigonometric entropy weights. *Technological Forecasting and Social Change*, *140*, 258–270. doi:10.1016/j.techfore.2018.12.009

Ceballos, B., Pelta, D. A., & Lamata, M. T. (2018). Rank reversal and the VIKOR method: An empirical evaluation. *International Journal of Information Technology & Decision Making*, *17*(02), 513–525. doi:10.1142/S0219622017500237

Certa, A., Enea, M., Galante, G. M., Izquierdo, J., & Fata, C. M. L. (2018). Food safety risk analysis from the producers' perspective: Prioritisation of production process stages by HACCP and TOPSIS. *International Journal of Management and Decision Making*, *17*(4), 396–414. doi:10.1504/IJMDM.2018.095720

Chakraborty, T., Majumder, M., & Khare, A. (2019). Application of AHP-VIKOR and GMDH framework to develop an indicator to identify utilisation potential of wave energy converter with respect to location. *International Journal of Spatio-Temporal Data Science*, *1*(1), 98–113. doi:10.1504/IJSTDS.2019.097603

Chang, C. C., & Chen, P. Y. (2018). Analysis of critical factors for social games based on extended technology acceptance model: A DEMATEL approach. *Behaviour & Information Technology*, *37*(8), 774–785. doi:10.1080/0144929X.2018.1480654

Chauhan, A., Singh, A., & Jharkharia, S. (2018). An interpretive structural modeling (ISM) and decision-making trail and evaluation laboratory (DEMATEL) method approach for the analysis of barriers of waste recycling in India. *Journal of the Air & Waste Management Association*, *68*(2), 100–110. doi:10.1080/10962247.2016.1249441 PMID:28278038

Chen, C. T., Huang, S. F., & Hung, W. Z. (2018). Linguistic VIKOR method for project evaluation of ambient intelligence product. *Journal of Ambient Intelligence and Humanized Computing*, 1–11.

Chen, T. Y. (2018). Remoteness index-based Pythagorean fuzzy VIKOR methods with a generalized distance measure for multiple criteria decision analysis. *Information Fusion*, *41*, 129–150. doi:10.1016/j.inffus.2017.09.003

Chen, W., Shen, Y., & Wang, Y. (2018). Evaluation of economic transformation and upgrading of resource-based cities in Shaanxi province based on an improved TOPSIS method. *Sustainable Cities and Society, 37*, 232-240.

Chen, Y. H., Wang, S. W., Lee, C., & Lin, C. T. (2018). Using the DEMATEL Method to Explore the Critical Factors That Influence Visitors to Purchase Museum Cultural Products. *Journal of Testing and Evaluation*, *46*(5).

Chou, Y. C., Yen, H. Y., Dang, V. T., & Sun, C. C. (2019). Assessing the Human Resource in Science and Technology for Asian Countries: Application of Fuzzy AHP and Fuzzy TOPSIS. *Symmetry*, *11*(2), 251. doi:10.3390ym11020251

Costa, F., Denis Granja, A., Fregola, A., Picchi, F., & Portioli Staudacher, A. (2019). Understanding Relative Importance of Barriers to Improving the Customer–Supplier Relationship within Construction Supply Chains Using DEMATEL Technique. *Journal of Management Engineering*, *35*(3), 04019002. doi:10.1061/(ASCE)ME.1943-5479.0000680

Cui, F. B., You, X. Y., Shi, H., & Liu, H. C. (2018). Optimal siting of electric vehicle charging stations using pythagorean fuzzy vikor approach. *Mathematical Problems in Engineering*, 2018.

Cui, L., Chan, H. K., Zhou, Y., Dai, J., & Lim, J. J. (2018). Exploring critical factors of green business failure based on grey-decision making trial and evaluation laboratory (DEMATEL). *Journal of Business Research*.

Dalapati, S., & Pramanik, S. (2018). A revisit to NC-VIKOR based MAGDM strategy in neutrosophic cubic set environment. *Neutrosophic Sets and Systems*, *21*, 131–141.

Daneshvar Rouyendegh, B., Yildizbasi, A., & Arikan, Ü. Z. (2018). Using intuitionistic fuzzy TOPSIS in site selection of wind power plants in Turkey. *Advances in Fuzzy Systems*.

Dev, S., Aherwar, A., & Patnaik, A. (2019). Material Selection for Automotive Piston Component Using Entropy-VIKOR Method. *Silicon*, 1-15.

Devadoss, A. V., Prabakaran, R., & Felix, A. (2018). A Hybrid Scenario FCM with VIKOR Technique for Ranking the Factors. *International Journal of Pure and Applied Mathematics*, *119*(9), 233–244.

Dincer, H. (2015). Profit-based stock selection approach in banking sector using Fuzzy AHP and MOORA method. *Global Business and Economics Research Journal*, *4*(2), 1–26.

Dincer, H. (2018). HHI-based evaluation of the European banking sector using an integrated fuzzy approach. *Kybernetes*.

Dinçer, H., Akdeniz, O. O., & Hacioglu, U. (2018). Competitive strategy selection in the European banking sector using a hybrid decision-making approach. *Zbornik Radova Ekonomski Fakultet u Rijeka*, *36*(1), 211–240.

Dinçer, H., Bozaykut-Buk, T., Emir, Ş., Yuksel, S., & Ashill, N. (2019). Using the fuzzy multicriteria decision making approach to evaluate brand equity: A study of privatized firms. *Journal of Product and Brand Management*.

Dinçer, H., & Görener, A. (2011). Performans değerlendirmesinde AHP-VIKOR ve AHP-TOPSIS yaklaşımları: Hizmet sektöründe bir uygulama. *Sigma: Mühendislik ve Fen Bilimleri Dergisi*, *29*, 244–260.

Dincer, H., & Hacioglu, U. (2013). Performance evaluation with fuzzy VIKOR and AHP method based on customer satisfaction in Turkish banking sector. *Kybernetes*, *42*(7), 1072–1085. doi:10.1108/K-02-2013-0021

Dincer, H., & Hacioglu, U. (2015). A comparative performance evaluation on bipolar risks in emerging capital markets using fuzzy AHP-TOPSIS and VIKOR approaches. *The Engineering Economist*, *26*(2), 118–129.

Dincer, H., & Hacioglu, U. (2017). Investigating the Economic Vulnerability Factors of Emerging Markets After the Global Financial Crisis of 2008 With a Hybrid Multi-Criteria Decision-Making Approach. In Handbook of Research on Economic, Financial, and Industrial Impacts on Infrastructure Development (pp. 313-333). IGI Global.

Dincer, H., Hacioglu, U., Tatoglu, E., & Delen, D. (2016). A fuzzy-hybrid analytic model to assess investors' perceptions for industry selection. *Decision Support Systems*, *86*, 24–34. doi:10.1016/j.dss.2016.03.005

Dincer, H., Hacioglu, U., & Yilmaz, R. (2013). *The effect of integrated marketing communication competencies on banking performance: analysis with fuzzy VIKOR method*. Academic Press.

Dinçer, H., Hacıoğlu, Ü., & Yüksel, S. (2017). Balanced scorecard based performance measurement of European airlines using a hybrid multicriteria decision making approach under the fuzzy environment. *Journal of Air Transport Management*, *63*, 17–33. doi:10.1016/j.jairtraman.2017.05.005

Dinçer, H., & Yüksel, S. (2018). Comparative Evaluation of BSC-Based New Service Development Competencies in Turkish Banking Sector with the Integrated Fuzzy Hybrid MCDM Using Content Analysis. *International Journal of Fuzzy Systems*, *20*(8), 2497–2516. doi:10.100740815-018-0519-y

Dinçer, H., & Yüksel, S. (2018). Financial Sector-Based Analysis of the G20 Economies Using the Integrated Decision-Making Approach with DEMATEL and TOPSIS. In *Emerging Trends in Banking and Finance* (pp. 210–223). Cham: Springer. doi:10.1007/978-3-030-01784-2_13

Dincer, H., & Yuksel, S. (2019). IT2-based Fuzzy Hybrid Decision Making Approach to Soft Computing. *IEEE Access*.

Dinçer, H., & Yüksel, S. (2019). Multidimensional evaluation of global investments on the renewable energy with the integrated fuzzy decision-making model under the hesitancy. *International Journal of Energy Research*.

Dinçer, H., Yuksel, S., & Bozaykut-Buk, T. (2018). Evaluation of Financial and Economic Effects on Green Supply Chain Management With Multi-Criteria Decision-Making Approach: Evidence From Companies Listed in BIST. In *Handbook of Research on Supply Chain Management for Sustainable Development* (pp. 144–175). IGI Global. doi:10.4018/978-1-5225-5757-9.ch009

Dinçer, H., Yüksel, S., & Çetiner, İ. T. (2019). Strategy Selection for Organizational Performance of Turkish Banking Sector With the Integrated Multi-Dimensional Decision-Making Approach. In *Handbook of Research on Contemporary Approaches in Management and Organizational Strategy* (pp. 273–291). IGI Global. doi:10.4018/978-1-5225-6301-3.ch014

Dinçer, H., Yüksel, S., & Martínez, L. (2019). Balanced scorecard-based Analysis about European Energy Investment Policies: A hybrid hesitant fuzzy decision-making approach with Quality Function Deployment. *Expert Systems with Applications*, *115*, 152–171. doi:10.1016/j.eswa.2018.07.072

Dinçer, H., Yüksel, S., & Martínez, L. (2019). Interval type 2-based hybrid fuzzy evaluation of financial services in E7 economies with DEMATEL-ANP and MOORA methods. *Applied Soft Computing*, *79*, 186–202. doi:10.1016/j.asoc.2019.03.018

Dinçer, H., Yüksel, S., & Pınarbaşı, F. (2019). SERVQUAL-Based Evaluation of Service Quality of Energy Companies in Turkey: Strategic Policies for Sustainable Economic Development. In The Circular Economy and Its Implications on Sustainability and the Green Supply Chain (pp. 142-167). IGI Global.

Dinçer, H., Yüksel, S., Pınarbaşı, F., & Çetiner, İ. T. (2019). Measurement of Economic and Banking Stability in Emerging Markets by Considering Income Inequality and Nonperforming Loans. In *Maintaining Financial Stability in Times of Risk and Uncertainty* (pp. 49–68). IGI Global. doi:10.4018/978-1-5225-7208-4.ch003

Ding, X. F., & Liu, H. C. (2018). A 2-dimension uncertain linguistic DEMATEL method for identifying critical success factors in emergency management. *Applied Soft Computing*, *71*, 386–395. doi:10.1016/j.asoc.2018.07.018

Dong, W., & Bao, X. (2018, August). Application of Improved Interval Numbers TOPSIS Method Based on Mahalanobis Distance in the Evaluation of SME Public Service Platform. In *2018 International Conference on Information Technology and Management Engineering (ICITME 2018)*. Atlantis Press. 10.2991/icitme-18.2018.47

dos Santos, B. M., Godoy, L. P., & Campos, L. M. (2019). Performance evaluation of green suppliers using entropy-TOPSIS-F. *Journal of Cleaner Production*, *207*, 498–509. doi:10.1016/j.jclepro.2018.09.235

Dwivedi, G., Srivastava, R. K., & Srivastava, S. K. (2018). A generalised fuzzy TOPSIS with improved closeness coefficient. *Expert Systems with Applications*, *96*, 185–195. doi:10.1016/j.eswa.2017.11.051

Emeç, Ş., & Akkaya, G. (2018). Stochastic AHP and fuzzy VIKOR approach for warehouse location selection problem. *Journal of Enterprise Information Management*, *31*(6), 950–962. doi:10.1108/JEIM-12-2016-0195

Ervural, B. C., Zaim, S., Demirel, O. F., Aydin, Z., & Delen, D. (2018). An ANP and fuzzy TOPSIS-based SWOT analysis for Turkey's energy planning. *Renewable & Sustainable Energy Reviews*, *82*, 1538–1550. doi:10.1016/j.rser.2017.06.095

Fei, L., Deng, Y., & Hu, Y. (2018). DS-VIKOR: A new multi-criteria decision-making method for supplier selection. *International Journal of Fuzzy Systems*, 1–19.

Feng, Y., Hong, Z., Tian, G., Li, Z., Tan, J., & Hu, H. (2018). Environmentally friendly MCDM of reliability-based product optimisation combining DEMATEL-based ANP, interval uncertainty and Vlse Kriterijumska Optimizacija Kompromisno Resenje (VIKOR). *Information Sciences*, *442*, 128–144. doi:10.1016/j.ins.2018.02.038

Ganesh Kumar, P., Meikandan, M., Sakthivadivel, D., & Vigneswaran, V. S. (2018). Selection of optimum glazing material for solar thermal applications using TOPSIS methodology. *International Journal of Ambient Energy*, 1-5.

Ganji, S. S., Rassafi, A. A., & Kordani, A. A. (2018). Vehicle safety analysis based on a hybrid approach integrating DEMATEL, ANP and ER. *KSCE Journal of Civil Engineering*, *22*(11), 4580–4592. doi:10.100712205-018-1720-0

Gardas, B. B., Raut, R. D., & Narkhede, B. (2018). Evaluating critical causal factors for post-harvest losses (PHL) in the fruit and vegetables supply chain in India using the DEMATEL approach. *Journal of Cleaner Production, 199*, 47–61. doi:10.1016/j.jclepro.2018.07.153

Gardas, B. B., Raut, R. D., & Narkhede, B. (2018). Modelling the challenges to sustainability in the textile and apparel (T&A) sector: A Delphi-DEMATEL approach. *Sustainable Production and Consumption, 15*, 96–108. doi:10.1016/j.spc.2018.05.001

Ghadikolaei, A. S., Madhoushi, M., & Divsalar, M. (2018). Extension of the VIKOR method for group decision making with extended hesitant fuzzy linguistic information. *Neural Computing & Applications, 30*(12), 3589–3602. doi:10.100700521-017-2944-5

Gopal, J., Sangaiah, A. K., Basu, A., & Gao, X. Z. (2018). Integration of fuzzy DEMATEL and FMCDM approach for evaluating knowledge transfer effectiveness with reference to GSD project outcome. *International Journal of Machine Learning and Cybernetics, 9*(2), 225–241. doi:10.100713042-015-0370-5

Gorener, A., Dincer, H., & Hacioglu, U. (2013). *Application of multi-objective optimization on the basis of ratio analysis (MOORA) method for bank branch location selection*. Academic Press.

Goyal, S., Routroy, S., & Singhal, A. (2018). Analyzing environment sustainability enablers using fuzzy DEMATEL for an Indian steel manufacturing company. *Journal of Engineering, Design and Technology.*

Gupta, H. (2018). Evaluating service quality of airline industry using hybrid best worst method and VIKOR. *Journal of Air Transport Management, 68*, 35–47. doi:10.1016/j.jairtraman.2017.06.001

Gupta, H., & Barua, M. K. (2018). A grey DEMATEL-based approach for modeling enablers of green innovation in manufacturing organizations. *Environmental Science and Pollution Research International*, 1–23. PMID:29357076

Hadi-Vencheh, A., Mohammadghasemi, A., Hosseinzadeh Lotfi, F., & Khalil Zadeh, M. (2018). Group multiple criteria ABC inventory classification using TOPSIS approach extended by Gaussian interval type-2 fuzzy sets and optimization programs. *Scientia Iranica, 0*(0), 0. doi:10.24200ci.2018.5539.1332

Han, C., Zhao, Y., Lin, Z., Ding, Y., Yang, L., Lin, G., ... Ye, X. (2018). Critical lines identification for skeleton-network of power systems under extreme weather conditions based on the modified VIKOR method. *Energies*, *11*(6), 1355. doi:10.3390/en11061355

Han, H., & Trimi, S. (2018). A fuzzy TOPSIS method for performance evaluation of reverse logistics in social commerce platforms. *Expert Systems with Applications*, *103*, 133–145. doi:10.1016/j.eswa.2018.03.003

Hashemi, H., Mousavi, S., Zavadskas, E., Chalekaee, A., & Turskis, Z. (2018). A new group decision model based on grey-intuitionistic fuzzy-ELECTRE and VIKOR for contractor assessment problem. *Sustainability*, *10*(5), 1635. doi:10.3390u10051635

Hatefi, S. M., & Tamošaitienė, J. (2019). An integrated fuzzy DEMATEL-fuzzy ANP model for evaluating construction projects by considering interrelationships among risk factors. *Journal of Civil Engineering and Management*, *25*(2), 114–131. doi:10.3846/jcem.2019.8280

Hu, J., Zhang, X., Yang, Y., Liu, Y., & Chen, X. (2018). New doctors ranking system based on VIKOR method. *International Transactions in Operational Research*. doi:10.1111/itor.12569

Hwang, C. L., & Yoon, K. S. (1981). *Multiple attribute decision making: Methods and applications*. Berlin: Springer-Verlag. doi:10.1007/978-3-642-48318-9

Ilgin, M. A. (2019). A DEMATEL-Based Disassembly Line Balancing Heuristic. *Journal of Manufacturing Science and Engineering*, *141*(2), 021002. doi:10.1115/1.4041925

Indahingwati, A., Barid, M., Wajdi, N., Susilo, D. E., Kurniasih, N., & Rahim, R. (2018). Comparison Analysis of TOPSIS and Fuzzy Logic Methods On Fertilizer Selection. *Int. J. Eng. Technol, 7*(2.3), 109-114.

Jain, V., Sangaiah, A. K., Sakhuja, S., Thoduka, N., & Aggarwal, R. (2018). Supplier selection using fuzzy AHP and TOPSIS: A case study in the Indian automotive industry. *Neural Computing & Applications*, *29*(7), 555–564. doi:10.100700521-016-2533-z

Janaki, D., Izadbakhsh, H., & Hatefi, S. (2018). The evaluation of supply chain performance in the Oil Products Distribution Company, using information technology indicators and fuzzy TOPSIS technique. *Management Science Letters*, *8*(8), 835–848. doi:10.5267/j.msl.2018.6.004

Ji, M. (2018, September). Analysis of Machine Failure Sorting Based on Directed Graph and DEMATEL. In *International Workshop of Advanced Manufacturing and Automation* (pp. 377-382). Springer.

Kaur, J., Sidhu, R., Awasthi, A., Chauhan, S., & Goyal, S. (2018). A DEMATEL based approach for investigating barriers in green supply chain management in Canadian manufacturing firms. *International Journal of Production Research*, *56*(1-2), 312–332. doi:10.1080/00207543.2017.1395522

Kazancoglu, Y., Kazancoglu, I., & Sagnak, M. (2018). Fuzzy DEMATEL-based green supply chain management performance: Application in cement industry. *Industrial Management & Data Systems*, *118*(2), 412–431. doi:10.1108/IMDS-03-2017-0121

Khan, M. S. A., Abdullah, S., Ali, A., & Amin, F. (2018). An extension of VIKOR method for multi-attribute decision-making under Pythagorean hesitant fuzzy setting. *Granular Computing*, 1-14.

Khedrigharibvand, H., Azadi, H., Bahrami, H., Tesfamariam, Z., Bazzazi, A. A., De Maeyer, P., & Witlox, F. (2018). Sustainable rangeland management in southwest Iran: Application of the AHP-TOPSIS approach in ranking livelihood alternatives. *The Rangeland Journal*, *40*(6), 603–614. doi:10.1071/RJ17038

Kiani, B., Liang, R. Y., & Gross, J. (2018). Material selection for repair of structural concrete using VIKOR method. *Case Studies in Construction Materials, 8*, 489-497.

Kim, J. H., & Ahn, B. S. (2019). Extended VIKOR method using incomplete criteria weights. *Expert Systems with Applications*, *126*, 124–132. doi:10.1016/j.eswa.2019.02.019

Koulinas, G. K., Demesouka, O. E., Marhavilas, P. K., Vavatsikos, A. P., & Koulouriotis, D. E. (2019). Risk Assessment Using Fuzzy TOPSIS and PRAT for Sustainable Engineering Projects. *Sustainability*, *11*(3), 615. doi:10.3390u11030615

Kumar, A., & Dixit, G. (2018). Evaluating critical barriers to implementation of WEEE management using DEMATEL approach. *Resources, Conservation and Recycling*, *131*, 101–121. doi:10.1016/j.resconrec.2017.12.024

Kumar, A., Kaviani, M. A., Bottani, E., Dash, M. K., & Zavadskas, E. K. (2018). Investigating the role of social media in polio prevention in India: A Delphi-DEMATEL approach. *Kybernetes*, *47*(5), 1053–1072. doi:10.1108/K-06-2017-0210

Kumar, A., Pal, A., Vohra, A., Gupta, S., Manchanda, S., & Dash, M. K. (2018). Construction of capital procurement decision making model to optimize supplier selection using Fuzzy Delphi and AHP-DEMATEL. *Benchmarking: An International Journal*, *25*(5), 1528–1547. doi:10.1108/BIJ-01-2017-0005

Kumar, K., & Garg, H. (2018). TOPSIS method based on the connection number of set pair analysis under interval-valued intuitionistic fuzzy set environment. *Computational & Applied Mathematics*, *37*(2), 1319–1329. doi:10.100740314-016-0402-0

Kwok, P. K., & Lau, H. Y. (2019). Hotel selection using a modified TOPSIS-based decision support algorithm. *Decision Support Systems*, *120*, 95–105. doi:10.1016/j.dss.2019.02.004

Lee, C. C., & Tseng, H. C. (2018, January). Integrating fuzzy membership function, entropy method and VIKOR to select qualified and stable employee. In *2018 International Conference on Information Management and Processing (ICIMP)* (pp. 26-31). IEEE. 10.1109/ICIMP1.2018.8325836

Leksono, E. B., Suparno, S., & Vanany, I. (2018). Development of Performance Indicators Relationships on Sustainable Healthcare Supply Chain Performance Measurement Using Balanced Scorecard and DEMATEL. *International Journal on Advanced Science Engineering Information Technology, 8*(1), 115-122.

Li, J., Fang, H., & Song, W. (2019). Sustainable supplier selection based on SSCM practices: A rough cloud TOPSIS approach. *Journal of Cleaner Production.*

Li, Y., & Mathiyazhagan, K. (2018). Application of DEMATEL approach to identify the influential indicators towards sustainable supply chain adoption in the auto components manufacturing sector. *Journal of Cleaner Production*, *172*, 2931–2941. doi:10.1016/j.jclepro.2017.11.120

Liang, D., Xu, Z., Liu, D., & Wu, Y. (2018). Method for three-way decisions using ideal TOPSIS solutions at Pythagorean fuzzy information. *Information Sciences*, *435*, 282–295. doi:10.1016/j.ins.2018.01.015

Liang, D., Zhang, Y., Xu, Z., & Jamaldeen, A. (2019). Pythagorean fuzzy VIKOR approaches based on TODIM for evaluating internet banking website quality of Ghanaian banking industry. *Applied Soft Computing*, *78*, 583–594. doi:10.1016/j.asoc.2019.03.006

Liang, W. Z., Zhao, G. Y., & Hong, C. S. (2018). Performance assessment of circular economy for phosphorus chemical firms based on VIKOR-QUALIFLEX method. *Journal of Cleaner Production*, *196*, 1365–1378. doi:10.1016/j.jclepro.2018.06.147

Lin, K. P., Tseng, M. L., & Pai, P. F. (2018). Sustainable supply chain management using approximate fuzzy DEMATEL method. *Resources, Conservation and Recycling*, *128*, 134–142. doi:10.1016/j.resconrec.2016.11.017

Lin, S., Li, C., Xu, F., Liu, D., & Liu, J. (2018). Risk identification and analysis for new energy power system in China based on D numbers and decision-making trial and evaluation laboratory (DEMATEL). *Journal of Cleaner Production*, *180*, 81–96. doi:10.1016/j.jclepro.2018.01.153

Liu, F., Aiwu, G., Lukovac, V., & Vukic, M. (2018). A multicriteria model for the selection of the transport service provider: A single valued neutrosophic DEMATEL multicriteria model. *Decision Making: Applications in Management and Engineering*, *1*(2), 121–130.

Liu, H. C. (2019). FMEA Using Combination Weighting and Fuzzy VIKOR and Its Application to General Anesthesia. In *Improved FMEA Methods for Proactive Healthcare Risk Analysis* (pp. 151–172). Singapore: Springer. doi:10.1007/978-981-13-6366-5_7

Liu, H. C., Wang, L. E., Li, Z., & Hu, Y. P. (2019). Improving Risk Evaluation in FMEA With Cloud Model and Hierarchical TOPSIS Method. *IEEE Transactions on Fuzzy Systems*, *27*(1), 84–95. doi:10.1109/TFUZZ.2018.2861719

Liu, J., & Wei, Q. (2018). Risk evaluation of electric vehicle charging infrastructure public-private partnership projects in China using fuzzy TOPSIS. *Journal of Cleaner Production*, *189*, 211–222. doi:10.1016/j.jclepro.2018.04.103

Liu, K., Liu, Y., & Qin, J. (2018). An integrated ANP-VIKOR methodology for sustainable supplier selection with interval type-2 fuzzy sets. *Granular Computing, 3*(3), 193–208. doi:10.100741066-017-0071-4

Liu, R., Sun, H., Zhang, L., Zhuang, Q., Zhang, L., Zhang, X., & Chen, Y. (2018). Low-Carbon Energy Planning: A Hybrid MCDM Method Combining DANP and VIKOR Approach. *Energies, 11*(12), 3401. doi:10.3390/en11123401

Liu, T., Deng, Y., & Chan, F. (2018). Evidential supplier selection based on DEMATEL and game theory. *International Journal of Fuzzy Systems, 20*(4), 1321–1333. doi:10.100740815-017-0400-4

Liu, Z., Ming, X., & Song, W. (2019). A framework integrating interval-valued hesitant fuzzy DEMATEL method to capture and evaluate co-creative value propositions for smart PSS. *Journal of Cleaner Production.*

Luan, B., Yin, R., Xu, P., Wang, X., Yang, X., Zhang, L., & Tang, X. (2019). Evaluating Green Stormwater Infrastructure strategies efficiencies in a rapidly urbanizing catchment using SWMM-based TOPSIS. *Journal of Cleaner Production.*

Luthra, S., Mangla, S. K., Shankar, R., Prakash Garg, C., & Jakhar, S. (2018). Modelling critical success factors for sustainability initiatives in supply chains in Indian context using Grey-DEMATEL. *Production Planning and Control, 29*(9), 705–728. doi:10.1080/09537287.2018.1448126

Ma, F., Shi, W., Yuen, K. F., Sun, Q., & Guo, Y. (2019). Multi-stakeholders' assessment of bike sharing service quality based on DEMATEL–VIKOR method. *International Journal of Logistics Research and Applications*, 1-24.

Majumdar, R., Kapur, P. K., & Khatri, S. K. (2019). Assessing software upgradation attributes and optimal release planning using DEMATEL and MAUT. *International Journal of Industrial and Systems Engineering, 31*(1), 70–94. doi:10.1504/IJISE.2019.096886

Mangla, S. K., Luthra, S., Jakhar, S. K., Tyagi, M., & Narkhede, B. E. (2018). Benchmarking the logistics management implementation using Delphi and fuzzy DEMATEL. *Benchmarking: An International Journal, 25*(6), 1795–1828. doi:10.1108/BIJ-01-2017-0006

Mao, N., Song, M., Pan, D., & Deng, S. (2018). Comparative studies on using RSM and TOPSIS methods to optimize residential air conditioning systems. *Energy*, *144*, 98–109. doi:10.1016/j.energy.2017.11.160

Mavi, R. K., & Standing, C. (2018). Critical success factors of sustainable project management in construction: A fuzzy DEMATEL-ANP approach. *Journal of Cleaner Production*, *194*, 751–765. doi:10.1016/j.jclepro.2018.05.120

Mohammed, A., Harris, I., Soroka, A., Naim, M. M., & Ramjaun, T. (2018). Evaluating Green and Resilient Supplier Performance: AHP-Fuzzy Topsis Decision-Making Approach. In ICORES (pp. 209-216). Academic Press.

Mousavizade, F., & Shakibazad, M. (2019). Identifying and ranking CSFs for KM implementation in urban water and sewage companies using ISM-DEMATEL technique. *Journal of Knowledge Management*, *23*(1), 200–218. doi:10.1108/JKM-05-2018-0321

Narayanamoorthy, S., Geetha, S., Rakkiyappan, R., & Joo, Y. H. (2019). Interval-valued intuitionistic hesitant fuzzy entropy based VIKOR method for industrial robots selection. *Expert Systems with Applications*, *121*, 28–37. doi:10.1016/j.eswa.2018.12.015

Nazari, M. A., Aslani, A., & Ghasempour, R. (2018). Analysis of solar farm site selection based on TOPSIS approach. *International Journal of Social Ecology and Sustainable Development*, *9*(1), 12–25. doi:10.4018/IJSESD.2018010102

Nguyen, P., Banh, L., Bui, V., & Hoang, D. (2018). Multi-response optimization of process parameters for powder mixed electro-discharge machining according to the surface roughness and surface micro-hardness using Taguchi-TOPSIS. *International Journal of Data and Network Science*, *2*(4), 109–119. doi:10.5267/j.ijdns.2018.9.001

Ocampo, L. A., Tan, T. A. G., & Sia, L. A. (2018). Using fuzzy DEMATEL in modeling the causal relationships of the antecedents of organizational citizenship behavior (OCB) in the hospitality industry: A case study in the Philippines. *Journal of Hospitality and Tourism Management*, *34*, 11–29. doi:10.1016/j.jhtm.2017.11.002

Ortega, R. G., Vázquez, M. L., Figueiredo, J. A., & Guijarro-Rodríguez, A. (2018). Sinos River basin social-environmental prospective assessment of water quality management using fuzzy cognitive maps and neutrosophic AHP-TOPSIS. *Neutrosophic Sets & Systems, 23*.

Ouenniche, J., Pérez-Gladish, B., & Bouslah, K. (2018). An out-of-sample framework for TOPSIS-based classifiers with application in bankruptcy prediction. *Technological Forecasting and Social Change*, *131*, 111–116. doi:10.1016/j.techfore.2017.05.034

Peng, X., & Dai, J. (2018). Approaches to single-valued neutrosophic MADM based on MABAC, TOPSIS and new similarity measure with score function. *Neural Computing & Applications*, *29*(10), 939–954. doi:10.100700521-016-2607-y

Pourjavad, E., & Shahin, A. (2018). Hybrid performance evaluation of sustainable service and manufacturing supply chain management: An integrated approach of fuzzy dematel and fuzzy inference system. *Intelligent Systems in Accounting, Finance & Management*, *25*(3), 134–147. doi:10.1002/isaf.1431

Pramanik, S., Dalapati, S., Alam, S., & Roy, T. K. (2018). NC-VIKOR Based MAGDM Strategy under Neutrosophic Cubic Set Environment. *Neutrosophic Sets and Systems*, *20*(1), 95–108.

Pramanik, S., & Mallick, R. (2018). VIKOR based MAGDM Strategy with Trapezoidal Neutrosophic Numbers. *Neutrosophic Sets and Systems*, 118.

Quezada, L. E., López-Ospina, H. A., Palominos, P. I., & Oddershede, A. M. (2018). Identifying causal relationships in strategy maps using ANP and DEMATEL. *Computers & Industrial Engineering*, *118*, 170–179. doi:10.1016/j.cie.2018.02.020

Rad, T. G., Sadeghi-Niaraki, A., Abbasi, A., & Choi, S. M. (2018). A methodological framework for assessment of ubiquitous cities using ANP and DEMATEL methods. *Sustainable Cities and Society*, *37*, 608-618.

Rahim, R., Supiyandi, S., Siahaan, A. P. U., Listyorini, T., Utomo, A. P., Triyanto, W. A., ... Khairunnisa, K. (2018, June). TOPSIS Method Application for Decision Support System in Internal Control for Selecting Best Employees. *Journal of Physics: Conference Series*, *1028*(1), 012052. doi:10.1088/1742-6596/1028/1/012052

Rajesh, R. (2018). Measuring the barriers to resilience in manufacturing supply chains using Grey Clustering and VIKOR approaches. *Measurement*, *126*, 259–273. doi:10.1016/j.measurement.2018.05.043

Rani, P., Jain, D., & Hooda, D. S. (2018). Shapley function based interval-valued intuitionistic fuzzy VIKOR technique for correlative multi-criteria decision making problems. *Iranian Journal of Fuzzy Systems*, *15*(1), 25–54.

Rao, M., Prasad, R. V., & Subbaiah, K. V. (2018). Experimental Investigation of Process Parameters While Milling of AA8011 Using MCDM/MADM Method-TOPSIS. *Journal of Production Research & Management*, *8*(2), 1–7.

Rostamzadeh, R., Ghorabaee, M. K., Govindan, K., Esmaeili, A., & Nobar, H. B. K. (2018). Evaluation of sustainable supply chain risk management using an integrated fuzzy TOPSIS-CRITIC approach. *Journal of Cleaner Production*, *175*, 651–669. doi:10.1016/j.jclepro.2017.12.071

Roy, J., Adhikary, K., Kar, S., & Pamucar, D. (2018). A rough strength relational DEMATEL model for analysing the key success factors of hospital service quality. *Decision Making: Applications in Management and Engineering*, *1*(1), 121–142.

Sajjad Ali Khan, M., Abdullah, S., Yousaf Ali, M., Hussain, I., & Farooq, M. (2018). Extension of TOPSIS method base on Choquet integral under interval-valued Pythagorean fuzzy environment. *Journal of Intelligent & Fuzzy Systems*, *34*(1), 267–282. doi:10.3233/JIFS-171164

Sasikumar, P., & Vimal, K. E. K. (2019). Evaluation and Selection of Green Suppliers Using Fuzzy VIKOR and Fuzzy TOPSIS. In *Emerging Applications in Supply Chains for Sustainable Business Development* (pp. 202–218). IGI Global. doi:10.4018/978-1-5225-5424-0.ch012

Şen, A. Y., Semiz, N., Güneş, B., Algül, D., Gergin, Z., & Dönmez, N. D. (2018, August). The Selection of a Process Management Software with Fuzzy Topsis Multiple Criteria Decision Making Method. In *The International Symposium for Production Research* (pp. 150-167). Springer.

Şengül, Ü., Eren, M., Shiraz, S. E., Gezder, V., & Şengül, A. B. (2015). Fuzzy TOPSIS method for ranking renewable energy supply systems in Turkey. *Renewable Energy*, *75*, 617–625. doi:10.1016/j.renene.2014.10.045

Sennaroglu, B., & Celebi, G. V. (2018). A military airport location selection by AHP integrated PROMETHEE and VIKOR methods. *Transportation Research Part D, Transport and Environment*, *59*, 160–173. doi:10.1016/j.trd.2017.12.022

Sennaroglu, B., Yilmazer, K. B., Tuzkaya, G., & Tuzkaya, U. R. (2018). A DEMATEL Integrated Interval Valued Intuitionistic Fuzzy PROMETHEE Approach for Parking Lots Evaluation. *Journal of Multiple-Valued Logic & Soft Computing, 30.*

Sepehri-Rad, A., Sadjadi, S., & Sadi-Nezhad, S. (2019). An application of DEMATEL for transaction authentication in online banking. *International Journal of Data and Network Science*, *3*(2), 71–76. doi:10.5267/j.ijdns.2019.1.002

Seyedmohammadi, J., Sarmadian, F., Jafarzadeh, A. A., Ghorbani, M. A., & Shahbazi, F. (2018). Application of SAW, TOPSIS and fuzzy TOPSIS models in cultivation priority planning for maize, rapeseed and soybean crops. *Geoderma*, *310*, 178–190. doi:10.1016/j.geoderma.2017.09.012

Shahi, E., Alavipoor, F. S., & Karimi, S. (2018). The development of nuclear power plants by means of modified model of Fuzzy DEMATEL and GIS in Bushehr, Iran. *Renewable & Sustainable Energy Reviews*, *83*, 33–49. doi:10.1016/j.rser.2017.10.073

Sharma, R., Sibal, R., & Sabharwal, S. (2019). Software Vulnerability Prioritization: A Comparative Study Using TOPSIS and VIKOR Techniques. In *System Performance and Management Analytics* (pp. 405–418). Singapore: Springer. doi:10.1007/978-981-10-7323-6_32

Sharma, Y. K., Mangla, S. K., Patil, P. P., & Uniyal, S. (2018). Sustainable Food Supply Chain Management Implementation Using DEMATEL Approach. In *Advances in Health and Environment Safety* (pp. 115–125). Singapore: Springer. doi:10.1007/978-981-10-7122-5_13

Shen, F., Ma, X., Li, Z., Xu, Z., & Cai, D. (2018). An extended intuitionistic fuzzy TOPSIS method based on a new distance measure with an application to credit risk evaluation. *Information Sciences*, *428*, 105–119. doi:10.1016/j.ins.2017.10.045

Shen, K. W., & Wang, J. Q. (2018). Z-VIKOR method based on a new comprehensive weighted distance measure of Z-number and its application. *IEEE Transactions on Fuzzy Systems*, *26*(6), 3232–3245. doi:10.1109/TFUZZ.2018.2816581

Shi, X., Li, J., Wang, F., Dinçer, H., & Yüksel, S. (2019). A Hybrid Decision-Making Approach for the Service and Financial-Based Measurement of Universal Health Coverage for the E7 Economies. *International Journal of Environmental Research and Public Health*, *16*(18), 3295. doi:10.3390/ijerph16183295 PMID:31500288

Shojaei, P., Haeri, S. A. S., & Mohammadi, S. (2018). Airports evaluation and ranking model using Taguchi loss function, best-worst method and VIKOR technique. *Journal of Air Transport Management*, *68*, 4–13. doi:10.1016/j.jairtraman.2017.05.006

Si, S. L., You, X. Y., Liu, H. C., & Zhang, P. (2018). DEMATEL technique: A systematic review of the state-of-the-art literature on methodologies and applications. *Mathematical Problems in Engineering*.

Sianturi, M., Wulan, S., Suginam, S., Rohminatin, R., & Mesran, M. (2018). Implementasi Metode VIKOR Untuk Menentukan Bahan Kulit Terbaik Dalam Pembuatan Ikat Pinggang. *JURIKOM*, *5*(1), 56–60.

Simab, M., Javadi, M. S., & Nezhad, A. E. (2018). Multi-objective programming of pumped-hydro-thermal scheduling problem using normal boundary intersection and VIKOR. *Energy*, *143*, 854–866. doi:10.1016/j.energy.2017.09.144

Siregar, D., Nurdiyanto, H., Sriadhi, S., Suita, D., Khair, U., Rahim, R., ... Siahaan, A. P. U. (2018, June). Multi-Attribute Decision Making with VIKOR Method for Any Purpose Decision. *Journal of Physics: Conference Series*, *1019*(1), 012034. doi:10.1088/1742-6596/1019/1/012034

Suganthi, L. (2018). Multi expert and multi criteria evaluation of sectoral investments for sustainable development: An integrated fuzzy AHP, VIKOR/DEA methodology. *Sustainable Cities and Society, 43*, 144-156.

Sun, G., Guan, X., Yi, X., & Zhou, Z. (2018). An innovative TOPSIS approach based on hesitant fuzzy correlation coefficient and its applications. *Applied Soft Computing*, *68*, 249–267. doi:10.1016/j.asoc.2018.04.004

Sutrikanti, N., Situmorang, H., Fachrurrazi, F., Nurdiyanto, H., & Mesran, M. (2018). Implementasi Pendukung Keputusan Dalam Pemilihan Calon Peserta Cerdas Cermat Tingkat SMA Menerapkan Metode VIKOR. *JURIKOM*, *5*(2), 109–113.

Taleai, M., Safarpour, M., & Javadi, G. (2019). Potential Evaluation for Establishment of Solar Power Plants Using Multi-Criteria Decision Making Methods: OWA and TOPSIS (case study: Qazvin-Iran). *The Journal of Spatial Planning*, *22*(4), 1–27.

Tang, H., Shi, Y., & Dong, P. (2019). Public blockchain evaluation using entropy and TOPSIS. *Expert Systems with Applications*, *117*, 204–210. doi:10.1016/j.eswa.2018.09.048

Tavana, M., Di Caprio, D., & Santos-Arteaga, F. J. (2018). An extended stochastic VIKOR model with decision maker's attitude towards risk. *Information Sciences*, *432*, 301–318. doi:10.1016/j.ins.2017.12.019

Tian, G., Liu, X., Zhang, M., Yang, Y., Zhang, H., Lin, Y., ... Li, Z. (2019). Selection of take-back pattern of vehicle reverse logistics in China via Grey-DEMATEL and Fuzzy-VIKOR combined method. *Journal of Cleaner Production*, *220*, 1088–1100. doi:10.1016/j.jclepro.2019.01.086

Tian, G., Zhang, H., Zhou, M., & Li, Z. (2018). AHP, gray correlation, and TOPSIS combined approach to green performance evaluation of design alternatives. *IEEE Transactions on Systems, Man, and Cybernetics. Systems*, *48*(7), 1093–1105. doi:10.1109/TSMC.2016.2640179

Tian, Z. P., Wang, J. Q., & Zhang, H. Y. (2018). An integrated approach for failure mode and effects analysis based on fuzzy best-worst, relative entropy, and VIKOR methods. *Applied Soft Computing*, *72*, 636–646. doi:10.1016/j.asoc.2018.03.037

Titiyal, R., Bhattacharya, S., & Thakkar, J. J. (2019). The distribution strategy selection for an e-tailer using a hybrid DANP VIKOR MCDM model. *Benchmarking. International Journal (Toronto, Ont.)*.

Torğul, B., & Paksoy, T. (2019). A New Multi Objective Linear Programming Model for Lean and Green Supplier Selection with Fuzzy TOPSIS. In *Lean and Green Supply Chain Management* (pp. 101–141). Cham: Springer. doi:10.1007/978-3-319-97511-5_4

Tsai, S. B. (2018). Using the DEMATEL model to explore the job satisfaction of research and development professionals in china's photovoltaic cell industry. *Renewable & Sustainable Energy Reviews*, *81*, 62–68. doi:10.1016/j.rser.2017.07.014

Ture, H., Dogan, S., & Kocak, D. (2018). Assessing Euro 2020 Strategy Using Multi-criteria Decision Making Methods: VIKOR and TOPSIS. *Social Indicators Research*, 1–21.

Umam, K., Sulastri, V. E., Andini, T., Sutiksno, D. U., & Mesran, M. (2018). Perancangan Sistem Pendukung Keputusan Penentuan Prioritas Produk Unggulan Daerah Menggunakan Metode VIKOR. *JURIKOM*, *5*(1), 43–49.

Uztürk, D., Büyüközkan, G., Negüs, A. F., & Öztek, M. Y. (2018). 2-Tuple Based VIKOR Methodology for Green Building Certification Selection. In *Proceedings of the World Congress on Engineering* (*Vol. 2*). Academic Press.

Vinodh, S., Balagi, T. S., & Patil, A. (2016). A hybrid MCDM approach for agile concept selection using fuzzy DEMATEL, fuzzy ANP and fuzzy TOPSIS. *International Journal of Advanced Manufacturing Technology*, *83*(9-12), 1979–1987. doi:10.100700170-015-7718-6

Wang, B., Song, J., Ren, J., Li, K., Duan, H., & Wang, X. E. (2019). Selecting sustainable energy conversion technologies for agricultural residues: A fuzzy AHP-VIKOR based prioritization from life cycle perspective. *Resources, Conservation and Recycling*, *142*, 78–87. doi:10.1016/j.resconrec.2018.11.011

Wang, J., Wei, G., & Lu, M. (2018). An extended VIKOR method for multiple criteria group decision making with triangular fuzzy neutrosophic numbers. *Symmetry*, *10*(10), 497. doi:10.3390ym10100497

Wang, L., Cao, Q., & Zhou, L. (2018). Research on the influencing factors in coal mine production safety based on the combination of DEMATEL and ISM. *Safety Science*, *103*, 51–61. doi:10.1016/j.ssci.2017.11.007

Wang, L., Zhang, H. Y., Wang, J. Q., & Li, L. (2018). Picture fuzzy normalized projection-based VIKOR method for the risk evaluation of construction project. *Applied Soft Computing*, *64*, 216–226. doi:10.1016/j.asoc.2017.12.014

Wang, S., Liu, Q., Yuksel, S., & Dincer, H. (2019). Hesitant Linguistic Term Sets-Based Hybrid Analysis for Renewable Energy Investments. *IEEE Access: Practical Innovations, Open Solutions*, *7*, 114223–114235. doi:10.1109/ACCESS.2019.2935427

Wang, Y., Chen, W., Zhao, M., & Wang, B. (2019). Analysis of the influencing factors on CO 2 emissions at different urbanization levels: Regional difference in China based on panel estimation. *Natural Hazards*, 1–19.

Wang, Z., Gao, J. M., Wang, R. X., Chen, K., Gao, Z. Y., & Zheng, W. (2018). Failure mode and effects analysis by using the house of reliability-based rough VIKOR approach. *IEEE Transactions on Reliability*, *67*(1), 230–248. doi:10.1109/TR.2017.2778316

Wu, M., Li, C., Fan, J., Wang, X., & Wu, Z. (2018). Assessing the global productive efficiency of Chinese banks using the cross-efficiency interval and VIKOR. *Emerging Markets Review*, *34*, 77–86. doi:10.1016/j.ememar.2017.10.005

Wu, T., Liu, X., & Liu, F. (2018). An interval type-2 fuzzy TOPSIS model for large scale group decision making problems with social network information. *Information Sciences*, *432*, 392–410. doi:10.1016/j.ins.2017.12.006

Wu, Y., Zhang, B., Xu, C., & Li, L. (2018). Site selection decision framework using fuzzy ANP-VIKOR for large commercial rooftop PV system based on sustainability perspective. *Sustainable Cities and Society, 40*, 454-470.

Wu, Z., Xu, J., Jiang, X., & Zhong, L. (2019). Two MAGDM models based on hesitant fuzzy linguistic term sets with possibility distributions: VIKOR and TOPSIS. *Information Sciences*, *473*, 101–120. doi:10.1016/j.ins.2018.09.038

Yadav, D. K., & Barve, A. (2018). Segmenting critical success factors of humanitarian supply chains using fuzzy DEMATEL. *Benchmarking: An International Journal*, *25*(2), 400–425. doi:10.1108/BIJ-10-2016-0154

Yadav, G., Seth, D., & Desai, T. N. (2018). Prioritising solutions for Lean Six Sigma adoption barriers through fuzzy AHP-modified TOPSIS framework. *International Journal of Lean Six Sigma*, *9*(3), 270–300. doi:10.1108/IJLSS-06-2016-0023

Yadegaridehkordi, E., Hourmand, M., Nilashi, M., Shuib, L., Ahani, A., & Ibrahim, O. (2018). Influence of big data adoption on manufacturing companies' performance: An integrated DEMATEL-ANFIS approach. *Technological Forecasting and Social Change*, *137*, 199–210. doi:10.1016/j.techfore.2018.07.043

Yang, C., Lan, S., & Tseng, M. L. (2019). Coordinated development path of metropolitan logistics and economy in Belt and Road using DEMATEL–Bayesian analysis. *International Journal of Logistics Research and Applications*, *22*(1), 1–24. doi:10.1080/13675567.2018.1439907

Yang, W., Pang, Y., Shi, J., & Wang, C. (2018). Linguistic hesitant intuitionistic fuzzy decision-making method based on VIKOR. *Neural Computing & Applications*, *29*(7), 613–626. doi:10.100700521-016-2526-y

Yang, W., Xu, K., Lian, J., Ma, C., & Bin, L. (2018). Integrated flood vulnerability assessment approach based on TOPSIS and Shannon entropy methods. *Ecological Indicators*, *89*, 269–280. doi:10.1016/j.ecolind.2018.02.015

Yazdi, M. (2018). Risk assessment based on novel intuitionistic fuzzy-hybrid-modified TOPSIS approach. *Safety Science*, *110*, 438–448. doi:10.1016/j.ssci.2018.03.005

Yildiz, A., & Uğur, L. (2018). Evaluation of 3D printers used in additive manufacturing by using interval type-2 fuzzy TOPSIS method. *Journal of Engineering Research and Applied Science*, *7*(2), 984–993.

Yüksel, S., Dinçer, H., & Emir, Ş. (2017). Comparing the performance of Turkish deposit banks by using DEMATEL, Grey Relational Analysis (GRA) and MOORA approaches. *World Journal of Applied Economics*, *3*(2), 26–47. doi:10.22440/wjae.3.2.2

Yüksel, S., Dinçer, H., & Meral, Y. (2019). Financial Analysis of International Energy Trade: A Strategic Outlook for EU-15. *Energies*, *12*(3), 431. doi:10.3390/en12030431

Yurdakul, M., & İç, Y. T. (2018). Development of a multi-level performance measurement model for manufacturing companies using a modified version of the fuzzy TOPSIS approach. *Soft Computing*, *22*(22), 7491–7503. doi:10.100700500-018-3449-6

Zare, A., Feylizadeh, M., Mahmoudi, A., & Liu, S. (2018). Suitable computerized maintenance management system selection using grey group TOPSIS and fuzzy group VIKOR: A case study. *Decision Science Letters*, *7*(4), 341–358. doi:10.5267/j.dsl.2018.3.002

Zareie, A., Sheikhahmadi, A., & Khamforoosh, K. (2018). Influence maximization in social networks based on TOPSIS. *Expert Systems with Applications*, *108*, 96–107. doi:10.1016/j.eswa.2018.05.001

Zeng, S., Chen, S. M., & Kuo, L. W. (2019). Multiattribute decision making based on novel score function of intuitionistic fuzzy values and modified VIKOR method. *Information Sciences*.

Zhao, J., & Gong, Y. (2018, April). Data Driven Topsis Method and Its Application in E-commerce APP. In *Proceedings of the 2018 International Conference on Big Data and Computing*(pp. 49-52). ACM. 10.1145/3220199.3220214

Zhou, F., Wang, X., & Goh, M. (2018). Fuzzy extended VIKOR-based mobile robot selection model for hospital pharmacy. *International Journal of Advanced Robotic Systems, 15*(4), 1729881418787315. doi:10.1177/1729881418787315

Zhou, F., Wang, X., Lim, M. K., He, Y., & Li, L. (2018). Sustainable recycling partner selection using fuzzy DEMATEL-AEW-FVIKOR: A case study in small-and-medium enterprises (SMEs). *Journal of Cleaner Production, 196*, 489–504. doi:10.1016/j.jclepro.2018.05.247

Zhou, W., Yin, W., Peng, X., Liu, F., & Yang, F. (2018). Comprehensive evaluation of land reclamation and utilisation schemes based on a modified VIKOR method for surface mines. *International Journal of Mining, Reclamation and Environment, 32*(2), 93–108. doi:10.1080/17480930.2016.1228031

# Chapter 6
# Analysis Results for the Effectiveness of Monetary Policies With Fuzzy Logic

## ABSTRACT

*This chapter aims to examine the effectiveness of central bank policies in E7 economies. For this purpose, five different monetary policy instruments (required reserve ratio, rediscount rate, open market operations, standing facilities, and asset purchase program) are defined as the criteria. On the other side, E7 countries are selected as the alternatives. In the analysis process, fuzzy DEMATEL approach is used to weight the criteria whereas fuzzy TOPSIS and fuzzy VIKOR methods are considered to rank E7 economies. The findings show that open market operations are the most important criterion. However, changing required reserve ratio does not have any powerful impact on the market. Therefore, it is recommended that E7 countries should prefer open market operations instead of required reserve ratio in order to influence the market in an effective manner. Additionally, it is defined that Indonesia has the best performance in the E7 economies while Brazil takes place on the last rank.*

## GENERAL INFORMATION ABOUT THE ANALYSIS

In this first analysis, effectiveness of the monetary policies in the central banks of E7 countries is measured. For this purpose, five different monetary policies are selected as the criteria. These are Required Reserve Ratio (C1), Rediscount Rate (C2), Open Market Operations (C3), Standing Facilities

DOI: 10.4018/978-1-7998-1643-0.ch006

(C4), Asset Purchase Programs (C5). In addition to this situation, Brazil (A1), Russia (A2), India (A3), China (A4), Mexico (A5), Indonesia (A6), Turkey (A7) are selected as the alternatives. Fuzzy DEMATEL approach is used to weight the dimensions. On the other side, alternatives are ranked by using fuzzy TOPSIS and fuzzy VIKOR. The details of this analysis are given in the following subtitles.

## IDENTIFYING THE WEIGHTS OF CRITERIA

**Step 1:** Define the multicriteria decision making problem: The effective use of monetary policy instruments is discussed for the emerging countries. A set of criteria is determined to measure the performance of the economies. So, 5 Monetary policy instruments are defined as Required Reserve Ratio (C1), Rediscount Rate (C2), Open Market Operations (C3), Standing Facilities (C4), Asset Purchase Programs (C5) are listed to evaluate the central bank success in the emerging economies. For this purpose, Brazil (A1), Russia (A2), India (A3), China (A4), Mexico (A5), Indonesia (A6), Turkey (A7) that are called E7 economies are selected as a set of the alternatives.

**Step 2:** Provide the evaluations of decision makers: 5 Decision makers that are experts in the field of financial markets in emerging economies are appointed to provide their linguistic evaluations for the criteria and alternatives. Linguistic evaluations are converted into the fuzzy numbers to compute the performance results of criteria and alternatives. By considering the evaluations, weights and ranking results are computed with the proposed multi criteria decision making model (Dinçer and Hacıoğlu, 2017; Dinçer et al., 2016). Table 1 and 2 define the linguistic scales and fuzzy numbers for criteria and alternatives respectively.

However, Tables 3-8 illustrate the linguistic opinions of each decision maker on the criteria and their fuzzy numbers for the impact-relationship of criteria respectively.

Table 9-16 represent the linguistic evaluations and fuzzy numbers of alternatives for the decision matrix.

*Table 1. Linguistic variables of the impact-relationship degrees*

| Influence Level | Triangular Fuzzy Numbers | | |
|---|---|---|---|
| No (N) | 0 | 0 | 0.25 |
| Low (L) | 0 | 0.25 | 0.5 |
| Medium (M) | 0.25 | 0.5 | 0.75 |
| High (H) | 0.5 | 0.75 | 1 |
| Very High (VH)) | 0.75 | 1 | 1 |

Source: Dinçer (2018)

*Table 2. Linguistic scales for rating of alternatives*

| Definition | Triangular Fuzzy Numbers | | |
|---|---|---|---|
| Worst (W) | 0 | 0 | 2.5 |
| Poor (P) | 0 | 2.5 | 5 |
| Fair (F) | 2.5 | 5 | 7.5 |
| Good (G) | 5 | 7.5 | 10 |
| Best (B) | 7.5 | 10 | 10 |

Source: Dinçer et. al. (2018)

Step 3: Weight the criteria: Monetary policy instruments defined as a set of criteria are weighted by using fuzzy DEMATEL. First, the averaged fuzzy values of decision makers evaluations have been computed to construct the initial direct-relation matrix by the equations (1) and (2). Table 17 defines the averaged results of the direct-relations matrix.

The normalized values of the matrix have been calculated by considering the averaged values of initial direct-relation matrix obtained from the decision makers as seen in Table 18. The results are provided by considering the formulas (3)-(5).

The crisp matrices have been constructed with the formula (6) and the results are shown in Tables 19, 20, and 21 accordingly.

Identity matrix, the differences, and inverse matrix have been constructed to compute the total influence matrix. Table 22-28 define the results respectively.

Total influence matrices have been calculated by using the formulas (7)-(12). The matrix results are seen in Tables 29-31.

Total-relation matrix based on triangular fuzzy numbers is represented in Table 32.

*Table 3. Linguistic evaluations of decision makers for direct relation matrix*

| | C1 | | | | | C2 | | | | | C3 | | | | | C4 | | | | | C5 | | | | |
|---|---|---|---|---|---|---|---|---|---|---|---|---|---|---|---|---|---|---|---|---|---|---|---|---|---|
| | DM1 | DM2 | DM3 | DM4 | DM5 | DM1 | DM2 | DM3 | DM4 | DM5 | DM1 | DM2 | DM3 | DM4 | DM5 | DM1 | DM2 | DM3 | DM4 | DM5 | DM1 | DM2 | DM3 | DM4 | DM5 |
| C1 | - | - | - | - | - | L | L | M | L | H | M | M | M | L | M | L | L | L | L | L | L | L | M | M | L |
| C2 | L | L | L | L | L | - | - | - | - | - | L | M | L | L | L | H | H | M | H | H | M | M | M | M | M |
| C3 | VH | VH | VH | VH | VH | VH | VH | VH | VH | VH | - | - | - | - | - | VH | VH | VH | H | VH | VH | H | VH | H | VH |
| C4 | H | VH | H | H | H | M | H | M | M | H | M | M | L | M | H | - | - | - | - | - | M | M | M | M | H |
| C5 | H | H | H | H | VH | H | H | H | H | H | L | L | L | L | L | L | M | L | M | L | - | - | - | - | - |

*Table 4. Triangular fuzzy numbers of decision maker 1 for direct relation matrix*

| Criteria | C1 | | | C2 | | | C3 | | | C4 | | | C5 | | |
|---|---|---|---|---|---|---|---|---|---|---|---|---|---|---|---|
| C1 | 0 | 0 | 0 | 0 | 0.25 | 0.5 | 0.25 | 0.5 | 0.75 | 0 | 0.25 | 0.5 | 0 | 0.25 | 0.5 |
| C2 | 0 | 0.25 | 0.5 | 0 | 0 | 0 | 0 | 0.25 | 0.5 | 0.5 | 0.75 | 1 | 0.25 | 0.5 | 0.75 |
| C3 | 0.75 | 1 | 1 | 0.75 | 1 | 1 | 0 | 0 | 0 | 0.75 | 1 | 1 | 0.75 | 1 | 1 |
| C4 | 0.5 | 0.75 | 1 | 0.25 | 0.5 | 0.75 | 0.25 | 0.5 | 0.75 | 0 | 0 | 0 | 0.25 | 0.5 | 0.75 |
| C5 | 0.5 | 0.75 | 1 | 0.5 | 0.75 | 1 | 0 | 0.25 | 0.5 | 0 | 0.25 | 0.5 | 0 | 0 | 0 |

*Table 5. Triangular fuzzy numbers of decision maker 2 for direct relation matrix*

| Criteria | C1 | | | C2 | | | C3 | | | C4 | | | C5 | | |
|---|---|---|---|---|---|---|---|---|---|---|---|---|---|---|---|
| C1 | 0 | 0 | 0 | 0 | 0.25 | 0.5 | 0.25 | 0.5 | 0.75 | 0 | 0.25 | 0.5 | 0 | 0.25 | 0.5 |
| C2 | 0 | 0.25 | 0.5 | 0 | 0 | 0 | 0.25 | 0.5 | 0.75 | 0.5 | 0.75 | 1 | 0.25 | 0.5 | 0.75 |
| C3 | 0.75 | 1 | 1 | 0.75 | 1 | 1 | 0 | 0 | 0 | 0.75 | 1 | 1 | 0.5 | 0.75 | 1 |
| C4 | 0.75 | 1 | 1 | 0.5 | 0.75 | 1 | 0.25 | 0.5 | 0.75 | 0 | 0 | 0 | 0.25 | 0.5 | 0.75 |
| C5 | 0.5 | 0.75 | 1 | 0.5 | 0.75 | 1 | 0 | 0.25 | 0.5 | 0.25 | 0.5 | 0.75 | 0 | 0 | 0 |

*Table 6. Triangular fuzzy numbers of decision maker 3 for direct relation matrix*

| Criteria | C1 | | | C2 | | | C3 | | | C4 | | | C5 | | |
|---|---|---|---|---|---|---|---|---|---|---|---|---|---|---|---|
| C1 | 0 | 0 | 0 | 0.25 | 0.5 | 0.75 | 0.25 | 0.5 | 0.75 | 0 | 0.25 | 0.5 | 0.25 | 0.5 | 0.75 |
| C2 | 0 | 0.25 | 0.5 | 0 | 0 | 0 | 0 | 0.25 | 0.5 | 0.25 | 0.5 | 0.75 | 0.25 | 0.5 | 0.75 |
| C3 | 0.75 | 1 | 1 | 0.75 | 1 | 1 | 0 | 0 | 0 | 0.75 | 1 | 1 | 0.75 | 1 | 1 |
| C4 | 0.5 | 0.75 | 1 | 0.25 | 0.5 | 0.75 | 0 | 0.25 | 0.5 | 0 | 0 | 0 | 0.25 | 0.5 | 0.75 |
| C5 | 0.5 | 0.75 | 1 | 0.5 | 0.75 | 1 | 0 | 0.25 | 0.5 | 0 | 0.25 | 0.5 | 0 | 0 | 0 |

*Table 7. Triangular fuzzy numbers of decision maker 4 for direct relation matrix*

| Criteria | C1 | | | C2 | | | C3 | | | C4 | | | C5 | | |
|---|---|---|---|---|---|---|---|---|---|---|---|---|---|---|---|
| C1 | 0 | 0 | 0 | 0 | 0.25 | 0.5 | 0 | 0.25 | 0.5 | 0 | 0.25 | 0.5 | 0.25 | 0.5 | 0.75 |
| C2 | 0 | 0.25 | 0.5 | 0 | 0 | 0 | 0 | 0.25 | 0.5 | 0.5 | 0.75 | 1 | 0.25 | 0.5 | 0.75 |
| C3 | 0.75 | 1 | 1 | 0.75 | 1 | 1 | 0 | 0 | 0 | 0.5 | 0.75 | 1 | 0.5 | 0.75 | 1 |
| C4 | 0.5 | 0.75 | 1 | 0.25 | 0.5 | 0.75 | 0.25 | 0.5 | 0.75 | 0 | 0 | 0 | 0.25 | 0.5 | 0.75 |
| C5 | 0.5 | 0.75 | 1 | 0.5 | 0.75 | 1 | 0 | 0.25 | 0.5 | 0.25 | 0.5 | 0.75 | 0 | 0 | 0 |

*Table 8. Triangular fuzzy numbers of decision maker 5 for direct relation matrix*

| Criteria | C1 | | | C2 | | | C3 | | | C4 | | | C5 | | |
|---|---|---|---|---|---|---|---|---|---|---|---|---|---|---|---|
| C1 | 0 | 0 | 0 | 0.5 | 0.75 | 1 | 0.25 | 0.5 | 0.75 | 0 | 0.25 | 0.5 | 0 | 0.25 | 0.5 |
| C2 | 0 | 0.25 | 0.5 | 0 | 0 | 0 | 0 | 0.25 | 0.5 | 0.5 | 0.75 | 1 | 0.25 | 0.5 | 0.75 |
| C3 | 0.75 | 1 | 1 | 0.75 | 1 | 1 | 0 | 0 | 0 | 0.75 | 1 | 1 | 0.75 | 1 | 1 |
| C4 | 0.5 | 0.75 | 1 | 0.5 | 0.75 | 1 | 0.5 | 0.75 | 1 | 0 | 0 | 0 | 0.5 | 0.75 | 1 |
| C5 | 0.75 | 1 | 1 | 0.5 | 0.75 | 1 | 0 | 0.25 | 0.5 | 0 | 0.25 | 0.5 | 0 | 0 | 0 |

Converting fuzzy data into crisp scores deffuzzification method is applied to convert the triangular fuzzy numbers $\tilde{f}_{ij} = \left(l_{ij}, m_{ij}, u_{ij}\right)$, $j$=1,...,$J$, the crisp value of the i-th criterion is determined by the equations (13)-(21). In this process, firstly, the values of $x_{lj}$, $x_{mj}$,and $x_{uj}$ have been calculated by the equations (13)-(17) as seen in Table 33.

Secondly, the values of $x_j^{ls}$ and $x_j^{rs}$ have been computed with the formulas (18) and (19). The details are shown in Table 34.

After that, the values of $x_j^{crisp}$ have been calculated by the equation (20). Table 35 demonstrate the crisp results.

At the final step of the defuzzification process, the values of $f_{ij}$ have been employed by the formula (21) to construct the defuzzified total relation matrix. Table 36 show the defuzzified total relation matrix results.

Impact and relationship map is represented by computing the values of $\left(\tilde{D}_i + \tilde{R}_i\right)^{def}$ and $\left(\tilde{D}_i - \tilde{R}_i\right)^{def}$. The values and weighting results are seen in Table 37.

According to the final results, C3 is the most influencing factor while C1 is the most influenced criteria among the monetary policy instruments. However, C3 is the most important factor as C1 has the weakest importance in the criteria set.

## RANKING THE MONETARY POLICIES OF E7 ECONOMIES

Central bank performances in the E7 economies are analyzed by considering fuzzy TOPSIS and fuzzy VIKOR comparatively. For this aim, the averaged values of decision makers are used for the fuzzy decision matrix with the equation (22) (Dinçer and Hacıoğlu, 2015; Dinçer et al., 2013; Dinçer and Hacıoğlu, 2013; Dinçer and Görener, 2011). Table 38 defines the averaged fuzzy decision matrix.

Table 9. Linguistic evaluations of decision makers for fuzzy decision matrix

| | C1 | | | | | C2 | | | | | C3 | | | | | C4 | | | | | C5 | | | | |
|---|---|---|---|---|---|---|---|---|---|---|---|---|---|---|---|---|---|---|---|---|---|---|---|---|---|
| | DM1 | DM2 | DM3 | DM4 | DM5 | DM1 | DM2 | DM3 | DM4 | DM5 | DM1 | DM2 | DM3 | DM4 | DM5 | DM1 | DM2 | DM3 | DM4 | DM5 | DM1 | DM2 | DM3 | DM4 | DM5 |
| A1 | F | W | P | W | P | F | W | F | P | F | G | F | F | F | F | P | W | F | F | F | P | P | P | F | F |
| A2 | F | F | G | P | F | F | P | F | F | F | F | F | P | P | F | F | P | F | P | F | F | P | P | F | F |
| A3 | G | F | F | G | F | F | F | G | G | F | F | G | G | G | F | F | G | F | F | F | F | F | F | F | F |
| A4 | G | G | G | B | G | G | G | F | F | G | F | F | F | G | F | G | F | F | G | G | F | F | F | G | G |
| A5 | G | G | F | F | F | F | G | F | G | F | G | F | G | G | G | F | F | G | G | F | F | F | G | F | F |
| A6 | G | G | F | F | F | F | G | F | G | F | F | G | F | G | G | G | F | G | F | F | F | F | G | G | F |
| A7 | P | P | P | F | F | F | F | F | F | F | G | P | F | F | F | F | F | P | P | F | F | F | P | P | P |

*Table 10. Fuzzy decision matrix of decision makers for alternative 1*

| Criteria | DM1 | | | DM2 | | | DM3 | | | DM4 | | | DM5 | | |
|---|---|---|---|---|---|---|---|---|---|---|---|---|---|---|---|
| C1 | 2.5 | 5 | 7.5 | 0 | 0 | 2.5 | 0 | 2.5 | 5 | 0 | 0 | 2.5 | 0 | 2.5 | 5 |
| C2 | 2.5 | 5 | 7.5 | 0 | 0 | 2.5 | 2.5 | 5 | 7.5 | 0 | 2.5 | 5 | 2.5 | 5 | 7.5 |
| C3 | 5 | 7.5 | 10 | 2.5 | 5 | 7.5 | 2.5 | 5 | 7.5 | 2.5 | 5 | 7.5 | 2.5 | 5 | 7.5 |
| C4 | 0 | 2.5 | 5 | 0 | 0 | 2.5 | 2.5 | 5 | 7.5 | 2.5 | 5 | 7.5 | 2.5 | 5 | 7.5 |
| C5 | 0 | 2.5 | 5 | 0 | 2.5 | 5 | 0 | 2.5 | 5 | 2.5 | 5 | 7.5 | 2.5 | 5 | 7.5 |

*Table 11. Fuzzy decision matrix of decision makers for alternative 2*

| Criteria | DM1 | | | DM2 | | | DM3 | | | DM4 | | | DM5 | | |
|---|---|---|---|---|---|---|---|---|---|---|---|---|---|---|---|
| C1 | 2.5 | 5 | 7.5 | 2.5 | 5 | 7.5 | 5 | 7.5 | 10 | 0 | 2.5 | 5 | 2.5 | 5 | 7.5 |
| C2 | 2.5 | 5 | 7.5 | 0 | 2.5 | 5 | 2.5 | 5 | 7.5 | 2.5 | 5 | 7.5 | 2.5 | 5 | 7.5 |
| C3 | 2.5 | 5 | 7.5 | 2.5 | 5 | 7.5 | 0 | 2.5 | 5 | 0 | 2.5 | 5 | 2.5 | 5 | 7.5 |
| C4 | 2.5 | 5 | 7.5 | 0 | 2.5 | 5 | 2.5 | 5 | 7.5 | 0 | 2.5 | 5 | 2.5 | 5 | 7.5 |
| C5 | 2.5 | 5 | 7.5 | 0 | 2.5 | 5 | 0 | 2.5 | 5 | 2.5 | 5 | 7.5 | 2.5 | 5 | 7.5 |

*Table 12. Fuzzy decision matrix of decision makers for alternative 3*

| Criteria | DM1 | | | DM2 | | | DM3 | | | DM4 | | | DM5 | | |
|---|---|---|---|---|---|---|---|---|---|---|---|---|---|---|---|
| C1 | 5 | 7.5 | 10 | 2.5 | 5 | 7.5 | 2.5 | 5 | 7.5 | 5 | 7.5 | 10 | 2.5 | 5 | 7.5 |
| C2 | 2.5 | 5 | 7.5 | 2.5 | 5 | 7.5 | 5 | 7.5 | 10 | 5 | 7.5 | 10 | 2.5 | 5 | 7.5 |
| C3 | 2.5 | 5 | 7.5 | 5 | 7.5 | 10 | 5 | 7.5 | 10 | 5 | 7.5 | 10 | 2.5 | 5 | 7.5 |
| C4 | 2.5 | 5 | 7.5 | 5 | 7.5 | 10 | 2.5 | 5 | 7.5 | 2.5 | 5 | 7.5 | 2.5 | 5 | 7.5 |
| C5 | 2.5 | 5 | 7.5 | 2.5 | 5 | 7.5 | 2.5 | 5 | 7.5 | 2.5 | 5 | 7.5 | 2.5 | 5 | 7.5 |

*Table 13. Fuzzy decision matrix of decision makers for alternative 4*

| Criteria | DM1 | | | DM2 | | | DM3 | | | DM4 | | | DM5 | | |
|---|---|---|---|---|---|---|---|---|---|---|---|---|---|---|---|
| C1 | 5 | 7.5 | 10 | 5 | 7.5 | 10 | 5 | 7.5 | 10 | 7.5 | 10 | 10 | 5 | 7.5 | 10 |
| C2 | 5 | 7.5 | 10 | 5 | 7.5 | 10 | 2.5 | 5 | 7.5 | 2.5 | 5 | 7.5 | 5 | 7.5 | 10 |
| C3 | 2.5 | 5 | 7.5 | 2.5 | 5 | 7.5 | 2.5 | 5 | 7.5 | 5 | 7.5 | 10 | 2.5 | 5 | 7.5 |
| C4 | 5 | 7.5 | 10 | 2.5 | 5 | 7.5 | 2.5 | 5 | 7.5 | 5 | 7.5 | 10 | 5 | 7.5 | 10 |
| C5 | 2.5 | 5 | 7.5 | 2.5 | 5 | 7.5 | 2.5 | 5 | 7.5 | 5 | 7.5 | 10 | 5 | 7.5 | 10 |

*Table 14. Fuzzy decision matrix of decision makers for alternative 5*

| Criteria | DM1 | | | DM2 | | | DM3 | | | DM4 | | | DM5 | | |
|---|---|---|---|---|---|---|---|---|---|---|---|---|---|---|---|
| C1 | 5 | 7.5 | 10 | 5 | 7.5 | 10 | 2.5 | 5 | 7.5 | 2.5 | 5 | 7.5 | 2.5 | 5 | 7.5 |
| C2 | 2.5 | 5 | 7.5 | 5 | 7.5 | 10 | 2.5 | 5 | 7.5 | 5 | 7.5 | 10 | 2.5 | 5 | 7.5 |
| C3 | 5 | 7.5 | 10 | 2.5 | 5 | 7.5 | 5 | 7.5 | 10 | 5 | 7.5 | 10 | 5 | 7.5 | 10 |
| C4 | 2.5 | 5 | 7.5 | 2.5 | 5 | 7.5 | 5 | 7.5 | 10 | 5 | 7.5 | 10 | 2.5 | 5 | 7.5 |
| C5 | 2.5 | 5 | 7.5 | 2.5 | 5 | 7.5 | 5 | 7.5 | 10 | 2.5 | 5 | 7.5 | 2.5 | 5 | 7.5 |

*Table 15. Fuzzy decision matrix of decision makers for alternative 6*

| Criteria | DM1 | | | DM2 | | | DM3 | | | DM4 | | | DM5 | | |
|---|---|---|---|---|---|---|---|---|---|---|---|---|---|---|---|
| C1 | 5 | 7.5 | 10 | 5 | 7.5 | 10 | 2.5 | 5 | 7.5 | 2.5 | 5 | 7.5 | 2.5 | 5 | 7.5 |
| C2 | 2.5 | 5 | 7.5 | 5 | 7.5 | 10 | 2.5 | 5 | 7.5 | 5 | 7.5 | 10 | 2.5 | 5 | 7.5 |
| C3 | 2.5 | 5 | 7.5 | 5 | 7.5 | 10 | 2.5 | 5 | 7.5 | 5 | 7.5 | 10 | 5 | 7.5 | 10 |
| C4 | 5 | 7.5 | 10 | 2.5 | 5 | 7.5 | 5 | 7.5 | 10 | 2.5 | 5 | 7.5 | 2.5 | 5 | 7.5 |
| C5 | 2.5 | 5 | 7.5 | 2.5 | 5 | 7.5 | 5 | 7.5 | 10 | 5 | 7.5 | 10 | 2.5 | 5 | 7.5 |

*Table 16. Fuzzy decision matrix of decision makers for alternative 7*

| Criteria | DM1 | | | DM2 | | | DM3 | | | DM4 | | | DM5 | | |
|---|---|---|---|---|---|---|---|---|---|---|---|---|---|---|---|
| C1 | 0 | 2.5 | 5 | 0 | 2.5 | 5 | 0 | 2.5 | 5 | 2.5 | 5 | 7.5 | 2.5 | 5 | 7.5 |
| C2 | 2.5 | 5 | 7.5 | 2.5 | 5 | 7.5 | 2.5 | 5 | 7.5 | 2.5 | 5 | 7.5 | 2.5 | 5 | 7.5 |
| C3 | 5 | 7.5 | 10 | 0 | 2.5 | 5 | 2.5 | 5 | 7.5 | 2.5 | 5 | 7.5 | 2.5 | 5 | 7.5 |
| C4 | 2.5 | 5 | 7.5 | 2.5 | 5 | 7.5 | 0 | 2.5 | 5 | 0 | 2.5 | 5 | 2.5 | 5 | 7.5 |
| C5 | 2.5 | 5 | 7.5 | 2.5 | 5 | 7.5 | 0 | 2.5 | 5 | 0 | 2.5 | 5 | 0 | 2.5 | 5 |

## Ranking the Alternatives With Fuzzy TOPSIS

Initially, fuzzy decision matrix has been normalized. In first step of the normalized process, the values of $c_{ij}^{*}$ have been computed by the formula (23), secondly, the values of $\tilde{r}_{ij}$ have been calculated with the formula (24) to construct the normalized values. The results are seen in Tables 39 and 40 respectively.

The weights of the criteria with fuzzy DEMATEL have been multiplied with the normalized values and weighted normalized matrix has been constructed as seen in Table 41.

*Table 17. Initial direct-relation fuzzy matrix*

| | C1 | | | C2 | | | C3 | | | C4 | | | C5 | | |
|---|---|---|---|---|---|---|---|---|---|---|---|---|---|---|---|
| C1 | 0.000 | 0.000 | 0.000 | 0.150 | 0.400 | 0.650 | 0.200 | 0.450 | 0.700 | 0.000 | 0.250 | 0.500 | 0.100 | 0.350 | 0.600 |
| C2 | 0.000 | 0.250 | 0.500 | 0.000 | 0.000 | 0.000 | 0.050 | 0.300 | 0.550 | 0.450 | 0.700 | 0.950 | 0.250 | 0.500 | 0.750 |
| C3 | 0.750 | 1.000 | 1.000 | 0.750 | 1.000 | 1.000 | 0.000 | 0.000 | 0.000 | 0.700 | 0.950 | 1.000 | 0.650 | 0.900 | 1.000 |
| C4 | 0.550 | 0.800 | 1.000 | 0.350 | 0.600 | 0.850 | 0.250 | 0.500 | 0.750 | 0.000 | 0.000 | 0.000 | 0.300 | 0.550 | 0.800 |
| C5 | 0.550 | 0.800 | 1.000 | 0.500 | 0.750 | 1.000 | 0.000 | 0.250 | 0.500 | 0.100 | 0.350 | 0.600 | 0.000 | 0.000 | 0.000 |

*Table 18. Normalized direct-relation fuzzy matrix*

| | C1 | | | C2 | | | C3 | | | C4 | | | C5 | | |
|---|---|---|---|---|---|---|---|---|---|---|---|---|---|---|---|
| C1 | 0.000 | 0.000 | 0.000 | 0.038 | 0.100 | 0.163 | 0.050 | 0.113 | 0.175 | 0.000 | 0.063 | 0.125 | 0.025 | 0.088 | 0.150 |
| C2 | 0.000 | 0.063 | 0.125 | 0.000 | 0.000 | 0.000 | 0.013 | 0.075 | 0.138 | 0.113 | 0.175 | 0.238 | 0.063 | 0.125 | 0.188 |
| C3 | 0.188 | 0.250 | 0.250 | 0.188 | 0.250 | 0.250 | 0.000 | 0.000 | 0.000 | 0.175 | 0.238 | 0.250 | 0.163 | 0.225 | 0.250 |
| C4 | 0.138 | 0.200 | 0.250 | 0.088 | 0.150 | 0.213 | 0.063 | 0.125 | 0.188 | 0.000 | 0.000 | 0.000 | 0.075 | 0.138 | 0.200 |
| C5 | 0.138 | 0.200 | 0.250 | 0.125 | 0.188 | 0.250 | 0.000 | 0.063 | 0.125 | 0.025 | 0.088 | 0.150 | 0.000 | 0.000 | 0.000 |

*Table 19. Normalized direct-relation fuzzy matrix (xl)*

| | C1 | C2 | C3 | C4 | C5 |
|---|---|---|---|---|---|
| C1 | 0.000 | 0.038 | 0.050 | 0.000 | 0.025 |
| C2 | 0.000 | 0.000 | 0.013 | 0.113 | 0.063 |
| C3 | 0.188 | 0.188 | 0.000 | 0.175 | 0.163 |
| C4 | 0.138 | 0.088 | 0.063 | 0.000 | 0.075 |
| C5 | 0.138 | 0.125 | 0.000 | 0.025 | 0.000 |

*Table 20. Normalized direct-relation fuzzy matrix (xm)*

| | C1 | C2 | C3 | C4 | C5 |
|---|---|---|---|---|---|
| C1 | 0.000 | 0.100 | 0.113 | 0.063 | 0.088 |
| C2 | 0.063 | 0.000 | 0.075 | 0.175 | 0.125 |
| C3 | 0.250 | 0.250 | 0.000 | 0.238 | 0.225 |
| C4 | 0.200 | 0.150 | 0.125 | 0.000 | 0.138 |
| C5 | 0.200 | 0.188 | 0.063 | 0.088 | 0.000 |

*Table 21. Normalized direct-relation fuzzy matrix (xu)*

| | C1 | C2 | C3 | C4 | C5 |
|---|---|---|---|---|---|
| C1 | 0.000 | 0.163 | 0.175 | 0.125 | 0.150 |
| C2 | 0.125 | 0.000 | 0.138 | 0.238 | 0.188 |
| C3 | 0.250 | 0.250 | 0.000 | 0.250 | 0.250 |
| C4 | 0.250 | 0.213 | 0.188 | 0.000 | 0.200 |
| C5 | 0.250 | 0.250 | 0.125 | 0.150 | 0.000 |

*Table 22. Identity matrix (I)*

| | C1 | C2 | C3 | C4 | C5 |
|---|---|---|---|---|---|
| C1 | 1 | 0 | 0 | 0 | 0 |
| C2 | 0 | 1 | 0 | 0 | 0 |
| C3 | 0 | 0 | 1 | 0 | 0 |
| C4 | 0 | 0 | 0 | 1 | 0 |
| C5 | 0 | 0 | 0 | 0 | 1 |

*Table 23. Difference matrix (I-xl)*

| | C1 | C2 | C3 | C4 | C5 |
|---|---|---|---|---|---|
| C1 | 1.000 | -0.038 | -0.050 | 0.000 | -0.025 |
| C2 | 0.000 | 1.000 | -0.013 | -0.113 | -0.063 |
| C3 | -0.188 | -0.188 | 1.000 | -0.175 | -0.163 |
| C4 | -0.138 | -0.088 | -0.063 | 1.000 | -0.075 |
| C5 | -0.138 | -0.125 | 0.000 | -0.025 | 1.000 |

*Table 24. Difference matrix (I-xm)*

| | C1 | C2 | C3 | C4 | C5 |
|---|---|---|---|---|---|
| C1 | 1.000 | -0.100 | -0.113 | -0.063 | -0.088 |
| C2 | -0.063 | 1.000 | -0.075 | -0.175 | -0.125 |
| C3 | -0.250 | -0.250 | 1.000 | -0.238 | -0.225 |
| C4 | -0.200 | -0.150 | -0.125 | 1.000 | -0.138 |
| C5 | -0.200 | -0.188 | -0.063 | -0.088 | 1.000 |

*Table 25. Difference matrix (I-xu)*

| | C1 | C2 | C3 | C4 | C5 |
|---|---|---|---|---|---|
| C1 | 1.000 | -0.163 | -0.175 | -0.125 | -0.150 |
| C2 | -0.125 | 1.000 | -0.138 | -0.238 | -0.188 |
| C3 | -0.250 | -0.250 | 1.000 | -0.250 | -0.250 |
| C4 | -0.250 | -0.213 | -0.188 | 1.000 | -0.200 |
| C5 | -0.250 | -0.250 | -0.125 | -0.150 | 1.000 |

*Table 26. Inverse matrix of (I-xl)*

| | C1 | C2 | C3 | C4 | C5 |
|---|---|---|---|---|---|
| C1 | 1.017 | 0.054 | 0.053 | 0.016 | 0.039 |
| C2 | 0.031 | 1.026 | 0.022 | 0.121 | 0.078 |
| C3 | 0.250 | 0.247 | 1.029 | 0.213 | 0.205 |
| C4 | 0.169 | 0.123 | 0.074 | 1.029 | 0.101 |
| C5 | 0.148 | 0.139 | 0.012 | 0.043 | 1.018 |

*Table 27. Inverse matrix of (I-xm)*

| | C1 | C2 | C3 | C4 | C5 |
|---|---|---|---|---|---|
| C1 | 1.129 | 0.217 | 0.176 | 0.167 | 0.188 |
| C2 | 0.213 | 1.146 | 0.159 | 0.272 | 0.235 |
| C3 | 0.496 | 0.488 | 1.173 | 0.432 | 0.428 |
| C4 | 0.365 | 0.320 | 0.227 | 1.157 | 0.282 |
| C5 | 0.328 | 0.317 | 0.158 | 0.213 | 1.133 |

*Table 28. Inverse matrix of (I-xu)*

| | C1 | C2 | C3 | C4 | C5 |
|---|---|---|---|---|---|
| C1 | 1.501 | 0.644 | 0.530 | 0.562 | 0.591 |
| C2 | 0.670 | 1.558 | 0.544 | 0.690 | 0.667 |
| C3 | 0.954 | 0.957 | 1.574 | 0.873 | 0.891 |
| C4 | 0.855 | 0.830 | 0.656 | 1.583 | 0.764 |
| C5 | 0.790 | 0.795 | 0.564 | 0.659 | 1.540 |

*Table 29. Total influence matrix for xl*

| | C1 | C2 | C3 | C4 | C5 |
|---|---|---|---|---|---|
| C1 | 0.017 | 0.054 | 0.053 | 0.016 | 0.039 |
| C2 | 0.031 | 0.026 | 0.022 | 0.121 | 0.078 |
| C3 | 0.250 | 0.247 | 0.029 | 0.213 | 0.205 |
| C4 | 0.169 | 0.123 | 0.074 | 0.029 | 0.101 |
| C5 | 0.148 | 0.139 | 0.012 | 0.043 | 0.018 |

*Table 30. Total influence matrix for xm*

| | C1 | C2 | C3 | C4 | C5 |
|---|---|---|---|---|---|
| C1 | 0.129 | 0.217 | 0.176 | 0.167 | 0.188 |
| C2 | 0.213 | 0.146 | 0.159 | 0.272 | 0.235 |
| C3 | 0.496 | 0.488 | 0.173 | 0.432 | 0.428 |
| C4 | 0.365 | 0.320 | 0.227 | 0.157 | 0.282 |
| C5 | 0.328 | 0.317 | 0.158 | 0.213 | 0.133 |

*Table 31. Total influence matrix for xu*

| | C1 | C2 | C3 | C4 | C5 |
|---|---|---|---|---|---|
| C1 | 0.501 | 0.644 | 0.530 | 0.562 | 0.591 |
| C2 | 0.670 | 0.558 | 0.544 | 0.690 | 0.667 |
| C3 | 0.954 | 0.957 | 0.574 | 0.873 | 0.891 |
| C4 | 0.855 | 0.830 | 0.656 | 0.583 | 0.764 |
| C5 | 0.790 | 0.795 | 0.564 | 0.659 | 0.540 |

The closeness coefficient values of each alternatives have been calculated by the formulas (25)-(28). Ranking results have been provided by considering the values of closeness coefficient in the decreasing order. Table 42 shows the performance results of the alternatives.

In Table 42, A4 has the best performance in the E7 economies while A1 has the worst performance in the efficiency of monetary policy instruments among the countries.

## Ranking the Alternatives With Fuzzy VIKOR

The fuzzy best value $\tilde{f}_j^*$ and fuzzy worst value $\tilde{f}_j^-$ of each criterion have been computed by the formula (30). The results are shown in Table 43.

The values of Si, Ri, and Qi have been calculated to rank the alternatives with the equations (31)-(33). Results of this process are demonstrated on Table 44.

Several values of v have been used between 1 and 0 for the weight of strategy of maximum group utility such as consensus, veto, and stability. Table 45 presents the results by the different values of v.

The ranking results with the values of v that are higher than 0.5 are close to the ranking results of fuzzy TOPSIS. This is a clear evidence that the results of comparative analysis are coherent and stable for the weight of strategy of maximum group utility.

## CONCLUSION

This analysis aims to measure the effectiveness of the central banks under fuzzy logic. Within this framework, five different monetary policy instruments (required reserve ratio, rediscount rate, open market operations, standing

*Table 32. Total-relation fuzzy matrix*

| | C1 | | | C2 | | | C3 | | | C4 | | | C5 | | |
|---|---|---|---|---|---|---|---|---|---|---|---|---|---|---|---|
| C1 | 0.017 | 0.129 | 0.501 | 0.054 | 0.217 | 0.644 | 0.053 | 0.176 | 0.530 | 0.016 | 0.167 | 0.562 | 0.039 | 0.188 | 0.591 |
| C2 | 0.031 | 0.213 | 0.670 | 0.026 | 0.146 | 0.558 | 0.022 | 0.159 | 0.544 | 0.121 | 0.272 | 0.690 | 0.078 | 0.235 | 0.667 |
| C3 | 0.250 | 0.496 | 0.954 | 0.247 | 0.488 | 0.957 | 0.029 | 0.173 | 0.574 | 0.213 | 0.432 | 0.873 | 0.205 | 0.428 | 0.891 |
| C4 | 0.169 | 0.365 | 0.855 | 0.123 | 0.320 | 0.830 | 0.074 | 0.227 | 0.656 | 0.029 | 0.157 | 0.583 | 0.101 | 0.282 | 0.764 |
| C5 | 0.148 | 0.328 | 0.790 | 0.139 | 0.317 | 0.795 | 0.012 | 0.158 | 0.564 | 0.043 | 0.213 | 0.659 | 0.018 | 0.133 | 0.540 |

*Table 33. The values of $x_{lj}$, $x_{mj}$, and $x_{uj}$*

| | $x_{lj}$ | $x_{mj}$ | $x_{uj}$ | $x_{lj}$ | $x_{mj}$ | $x_{uj}$ | $x_{lj}$ | $x_{mj}$ | $x_{uj}$ | $x_{lj}$ | $x_{mj}$ | $x_{uj}$ | $x_{lj}$ | $x_{mj}$ | $x_{uj}$ |
|---|---|---|---|---|---|---|---|---|---|---|---|---|---|---|---|
| C1 | 0.002 | 0.179 | 0.773 | 0.061 | 0.320 | 1.000 | 0.058 | 0.254 | 0.820 | 0.000 | 0.240 | 0.869 | 0.036 | 0.274 | 0.916 |
| C2 | 0.014 | 0.285 | 0.970 | 0.005 | 0.185 | 0.803 | 0.000 | 0.204 | 0.782 | 0.149 | 0.374 | 1.000 | 0.083 | 0.319 | 0.965 |
| C3 | 0.239 | 0.503 | 0.997 | 0.235 | 0.495 | 1.000 | 0.000 | 0.156 | 0.587 | 0.198 | 0.435 | 0.910 | 0.190 | 0.430 | 0.929 |
| C4 | 0.170 | 0.406 | 1.000 | 0.113 | 0.352 | 0.971 | 0.054 | 0.240 | 0.759 | 0.000 | 0.155 | 0.671 | 0.087 | 0.306 | 0.891 |
| C5 | 0.174 | 0.405 | 0.994 | 0.162 | 0.390 | 1.000 | 0.000 | 0.187 | 0.705 | 0.040 | 0.257 | 0.827 | 0.007 | 0.155 | 0.675 |

*Table 34. The values of $x_j^{ls}$ and $x_j^{rs}$*

| | $x_j^{ls}$ | $x_j^{rs}$ | $x_j^{ls}$ | $x_j^{rs}$ | $x_j^{ls}$ | $x_j^{rs}$ | $x_j^{ls}$ | $x_j^{rs}$ | $x_j^{ls}$ | $x_j^{rs}$ |
|---|---|---|---|---|---|---|---|---|---|---|
| C1 | 0.152 | 0.485 | 0.254 | 0.595 | 0.213 | 0.524 | 0.194 | 0.534 | 0.222 | 0.558 |
| C2 | 0.225 | 0.576 | 0.157 | 0.496 | 0.170 | 0.496 | 0.305 | 0.615 | 0.258 | 0.586 |
| C3 | 0.398 | 0.667 | 0.393 | 0.664 | 0.135 | 0.410 | 0.352 | 0.617 | 0.347 | 0.620 |
| C4 | 0.329 | 0.628 | 0.284 | 0.600 | 0.202 | 0.500 | 0.134 | 0.442 | 0.251 | 0.562 |
| C5 | 0.329 | 0.625 | 0.317 | 0.621 | 0.157 | 0.464 | 0.211 | 0.527 | 0.135 | 0.444 |

*Table 35. The values of $x_j^{crisp}$*

| | | | | | |
|---|---|---|---|---|---|
| **C1** | 0.273 | 0.406 | 0.337 | 0.329 | 0.362 |
| **C2** | 0.374 | 0.283 | 0.292 | 0.451 | 0.403 |
| **C3** | 0.540 | 0.535 | 0.223 | 0.481 | 0.480 |
| **C4** | 0.473 | 0.428 | 0.317 | 0.239 | 0.385 |
| **C5** | 0.472 | 0.462 | 0.267 | 0.337 | 0.240 |

*Table 36. The values of $f_{ij}$*

| | | | | | |
|---|---|---|---|---|---|
| **C1** | 0.188 | 0.271 | 0.228 | 0.223 | 0.243 |
| **C2** | 0.272 | 0.211 | 0.217 | 0.323 | 0.291 |
| **C3** | 0.530 | 0.525 | 0.236 | 0.475 | 0.474 |
| **C4** | 0.420 | 0.383 | 0.291 | 0.226 | 0.347 |
| **C5** | 0.381 | 0.373 | 0.220 | 0.276 | 0.200 |

*Table 37. Defuzzified total relation matrix and weights*

| | **C1** | **C2** | **C3** | **C4** | **C5** | $(\tilde{D}_i + \tilde{R}_i)^{def}$ | $(\tilde{D}_i - \tilde{R}_i)^{def}$ | **Weights** |
|---|---|---|---|---|---|---|---|---|
| C1 | 0.188 | 0.271 | 0.228 | 0.223 | 0.243 | 2.942 | -0.638 | 0.188 |
| C2 | 0.272 | 0.211 | 0.217 | 0.323 | 0.291 | 3.076 | -0.449 | 0.197 |
| C3 | 0.530 | 0.525 | 0.236 | 0.475 | 0.474 | 3.431 | 1.048 | 0.219 |
| C4 | 0.420 | 0.383 | 0.291 | 0.226 | 0.347 | 3.189 | 0.143 | 0.204 |
| C5 | 0.381 | 0.373 | 0.220 | 0.276 | 0.200 | 3.005 | -0.104 | 0.192 |

*Table 38. Averaged fuzzy decision matrix*

| | C1 | | | C2 | | | C3 | | | C4 | | | C5 | | |
|---|---|---|---|---|---|---|---|---|---|---|---|---|---|---|---|
| A1 | 0.50 | 2.00 | 4.50 | 1.50 | 3.50 | 6.00 | 3.00 | 5.50 | 8.00 | 1.50 | 3.50 | 6.00 | 1.00 | 3.50 | 6.00 |
| A2 | 2.50 | 5.00 | 7.50 | 2.00 | 4.50 | 7.00 | 1.50 | 4.00 | 6.50 | 1.50 | 4.00 | 6.50 | 1.50 | 4.00 | 6.50 |
| A3 | 3.50 | 6.00 | 8.50 | 3.50 | 6.00 | 8.50 | 4.00 | 6.50 | 9.00 | 3.00 | 5.50 | 8.00 | 2.50 | 5.00 | 7.50 |
| A4 | 5.50 | 8.00 | 10.00 | 4.00 | 6.50 | 9.00 | 3.00 | 5.50 | 8.00 | 4.00 | 6.50 | 9.00 | 3.50 | 6.00 | 8.50 |
| A5 | 3.50 | 6.00 | 8.50 | 3.50 | 6.00 | 8.50 | 4.50 | 7.00 | 9.50 | 3.50 | 6.00 | 8.50 | 3.00 | 5.50 | 8.00 |
| A6 | 3.50 | 6.00 | 8.50 | 3.50 | 6.00 | 8.50 | 4.00 | 6.50 | 9.00 | 3.50 | 6.00 | 8.50 | 3.50 | 6.00 | 8.50 |
| A7 | 1.00 | 3.50 | 6.00 | 2.50 | 5.00 | 7.50 | 2.50 | 5.00 | 7.50 | 1.50 | 4.00 | 6.50 | 1.00 | 3.50 | 6.00 |

*Table 39. The values of* $c_{ij}^{*}$

| | | | | | |
|---|---|---|---|---|---|
| **A1** | 20.25 | 36.00 | 64.00 | 36.00 | 36.00 |
| **A2** | 56.25 | 49.00 | 42.25 | 42.25 | 42.25 |
| **A3** | 72.25 | 72.25 | 81.00 | 64.00 | 56.25 |
| **A4** | 100.00 | 81.00 | 64.00 | 81.00 | 72.25 |
| **A5** | 72.25 | 72.25 | 90.25 | 72.25 | 64.00 |
| **A6** | 72.25 | 72.25 | 81.00 | 72.25 | 72.25 |
| **A7** | 36.00 | 56.25 | 56.25 | 42.25 | 36.00 |
| **Total** | 20.72 | 20.95 | 21.88 | 20.25 | 19.47 |

*Table 40. Normalized fuzzy decision matrix*

| | C1 | | | C2 | | | C3 | | | C4 | | | C5 | | |
|---|---|---|---|---|---|---|---|---|---|---|---|---|---|---|---|
| A1 | 0.02 | 0.10 | 0.22 | 0.07 | 0.17 | 0.29 | 0.14 | 0.25 | 0.37 | 0.07 | 0.17 | 0.30 | 0.05 | 0.18 | 0.31 |
| A2 | 0.12 | 0.24 | 0.36 | 0.10 | 0.21 | 0.33 | 0.07 | 0.18 | 0.30 | 0.07 | 0.20 | 0.32 | 0.08 | 0.21 | 0.33 |
| A3 | 0.17 | 0.29 | 0.41 | 0.17 | 0.29 | 0.41 | 0.18 | 0.30 | 0.41 | 0.15 | 0.27 | 0.40 | 0.13 | 0.26 | 0.39 |
| A4 | 0.27 | 0.39 | 0.48 | 0.19 | 0.31 | 0.43 | 0.14 | 0.25 | 0.37 | 0.20 | 0.32 | 0.44 | 0.18 | 0.31 | 0.44 |
| A5 | 0.17 | 0.29 | 0.41 | 0.17 | 0.29 | 0.41 | 0.21 | 0.32 | 0.43 | 0.17 | 0.30 | 0.42 | 0.15 | 0.28 | 0.41 |
| A6 | 0.17 | 0.29 | 0.41 | 0.17 | 0.29 | 0.41 | 0.18 | 0.30 | 0.41 | 0.17 | 0.30 | 0.42 | 0.18 | 0.31 | 0.44 |
| A7 | 0.05 | 0.17 | 0.29 | 0.12 | 0.24 | 0.36 | 0.11 | 0.23 | 0.34 | 0.07 | 0.20 | 0.32 | 0.05 | 0.18 | 0.31 |

*Table 41. Weighted normalized fuzzy decision matrix*

| | C1 | | | C2 | | | C3 | | | C4 | | | C5 | | |
|---|---|---|---|---|---|---|---|---|---|---|---|---|---|---|---|
| A1 | 0.00 | 0.02 | 0.04 | 0.01 | 0.03 | 0.06 | 0.03 | 0.06 | 0.08 | 0.02 | 0.04 | 0.06 | 0.01 | 0.03 | 0.06 |
| A2 | 0.02 | 0.05 | 0.07 | 0.02 | 0.04 | 0.07 | 0.02 | 0.04 | 0.07 | 0.02 | 0.04 | 0.07 | 0.01 | 0.04 | 0.06 |
| A3 | 0.03 | 0.05 | 0.08 | 0.03 | 0.06 | 0.08 | 0.04 | 0.07 | 0.09 | 0.03 | 0.06 | 0.08 | 0.02 | 0.05 | 0.07 |
| A4 | 0.05 | 0.07 | 0.09 | 0.04 | 0.06 | 0.08 | 0.03 | 0.06 | 0.08 | 0.04 | 0.07 | 0.09 | 0.03 | 0.06 | 0.08 |
| A5 | 0.03 | 0.05 | 0.08 | 0.03 | 0.06 | 0.08 | 0.05 | 0.07 | 0.10 | 0.04 | 0.06 | 0.09 | 0.03 | 0.05 | 0.08 |
| A6 | 0.03 | 0.05 | 0.08 | 0.03 | 0.06 | 0.08 | 0.04 | 0.07 | 0.09 | 0.04 | 0.06 | 0.09 | 0.03 | 0.06 | 0.08 |
| A7 | 0.01 | 0.03 | 0.05 | 0.02 | 0.05 | 0.07 | 0.03 | 0.05 | 0.08 | 0.02 | 0.04 | 0.07 | 0.01 | 0.03 | 0.06 |

*Table 42. The values of closeness coefficient and ranking results*

| | $D_i^*$ | $D_i^-$ | $CC_i$ | **Ranking** |
|---|---|---|---|---|
| A1 | 4.819 | 0.205 | 0.041 | 7 |
| A2 | 4.794 | 0.230 | 0.046 | 5 |
| A3 | 4.720 | 0.298 | 0.059 | 4 |
| A4 | 4.689 | 0.327 | 0.065 | 1 |
| A5 | 4.705 | 0.312 | 0.062 | 2 |
| A6 | 4.705 | 0.312 | 0.062 | 3 |
| A7 | 4.797 | 0.227 | 0.045 | 6 |

*Table 43. The fuzzy best and worst value*

| | $\tilde{f}_j^*$ | | | $\tilde{f}_j^-$ | | |
|---|---|---|---|---|---|---|
| C1 | 5.50 | 8.00 | 10.00 | 0.50 | 2.00 | 4.50 |
| C2 | 4.00 | 6.50 | 9.00 | 1.50 | 3.50 | 6.00 |
| C3 | 4.50 | 7.00 | 9.50 | 1.50 | 4.00 | 6.50 |
| C4 | 4.00 | 6.50 | 9.00 | 1.50 | 3.50 | 6.00 |
| C5 | 3.50 | 6.00 | 8.50 | 1.00 | 3.50 | 6.00 |

*Table 44. The values of Si, Ri, and Qi (v:0.5)*

| Alternatives | Si | Ri | Qi | Ranking |
|---|---|---|---|---|
| A1 | 0.890 | 0.204 | 0.950 | 7 |
| A2 | 0.792 | 0.219 | 0.937 | 6 |
| A3 | 0.284 | 0.078 | 0.159 | 4 |
| A4 | 0.110 | 0.110 | 0.148 | 3 |
| A5 | 0.173 | 0.063 | 0.040 | 2 |
| A6 | 0.171 | 0.063 | 0.039 | 1 |
| A7 | 0.773 | 0.196 | 0.851 | 5 |

*Table 45a. The values of Qi and ranking results by the different values of v*

| v:0 | | v:0.1 | | v:0.2 | | v:0.3 | | v:0.4 | | v:0.5 | |
|---|---|---|---|---|---|---|---|---|---|---|---|
| Qi | Ranking | Qi | Ranking | Qi | Ranking | Qi | Ranking | Qi | Ranking | Qi | Ranking |
| 0.901 | 6 | 0.911 | 6 | 0.921 | 6 | 0.930 | 6 | 0.940 | 6 | 0.950 | 7 |
| 1.000 | 7 | 0.987 | 7 | 0.975 | 7 | 0.962 | 7 | 0.949 | 7 | 0.937 | 6 |
| 0.095 | 3 | 0.108 | 3 | 0.121 | 3 | 0.134 | 3 | 0.147 | 3 | 0.159 | 4 |
| 0.295 | 4 | 0.266 | 4 | 0.236 | 4 | 0.207 | 4 | 0.177 | 4 | 0.148 | 3 |
| 0.000 | 1 | 0.008 | 2 | 0.016 | 2 | 0.024 | 2 | 0.032 | 2 | 0.040 | 2 |
| 0.000 | 1 | 0.008 | 1 | 0.016 | 1 | 0.024 | 1 | 0.031 | 1 | 0.039 | 1 |
| 0.852 | 5 | 0.852 | 5 | 0.852 | 5 | 0.852 | 5 | 0.851 | 5 | 0.851 | 5 |

*Table 45b. The values of Qi and ranking results by the different values of v*

| v:0.6 | | v:0.7 | | v:0.8 | | v:0.9 | | v:1 | |
|---|---|---|---|---|---|---|---|---|---|
| Qi | Ranking | Qi | Ranking | Qi | Ranking | Qi | Ranking | Qi | Ranking |
| 0.960 | 7 | 0.970 | 7 | 0.980 | 7 | 0.990 | 7 | 1.000 | 7 |
| 0.924 | 6 | 0.911 | 6 | 0.899 | 6 | 0.886 | 6 | 0.873 | 6 |
| 0.172 | 4 | 0.185 | 4 | 0.198 | 4 | 0.210 | 4 | 0.223 | 4 |
| 0.118 | 3 | 0.089 | 3 | 0.059 | 1 | 0.030 | 1 | - | 1 |
| 0.048 | 2 | 0.057 | 2 | 0.065 | 3 | 0.073 | 3 | 0.081 | 3 |
| 0.047 | 1 | 0.055 | 1 | 0.063 | 2 | 0.071 | 2 | 0.078 | 2 |
| 0.851 | 5 | 0.851 | 5 | 0.851 | 5 | 0.850 | 5 | 0.850 | 5 |

facilities and asset purchase program) are defined as the criteria. Additionally, E7 countries are selected as the alternatives. Moreover, fuzzy DEMATEL methodology is taken into consideration to weight the criteria according to their importance. Similarly, fuzzy TOPSIS and fuzzy VIKOR approaches are used in order to rank the alternatives related to the monetary policy effectiveness.

According to the results of fuzzy DEMATEL approach, it is determined that open market operations (C3) is the most influencing factor. On the other side, it is also concluded that required reserve ratio (C1) is the most influenced criteria among the monetary policy instruments. The results explain that when central banks implement an active monetary policy, such as open market operations, it affects other monetary policies as well. On the other hand, the passive monetary policy is influenced by other monetary policy instruments.

In addition to them, it is also defined that open market operations (C3) is the most important criterion. Nevertheless, required reserve ratio (C1) has the lowest significance. The findings show that central banks should prefer to implement active monetary policy instruments. With the help of this issue, it can be much easier to influence the market. Otherwise, changing required reserve ratio does not have any powerful impact on the market. Because emerging economies can face volatility in the market, central banks should play a very active role in order to solve the problems in the market. In this circumstance, they should prefer open market operations instead of required reserve ratio.

According to the results of fuzzy TOPSIS methods, it is defined that Indonesia (A4) has the best performance in the E7 economies. Similar to this company, Mexico (A5) is the second most successful company with respect to the effectiveness of the central bank policies. On the other side, Brazil (A1) takes place on the last rank. Parallel to this aspect, the ranking results of fuzzy VIKOR with the values of v that are higher than 0.5 are close to the ranking results of fuzzy TOPSIS. This condition gives information that the results of comparative analysis are coherent and stable for the weight of strategy of maximum group utility. While looking at these results, it is recommended that countries that takes place on the last ranks should implement more active monetary policies, such as open market operations. Therefore, it can be much easier to increase the effectiveness of monetary policies.

## REFERENCES

Dincer, H. (2018). HHI-based evaluation of the European banking sector using an integrated fuzzy approach. *Kybernetes*.

Dinçer, H., Akdeniz, O. O., & Hacioglu, U. (2018). Competitive strategy selection in the European banking sector using a hybrid decision-making approach. *Zbornik Radova Ekonomski Fakultet u Rijeka*, *36*(1), 211–240.

Dinçer, H., & Görener, A. (2011). Performans değerlendirmesinde AHP-VIKOR ve AHP-TOPSIS yaklaşımları: Hizmet sektöründe bir uygulama. *Sigma: Mühendislik ve Fen Bilimleri Dergisi*, *29*, 244–260.

Dincer, H., & Hacioglu, U. (2013). Performance evaluation with fuzzy VIKOR and AHP method based on customer satisfaction in Turkish banking sector. *Kybernetes*, *42*(7), 1072–1085. doi:10.1108/K-02-2013-0021

Dincer, H., & Hacioglu, U. (2015). A comparative performance evaluation on bipolar risks in emerging capital markets using fuzzy AHP-TOPSIS and VIKOR approaches. *The Engineering Economist*, *26*(2), 118–129.

Dincer, H., & Hacioglu, U. (2017). Investigating the Economic Vulnerability Factors of Emerging Markets After the Global Financial Crisis of 2008 With a Hybrid Multi-Criteria Decision-Making Approach. In Handbook of Research on Economic, Financial, and Industrial Impacts on Infrastructure Development (pp. 313-333). IGI Global.

Dincer, H., Hacioglu, U., Tatoglu, E., & Delen, D. (2016). A fuzzy-hybrid analytic model to assess investors' perceptions for industry selection. *Decision Support Systems*, *86*, 24–34. doi:10.1016/j.dss.2016.03.005

Dincer, H., Hacioglu, U., & Yilmaz, R. (2013). *The effect of integrated marketing communication competencies on banking performance: analysis with fuzzy VIKOR method*. Academic Press.

# Chapter 7
# Analysis Results for the Effectiveness of Monetary Policies With Cointegration and Causality Analyses


## ABSTRACT

*The aim of this chapter is to examine the effectiveness of the monetary policies in E7 economies. For this purpose, two different variables are selected, which are central bank interest rate and inflation rate. These variables are tested with the help of Kao panel cointegration analysis, Pedroni panel cointegration analysis, and Dumitrescu Hurlin panel causality analysis. Additionally, monthly data of these variables for the periods between 1996:01-2019:02 is used in the analysis process. The findings show that there is a long-term relationship between interest rate and inflation rate for E7 economies. This situation gives information that monetary policies are used effectively in these countries. On the other side, for all three different lags, it is concluded that interest is the main cause of the inflation rate. This situation gives information that interest rate decisions of the central banks in E7 economies are very successful to control the inflation rate.*


DOI: 10.4018/978-1-7998-1643-0.ch007

## PEDRONI PANEL COINTEGRATION ANALYSIS

Cointegration analysis aims to identify long term relationship between the variables. Therefore, the main purpose of this methodology in comparison with the similar approaches is that it can be used for panel data (Eti and İnel, 2016). There are 7 different tests in the process of Pedroni panel cointegration analysis that are Panel v-Statistic, Panel rho-Statistic, Panel PP-Statistic, Panel ADF-Statistic, Group rho-Statistic, Group PP-Statistic and Group ADF-Statistic. The system provides probability values for each of these tests. On the other side, if the probability value is lower than 0.05, it means that the test is significant. In order to have a long-term relationship between the variables, at least four of them should be significant (Pedroni, 2004). This method was widely preferred in the literature. Some recent studies are illustrated on Table 1.

*Table 1. Studies related to Pedroni panel cointegration analysis*

| Author | Subject |
|---|---|
| Nguyen & Kakinaka (2019) | renewable energy consumption |
| Jäger & Schmidt (2016) | political economy of public investment |
| Hassler & Hosseinkouchack (2016) | in the presence of linear time trends |
| Liu et al. (2016) | economic growth and carbon dioxide emissions |
| Wang et al. (2016) | urbanization, energy use and carbon emissions |
| Lu (2017) | energy consumption and economic growth |
| Balcioglu (2016) | foreign aid and economic growth |
| Saeed & Hassan (2018) | liquidity and stock returns |
| Li et al. (2018) | economic development and energy factors |
| Kirikkaleli et al. (2018) | internet, electricity consumption and economic growth |
| Karanfil & Li (2015) | electricity consumption and economic growth |
| Ozcan & Ozturk (2019) | renewable energy consumption-economic growth |
| Salahuddin et al. (2016) | internet usage and economic growth |
| Khan & Abbas (2016) | electricity demand in Pakistan |
| Wang et al. (2015) | urban development intensity and carbon dioxide emissions |
| Saidi & Mbarek (2016) | nuclear energy and economic growth |
| Saleh et al. (2015) | the impact of tourism on economic growth |
| Kizilkaya et al. (2016) | foreign direct investments and economic growth |
| Dong et al. (2017) | impact of natural gas consumption on co2 emissions |

*continues on following page*

*Table 1. Continued*

| Author | Subject |
|---|---|
| Hassan (2018) | long run energy demand |
| Sharif et al. (2019) | renewable and nonrenewable energy consumption |
| Saridakis et al. (2016) | self-employment and unemployment |
| Afolabi et al. (2016) | openness and regional trade |
| Jin & Kim (2018) | mitigating carbon emissions |
| Dogan & Inglesi-Lotz (2017) | the effects of real income on carbon emissions |
| Abdlaziz et al. (2018) | the effect of oil price on agriculture sector |
| Abdullah et al. (2017) | health care in Asian countries |
| Ali et al. (2018) | biomass energy consumption and economic growth |
| Pradhan et al. (2018) | information communication technology infrastructure and economic growth |
| Işık & Shahbaz (2015) | energy consumption and economic growth |
| Tugcu (2018) | energy growth |
| Ladu & Meleddu (2016) | wage and inflation relationship |
| Osman et al. (2016) | electricity consumption and economic growth |
| Rasoulinezhad & Kang (2016) | South Korea's trade with OPEC member countries |
| Mahmoodi (2017) | economic growth and renewable energy |
| Jayaraman et al. (2018) | financial sector development |
| Appiah et al. (2019) | energy use and carbon emissions |
| Shafighi et al. (2016) | financial integration |
| Li & Zhou (2019) | the impacts of demographic structure on co2 emissions |
| Neuts (2019) | tourism and urban economic growth |
| Ali et al. (2018) | bank stock prices |
| Afolabi et al. (2017) | regional integration and trade effect |
| Ibhagui (2019) | long-run monetary model |
| Rahnama et al. (2019) | tourism and equality in income distribution |
| Loganathan et al. (2017) | taxation, growth and the stock traded nexus |
| Pradhan et al. (2018) | innovation and financial development |
| Vidyarthi (2015) | energy consumption and growth |
| Nasre Esfahani & Rasoulinezhad (2015) | new co2 emitters in the future |
| Nasreen & Anwar (2018) | financial stability and economic development |
| Alsaleh & Abdul-Rahim (2018) | bioenergy industry and the growth of the energy sector |
| Rasoulinezhad & Saboori (2018) | renewable and non-renewable energy consumption |
| Rahman & Mustafa (2017) | financial deepening and stock market returns |

## KAO PANEL COINTEGRATION ANALYSIS

Similar to Pedroni panel cointegration analysis, Kao cointegration analysis also aims to understand whether there is a long-term relationship between the variables. This approach is also suitable for panel data analysis. On the other hand, there is only one test in this methodology (Ersin, 2018). Therefore, if the probability value of this test is lower than 0.05, it means that the test is significant (Kao and Chiang, 2001). Some recent studies related to Kao panel cointegration analysis are given on Table 2.

*Table 2. Studies related to Kao panel cointegration analysis*

| Author | Subject |
|---|---|
| Abidin et al. (2015) | trade relationship between Malaysia and the OIC member countries |
| Rodriguez Garcia et al. (2018) | agricultural intensification and land use change |
| Mosikari et al. (2016) | manufactured exports and economic growth |
| Egbetunde & Akinlo (2015) | financial globalization and economic growth |
| Moutinho et al. (2018) | the environment–growth dilemma |
| Hartani et al. (2015) | female labor force participation |
| Wang et al. (2017) | the impacts of population-related factors on $CO_2$ emissions |
| Inglesi-Lotz & Dogan (2018) | renewable versus non-renewable energy |
| Rahman & Grewal (2017) | foreign direct investment and international trade |
| Carreras et al. (2018) | macroprudential tools |
| Kais & Mounir (2017) | nuclear energy and economic development |
| Razak et al. (2017) | determinants of environmental quality |
| Wang et al. (2019) | the influencing factors on carbon emission |
| Tiba & Frikha (2018) | analysis of African economy |
| Liu et al. (2016) | the impact of foreign direct investment on total factor productivity |
| Aye & Edoja (2017) | effect of economic growth on carbon emission |
| Abimelech Paye Gbatu et al. (2018) | carbon emissions |
| Guy (2018) | forecast of electricity demand |
| Baiardi et al. (2015) | the price and income elasticities |
| Zaman et al. (2016) | energy consumption, environment, health and wealth |
| Dogan & Seker (2016) | renewable and non-renewable energy, trade |
| Gbatu et al. (2018) | carbon emissions |
| Popescu et al. (2018) | determinants of the energy paradigm changes |
| Arun & Yıldırım (2017) | effects of foreign direct investment on intellectual property |
| Sayari et al. (2018) | components of economic growth |

*continues on following page*

*Table 2. Continued*

| Author | Subject |
|---|---|
| Zhang & Zhou (2016) | foreign direct investment and carbon emissions |
| Song & Mi (2016) | regional economic growth |
| Narayan & Rehman (2018) | portfolio diversification opportunities |
| Arshad et al. (2018) | macroeconomic determinants |
| Mahmoodi & Mahmoodi (2018) | environmental quality and renewable energy |
| Andrea (2015) | monetary exchange rate models |
| Al-Mulali et al. (2015) | the influence of economic growth on pollution |
| Anastasiou et al. (2019) | nonperforming loans in the euro area |
| Ali et al. (2019) | road traffic fatalities |
| Andrei et al. (2017) | the determinants of the energy paradigm |
| Albaity & Mustafa (2018) | macroeconomic determinants of oil price |
| Ketenci (2016) | literature review |
| Sezer & Abasiz (2016) | the effect of technology on economic improvement |
| Siddiqui & Rehman (2017) | the human capital and economic growth nexus |
| Ssali et al. (2019) | environmental pollution and economic growth |
| Kapingura (2018) | domestic investment and savings |
| Rehman et al. (2019) | commonalities of equity market fundamentals |

## DUMITRESCU HURLIN PANEL CAUSALITY ANALYSIS

Dumitrescu Hurlin panel causality test is used to see whether there is causal relationship between the variables. It is an advanced form of Granger causality analysis. The main benefit of this method is that it is appropriate for panel data (Dumitrescu and Hurlin, 2012; Ersin and Ergeç, 2018; Ergeç and Ersin, 2019). Some recent studies which considered Dumitrescu Hurlin panel causality test are demonstrated on Table 3.

## GENERAL INFORMATION ABOUT THE ANALYSIS

In this study, effectiveness of the monetary policies in E7 economies is examined with the help of Kao panel cointegration analysis, Pedroni panel cointegration analysis and Dumitrescu Hurlin panel causality analysis. Because of using these cointegration and causality tests, it is necessary to consider the stationary variables. Therefore, before making these analyses, panel unit root

*Table 3. Studies related to Dumitrescu Hurlin panel causality analysis*

| Author | Subject |
|---|---|
| Ng et al. (2019) | the impact of electricity production |
| Dogan & Aslan (2017) | energy consumption and tourism |
| Yüksel (2017) | research and development expenses |
| Aydin & Malcioglu (2016) | financial development and economic growth |
| Furuoka (2017) | renewable electricity consumption |
| Dogan et al. (2016) | agricultural electricity consumption |
| Lau et al. (2018) | nuclear energy clean |
| Tuna et al. (2017) | oil and stock prices |
| Zaman et al. (2017) | tourism transportation expenditures |
| Dinçer et al. (2017) | energy consumption and economic growth |
| Rahimi & Rad (2017) | internet usage, electricity consumption and economic growth |
| Aydin (2019) | renewable and non-renewable electricity consumption |
| Magazzino (2018) | fiscal sustainability |
| Ayad (2019) | current account balance |
| Adalı & Yüksel (2017) | foreign direct investments and economic improvement |
| Kilic (2015) | effects of globalization on economic growth |
| Lopez & Weber (2018) | literature review |
| Dinçer et al. (2018) | non-performing loans |
| Rahim et al. (2018) | electric consumption and economic growth |
| Mansour et al. (2017) | foreign direct investment |
| Dinçer et al. (2019) | research and development and technology investments |
| Huang et al. (2018) | oil prices and tourist arrivals |
| Aderemi et al. (2018) | foreign direct investment and economic growth |
| Evans (2019) | internet and democracy |
| Lv (2019) | the effects of tourism on regional inequality |
| Tunay et al. (2015) | interaction between internet banking and bank performance |
| Akram & Rath (2019) | fiscal synchronization |
| Dinçer et al. (2019) | Islamic stock development |
| Dogan et al. (2017) | the impacts of energy consumption |
| Bhat et al. (2018) | state domestic product |
| Miljkovic et al. (2018) | the impact on mortality arising from climate change |
| Yu (2016) | examining inflation problem |
| Dinçer et al. (2019) | effects of demographic characteristics on business success |
| Dinçer et al. (2018) | conflict risk and defense expenses |
| Zaman et al. (2016) | tourism development and energy consumption |

*continues on following page*

*Table 3. Continued*

| Author | Subject |
|---|---|
| Dinçer et al. (2019) | income inequality and nonperforming loans. |
| Gorus & Aslan (2019) | impacts of economic indicators on environmental degradation |
| Tunay et al. (2018) | international insurance industry and systemic risk |
| Zaghdoudi (2017) | electricity consumption and economic growth |
| Bildirici (2018) | impact of military on biofuels consumption |
| Haseeb et al. (2019) | environmental quality |
| Ndlovu et al. (2018) | the impact macroeconomic variables on stock returns |
| Can & Gozgor (2018) | revisiting the tourism-growth nexus |
| Moreira (2019) | inflation and real exchange rate |
| Sekmen & Gokirmak (2018) | internet use and economic development |
| Maroof et al. (2018) | determinants of industrial development |
| Tabassum & Alam (2018) | trade openness and size of city |
| Akhtar et al. (2016) | financial development, energy consumption and trade openness nexus |
| Bayramoğlu & Öztürk (2018) | triple deficit hypotheses in developing economies |
| Yüksel & Oktar (2017) | Okun's law |
| Dinçer and Yüksel (2018) | health expenditure and economic growth |

tests are performed for these variables. Hence, in this section, firstly, data and scope are defined. After that, panel unit root test results are given. Finally, Kao panel cointegration analysis, Pedroni panel cointegration analysis and Dumitrescu Hurlin panel causality analysis results are presented. The details of this process are demonstrated in the following subtitles.

## DATA AND SCOPE

In this analysis, it is aimed to understand whether central banks of E7 economies are successful to implement monetary policies. Therefore, in order to reach this objective, two different variables are selected which are central bank interest rate and inflation rate. Additionally, montly data of these variables for the periods between 1996:01-2019:02 is taken into consideration. Moreover, Kao panel cointegration analysis, Pedroni panel cointegration analysis and Dumitrescu Hurlin panel causality analysis are performed so as to reach this objective. Before implementing these tests, panel unit root tests are performed to see whether these variables are stationary or not.

## RESULTS OF PANEL UNIT ROOT TESTS

In the analysis process, firstly, stationary analysis is performed for the variables. Within this framework, five different panel unit root analysis techniques are considered. The unit root test results for the inflation is given on Table 4.

Table 4 gives information that probability values are lower than 0.05 for all different panel unit root test results. This situation explains that inflation is stationary on its level value. Therefore, this variable is used in the analysis without making any changes. On the other side, Table 5 identifies that panel unit root test results of the variable on central bank interest rates.

Table 5 shows that probability values for two different tests (Levin, Lin & Chu, Breitung t-stat) are greater than 0.05. On the other hand, these values are lower than 0.05 for other three different tests (Im, Pesaran and Shin W-stat, ADF - Fisher Chi-square, PP - Fisher Chi-square). Therefore, the first difference of this variable is taken to make it stationary. The new test results are demonstrated on Table 6.

*Table 4. Panel unit root test results for the inflation*

| Panel unit root test: Summary | | | | |
|---|---|---|---|---|
| Series: INFLATION | | | | |
| Date: 03/20/19 Time: 14:13 | | | | |
| Sample: 1996M01 2019M02 | | | | |
| Exogenous variables: Individual effects, individual linear trends | | | | |
| User-specified lags: 4 | | | | |
| Newey-West automatic bandwidth selection and Bartlett kernel | | | | |
| **Method** | **Statistic** | **Prob.**** | | **Obs** |
| **Null: Unit Root (Assumes Common Unit Root Process)** | | | | |
| Levin, Lin & Chu t* | -3.69703 | 0.0001 | 7 | 1909 |
| Breitung t-stat | -2.69277 | 0.0035 | 7 | 1902 |
| **Null: Unit Root (Assumes Individual Unit Root Process)** | | | | |
| Im, Pesaran and Shin W-stat | -6.64265 | 0.0000 | 7 | 1909 |
| ADF - Fisher Chi-square | 83.8815 | 0.0000 | 7 | 1909 |
| PP - Fisher Chi-square | 102.511 | 0.0000 | 7 | 1937 |

** Probabilities for Fisher tests are computed using an asymptotic Chi-square distribution. All other tests assume asymptotic normality.

## Table 5. Panel unit root test results for the central bank interest rate

| Panel unit root test: Summary | | | | |
|---|---|---|---|---|
| Series: INTEREST | | | | |
| Date: 03/20/19 Time: 14:14 | | | | |
| Sample: 1996M01 2019M02 | | | | |
| Exogenous variables: Individual effects, individual linear trends | | | | |
| User-specified lags: 4 | | | | |
| Newey-West automatic bandwidth selection and Bartlett kernel | | | | |
| **Method** | **Statistic** | **Prob.**** | | **Obs** |
| **Null: Unit Root (Assumes Common Unit Root Process)** | | | | |
| Levin, Lin & Chu t* | -0.62685 | 0.2654 | 7 | 1909 |
| Breitung t-stat | 0.15180 | 0.5603 | 7 | 1902 |
| **Null: Unit Root (Assumes Individual Unit Root Process)** | | | | |
| Im, Pesaran and Shin W-stat | -2.72920 | 0.0032 | 7 | 1909 |
| ADF - Fisher Chi-square | 47.3652 | 0.0000 | 7 | 1909 |
| PP - Fisher Chi-square | 67.8173 | 0.0000 | 7 | 1937 |

** Probabilities for Fisher tests are computed using an asymptotic Chi-square distribution. All other tests assume asymptotic normality.

## Table 6. Panel unit root test results for the Central Bank interest rate (first difference)

| Panel unit root test: Summary | | | | |
|---|---|---|---|---|
| Series: D(INTEREST) | | | | |
| Date: 03/20/19 Time: 14:15 | | | | |
| Sample: 1996M01 2019M02 | | | | |
| Exogenous variables: Individual effects | | | | |
| User-specified lags: 4 | | | | |
| Newey-West automatic bandwidth selection and Bartlett kernel | | | | |
| **Method** | **Statistic** | **Prob.**** | | **Obs** |
| **Null: Unit Root (Assumes Common Unit Root Process)** | | | | |
| Levin, Lin & Chu t* | -8.54379 | 0.0000 | 7 | 1902 |
| **Null: Unit Root (Assumes Individual Unit Root Process)** | | | | |
| Im, Pesaran and Shin W-stat | -16.8880 | 0.0000 | 7 | 1902 |
| ADF - Fisher Chi-square | 293.765 | 0.0000 | 7 | 1902 |
| PP - Fisher Chi-square | 848.876 | 0.0000 | 7 | 1930 |

** Probabilities for Fisher tests are computed using an asymptotic Chi- square distribution. All other tests assume asymptotic normality.

## RESULTS OF KAO PANEL COINTEGRATION TESTS

After making panel unit root tests, long run relationship between the variables is evaluated with the help of Kao panel cointegration analysis. The test results are given on Table 7.

Table 7 gives information about the results of Kao panel cointegration analysis. Because the probability value (0.0000) is lower than 0.05, it shows that there is a long run relationship between the variables. It is determined that monetary policies are used effectively in these countries.

*Table 7. Kao panel cointegration analysis results*

| Kao Residual Cointegration Test | | | | |
|---|---|---|---|---|
| Series: DINT INFLATION | | | | |
| Date: 03/20/19 Time: 14:17 | | | | |
| Sample: 1996M01 2019M02 | | | | |
| Included observations: 1944 | | | | |
| Null Hypothesis: No cointegration | | | | |
| Trend assumption: No deterministic trend | | | | |
| User-specified lag length: 1 | | | | |
| Newey-West automatic bandwidth selection and Bartlett kernel | | | | |
| | | | **t-Statistic** | **Prob.** |
| ADF | | | -18.01150 | 0.0000 |
| Residual variance | | | 33.17780 | |
| HAC variance | | | 3.048026 | |
| Augmented Dickey-Fuller Test Equation | | | | |
| Dependent Variable: D(RESID) | | | | |
| Method: Least Squares | | | | |
| Date: 03/20/19 Time: 14:17 | | | | |
| Sample (adjusted): 1996M04 2019M02 | | | | |
| Included observations: 1923 after adjustments | | | | |
| **Variable** | **Coefficient** | **Std. Error** | **t-Statistic** | **Prob.** |
| RESID(-1) | -1.519193 | 0.035014 | -43.38783 | 0.0000 |
| D(RESID(-1)) | 0.192005 | 0.021658 | 8.865133 | 0.0000 |
| R-squared | 0.651558 | Mean dependent var | | 0.000846 |
| Adjusted R-squared | 0.651377 | S.D. dependent var | | 5.691966 |
| S.E. of regression | 3.360781 | Akaike info criterion | | 5.263264 |
| Sum squared resid | 21697.41 | Schwarz criterion | | 5.269048 |
| Log likelihood | -5058.628 | Hannan-Quinn criter. | | 5.265392 |

## RESULTS OF PEDRONI PANEL COINTEGRATION TESTS

In addition to Kao panel cointegration analysis, another test is also performed by using Pedroni panel cointegration analysis. Analysis results of this test are demonstrated on Table 8.

Table 8 gives information about the Pedroni panel cointegration analysis. As it can be seen from this table, there are seven different tests in this cointegration analysis. It is understood that probability values of all these tests are lower than 0.05. Therefore, it is concluded that there is long term relationship between interest rate and inflation rate for E7 economies. Hence, it is concluded that monetary policies are used effectively in these countries.

*Table 8. Pedroni panel cointegration analysis results*

| Pedroni Residual Cointegration Test | | | | |
|---|---|---|---|---|
| Series: DINT INFLATION | | | | |
| Date: 03/20/19 Time: 14:17 | | | | |
| Sample: 1996M01 2019M02 | | | | |
| Included observations: 1944 | | | | |
| Cross-sections included: 7 | | | | |
| Null Hypothesis: No cointegration | | | | |
| Trend assumption: No deterministic trend | | | | |
| User-specified lag length: 1 | | | | |
| Newey-West automatic bandwidth selection and Bartlett kernel | | | | |
| **Alternative Hypothesis: Common AR Coefs. (within-dimension)** | | | | |
| | **Statistic** | **Prob.** | **Weighted Statistic** | **Prob.** |
| Panel v-Statistic | 5.904916 | 0.0000 | 2.377600 | 0.0087 |
| Panel rho-Statistic | -147.7635 | 0.0000 | -105.8282 | 0.0000 |
| Panel PP-Statistic | -60.55611 | 0.0000 | -37.19487 | 0.0000 |
| Panel ADF-Statistic | -40.89816 | 0.0000 | -27.52776 | 0.0000 |
| **Alternative Hypothesis: Individual AR Coefs. (between-dimension)** | | | | |
| | **Statistic** | **Prob.** | | |
| Group rho-Statistic | -108.6308 | 0.0000 | | |
| Group PP-Statistic | -47.24313 | 0.0000 | | |
| Group ADF-Statistic | -33.49050 | 0.0000 | | |

## RESULTS OF DUMITRESCU HURLIN PANEL CAUSALITY TESTS

In the last stage of the analysis, Dumitrescu Hurlin panel causality analysis is performed to understand whether there is a causal relationship between interest rate and inflation rate. In this framework, three different lags are taken into consideration in order to reach more appropriate results. Analysis results for three different lags are given on Table 9-11.

Tables explain that only for lag 1, inflation does not homogeneously cause interest rate. The main reason is that probability value is greater than 0.05. In addition to this issue, for other lags, it is understood that inflation is the main cause of the interest rate. On the other side, for all three different lags, it is concluded that interest is the main cause of the inflation rate. This situation gives information that interest rate decisions of the central banks in E7 economies are very successful to control the inflation rate.

*Table 9. Dumitrescu Hurlin panel causality analysis results (lag=1)*

| Pairwise Dumitrescu Hurlin Panel Causality Tests | | | |
|---|---|---|---|
| Date: 03/20/19 Time: 14:18 | | | |
| Sample: 1996M01 2019M02 | | | |
| Lags: 1 | | | |
| **Null Hypothesis** | **W-Stat.** | **Zbar-Stat.** | **Prob.** |
| INFLATION does not homogeneously cause INTEREST | 1.00624 | -0.00212 | 0.9983 |
| INTEREST does not homogeneously cause INFLATION | 2.94944 | 3.58663 | 0.0003 |

*Table 10. Dumitrescu Hurlin panel causality analysis results (lag=2)*

| Pairwise Dumitrescu Hurlin Panel Causality Tests | | | |
|---|---|---|---|
| Date: 03/20/19 Time: 14:18 | | | |
| Sample: 1996M01 2019M02 | | | |
| Lags: 2 | | | |
| **Null Hypothesis** | **W-Stat.** | **Zbar-Stat.** | **Prob** |
| INFLATION does not homogeneously cause INTEREST | 4.57564 | 3.33734 | 0.0008 |
| INTEREST does not homogeneously cause INFLATION | 5.84570 | 4.99260 | 6.E-07 |

*Table 11. Dumitrescu Hurlin panel causality analysis results (lag=3)*

| Pairwise Dumitrescu Hurlin Panel Causality Tests | | | |
|---|---|---|---|
| Date: 03/20/19 Time: 14:18 | | | |
| Sample: 1996M01 2019M02 | | | |
| Lags: 3 | | | |
| **Null Hypothesis** | **W-Stat.** | **Zbar-Stat.** | **Prob.** |
| INFLATION does not homogeneously cause INTEREST | 6.19385 | 3.36769 | 0.0008 |
| INTEREST does not homogeneously cause INFLATION | 8.95641 | 6.30143 | 3.E-10 |

## CONCLUSION

In this second analysis, effectiveness of the monetary policies in E7 economies is examined with the help of Kao panel cointegration analysis, Pedroni panel cointegration analysis and Dumitrescu Hurlin panel causality analysis. In the first analysis, fuzzy logic is used whereas econometric models are taken into consideration in this second analysis. For this purpose, two different variables are selected which are central bank interest rate and inflation rate. Additionally, monthly data of these variables for the periods between 1996:01-2019:02 is used in the analysis process.

According to the Kao panel cointegration analysis results, it is understood that there is a long run relationship between the variables. Similarly, as a result of Pedroni panel cointegration analysis, it is concluded that there is long term relationship between interest rate and inflation rate for E7 economies. While considering these results, it is determined that monetary policies are used effectively in these countries.

In addition to these methods, Dumitrescu Hurlin panel causality test is also considered in the analysis process. It is identified that only for lag 1, inflation does not homogeneously cause interest rate. The main reason is that probability value is greater than 0.05. In addition to this issue, for other lags, it is understood that inflation is the main cause of the interest rate. On the other side, for all three different lags, it is concluded that interest is the main cause of the inflation rate. This situation gives information that interest rate decisions of the central banks in E7 economies are very successful to control the inflation rate.

## REFERENCES


Abdlaziz, R. A., Naseem, N. A. M., & Slesman, L. (2018). Dutch Disease effect of Oil Price on Agriculture Sector: Evidence from Panel Cointegration of Oil Exporting Countries. *International Journal of Energy Economics and Policy*, *8*(5), 241–250.

Abdullah, S. M., Siddiqua, S., & Huque, R. (2017). Is health care a necessary or luxury product for Asian countries? An answer using panel approach. *Health Economics Review*, *7*(1), 4. doi:10.118613561-017-0144-8 PMID:28124312

Abidin, I. S. Z., Bakar, N. A., & Haseeb, M. (2015). Exploring trade relationship between Malaysia and the OIC member countries: A panel cointegration approach (1995-2012). *Asian Journal of Scientific Research*, *8*(1), 107–121. doi:10.3923/ajsr.2015.107.121

Abimelech Paye Gbatu, Z. W., Wesseh Jr, P. K., & Sesay, V. A. (2018). *What precipitates growth in CO2 emissions?: New evidence from a panel of economic community of West African states (ECOWAS). International Journal of Energy Sector Management*. doi:10.1108/IJESM-09-2017-0001

Adalı, Z., & Yüksel, S. (2017). *Causality relationship between foreign direct investments and economic improvement for developing economies*. Academic Press.

Aderemi, T. A., Adebayo, A. G., Jolayemi, A. L., & Kalejaiye, G. T. (2018). Panel Cointegration and Granger Causality Approach to Foreign Direct Investment and Economic Growth in BRICS Countries. *Acta Universitatis Danubius. Œconomica, 15*(2).

Afolabi, L. O., Abu, B. N., & Azman, A. M. (2016). Openness and ECOWAS regional trade: a panel cointegration analysis using a gravity model. *Актуальні проблеми економіки*, (3), 319-328.

Afolabi, L. O., Aznin, A. B., & Izraf, A. A. (2017). ECOWAS Regional Integration and Trade Effect: A Dynamic Panel Cointegration Method Using the Gravity Model. *International Journal of Economic Perspectives, 11*(1).

Akhtar, M. H., Sheikh, M. R., & Anam, A. (2016). Financial Development, Energy Consumption and Trade Openness Nexus: Empirical Evidence from Selected South Asian Countries. *Pakistan Journal of Social Sciences*, *36*(1).

Akram, V., & Rath, B. N. (2019). Is there any evidence of tax-and-spend, spend-and-tax or fiscal synchronization from panel of Indian state? *Applied Economics Letters*, 1–4.

Al-Mulali, U., Ozturk, I., & Lean, H. H. (2015). The influence of economic growth, urbanization, trade openness, financial development, and renewable energy on pollution in Europe. *Natural Hazards*, *79*(1), 621–644. doi:10.100711069-015-1865-9

Albaity, M., & Mustafa, H. (2018). International and Macroeconomic Determinants of Oil Price: Evidence from Gulf Cooperation Council Countries. *International Journal of Energy Economics and Policy*, *8*(1), 69–81.

Ali, H. S., Adaa, A. H. M. A., Lin, W. L., & Youssouf, M. A. (2018). Biomass energy consumption and economic growth: Panel data evidence from ASEAN member countries. *GeoJournal*, *83*(6), 1339–1348. doi:10.100710708-017-9839-y

Ali, Q., Yaseen, M. R., & Khan, M. T. I. (2019). The causality of road traffic fatalities with its determinants in upper middle income countries: A continent-wide comparison. *Transportation Research Part A, Policy and Practice*, *119*, 301–312. doi:10.1016/j.tra.2018.12.002

Ali, S., Bashir, T., Ahmed, T., Ishaq, A., & Shahzad, S. J. H. (2018). The Determinants of Bank Stock Prices: A Panel Approach. *South Asian Journal of Management Sciences*, *12*(2), 116–129. doi:10.21621ajms.2018122.01

Alsaleh, M., & Abdul-Rahim, A. S. (2018). Bioenergy industry and the growth of the energy sector in the EU-28 region: Evidence from panel cointegration analysis. *Journal of Renewable and Sustainable Energy*, *10*(5), 053103. doi:10.1063/1.5032323

Anastasiou, D., Louri, H., & Tsionas, M. (2019). Nonperforming loans in the euro area: A re core–periphery banking markets fragmented? *International Journal of Finance & Economics*, *24*(1), 97–112. doi:10.1002/ijfe.1651

Andrea, S. (2015). Testing Monetary Exchange Rate Models With Panel Cointegration Tests. *Annals of the University of Oradea: Economic Science*, *25*(1), 643–651.

Andrei, J. V., Mieila, M., & Panait, M. (2017). The impact and determinants of the energy paradigm on economic growth in European Union. *PLoS One*, *12*(3), e0173282. doi:10.1371/journal.pone.0173282 PMID:28301505

Appiah, K., Du, J., Yeboah, M., & Appiah, R. (2019). Causal correlation between energy use and carbon emissions in selected emerging economies—panel model approach. *Environmental Science and Pollution Research International*, 1–17. PMID:30684181

Arshad, N., Ismail, M. T., & Rahman, R. A. (2018, June). Macroeconomic determinants of selected Asia housing market. In. AIP Conference Proceedings: Vol. 1974. *No. 1* (p. 040001). AIP Publishing. doi:10.1063/1.5041675

Arun, K., & Yıldırım, D. Ç. (2017). Effects of foreign direct investment on intellectual property, patents and R&D. *Queen Mary Journal of Intellectual Property*, *7*(2), 226–241. doi:10.4337/qmjip.2017.02.05

Ayad, H. (2019). The effect of terms of trade on current account balance: Harberger-Laursen-Metzler effect in Arabic countries. *Journal of Smart Economic Growth*, *4*(1).

Aydin, M. (2019). Renewable and non-renewable electricity consumption–economic growth nexus: Evidence from OECD countries. *Renewable Energy*, *136*, 599–606. doi:10.1016/j.renene.2019.01.008

Aydin, M., & Malcioglu, G. (2016). Financial development and economic growth relationship: The case of OECD countries. *Journal of Applied Research in Finance and Economics*, *2*(1), 1–7.

Aye, G. C., & Edoja, P. E. (2017). Effect of economic growth on CO2 emission in developing countries: Evidence from a dynamic panel threshold model. *Cogent Economics & Finance*, *5*(1), 1379239. doi:10.1080/23322039.2017.1379239

Baiardi, D., Bianchi, C., & Lorenzini, E. (2015). The price and income elasticities of the top clothing exporters: Evidence from a panel data analysis. *Journal of Asian Economics*, *38*, 14–30. doi:10.1016/j.asieco.2015.03.003

Balcioglu, H. (2016). Foreign Aid and Economic Growth: A Panel Cointegration for Selected Turkic Republics. *International Journal of Business and Social Research*, *6*(6), 17–23. doi:10.18533/ijbsr.v6i6.947

Bayramoğlu, A. T., & Öztürk, Z. (2018). Assessing the Twin and Triple Deficit Hypotheses in Developing Economies: A Panel Causality Analysis. In *Global Approaches in Financial Economics, Banking, and Finance* (pp. 209–225). Cham: Springer. doi:10.1007/978-3-319-78494-6_10

Bhat, S. A., Ganaie, A. A., Khan, N. A., & Kamaiah, B. (2018). Grants-in-Aid and State Domestic Product: An Empirical Analysis in India. In *Challenges and Issues in Indian Fiscal Federalism* (pp. 107–120). Singapore: Springer. doi:10.1007/978-981-10-6217-9_9

Bildirici, M. (2018). Impact of military on biofuels consumption and GHG emissions: The evidence from G7 countries. *Environmental Science and Pollution Research International*, *25*(14), 13560–13568. doi:10.100711356-018-1545-x PMID:29492823

Can, M., & Gozgor, G. (2018). Revisiting the tourism-growth nexus: Evidence from a new index for the market diversification of tourist arrivals. *Current Issues in Tourism*, *21*(10), 1157–1170. doi:10.1080/13683500.2016.1268103

Carreras, O., Davis, E. P., & Piggott, R. (2018). Assessing macroprudential tools in OECD countries within a cointegration framework. *Journal of Financial Stability*, *37*, 112–130. doi:10.1016/j.jfs.2018.04.004

Dincer, H., Hacioglu, U., Tatoglu, E., & Delen, D. (2016). A fuzzy-hybrid analytic model to assess investors' perceptions for industry selection. *Decision Support Systems*, *86*, 24–34. doi:10.1016/j.dss.2016.03.005

Dinçer, H., Hacıoğlu, Ü., & Yüksel, S. (2018). Conflict Risk and Defense Expenses and Their Impact on the Economic Growth. In *Handbook of Research on Military Expenditure on Economic and Political Resources* (pp. 1–23). IGI Global. doi:10.4018/978-1-5225-4778-5.ch001

Dinçer, H., & Yüksel, S. (2019). Identifying the Causality Relationship between Health Expenditure and Economic Growth: An Application on E7 Countries. *Journal of Health Systems And Policies*, *1*, 5.

Dinçer, H., Yüksel, S., & Adalı, Z. (2017). Identifying Causality Relationship between Energy Consumption and Economic Growth in Developed Countries. *International Business and Accounting Research Journal*, *1*(2), 71–81. doi:10.15294/ibarj.v1i2.9

Dinçer, H., Yuksel, S., & Adalı, Z. (2018). Relationship Between Non-Performing Loans, Industry, and Economic Growth of the African Economies and Policy Recommendations for Global Growth. In *Globalization and Trade Integration in Developing Countries* (pp. 203–228). IGI Global. doi:10.4018/978-1-5225-4032-8.ch009

Dinçer, H., Yüksel, S., & Adalı, Z. (2019). Economic Effects in Islamic Stock Development of the European Countries: Policy Recommendations for Ethical Behaviors. In Handbook of Research on Managerial Thinking in Global Business Economics (pp. 58-78). IGI Global.

Dinçer, H., Yüksel, S., Adalı, Z., & Aydın, R. (2019). Evaluating the Role of Research and Development and Technology Investments on Economic Development of E7 Countries. In Organizational Transformation and Managing Innovation in the Fourth Industrial Revolution (pp. 245-263). IGI Global.

Dinçer, H., Yüksel, S., Eti, S., & Tula, A. (2019). Effects of Demographic Characteristics on Business Success: An Evidence From Turkish Banking Sector. In *Handbook of Research on Business Models in Modern Competitive Scenarios* (pp. 304–324). IGI Global. doi:10.4018/978-1-5225-7265-7.ch016

Dinçer, H., Yüksel, S., Korsakienė, R., Raišienė, A. G., & Bilan, Y. (2019). IT2 Hybrid Decision-Making Approach to Performance Measurement of Internationalized Firms in the Baltic States. *Sustainability*, *11*(1), 296. doi:10.3390u11010296

Dinçer, H., Yüksel, S., & Şenel, S. (2018). Analyzing the Global Risks for the Financial Crisis after the Great Depression Using Comparative Hybrid Hesitant Fuzzy Decision-Making Models: Policy Recommendations for Sustainable Economic Growth. *Sustainability*, *10*(9), 3126. doi:10.3390u10093126

Dogan, E., & Aslan, A. (2017). Exploring the relationship among CO2 emissions, real GDP, energy consumption and tourism in the EU and candidate countries: Evidence from panel models robust to heterogeneity and cross-sectional dependence. *Renewable & Sustainable Energy Reviews*, *77*, 239–245. doi:10.1016/j.rser.2017.03.111

Dogan, E., & Inglesi-Lotz, R. (2017). Analyzing the effects of real income and biomass energy consumption on carbon dioxide (CO2) emissions: Empirical evidence from the panel of biomass-consuming countries. *Energy*, *138*, 721–727. doi:10.1016/j.energy.2017.07.136

Dogan, E., Sebri, M., & Turkekul, B. (2016). Exploring the relationship between agricultural electricity consumption and output: New evidence from Turkish regional data. *Energy Policy*, *95*, 370–377. doi:10.1016/j.enpol.2016.05.018

Dogan, E., & Seker, F. (2016). The influence of real output, renewable and non-renewable energy, trade and financial development on carbon emissions in the top renewable energy countries. *Renewable & Sustainable Energy Reviews*, *60*, 1074–1085. doi:10.1016/j.rser.2016.02.006

Dogan, E., Seker, F., & Bulbul, S. (2017). Investigating the impacts of energy consumption, real GDP, tourism and trade on CO2 emissions by accounting for cross-sectional dependence: A panel study of OECD countries. *Current Issues in Tourism*, *20*(16), 1701–1719. doi:10.1080/13683500.2015.1119103

Dong, K., Sun, R., Hochman, G., Zeng, X., Li, H., & Jiang, H. (2017). Impact of natural gas consumption on CO2 emissions: Panel data evidence from China's provinces. *Journal of Cleaner Production*, *162*, 400–410. doi:10.1016/j.jclepro.2017.06.100

Dumitrescu, E. I., & Hurlin, C. (2012). Testing for Granger non-causality in heterogeneous panels. *Economic Modelling*, *29*(4), 1450–1460. doi:10.1016/j.econmod.2012.02.014

Egbetunde, T., & Akinlo, A. E. (2015). Financial globalization and economic growth in Sub-Saharan Africa: Evidence from panel cointegration tests. *African Development Review*, *27*(3), 187–198. doi:10.1111/1467-8268.12140

Ergeç, E. H., & Ersin, İ. (2019). The Relationships between Public Expenditure and Sectorial Employment in Turkey. *BİLTÜRK Ekonomi ve İlişkili Çalışmalar Dergisi*, *1*(2), 150–168.

Ersin, İ. (2018). İhracata Dayalı Büyüme Hipotezinin Test Edilmesi: MINT Ülkeleri Örneği. *Ekonomi, İşletme ve Maliye Araştırmaları Dergisi*, *1*(1), 26–38.

Ersin, İ., & Ergeç, E. H. (2018). Harcama Bileşenleri Ve Sektörel İstihdam Arasindaki Nedensellik İlişkisi. *Yönetim ve Ekonomi Araştırmaları Dergisi*, *16*(Özel Sayı 1), 161-180.

Eti, S., & İnel, M. N. (2016). A research on comparison of regression models explaining the profitability base on financial data. *International Journal of Business and Management*, *4*(10), 470–475.

Evans, O. (2019). Digital politics: Internet and democracy in Africa. *Journal of Economic Studies (Glasgow, Scotland)*, *46*(1), 169–191. doi:10.1108/JES-08-2017-0234

Furuoka, F. (2017). Renewable electricity consumption and economic development: New findings from the Baltic countries. *Renewable & Sustainable Energy Reviews*, *71*, 450–463. doi:10.1016/j.rser.2016.12.074

Gbatu, A. P., Wang, Z., Wesseh Jr, P. K., & Sesay, V. A. (2018). What precipitates growth in CO2 emissions? New evidence from a panel of economic community of West African states (ECOWAS). *International Journal of Energy Sector Management*.

Gorus, M. S., & Aslan, M. (2019). Impacts of economic indicators on environmental degradation: Evidence from MENA countries. *Renewable & Sustainable Energy Reviews*, *103*, 259–268. doi:10.1016/j.rser.2018.12.042

Guy, D. B. (2018). Empirical Analysis and Forecast of Electricity Demand in West African Economic and Monetary Zone: Evidence from Panel ADRL Modelling. *Asian Journal of Economic Modelling*, *6*(3), 257–273. doi:10.18488/journal.8.2018.63.257.273

Hartani, N. H., Bakar, N. A. A., & Haseeb, M. (2015). The nexus between female labor force participation and female total fertility rate in selected ASEAN countries: Panel cointegration approach. *Modern Applied Science*, *9*(8), 29.

Haseeb, A., Xia, E., Saud, S., Ahmad, A., & Khurshid, H. (2019). Does information and communication technologies improve environmental quality in the era of globalization? An empirical analysis. *Environmental Science and Pollution Research International*, 1–15. PMID:30710332

Hassan, S. (2018). Long Run Energy Demand and Its Determinants: A Panel Cointegration Analysis of the Association of Southeast Asian Nations-5. *International Journal of Energy Economics and Policy*, *8*(4), 270–279.

Hassler, U., & Hosseinkouchack, M. (2016). Panel cointegration testing in the presence of linear time trends. *Econometrics*, *4*(4), 45. doi:10.3390/econometrics4040045

Huang, X., Silva, E., & Hassani, H. (2018). Causality between Oil Prices and Tourist Arrivals. *Stats*, *1*(1), 134–154. doi:10.3390tats1010010

Ibhagui, O. W. (2019). Does the long-run monetary model hold for Sub-Saharan Africa? A time series and panel-cointegration study. *Research in International Business and Finance*, *47*, 279–303. doi:10.1016/j.ribaf.2018.08.004

Inglesi-Lotz, R., & Dogan, E. (2018). The role of renewable versus non-renewable energy to the level of CO2 emissions a panel analysis of sub-Saharan Africa's Big 10 electricity generators. *Renewable Energy*, *123*, 36–43. doi:10.1016/j.renene.2018.02.041

Işık, C., & Shahbaz, M. (2015). Energy consumption and economic growth: A panel data aproach to OECD countries. *International Journal of Energy Science*, *5*(1), 1–5. doi:10.12783/ijes.2015.0501.01

Jäger, P., & Schmidt, T. (2016). The political economy of public investment when population is aging: A panel cointegration analysis. *European Journal of Political Economy*, *43*, 145–158. doi:10.1016/j.ejpoleco.2016.04.004

Jayaraman, T. K., Lau, L. S., & Ng, C. F. (2018). Role of Financial Sector Development as a Contingent Factor in the Remittances and Growth Nexus: A Panel Study of Pacific Island Countries. *Remittances Review*, *3*(1), 51–74. doi:10.33182/rr.v3i1.426

Jin, T., & Kim, J. (2018). What is better for mitigating carbon emissions–Renewable energy or nuclear energy? A panel data analysis. *Renewable & Sustainable Energy Reviews*, *91*, 464–471. doi:10.1016/j.rser.2018.04.022

Kais, S., & Mounir, B. M. (2017). Causal interactions between environmental degradation, renewable energy, nuclear energy and real GDP: A dynamic panel data approach. *Environment Systems & Decisions*, *37*(1), 51–67. doi:10.100710669-016-9619-0

Kao, C., & Chiang, M. H. (2001). On the estimation and inference of a cointegrated regression in panel data. In *Nonstationary panels, panel cointegration, and dynamic panels* (pp. 179–222). Emerald Group Publishing Limited.

Kapingura, F. M. (2018). Relationship between foreign capital flows, domestic investment and savings in the SADC region. *Development Southern Africa*, *35*(4), 554–568. doi:10.1080/0376835X.2018.1487279

Karanfil, F., & Li, Y. (2015). Electricity consumption and economic growth: Exploring panel-specific differences. *Energy Policy*, *82*, 264–277. doi:10.1016/j.enpol.2014.12.001

Ketenci, N. (2016). The Feldstein–Horioka Puzzle and structural breaks: Evidence from the largest countries of Asia. *Margin - the Journal of Applied Economic Research*, *10*(3), 337–354. doi:10.1177/0973801016645216

Khan, M. A., & Abbas, F. (2016). The dynamics of electricity demand in Pakistan: A panel cointegration analysis. *Renewable & Sustainable Energy Reviews*, *65*, 1159–1178. doi:10.1016/j.rser.2016.06.054

Kilic, C. (2015). Effects of Globalization on Economic Growth: Panel Data Analysis for Developing Countries. *Petroleum-Gas University of Ploiesti Bulletin, Technical Series, 67*(1).

Kirikkaleli, D., Sokri, A., Candemir, M., & Ertugrul, H. M. (2018). Panel cointegration: Long-run relationship between internet, electricity consumption and economic growth. Evidence from oecd countries. *Investigacion Economica*, *77*(303), 161–176. doi:10.22201/fe.01851667p.2018.303.64158

Kizilkaya, O., Ay, A., & Akar, G. (2016). Dynamic relationship among foreign direct investments, human capital, economic freedom and economic growth: Evidence from panel cointegration and panel causality analysis. *Theoretical & Applied Economics, 23*(3).

Ladu, M. G., & Meleddu, M. (2016). Productivity, Wage and Inflation Relationship for a Sample of Developed Countries: New Evidence from Panel Cointegration Tests with Multiple Structural Breaks. *International Journal of Applied Economics*, *13*, 15–31.

Lau, L. S., Choong, C. K., Ng, C. F., Liew, F. M., & Ching, S. L. (2018). Is nuclear energy clean? Revisit of Environmental Kuznets Curve hypothesis in OECD countries. *Economic Modelling*.

Li, H., Li, F., Shi, D., Yu, X., & Shen, J. (2018). Carbon Emission Intensity, Economic Development and Energy Factors in 19 G20 Countries: Empirical Analysis Based on a Heterogeneous Panel from 1990 to 2015. *Sustainability*, *10*(7), 2330. doi:10.3390u10072330

Li, S., & Zhou, C. (2019). What are the impacts of demographic structure on CO2 emissions? A regional analysis in China via heterogeneous panel estimates. *The Science of the Total Environment*, *650*, 2021–2031. doi:10.1016/j.scitotenv.2018.09.304 PMID:30290345

Liu, W. S., Agbola, F. W., & Dzator, J. A. (2016). The impact of FDI spillover effects on total factor productivity in the Chinese electronic industry: A panel data analysis. *Journal of the Asia Pacific Economy*, *21*(2), 217–234. doi:10.1080/13547860.2015.1137473

Liu, Y., Yan, B., & Zhou, Y. (2016). Urbanization, economic growth, and carbon dioxide emissions in China: A panel cointegration and causality analysis. *Journal of Geographical Sciences*, *26*(2), 131–152. doi:10.100711442-016-1259-2

Loganathan, N., Taha, R., Ahmad, N., & Subramaniam, T. (2017). Taxation, growth and the stock traded nexus in emerging Asian countries: Heterogeneous and semi-parametric panel estimates. *Economic research-. Ekonomska Istrazivanja*, *30*(1), 566–580. doi:10.1080/1331677X.2017.1305789

Lopez, L., & Weber, S. (2018). Testing for Granger causality in panel data. *The Stata Journal*, *17*(4), 972–984. doi:10.1177/1536867X1801700412

Lu, W. C. (2017). Greenhouse gas emissions, energy consumption and economic growth: A panel cointegration analysis for 16 Asian countries. *International Journal of Environmental Research and Public Health*, *14*(11), 1436. doi:10.3390/ijerph14111436 PMID:29165399

Lv, Z. (2019). Deepening or lessening? The effects of tourism on regional inequality. *Tourism Management*, *72*, 23–26. doi:10.1016/j.tourman.2018.11.009

Magazzino, C. (2018). Fiscal Sustainability in the EU. *Atlantic Economic Journal*, *46*(3), 297–311. doi:10.100711293-018-9588-4

Mahmoodi, M. (2017). The Relationship between economic growth, renewable energy, and CO2 emissions: Evidence from panel data approach. *International Journal of Energy Economics and Policy*, *7*(6), 96–102.

Mahmoodi, M., & Mahmoodi, E. (2018). Environmental quality, renewable energy, trade openness and economic growth: Evidence from two groups of developing countries. *Asian Journal of Water, Environment and Pollution*, *15*(2), 177–185. doi:10.3233/AJW-180030

Mansour, A., Musaad, H., Zhang Ya, B., & Ameer, W. (2017). The Long-Run Effect of Outward Foreign Direct Investment and Macroeconomic Variables on Domestic Investment: Evidence from World Major Economies Using Panel ARDL Approach. *JL Pol'y & Globalization*, *63*, 39.

Maroof, Z., Hussain, S., Jawad, M., & Naz, M. (2018). Determinants of industrial development: A panel analysis of South Asian economies. *Quality & Quantity*, 1–29.

Miljkovic, T., Miljkovic, D., & Maurer, K. (2018). Examining the impact on mortality arising from climate change: Important findings for the insurance industry. *European Actuarial Journal*, *8*(2), 363–381. doi:10.100713385-018-0178-2

Moreira, R. (2019). Inflation and real exchange rate and macroeconomic gaps: Causality for 50 emerging and developing countries. *Economic Bulletin*, *39*(1), 142–158.

Mosikari, T. J., Senosi, M. C., & Eita, J. H. (2016). Manufactured exports and economic growth in Southern African Development Community (SADC) region: A panel cointegration approach. *Acta Universitatis Danubius: Oeconomica*, *12*(5).

Moutinho, V., Varum, C., & Mota, J. (2018). The environment–growth dilemma: New evidence using a panel cointegration approach. *Journal of Environmental Economics and Policy*, *7*(2), 166–183. doi:10.1080/21606544.2017.1383312

Narayan, S. W., & Rehman, M. U. (2018). Portfolio Diversification Opportunities Within Emerging and Frontier Stock Markets: Evidence from Ten Asian Countries. *Buletin Ekonomi Moneter dan Perbankan, 21*(1), 1-22.

Nasre Esfahani, M., & Rasoulinezhad, E. (2015). Will be there new CO2 emitters in the future? Evidence of long-run panel co-integration for N-11 countries. *International Journal of Energy Economics and Policy*, *6*(3), 463–470.

Nasreen, S., & Anwar, S. (2018). How Financial Stability Affects Economic Development in South Asia: A Panel data Analysis. *European Online Journal of Natural and Social Sciences, 7*(1), 54.

Ndlovu, B., Faisa, F., Resatoglu, N. G., & Türsoy, T. (2018). The Impact Macroeconomic Variables on Stock Returns: A Case of the Johannesburg Stock Exchange. *Romanian Statistical Review*, (2).

Neuts, B. (2019). Tourism and urban economic growth: A panel analysis of German cities. *Tourism Economics*.

Ng, C. F., Choong, C. K., Ching, S. L., & Lau, L. S. (2019). The Impact of Electricity Production From Renewable And Non-Renewable Sources On Co2 Emissions: Evidence From OECD Countries. *International Journal Of Business And Society*, *20*(1), 365–382.

Nguyen, K. H., & Kakinaka, M. (2019). Renewable energy consumption, carbon emissions, and development stages: Some evidence from panel cointegration analysis. *Renewable Energy*, *132*, 1049–1057. doi:10.1016/j.renene.2018.08.069

Osman, M., Gachino, G., & Hoque, A. (2016). Electricity consumption and economic growth in the GCC countries: Panel data analysis. *Energy Policy*, *98*, 318–327. doi:10.1016/j.enpol.2016.07.050

Ozcan, B., & Ozturk, I. (2019). Renewable energy consumption-economic growth nexus in emerging countries: A bootstrap panel causality test. *Renewable & Sustainable Energy Reviews*, *104*, 30–37. doi:10.1016/j.rser.2019.01.020

Pedroni, P. (2004). Panel cointegration: Asymptotic and finite sample properties of pooled time series tests with an application to the PPP hypothesis. *Econometric Theory*, *20*(3), 597–625. doi:10.1017/S0266466604203073

Popescu, G. H., Mieila, M., Nica, E., & Andrei, J. V. (2018). The emergence of the effects and determinants of the energy paradigm changes on European Union economy. *Renewable & Sustainable Energy Reviews*, *81*, 768–774. doi:10.1016/j.rser.2017.08.055

Pradhan, R. P., Arvin, M. B., & Bahmani, S. (2018). Are innovation and financial development causative factors in economic growth? Evidence from a panel granger causality test. *Technological Forecasting and Social Change*, *132*, 130–142. doi:10.1016/j.techfore.2018.01.024

Pradhan, R. P., Mallik, G., & Bagchi, T. P. (2018). Information communication technology (ICT) infrastructure and economic growth: A causality evinced by cross-country panel data. *IIMB Management Review*, *30*(1), 91–103. doi:10.1016/j.iimb.2018.01.001

Rahim, M., Adam, P., Saenong, Z., Atmodjo, E., Rumbia, W. A., & Tamburaka, I. P. (2018). Causal Relationship between Electric Consumption and Economic Growth in South East Sulawesi. *International Journal of Energy Economics and Policy*, *8*(6), 29–34.

Rahimi, M., & Rad, A. A. (2017). Internet usage, electricity consumption and economic growth: Evidence from a panel of developing-8 countries. *International Journal of Energy Economics and Policy*, *7*(3), 152–156.

Rahman, M., & Mustafa, M. (2017). Financial deepening and stock market returns: Panel data analyses for selected developed and developing economies. *International Journal of Monetary Economics and Finance*, *10*(1), 96–109. doi:10.1504/IJMEF.2017.081287

Rahman, M. N., & Grewal, H. S. (2017). Foreign direct investment and international trade in BIMSTEC: Panel causality analysis. *Transnational Corporations Review*, *9*(2), 112–121. doi:10.1080/19186444.2017.1326720

Rahnama, A., Astaneh, H., & Hajian, M. (2019). The relationship between tourism and equality in income distribution in developed and developing countries: An application of Panel VAR model. *European Journal of Tourism Research*, *21*(21), 124–131.

Rasoulinezhad, E., & Kang, G. S. (2016). A panel data analysis of South Korea's trade with OPEC member countries: The gravity model approach. *Indian Economic Review*, *20*(2), 203–224.

Rasoulinezhad, E., & Saboori, B. (2018). Panel estimation for renewable and non-renewable energy consumption, economic growth, CO 2 emissions, the composite trade intensity, and financial openness of the commonwealth of independent states. *Environmental Science and Pollution Research International*, *25*(18), 17354–17370. doi:10.100711356-018-1827-3 PMID:29654460

Razak, M. I. M., Ridzuan, A. R., Masdek, N. R. N. M., Rasid, M. F. R. M., Ibrahim, Z., & Talib, A. H. (2017). Determinants of Environmental Quality in Selected Asia Pacific Countries Based on Panel Estimation. *Advanced Science Letters*, *23*(9), 9215–9219. doi:10.1166/asl.2017.10057

Rehman, M. U., Shah, S. M. A., & Hussain, J. G. (2019). Commonalities of Equity Market Fundamentals and Return Comovements: An Emerging and Frontier Market Perspective. *Revista Evidenciação Contábil & Finanças*, *7*(1), 133–151. doi:10.22478/ufpb.2318-1001.2019v7n1.37062

Rodriguez Garcia, V., Meyfroidt, P., & Gaspart, F. (2018). *Agricultural intensification and land use change: A panel cointegration approach to test induced intensification, land sparing and rebound-effect*. Academic Press.

Saeed, S., & Hassan, A. (2018). Inter-linkages between liquidity and stock returns: An empirical investigation through panel cointegration. *Pakistan Journal of Commerce and Social Sciences*, *12*(2), 617–637.

Saidi, K., & Mbarek, M. B. (2016). Nuclear energy, renewable energy, CO2 emissions, and economic growth for nine developed countries: Evidence from panel Granger causality tests. *Progress in Nuclear Energy*, *88*, 364–374. doi:10.1016/j.pnucene.2016.01.018

Salahuddin, M., Alam, K., & Ozturk, I. (2016). The effects of Internet usage and economic growth on CO2 emissions in OECD countries: A panel investigation. *Renewable & Sustainable Energy Reviews*, *62*, 1226–1235. doi:10.1016/j.rser.2016.04.018

Saleh, A. S., Assaf, A. G., Ihalanayake, R., & Lung, S. (2015). A panel cointegration analysis of the impact of tourism on economic growth: Evidence from the Middle East region. *International Journal of Tourism Research*, *17*(3), 209–220. doi:10.1002/jtr.1976

Saridakis, G., Mendoza, M. A., Muñoz Torres, R. I., & Glover, J. (2016). The relationship between self-employment and unemployment in the long-run: A panel cointegration approach allowing for breaks. *Journal of Economic Studies (Glasgow, Scotland)*, *43*(3), 358–379. doi:10.1108/JES-11-2013-0169

Sayari, N., Sari, R., & Hammoudeh, S. (2018). The impact of value added components of GDP and FDI on economic freedom in Europe. *Economic Systems*, *42*(2), 282–294. doi:10.1016/j.ecosys.2017.03.003

Sekmen, F., & Gokirmak, H. (2018). Causal relationship between internet use and economic development for selected Central Asian economies. *Theoretical and Applied Economics, 22*(616), 145-152.

Sezer, S., & Abasiz, T. (2016). The Effect Of Information And Communication Technologies On Economic Growth In Oecd Countries. *Annals-Economy Series*, *6*, 31–36.

Shafighi, N., Shaari, A. H., Gharleghi, B., Sarmidi, T., & Omar, K. (2016). Financial integration via panel cointegration approaches in ASEAN+ 5. *Journal of Economic Studies (Glasgow, Scotland)*, *43*(1), 2–15. doi:10.1108/JES-08-2014-0141

Sharif, A., Raza, S. A., Ozturk, I., & Afshan, S. (2019). The dynamic relationship of renewable and nonrenewable energy consumption with carbon emission: A global study with the application of heterogeneous panel estimations. *Renewable Energy*, *133*, 685–691. doi:10.1016/j.renene.2018.10.052

Siddiqui, A., & Rehman, A. U. (2017). The human capital and economic growth nexus: In East and South Asia. *Applied Economics*, *49*(28), 2697–2710. doi:10.1080/00036846.2016.1245841

Song, L., & Mi, J. (2016). Port infrastructure and regional economic growth in China: A Granger causality analysis. *Maritime Policy & Management*, *43*(4), 456–468. doi:10.1080/03088839.2015.1134831

Ssali, M. W., Du, J., Mensah, I. A., & Hongo, D. O. (2019). Investigating the nexus among environmental pollution, economic growth, energy use, and foreign direct investment in 6 selected sub-Saharan African countries. *Environmental Science and Pollution Research International*, 1–16. PMID:30796658

Tabassum, U., & Alam, S. (2018). Two way Panel Causality Analysis for Degree of Trade Openness and Size of City. *Journal of Basic and Applied Sciences*, *14*, 32–44. doi:10.6000/1927-5129.2018.14.06

Tiba, S., & Frikha, M. (2018). Africa Is Rich, Africans Are Poor! A Blessing or Curse: An Application of Cointegration Techniques. *Journal of the Knowledge Economy*, 1-26.

Tugcu, C. T. (2018). Panel Data Analysis in the Energy-Growth Nexus (EGN). In The Economics and Econometrics of the Energy-Growth Nexus (pp. 255-271). Academic Press.

Tuna, G., Göleç, N., & Tuna, V. E. (2017). The relationship between oil and stock prices: The case of developing and developed countries. *Theoretical & Applied Economics, 24*(4).

Tunay, K. B., Tunay, N., & Akhisar, İ. (2015). Interaction between Internet banking and bank performance: The case of Europe. *Procedia: Social and Behavioral Sciences*, *195*, 363–368. doi:10.1016/j.sbspro.2015.06.335

Tunay, K. B., & Yüksel, S. (2017). The relationship between corporate governance and foreign ownership of the banks in developing countries. *Contaduría y Administración*, *62*(5), 1627–1642. doi:10.1016/j.cya.2017.05.007

Tunay, N., Tunay, K. B., & Özataç, N. (2018). International Insurance Industry and Systemic Risk. In *Emerging Trends in Banking and Finance* (pp. 241–249). Cham: Springer. doi:10.1007/978-3-030-01784-2_15

Vidyarthi, H. (2015). Energy consumption and growth in South Asia: Evidence from a panel error correction model. *International Journal of Energy Sector Management*, *9*(3), 295–310. doi:10.1108/IJESM-10-2013-0002

Wang, S., Fang, C., Wang, Y., Huang, Y., & Ma, H. (2015). Quantifying the relationship between urban development intensity and carbon dioxide emissions using a panel data analysis. *Ecological Indicators*, *49*, 121–131. doi:10.1016/j.ecolind.2014.10.004

Wang, Y., Chen, L., & Kubota, J. (2016). The relationship between urbanization, energy use and carbon emissions: Evidence from a panel of Association of Southeast Asian Nations (ASEAN) countries. *Journal of Cleaner Production*, *112*, 1368–1374. doi:10.1016/j.jclepro.2015.06.041

Wang, Y., Kang, Y., Wang, J., & Xu, L. (2017). Panel estimation for the impacts of population-related factors on CO2 emissions: A regional analysis in China. *Ecological Indicators*, *78*, 322–330. doi:10.1016/j.ecolind.2017.03.032

Wang, Z., Xu, G., Wang, H., & Ren, J. (2019). Distributed energy system for sustainability transition: A comprehensive assessment under uncertainties based on interval multi-criteria decision making method by coupling interval DEMATEL and interval VIKOR. *Energy*, *169*, 750–761. doi:10.1016/j.energy.2018.12.105

Yu, C. P. (2016). Why are there always inconsistent answers to the relation between the PPI and CPI? Re-examination using Panel Data Analysis. *International Review of Accounting, Banking & Finance, 8*(1).

Yüksel, S. (2016a). Bankacılık Krizlerinin Erken Uyarı Sinyalleri: Türkiye Üzerine Bir Uygulama. *Akademisyen Kitabevi, 1*.

Yüksel, S. (2016b). Rusya Ekonomisinde Büyüme, Issizlik ve Enflasyon Arasindaki Nedensellik Iliskileri/The Causality Relationship Between Growth, Unemployment and Inflation in Russian Economy. *Finans Politik & Ekonomik Yorumlar*, *53*(614), 43.

Yüksel, S., Mukhtarov, S., & Mammadov, E. (2016). Comparing the efficiency of Turkish and Azerbaijani banks: An application with data envelopment analysis. *International Journal of Economics and Financial Issues*, *6*(3).

Yüksel, S., Mukhtarov, S., Mammadov, E., & Özsarı, M. (2018). Determinants of Profitability in the Banking Sector: An Analysis of Post-Soviet Countries. *Economies*, *6*(3), 41. doi:10.3390/economies6030041

Yüksel, S., & Oktar, S. (2017). *Okun yasasının farklı gelişme düzeyindeki ülkelere ilişkin ekonometrik analizi*. Academic Press.

Yuksel, S., & Zengin, S. (2017). Influencing factors of net interest margin in Turkish banking sector. *International Journal of Economics and Financial Issues*, *7*(1).

Zaghdoudi, T. (2017). Internet usage, renewable energy, electricity consumption and economic growth: Evidence from developed countries. *Economics Bulletin Access Econ*, *37*(3), 1612–1619.

Zaman, K., Abdullah, A., Khan, A., Nasir, M. R. M., Hamzah, T. A. A. T., & Hussain, S. (2016). Dynamic linkages among energy consumption, environment, health and wealth in BRICS countries: Green growth key to sustainable development. *Renewable & Sustainable Energy Reviews*, *56*, 1263–1271. doi:10.1016/j.rser.2015.12.010

Zaman, K., Moemen, M. A. E., & Islam, T. (2017). Dynamic linkages between tourism transportation expenditures, carbon dioxide emission, energy consumption and growth factors: Evidence from the transition economies. *Current Issues in Tourism*, *20*(16), 1720–1735. doi:10.1080/13683500.2015.1135107

Zaman, K., Shahbaz, M., Loganathan, N., & Raza, S. A. (2016). Tourism development, energy consumption and Environmental Kuznets Curve: Trivariate analysis in the panel of developed and developing countries. *Tourism Management*, *54*, 275–283. doi:10.1016/j.tourman.2015.12.001

Zhang, C., & Zhou, X. (2016). Does foreign direct investment lead to lower CO2 emissions? Evidence from a regional analysis in China. *Renewable & Sustainable Energy Reviews*, *58*, 943–951. doi:10.1016/j.rser.2015.12.226

# APPENDIX

*Table 12. Inflation and Central Bank's interest rates of E7 economies*

| Date | Brazil | | China | | India | | Indonesia | | Mexico | | Russia | | Turkey | |
|---|---|---|---|---|---|---|---|---|---|---|---|---|---|---|
| | Inflation | Interest | Inflation | Interest | Inflation | Interest | Inflation | Interest | Inflation | Interest | Inflation | Interest | Inflation | Interest |
| 1996-01 | 21.97 | 33.93 | 9.00 | 12.06 | 11.08 | 12.00 | 9.00 | 12.75 | 51.72 | 8.55 | 104.50 | 160.00 | 78.11 | 48.00 |
| 1996-02 | 21.99 | 34.38 | 9.30 | 12.06 | 11.12 | 12.00 | 8.59 | 12.75 | 48.95 | 9.29 | 89.34 | 120.00 | 77.49 | 48.00 |
| 1996-03 | 20.55 | 29.83 | 9.80 | 12.06 | 9.69 | 12.00 | 8.87 | 12.75 | 43.75 | 10.03 | 78.66 | 120.00 | 79.34 | 48.00 |
| 1996-04 | 19.17 | 25.97 | 9.70 | 12.06 | 8.20 | 12.00 | 9.83 | 12.75 | 36.93 | 10.77 | 68.27 | 120.00 | 80.83 | 48.00 |
| 1996-05 | 17.49 | 28.75 | 8.90 | 10.98 | 8.38 | 12.00 | 9.33 | 12.75 | 33.83 | 11.51 | 58.40 | 120.00 | 82.93 | 46.00 |
| 1996-06 | 16.26 | 24.39 | 8.60 | 10.98 | 7.38 | 12.00 | 8.82 | 12.75 | 31.82 | 12.25 | 50.25 | 120.00 | 82.86 | 46.00 |
| 1996-07 | 14.84 | 22.90 | 8.30 | 10.98 | 7.37 | 12.00 | 8.31 | 12.75 | 31.03 | 12.99 | 43.60 | 110.00 | 81.20 | 46.00 |
| 1996-08 | 14.21 | 24.06 | 8.10 | 10.08 | 6.97 | 12.00 | 8.89 | 12.75 | 30.60 | 13.73 | 37.05 | 80.00 | 82.66 | 44.00 |
| 1996-09 | 13.26 | 25.05 | 7.40 | 10.08 | 6.82 | 12.00 | 8.52 | 12.75 | 30.00 | 14.47 | 31.63 | 80.00 | 79.32 | 44.00 |
| 1996-10 | 12.02 | 22.95 | 7.00 | 10.08 | 6.52 | 12.00 | 8.46 | 12.75 | 28.97 | 15.21 | 27.21 | 60.00 | 79.59 | 48.00 |
| 1996-11 | 10.75 | 24.90 | 6.90 | 10.08 | 6.54 | 12.00 | 8.72 | 12.75 | 27.77 | 15.95 | 23.95 | 60.00 | 80.38 | 48.00 |
| 1996-12 | 9.56 | 23.00 | 7.00 | 10.08 | 6.03 | 12.00 | 10.41 | 12.75 | 27.70 | 16.69 | 21.81 | 48.00 | 79.76 | 48.00 |

*continues on following page*

*Table 12. Continued*

| Date | Brazil | | China | | India | | Indonesia | | Mexico | | Russia | | Turkey | |
|---|---|---|---|---|---|---|---|---|---|---|---|---|---|---|
| | Inflation | Interest | Inflation | Interest | Inflation | Interest | Inflation | Interest | Inflation | Interest | Inflation | Interest | Inflation | Interest |
| 1997-01 | 9.39 | 21.30 | 5.90 | 10.08 | 4.61 | 12.00 | 11.11 | 12.75 | 26.44 | 17.43 | 19.74 | 48.00 | 75.72 | 48.00 |
| 1997-02 | 8.82 | 25.92 | 5.60 | 10.08 | 3.99 | 12.00 | 10.76 | 12.75 | 25.64 | 18.17 | 18.28 | 42.00 | 77.65 | 46.00 |
| 1997-03 | 8.99 | 23.76 | 4.00 | 10.08 | 4.74 | 12.00 | 10.03 | 12.75 | 24.46 | 18.91 | 16.71 | 42.00 | 77.30 | 46.00 |
| 1997-04 | 8.58 | 20.70 | 3.20 | 10.08 | 4.88 | 11.00 | 9.26 | 12.75 | 22.33 | 19.65 | 15.34 | 36.00 | 77.16 | 46.00 |
| 1997-05 | 7.71 | 21.84 | 2.80 | 10.08 | 4.50 | 11.00 | 7.32 | 12.75 | 21.23 | 20.39 | 14.59 | 36.00 | 77.46 | 44.00 |
| 1997-06 | 7.02 | 20.70 | 2.80 | 10.08 | 5.24 | 10.00 | 6.61 | 12.75 | 20.35 | 21.13 | 14.51 | 24.00 | 78.05 | 44.00 |
| 1997-07 | 6.08 | 18.74 | 2.70 | 10.08 | 5.37 | 10.00 | 5.60 | 12.75 | 19.70 | 21.87 | 14.75 | 24.00 | 85.23 | 48.00 |
| 1997-08 | 5.59 | 20.70 | 1.90 | 10.08 | 6.40 | 10.00 | 4.66 | 12.75 | 19.18 | 22.61 | 14.83 | 24.00 | 87.04 | 48.00 |
| 1997-09 | 5.50 | 19.67 | 1.80 | 10.08 | 7.33 | 10.00 | 4.94 | 12.75 | 18.76 | 23.35 | 14.11 | 24.00 | 89.86 | 48.00 |
| 1997-10 | 5.42 | 38.98 | 1.50 | 8.64 | 8.40 | 9.00 | 5.49 | 12.75 | 18.24 | 24.09 | 12.95 | 21.00 | 93.16 | 48.00 |
| 1997-11 | 5.27 | 46.02 | 1.10 | 8.64 | 8.79 | 9.00 | 4.87 | 12.75 | 17.77 | 24.83 | 11.54 | 28.00 | 95.82 | 46.00 |
| 1997-12 | 5.22 | 38.74 | 0.40 | 8.64 | 10.32 | 9.00 | 6.29 | 12.75 | 15.72 | 25.57 | 11.03 | 28.00 | 99.09 | 46.00 |

*continues on following page*

*Table 12. Continued*

| Date | Brazil | | China | | India | | Indonesia | | Mexico | | Russia | | Turkey | |
|---|---|---|---|---|---|---|---|---|---|---|---|---|---|---|
| | Inflation | Interest | Inflation | Interest | Inflation | Interest | Inflation | Interest | Inflation | Interest | Inflation | Interest | Inflation | Interest |
| 1998-01 | 4.73 | 34.50 | 0.30 | 8.64 | 16.24 | 11.00 | 9.71 | 12.75 | 15.27 | 26.31 | 10.13 | 28.00 | 101.62 | 46.00 |
| 1998-02 | 4.69 | 34.50 | -1.00 | 8.64 | 30.00 | 11.00 | 9.14 | 12.75 | 15.35 | 27.05 | 9.43 | 39.00 | 99.25 | 44.00 |
| 1998-03 | 4.52 | 28.00 | 0.70 | 7.92 | 36.83 | 10.50 | 8.26 | 12.75 | 15.27 | 27.79 | 8.57 | 30.00 | 97.18 | 44.00 |
| 1998-04 | 3.85 | 23.25 | -0.30 | 7.92 | 42.66 | 9.00 | 8.19 | 12.75 | 15.10 | 28.53 | 7.95 | 30.00 | 93.57 | 48.00 |
| 1998-05 | 3.95 | 21.75 | -1.00 | 7.92 | 49.66 | 9.00 | 10.51 | 12.75 | 14.97 | 29.27 | 7.48 | 150.00 | 91.37 | 48.00 |
| 1998-06 | 3.41 | 21.00 | -1.30 | 7.92 | 56.66 | 9.00 | 12.39 | 12.75 | 15.31 | 30.01 | 6.40 | 80.00 | 90.55 | 48.00 |
| 1998-07 | 3.06 | 19.75 | -1.40 | 6.93 | 68.73 | 9.00 | 14.80 | 12.75 | 15.41 | 30.75 | 5.59 | 60.00 | 85.35 | 48.00 |
| 1998-08 | 2.55 | 19.75 | -1.40 | 6.93 | 77.70 | 9.00 | 15.04 | 12.75 | 15.50 | 31.49 | 9.62 | 60.00 | 81.43 | 46.00 |
| 1998-09 | 2.27 | 19.00 | -1.50 | 6.93 | 82.42 | 9.00 | 16.34 | 12.75 | 15.92 | 32.23 | 52.21 | 60.00 | 80.43 | 46.00 |
| 1998-10 | 2.05 | 19.00 | -1.10 | 6.93 | 79.44 | 9.00 | 18.63 | 12.75 | 16.65 | 32.97 | 58.85 | 60.00 | 76.64 | 46.00 |
| 1998-11 | 1.76 | 19.00 | -1.20 | 6.93 | 78.16 | 9.00 | 19.67 | 12.75 | 17.41 | 34.37 | 66.84 | 60.00 | 72.77 | 44.00 |
| 1998-12 | 1.65 | 29.00 | -1.00 | 6.39 | 77.61 | 9.00 | 15.32 | 12.75 | 18.61 | 33.14 | 84.44 | 60.00 | 69.73 | 44.00 |

*continues on following page*

*Table 12. Continued*

| Date | Brazil | | China | | India | | Indonesia | | Mexico | | Russia | | Turkey | |
|---|---|---|---|---|---|---|---|---|---|---|---|---|---|---|
| | Inflation | Interest | Inflation | Interest | Inflation | Interest | Inflation | Interest | Inflation | Interest | Inflation | Interest | Inflation | Interest |
| 1999-01 | 1.65 | 25.00 | -1.20 | 6.39 | 70.64 | 9.00 | 9.38 | 12.75 | 19.02 | 35.85 | 96.92 | 60.00 | 65.90 | 48.00 |
| 1999-02 | 2.24 | 25.00 | -1.30 | 6.39 | 53.41 | 9.00 | 8.64 | 12.75 | 18.54 | 28.46 | 103.24 | 60.00 | 63.93 | 48.00 |
| 1999-03 | 3.02 | 42.00 | -1.80 | 6.39 | 45.42 | 8.00 | 8.95 | 12.75 | 18.26 | 22.96 | 107.58 | 60.00 | 63.54 | 48.00 |
| 1999-04 | 3.35 | 32.00 | -1.30 | 6.39 | 37.97 | 8.00 | 8.36 | 12.75 | 18.23 | 20.24 | 113.06 | 60.00 | 63.85 | 48.00 |
| 1999-05 | 3.14 | 23.50 | -2.20 | 6.39 | 30.74 | 8.00 | 7.71 | 12.75 | 18.01 | 21.78 | 116.71 | 60.00 | 62.97 | 46.00 |
| 1999-06 | 3.32 | 21.00 | -2.68 | 5.85 | 24.53 | 8.00 | 5.26 | 12.75 | 17.39 | 21.01 | 120.67 | 55.00 | 64.27 | 46.00 |
| 1999-07 | 4.57 | 19.50 | -1.40 | 5.85 | 13.50 | 8.00 | 3.16 | 12.75 | 17.04 | 21.90 | 126.51 | 55.00 | 65.00 | 46.00 |
| 1999-08 | 5.69 | 19.50 | -1.70 | 5.85 | 5.78 | 8.00 | 3.15 | 12.75 | 16.58 | 19.51 | 121.03 | 55.00 | 65.40 | 44.00 |
| 1999-09 | 6.25 | 19.00 | -0.80 | 5.85 | 1.25 | 8.00 | 2.14 | 12.75 | 15.83 | 18.90 | 62.03 | 55.00 | 64.27 | 44.00 |
| 1999-10 | 7.50 | 19.00 | -0.60 | 5.85 | 1.57 | 8.00 | 0.92 | 12.75 | 14.91 | 17.78 | 57.12 | 55.00 | 64.70 | 48.00 |
| 1999-11 | 8.65 | 19.00 | -0.90 | 5.85 | 1.59 | 8.00 | 0.00 | 12.75 | 13.92 | 19.97 | 50.52 | 55.00 | 64.55 | 48.00 |
| 1999-12 | 8.94 | 19.00 | -1.00 | 5.85 | 1.93 | 8.00 | 0.47 | 12.75 | 12.32 | 18.39 | 36.56 | 55.00 | 68.79 | 48.00 |

*continues on following page*

*Table 12. Continued*

| Date | Brazil | | China | | India | | Indonesia | | Mexico | | Russia | | Turkey | |
|---|---|---|---|---|---|---|---|---|---|---|---|---|---|---|
| | **Inflation** | **Interest** | **Inflation** | **Interest** | **Inflation** | **Interest** | **Inflation** | **Interest** | **Inflation** | **Interest** | **Inflation** | **Interest** | **Inflation** | **Interest** |
| 2000-01 | 8.85 | 19.00 | -0.20 | 5.85 | 0.29 | 8.00 | 2.62 | 12.75 | 11.02 | 19.25 | 28.93 | 45.00 | 68.88 | 48.00 |
| 2000-02 | 7.86 | 19.00 | 0.70 | 5.85 | -0.90 | 8.00 | 3.61 | 12.75 | 10.52 | 17.38 | 25.11 | 45.00 | 69.75 | 46.00 |
| 2000-03 | 6.92 | 18.50 | -0.20 | 5.85 | -1.17 | 8.00 | 4.83 | 12.75 | 10.11 | 13.87 | 22.49 | 33.00 | 67.90 | 46.00 |
| 2000-04 | 6.77 | 18.50 | -0.30 | 5.85 | 0.06 | 7.00 | 5.54 | 12.75 | 9.73 | 14.46 | 19.95 | 33.00 | 63.82 | 46.00 |
| 2000-05 | 6.47 | 18.50 | 0.10 | 5.85 | 1.20 | 7.00 | 5.01 | 12.75 | 9.48 | 16.23 | 19.40 | 33.00 | 62.67 | 44.00 |
| 2000-06 | 6.51 | 17.50 | 0.50 | 5.85 | 2.03 | 7.00 | 5.24 | 12.75 | 9.41 | 18.06 | 20.15 | 33.00 | 58.62 | 44.00 |
| 2000-07 | 7.06 | 16.50 | 0.50 | 5.85 | 4.46 | 8.00 | 4.95 | 12.75 | 9.12 | 13.75 | 18.94 | 28.00 | 56.21 | 48.00 |
| 2000-08 | 7.86 | 16.50 | 0.30 | 5.85 | 5.96 | 8.00 | 3.99 | 12.75 | 9.10 | 15.51 | 18.73 | 28.00 | 53.17 | 48.00 |
| 2000-09 | 7.77 | 16.50 | 0.00 | 5.85 | 6.64 | 8.00 | 3.50 | 12.75 | 8.85 | 15.89 | 18.54 | 28.00 | 48.96 | 48.00 |
| 2000-10 | 6.65 | 16.50 | 0.00 | 5.85 | 7.81 | 8.00 | 2.75 | 12.75 | 8.91 | 17.09 | 19.41 | 28.00 | 44.44 | 48.00 |
| 2000-11 | 5.99 | 16.50 | 1.30 | 5.85 | 9.13 | 8.00 | 2.74 | 12.75 | 8.87 | 17.90 | 19.75 | 25.00 | 43.76 | 46.00 |
| 2000-12 | 5.97 | 15.75 | 0.40 | 5.85 | 9.34 | 8.00 | 3.48 | 12.75 | 8.96 | 18.79 | 20.20 | 25.00 | 39.03 | 46.00 |

*continues on following page*

*Table 12. Continued*

| Date | Brazil | | China | | India | | Indonesia | | Mexico | | Russia | | Turkey | |
|---|---|---|---|---|---|---|---|---|---|---|---|---|---|---|
| | Inflation | Interest | Inflation | Interest | Inflation | Interest | Inflation | Interest | Inflation | Interest | Inflation | Interest | Inflation | Interest |
| 2001-01 | 5.92 | 15.25 | 1.20 | 5.85 | 8.28 | 8.00 | 3.25 | 12.75 | 8.11 | 17.72 | 20.71 | 25.00 | 35.92 | 46.00 |
| 2001-02 | 6.27 | 15.25 | 0.00 | 5.85 | 9.12 | 7.50 | 3.02 | 12.75 | 7.09 | 16.86 | 22.19 | 25.00 | 33.42 | 44.00 |
| 2001-03 | 6.44 | 15.75 | 0.80 | 5.85 | 10.61 | 7.00 | 2.53 | 12.75 | 7.17 | 16.32 | 23.67 | 25.00 | 37.51 | 44.00 |
| 2001-04 | 6.61 | 16.25 | 1.60 | 5.85 | 10.51 | 8.75 | 2.28 | 12.75 | 7.11 | 15.00 | 24.77 | 25.00 | 48.27 | 48.00 |
| 2001-05 | 7.04 | 16.75 | 1.70 | 5.85 | 10.83 | 8.75 | 2.50 | 12.75 | 6.95 | 11.47 | 24.81 | 25.00 | 52.39 | 48.00 |
| 2001-06 | 7.35 | 18.25 | 1.40 | 5.85 | 12.12 | 8.50 | 3.39 | 12.75 | 6.57 | 10.25 | 23.68 | 25.00 | 56.10 | 48.00 |
| 2001-07 | 7.05 | 19.00 | 1.50 | 5.85 | 13.03 | 8.50 | 4.04 | 12.75 | 5.88 | 9.27 | 22.05 | 25.00 | 56.33 | 48.00 |
| 2001-08 | 6.41 | 19.00 | 1.00 | 5.85 | 12.24 | 8.50 | 5.19 | 12.75 | 5.93 | 8.94 | 20.88 | 25.00 | 57.50 | 46.00 |
| 2001-09 | 6.46 | 19.00 | -0.10 | 5.85 | 13.01 | 8.50 | 4.73 | 12.75 | 6.14 | 10.36 | 20.02 | 25.00 | 61.80 | 46.00 |
| 2001-10 | 7.19 | 19.00 | 0.20 | 5.85 | 12.47 | 8.50 | 4.23 | 12.75 | 5.89 | 8.08 | 18.82 | 25.00 | 66.47 | 46.00 |
| 2001-11 | 7.61 | 19.00 | -0.30 | 5.85 | 12.91 | 8.50 | 4.89 | 12.75 | 5.39 | 7.24 | 18.63 | 25.00 | 67.29 | 44.00 |
| 2001-12 | 7.67 | 19.00 | -0.30 | 5.85 | 12.54 | 8.50 | 5.16 | 12.75 | 4.40 | 8.04 | 18.58 | 25.00 | 68.53 | 44.00 |

*continues on following page*

*Table 12. Continued*

| Date | Brazil | | China | | India | | Indonesia | | Mexico | | Russia | | Turkey | |
|---|---|---|---|---|---|---|---|---|---|---|---|---|---|---|
| | Inflation | Interest | Inflation | Interest | Inflation | Interest | Inflation | Interest | Inflation | Interest | Inflation | Interest | Inflation | Interest |
| 2002-01 | 7.62 | 19.00 | -1.00 | 5.85 | 14.56 | 8.50 | 4.94 | 12.75 | 4.79 | 8.08 | 18.96 | 25.00 | 73.16 | 44.00 |
| 2002-02 | 7.51 | 18.75 | 0.00 | 5.31 | 14.88 | 8.50 | 5.19 | 12.75 | 4.79 | 7.63 | 17.66 | 25.00 | 73.08 | 57.00 |
| 2002-03 | 7.75 | 18.50 | -0.80 | 5.31 | 14.21 | 8.00 | 5.17 | 12.75 | 4.66 | 7.11 | 16.76 | 25.00 | 65.11 | 54.00 |
| 2002-04 | 7.98 | 18.50 | -1.30 | 5.31 | 13.44 | 8.00 | 4.69 | 12.75 | 4.70 | 5.47 | 16.04 | 23.00 | 52.72 | 48.00 |
| 2002-05 | 7.77 | 18.50 | -1.10 | 5.31 | 13.09 | 8.00 | 4.66 | 12.75 | 4.68 | 7.33 | 15.94 | 23.00 | 46.22 | 48.00 |
| 2002-06 | 7.66 | 18.50 | -0.80 | 5.31 | 11.57 | 8.00 | 4.16 | 12.75 | 4.94 | 8.13 | 14.69 | 23.00 | 42.60 | 48.00 |
| 2002-07 | 7.51 | 18.00 | -0.90 | 5.31 | 10.02 | 8.00 | 3.89 | 12.75 | 5.51 | 5.37 | 15.00 | 23.00 | 41.28 | 48.00 |
| 2002-08 | 7.46 | 18.00 | -0.70 | 5.31 | 10.57 | 8.00 | 3.86 | 12.75 | 5.29 | 6.64 | 15.09 | 21.00 | 40.24 | 46.00 |
| 2002-09 | 7.93 | 18.00 | -0.70 | 5.31 | 10.54 | 8.00 | 4.30 | 12.75 | 4.95 | 8.05 | 14.86 | 21.00 | 37.05 | 46.00 |
| 2002-10 | 8.45 | 21.00 | -0.80 | 5.31 | 10.34 | 8.00 | 4.06 | 12.75 | 4.94 | 7.72 | 14.84 | 21.00 | 33.45 | 46.00 |
| 2002-11 | 10.93 | 22.00 | -0.70 | 5.31 | 10.40 | 7.50 | 3.60 | 12.75 | 5.39 | 7.00 | 15.12 | 21.00 | 31.77 | 44.00 |
| 2002-12 | 12.53 | 25.00 | -0.40 | 5.31 | 9.92 | 7.50 | 3.20 | 12.75 | 5.70 | 8.25 | 15.06 | 21.00 | 29.75 | 44.00 |

*continues on following page*

*Table 12. Continued*

| Date | Brazil | | China | | India | | Indonesia | | Mexico | | Russia | | Turkey | |
|---|---|---|---|---|---|---|---|---|---|---|---|---|---|---|
| | Inflation | Interest | Inflation | Interest | Inflation | Interest | Inflation | Interest | Inflation | Interest | Inflation | Interest | Inflation | Interest |
| 2003-01 | 14.47 | 25.50 | 0.40 | 5.31 | 8.66 | 7.50 | 3.43 | 12.75 | 5.16 | 9.01 | 14.29 | 21.00 | 26.38 | 44.00 |
| 2003-02 | 15.85 | 26.50 | 0.20 | 5.31 | 7.64 | 7.50 | 3.86 | 12.75 | 5.52 | 9.27 | 14.82 | 18.00 | 26.12 | 44.00 |
| 2003-03 | 16.57 | 26.50 | 0.90 | 5.31 | 7.11 | 7.00 | 4.06 | 12.75 | 5.64 | 8.92 | 14.78 | 18.00 | 27.08 | 44.00 |
| 2003-04 | 16.77 | 26.50 | 1.00 | 5.31 | 7.63 | 7.00 | 5.12 | 12.75 | 5.25 | 5.85 | 14.62 | 18.00 | 25.76 | 41.00 |
| 2003-05 | 17.24 | 26.50 | 0.70 | 5.31 | 7.07 | 7.00 | 4.66 | 12.75 | 4.70 | 4.79 | 13.62 | 18.00 | 26.23 | 41.00 |
| 2003-06 | 16.57 | 26.00 | 0.30 | 5.31 | 6.94 | 7.00 | 4.41 | 12.75 | 4.27 | 4.36 | 13.93 | 16.00 | 25.60 | 38.00 |
| 2003-07 | 15.43 | 24.50 | 0.50 | 5.31 | 6.20 | 7.00 | 4.16 | 12.75 | 4.13 | 4.07 | 13.91 | 16.00 | 23.58 | 35.00 |
| 2003-08 | 15.07 | 22.00 | 0.90 | 5.31 | 6.59 | 7.00 | 3.10 | 12.75 | 4.04 | 4.57 | 13.35 | 16.00 | 21.13 | 32.00 |
| 2003-09 | 15.14 | 20.00 | 1.10 | 5.31 | 6.34 | 7.00 | 2.89 | 12.75 | 4.04 | 4.30 | 13.28 | 16.00 | 18.64 | 29.00 |
| 2003-10 | 13.98 | 19.00 | 1.80 | 5.31 | 6.41 | 7.00 | 3.29 | 12.75 | 3.96 | 4.73 | 13.20 | 16.00 | 15.93 | 26.00 |
| 2003-11 | 11.02 | 17.50 | 3.00 | 5.31 | 5.53 | 7.00 | 3.07 | 12.75 | 3.98 | 6.26 | 12.48 | 16.00 | 14.08 | 26.00 |
| 2003-12 | 9.30 | 16.50 | 3.20 | 5.31 | 5.16 | 7.00 | 3.72 | 12.75 | 3.98 | 6.12 | 11.99 | 16.00 | 12.71 | 26.00 |

*continues on following page*

*Table 12. Continued*

| Date | Brazil | | China | | India | | Indonesia | | Mexico | | Russia | | Turkey | |
|---|---|---|---|---|---|---|---|---|---|---|---|---|---|---|
| | Inflation | Interest | Inflation | Interest | Inflation | Interest | Inflation | Interest | Inflation | Interest | Inflation | Interest | Inflation | Interest |
| 2004-01 | 7.71 | 16.50 | 3.20 | 5.31 | 4.84 | 7.00 | 4.35 | 12.75 | 4.20 | 5.20 | 11.28 | 14.00 | 10.59 | 26.00 |
| 2004-02 | 6.69 | 16.50 | 2.10 | 5.31 | 4.55 | 7.00 | 4.13 | 12.75 | 4.53 | 6.71 | 10.58 | 14.00 | 9.48 | 24.00 |
| 2004-03 | 5.89 | 16.25 | 3.00 | 5.31 | 5.13 | 6.00 | 3.49 | 12.75 | 4.23 | 6.13 | 10.25 | 14.00 | 8.40 | 22.00 |
| 2004-04 | 5.26 | 16.00 | 3.80 | 5.31 | 5.87 | 6.00 | 2.23 | 12.75 | 4.21 | 6.26 | 10.22 | 14.00 | 7.87 | 22.00 |
| 2004-05 | 5.15 | 16.00 | 4.40 | 5.31 | 6.50 | 6.00 | 2.83 | 12.75 | 4.29 | 6.35 | 10.15 | 14.00 | 7.31 | 22.00 |
| 2004-06 | 6.06 | 16.00 | 5.00 | 5.31 | 6.78 | 6.00 | 3.02 | 12.75 | 4.37 | 6.53 | 10.13 | 13.00 | 7.08 | 22.00 |
| 2004-07 | 6.81 | 16.00 | 5.30 | 5.31 | 7.26 | 6.00 | 3.19 | 12.75 | 4.49 | 6.76 | 10.36 | 13.00 | 7.80 | 22.00 |
| 2004-08 | 7.18 | 16.00 | 5.30 | 5.31 | 6.63 | 6.00 | 4.61 | 12.75 | 4.82 | 7.17 | 11.28 | 13.00 | 8.44 | 22.00 |
| 2004-09 | 6.70 | 16.25 | 5.20 | 5.31 | 6.24 | 6.00 | 4.81 | 12.75 | 5.06 | 7.62 | 11.38 | 13.00 | 8.01 | 20.00 |
| 2004-10 | 6.86 | 16.75 | 4.30 | 5.58 | 6.21 | 6.00 | 4.57 | 12.75 | 5.40 | 7.81 | 11.53 | 13.00 | 9.43 | 20.00 |
| 2004-11 | 7.24 | 17.25 | 2.80 | 5.58 | 6.23 | 6.00 | 4.17 | 12.75 | 5.43 | 8.27 | 11.70 | 13.00 | 9.47 | 20.00 |
| 2004-12 | 7.60 | 17.75 | 2.40 | 5.58 | 6.47 | 6.00 | 3.78 | 12.75 | 5.19 | 8.75 | 11.74 | 13.00 | 9.35 | 18.00 |

*continues on following page*

Table 12. Continued

| Date | Brazil | | China | | India | | Indonesia | | Mexico | | Russia | | Turkey | |
|---|---|---|---|---|---|---|---|---|---|---|---|---|---|---|
| | Inflation | Interest | Inflation | Interest | Inflation | Interest | Inflation | Interest | Inflation | Interest | Inflation | Interest | Inflation | Interest |
| 2005-01 | 7.41 | 18.25 | 1.90 | 5.58 | 7.23 | 6.00 | 4.37 | 12.75 | 4.54 | 8.82 | 12.70 | 13.00 | 9.24 | 17.00 |
| 2005-02 | 7.39 | 18.75 | 3.90 | 5.58 | 7.16 | 6.00 | 4.17 | 12.75 | 4.27 | 9.21 | 12.96 | 13.00 | 8.69 | 16.50 |
| 2005-03 | 7.54 | 19.25 | 2.70 | 5.58 | 8.85 | 6.00 | 4.17 | 12.75 | 4.39 | 9.51 | 13.63 | 13.00 | 7.94 | 15.50 |
| 2005-04 | 8.07 | 19.50 | 1.80 | 5.58 | 8.13 | 6.00 | 4.96 | 12.75 | 4.60 | 9.60 | 13.77 | 13.00 | 8.18 | 15.00 |
| 2005-05 | 8.05 | 19.75 | 1.80 | 5.58 | 7.40 | 6.00 | 3.74 | 12.75 | 4.60 | 9.75 | 13.84 | 13.00 | 8.70 | 14.50 |
| 2005-06 | 7.27 | 19.75 | 1.60 | 5.58 | 7.46 | 6.00 | 3.32 | 12.75 | 4.33 | 9.76 | 13.68 | 13.00 | 8.95 | 14.25 |
| 2005-07 | 6.57 | 19.75 | 1.80 | 5.58 | 7.81 | 6.00 | 4.06 | 8.50 | 4.47 | 9.75 | 13.16 | 13.00 | 7.82 | 14.25 |
| 2005-08 | 6.02 | 19.75 | 1.30 | 5.58 | 8.32 | 6.00 | 3.45 | 8.75 | 3.95 | 9.51 | 12.53 | 13.00 | 7.91 | 14.25 |
| 2005-09 | 6.04 | 19.50 | 0.90 | 5.58 | 9.06 | 6.00 | 3.63 | 10.00 | 3.51 | 9.26 | 12.33 | 13.00 | 7.99 | 14.25 |
| 2005-10 | 6.36 | 19.00 | 1.20 | 5.58 | 17.93 | 6.25 | 4.18 | 11.00 | 3.05 | 9.01 | 11.68 | 13.00 | 7.52 | 14.00 |
| 2005-11 | 6.22 | 18.50 | 1.30 | 5.58 | 18.35 | 6.25 | 5.33 | 12.25 | 2.91 | 8.76 | 11.27 | 13.00 | 7.61 | 13.75 |
| 2005-12 | 5.69 | 18.00 | 1.60 | 5.58 | 17.08 | 6.25 | 5.57 | 12.75 | 3.33 | 8.27 | 10.91 | 12.00 | 7.72 | 13.50 |

*continues on following page*

*Table 12. Continued*

| Date | Brazil | | China | | India | | Indonesia | | Mexico | | Russia | | Turkey | |
|---|---|---|---|---|---|---|---|---|---|---|---|---|---|---|
| | Inflation | Interest | Inflation | Interest | Inflation | Interest | Inflation | Interest | Inflation | Interest | Inflation | Interest | Inflation | Interest |
| 2006-01 | 5.70 | 17.25 | 1.90 | 5.58 | 17.06 | 6.50 | 4.37 | 12.75 | 3.94 | 7.77 | 10.71 | 12.00 | 7.93 | 13.50 |
| 2006-02 | 5.51 | 17.25 | 0.90 | 5.58 | 17.94 | 6.50 | 4.57 | 12.75 | 3.75 | 7.51 | 11.18 | 12.00 | 8.15 | 13.50 |
| 2006-03 | 5.32 | 16.50 | 0.80 | 5.58 | 15.73 | 6.50 | 4.57 | 12.75 | 3.41 | 7.27 | 10.61 | 12.00 | 8.16 | 13.50 |
| 2006-04 | 4.63 | 15.75 | 1.20 | 5.85 | 15.40 | 6.50 | 4.65 | 12.75 | 3.20 | 7.05 | 9.77 | 12.00 | 8.83 | 13.25 |
| 2006-05 | 4.23 | 15.75 | 1.40 | 5.85 | 15.59 | 6.50 | 5.93 | 12.50 | 3.00 | 7.02 | 9.42 | 12.00 | 9.86 | 13.25 |
| 2006-06 | 4.03 | 15.25 | 1.50 | 5.85 | 15.54 | 6.75 | 7.27 | 12.50 | 3.18 | 7.03 | 9.03 | 11.50 | 10.12 | 17.25 |
| 2006-07 | 3.97 | 14.75 | 1.00 | 5.85 | 15.16 | 7.00 | 6.33 | 12.25 | 3.06 | 7.03 | 9.26 | 11.50 | 11.69 | 17.50 |
| 2006-08 | 3.84 | 14.25 | 1.30 | 6.12 | 14.90 | 7.00 | 5.94 | 11.75 | 3.47 | 7.03 | 9.62 | 11.50 | 10.26 | 17.50 |
| 2006-09 | 3.70 | 14.25 | 1.50 | 6.12 | 14.56 | 7.00 | 6.40 | 11.25 | 4.09 | 7.05 | 9.44 | 11.50 | 10.55 | 17.50 |
| 2006-10 | 3.26 | 13.75 | 1.40 | 6.12 | 6.29 | 7.25 | 6.92 | 10.75 | 4.29 | 7.04 | 9.15 | 11.00 | 9.98 | 17.50 |
| 2006-11 | 3.02 | 13.25 | 1.90 | 6.12 | 5.27 | 7.25 | 5.95 | 10.25 | 4.09 | 7.05 | 9.03 | 11.00 | 9.86 | 17.50 |
| 2006-12 | 3.14 | 13.25 | 2.80 | 6.12 | 6.60 | 7.25 | 6.53 | 9.75 | 4.05 | 7.02 | 9.00 | 11.00 | 9.65 | 17.50 |

*continues on following page*

*Table 12. Continued*

| Date | Brazil | | China | | India | | Indonesia | | Mexico | | Russia | | Turkey | |
|---|---|---|---|---|---|---|---|---|---|---|---|---|---|---|
| | Inflation | Interest | Inflation | Interest | Inflation | Interest | Inflation | Interest | Inflation | Interest | Inflation | Interest | Inflation | Interest |
| 2007-01 | 2.99 | 13.00 | 2.20 | 6.12 | 6.26 | 7.50 | 6.72 | 9.50 | 3.98 | 7.02 | 8.20 | 10.50 | 9.93 | 17.50 |
| 2007-02 | 3.02 | 13.00 | 2.70 | 6.12 | 6.30 | 7.50 | 7.56 | 9.25 | 4.11 | 7.08 | 7.61 | 10.50 | 10.16 | 17.50 |
| 2007-03 | 2.96 | 12.75 | 3.30 | 6.39 | 6.51 | 7.50 | 6.72 | 9.00 | 4.21 | 7.04 | 7.37 | 10.50 | 10.86 | 17.50 |
| 2007-04 | 3.00 | 12.50 | 3.00 | 6.39 | 6.30 | 7.75 | 6.67 | 9.00 | 3.99 | 7.26 | 7.60 | 10.50 | 10.72 | 17.50 |
| 2007-05 | 3.18 | 12.50 | 3.40 | 6.57 | 6.00 | 7.75 | 6.61 | 8.75 | 3.95 | 7.30 | 7.76 | 10.50 | 9.23 | 17.50 |
| 2007-06 | 3.69 | 12.00 | 4.40 | 6.57 | 5.77 | 7.75 | 5.69 | 8.50 | 3.98 | 7.30 | 8.48 | 10.00 | 8.60 | 17.50 |
| 2007-07 | 3.74 | 11.50 | 5.60 | 6.84 | 6.06 | 7.75 | 6.45 | 8.25 | 4.14 | 7.29 | 8.70 | 10.00 | 6.90 | 17.50 |
| 2007-08 | 4.18 | 11.50 | 6.50 | 7.02 | 6.50 | 7.75 | 7.26 | 8.25 | 4.03 | 7.29 | 8.59 | 10.00 | 7.39 | 17.50 |
| 2007-09 | 4.15 | 11.25 | 6.20 | 7.29 | 6.96 | 7.75 | 6.40 | 8.25 | 3.79 | 7.28 | 9.35 | 10.00 | 7.12 | 17.25 |
| 2007-10 | 4.12 | 11.25 | 6.50 | 7.29 | 6.87 | 7.75 | 5.51 | 8.25 | 3.74 | 7.49 | 10.83 | 10.00 | 7.70 | 16.75 |
| 2007-11 | 4.19 | 11.25 | 6.90 | 7.29 | 6.72 | 7.75 | 5.51 | 8.25 | 3.93 | 7.51 | 11.49 | 10.00 | 8.40 | 16.25 |
| 2007-12 | 4.46 | 11.25 | 6.50 | 7.47 | 6.58 | 7.75 | 5.51 | 8.00 | 3.76 | 7.57 | 11.87 | 10.00 | 8.39 | 15.75 |

*continues on following page*

*Table 12. Continued*

| Date | Brazil | | China | | India | | Indonesia | | Mexico | | Russia | | Turkey | |
|---|---|---|---|---|---|---|---|---|---|---|---|---|---|---|
| | Inflation | Interest | Inflation | Interest | Inflation | Interest | Inflation | Interest | Inflation | Interest | Inflation | Interest | Inflation | Interest |
| 2008-01 | 4.56 | 11.25 | 7.10 | 7.47 | 7.36 | 7.75 | 5.51 | 8.00 | 3.70 | 7.50 | 12.56 | 10.00 | 8.17 | 15.50 |
| 2008-02 | 4.61 | 11.25 | 8.70 | 7.47 | 7.40 | 7.75 | 5.47 | 8.00 | 3.72 | 7.50 | 12.66 | 10.25 | 9.10 | 15.25 |
| 2008-03 | 4.73 | 11.25 | 8.30 | 7.47 | 8.17 | 7.75 | 7.87 | 8.00 | 4.25 | 7.50 | 13.35 | 10.25 | 9.15 | 15.25 |
| 2008-04 | 5.04 | 11.75 | 8.50 | 7.47 | 8.97 | 7.75 | 7.81 | 8.00 | 4.55 | 7.50 | 14.30 | 10.50 | 9.66 | 15.25 |
| 2008-05 | 5.58 | 11.75 | 7.70 | 7.47 | 10.39 | 7.75 | 7.75 | 8.25 | 4.95 | 7.50 | 15.12 | 10.50 | 10.74 | 15.75 |
| 2008-06 | 6.06 | 12.25 | 7.10 | 7.47 | 11.28 | 8.50 | 7.69 | 8.50 | 5.26 | 7.75 | 15.14 | 10.75 | 10.61 | 16.25 |
| 2008-07 | 6.37 | 13.00 | 6.30 | 7.47 | 12.00 | 9.00 | 8.33 | 8.75 | 5.39 | 8.00 | 14.73 | 11.00 | 12.06 | 16.75 |
| 2008-08 | 6.17 | 13.00 | 4.90 | 7.47 | 11.75 | 9.00 | 9.02 | 9.00 | 5.57 | 8.25 | 15.04 | 11.00 | 11.77 | 16.75 |
| 2008-09 | 6.25 | 13.75 | 4.60 | 7.20 | 11.93 | 9.00 | 9.77 | 9.25 | 5.47 | 8.25 | 15.05 | 11.00 | 11.13 | 16.75 |
| 2008-10 | 6.41 | 13.75 | 4.00 | 6.66 | 11.55 | 8.00 | 10.45 | 9.50 | 5.78 | 8.25 | 14.23 | 11.00 | 11.99 | 16.75 |
| 2008-11 | 6.39 | 13.75 | 2.40 | 5.58 | 11.48 | 7.50 | 10.45 | 9.50 | 6.23 | 8.25 | 13.78 | 12.00 | 10.76 | 16.25 |
| 2008-12 | 5.90 | 13.75 | 1.20 | 5.31 | 10.23 | 6.50 | 9.70 | 9.25 | 6.53 | 8.25 | 13.28 | 13.00 | 10.06 | 15.00 |

*continues on following page*

*Table 12. Continued*

| Date | Brazil | | China | | India | | Indonesia | | Mexico | | Russia | | Turkey | |
|---|---|---|---|---|---|---|---|---|---|---|---|---|---|---|
| | Inflation | Interest | Inflation | Interest | Inflation | Interest | Inflation | Interest | Inflation | Interest | Inflation | Interest | Inflation | Interest |
| 2009-01 | 5.84 | 12.75 | 1.00 | 5.31 | 8.24 | 5.50 | 10.45 | 8.75 | 6.28 | 7.75 | 13.35 | 13.00 | 9.50 | 13.00 |
| 2009-02 | 5.90 | 12.75 | -1.60 | 5.31 | 7.76 | 5.50 | 9.63 | 8.25 | 6.20 | 7.50 | 13.85 | 13.00 | 7.73 | 11.50 |
| 2009-03 | 5.61 | 11.25 | -1.20 | 5.31 | 6.97 | 5.00 | 8.03 | 7.75 | 6.04 | 6.75 | 13.98 | 13.00 | 7.89 | 10.50 |
| 2009-04 | 5.53 | 10.25 | -1.50 | 5.31 | 6.04 | 4.75 | 8.70 | 7.50 | 6.17 | 6.00 | 13.16 | 12.50 | 6.13 | 9.75 |
| 2009-05 | 5.20 | 10.25 | -1.40 | 5.31 | 4.62 | 4.75 | 8.63 | 7.25 | 5.98 | 5.25 | 12.28 | 12.00 | 5.24 | 9.25 |
| 2009-06 | 4.80 | 9.25 | -1.70 | 5.31 | 3.65 | 4.75 | 9.29 | 7.00 | 5.74 | 4.75 | 11.87 | 11.50 | 5.73 | 8.75 |
| 2009-07 | 4.50 | 8.75 | -1.80 | 5.31 | 2.71 | 4.75 | 11.89 | 6.75 | 5.44 | 4.50 | 12.01 | 11.00 | 5.39 | 8.25 |
| 2009-08 | 4.36 | 8.75 | -1.20 | 5.31 | 2.75 | 4.75 | 11.72 | 6.50 | 5.08 | 4.50 | 11.60 | 10.75 | 5.33 | 7.75 |
| 2009-09 | 4.34 | 8.75 | -0.80 | 5.31 | 2.83 | 4.75 | 11.64 | 6.50 | 4.89 | 4.50 | 10.69 | 10.00 | 5.27 | 7.25 |
| 2009-10 | 4.17 | 8.75 | -0.50 | 5.31 | 2.57 | 4.75 | 11.49 | 6.50 | 4.50 | 4.50 | 9.69 | 9.50 | 5.08 | 6.75 |
| 2009-11 | 4.22 | 8.75 | 0.60 | 5.31 | 2.41 | 4.75 | 13.51 | 6.50 | 3.86 | 4.50 | 9.10 | 9.00 | 5.53 | 6.50 |
| 2009-12 | 4.31 | 8.75 | 1.90 | 5.31 | 2.78 | 4.75 | 14.97 | 6.50 | 3.57 | 4.50 | 8.80 | 8.75 | 6.53 | 6.50 |

*continues on following page*

*Table 12. Continued*

| Date | Brazil | | China | | India | | Indonesia | | Mexico | | Russia | | Turkey | |
|---|---|---|---|---|---|---|---|---|---|---|---|---|---|---|
| | Inflation | Interest | Inflation | Interest | Inflation | Interest | Inflation | Interest | Inflation | Interest | Inflation | Interest | Inflation | Interest |
| 2010-01 | 4.59 | 8.75 | 1.50 | 5.31 | 3.72 | 4.75 | 16.22 | 6.50 | 4.46 | 4.50 | 8.02 | 8.75 | 8.19 | 6.50 |
| 2010-02 | 4.83 | 8.75 | 2.70 | 5.31 | 3.82 | 4.75 | 14.86 | 6.50 | 4.83 | 4.50 | 7.18 | 8.50 | 10.13 | 6.50 |
| 2010-03 | 5.17 | 8.75 | 2.40 | 5.31 | 3.43 | 5.00 | 14.86 | 6.50 | 4.97 | 4.50 | 6.46 | 8.25 | 9.56 | 6.50 |
| 2010-04 | 5.26 | 9.50 | 2.80 | 5.31 | 3.91 | 5.25 | 13.33 | 6.50 | 4.27 | 4.50 | 6.04 | 8.00 | 10.19 | 6.50 |
| 2010-05 | 5.22 | 9.50 | 3.10 | 5.31 | 4.16 | 5.25 | 13.91 | 6.50 | 3.92 | 4.50 | 5.97 | 7.75 | 9.10 | 7.00 |
| 2010-06 | 4.84 | 10.25 | 2.90 | 5.31 | 5.05 | 5.25 | 13.73 | 6.50 | 3.69 | 4.50 | 5.74 | 7.75 | 8.37 | 7.00 |
| 2010-07 | 4.60 | 10.75 | 3.30 | 5.31 | 6.22 | 5.75 | 11.25 | 6.50 | 3.64 | 4.50 | 5.46 | 7.75 | 7.58 | 7.00 |
| 2010-08 | 4.49 | 10.75 | 3.50 | 5.31 | 6.44 | 5.75 | 9.88 | 6.50 | 3.68 | 4.50 | 6.04 | 7.75 | 8.33 | 7.00 |
| 2010-09 | 4.70 | 10.75 | 3.60 | 5.31 | 5.80 | 6.00 | 9.82 | 6.50 | 3.70 | 4.50 | 6.96 | 7.75 | 9.24 | 7.00 |
| 2010-10 | 5.20 | 10.75 | 4.40 | 5.56 | 5.67 | 6.00 | 9.70 | 6.50 | 4.02 | 4.50 | 7.50 | 7.75 | 8.62 | 7.00 |
| 2010-11 | 5.63 | 10.75 | 5.10 | 5.56 | 6.33 | 6.25 | 8.33 | 6.50 | 4.32 | 4.50 | 8.06 | 7.75 | 7.29 | 7.00 |
| 2010-12 | 5.91 | 10.75 | 4.60 | 5.81 | 6.96 | 6.25 | 9.47 | 6.50 | 4.40 | 4.50 | 8.78 | 7.75 | 6.40 | 6.50 |

*continues on following page*

*Table 12. Continued*

| Date | Brazil | | China | | India | | Indonesia | | Mexico | | Russia | | Turkey | |
|---|---|---|---|---|---|---|---|---|---|---|---|---|---|---|
| | Inflation | Interest | Inflation | Interest | Inflation | Interest | Inflation | Interest | Inflation | Interest | Inflation | Interest | Inflation | Interest |
| 2011-01 | 5.99 | 11.25 | 4.90 | 5.81 | 7.02 | 6.50 | 9.30 | 6.50 | 3.78 | 4.50 | 9.56 | 7.75 | 4.90 | 6.25 |
| 2011-02 | 6.01 | 11.25 | 4.90 | 6.06 | 6.83 | 6.50 | 8.82 | 6.75 | 3.57 | 4.50 | 9.47 | 8.00 | 4.16 | 6.25 |
| 2011-03 | 6.30 | 11.75 | 5.40 | 6.06 | 6.65 | 6.75 | 8.82 | 6.75 | 3.04 | 4.50 | 9.46 | 8.00 | 3.99 | 6.25 |
| 2011-04 | 6.51 | 12.00 | 5.30 | 6.31 | 6.16 | 6.75 | 9.41 | 6.75 | 3.36 | 4.50 | 9.61 | 8.00 | 4.26 | 6.25 |
| 2011-05 | 6.55 | 12.00 | 5.50 | 6.31 | 5.98 | 7.25 | 8.72 | 6.75 | 3.25 | 4.50 | 9.59 | 8.25 | 7.17 | 6.25 |
| 2011-06 | 6.71 | 12.25 | 6.40 | 6.31 | 5.54 | 7.50 | 8.62 | 6.75 | 3.28 | 4.50 | 9.42 | 8.25 | 6.24 | 6.25 |
| 2011-07 | 6.87 | 12.50 | 6.50 | 6.56 | 4.61 | 8.00 | 8.43 | 6.75 | 3.55 | 4.50 | 9.01 | 8.25 | 6.31 | 6.25 |
| 2011-08 | 7.23 | 12.50 | 6.20 | 6.56 | 4.79 | 8.00 | 8.99 | 6.75 | 3.42 | 4.50 | 8.16 | 8.25 | 6.65 | 5.75 |
| 2011-09 | 7.31 | 12.00 | 6.10 | 6.56 | 4.61 | 8.25 | 10.06 | 6.75 | 3.14 | 4.50 | 7.21 | 8.25 | 6.15 | 5.75 |
| 2011-10 | 6.97 | 11.50 | 5.50 | 6.56 | 4.42 | 8.50 | 9.39 | 6.50 | 3.20 | 4.50 | 7.19 | 8.25 | 7.66 | 5.75 |
| 2011-11 | 6.64 | 11.50 | 4.20 | 6.56 | 4.15 | 8.50 | 9.34 | 6.00 | 3.48 | 4.50 | 6.78 | 8.25 | 9.48 | 5.75 |
| 2011-12 | 6.50 | 11.00 | 4.10 | 6.56 | 3.79 | 8.50 | 6.49 | 6.00 | 3.82 | 4.50 | 6.10 | 8.00 | 10.45 | 5.75 |

*continues on following page*

*Table 12. Continued*

| Date | Brazil | | China | | India | | Indonesia | | Mexico | | Russia | | Turkey | |
|---|---|---|---|---|---|---|---|---|---|---|---|---|---|---|
| | Inflation | Interest | Inflation | Interest | Inflation | Interest | Inflation | Interest | Inflation | Interest | Inflation | Interest | Inflation | Interest |
| 2012-01 | 6.22 | 10.50 | 4.50 | 6.56 | 3.65 | 8.50 | 5.32 | 6.00 | 4.05 | 4.50 | 4.16 | 8.00 | 10.61 | 5.75 |
| 2012-02 | 5.85 | 10.50 | 3.20 | 6.56 | 3.56 | 8.50 | 7.57 | 5.75 | 3.87 | 4.50 | 3.74 | 8.00 | 10.43 | 5.75 |
| 2012-03 | 5.24 | 9.75 | 3.60 | 6.56 | 3.97 | 8.50 | 8.65 | 5.75 | 3.73 | 4.50 | 3.70 | 8.00 | 10.43 | 5.75 |
| 2012-04 | 5.11 | 9.00 | 3.40 | 6.56 | 4.50 | 8.00 | 10.22 | 5.75 | 3.41 | 4.50 | 3.57 | 8.00 | 11.14 | 5.75 |
| 2012-05 | 4.99 | 8.50 | 3.00 | 6.56 | 4.45 | 8.00 | 10.16 | 5.75 | 3.85 | 4.50 | 3.61 | 8.00 | 8.28 | 5.75 |
| 2012-06 | 4.91 | 8.50 | 2.20 | 6.31 | 4.53 | 8.00 | 10.05 | 5.75 | 4.34 | 4.50 | 4.30 | 8.25 | 8.87 | 5.75 |
| 2012-07 | 5.20 | 8.00 | 1.80 | 6.00 | 4.56 | 8.00 | 9.84 | 5.75 | 4.42 | 4.50 | 5.59 | 8.00 | 9.07 | 5.75 |
| 2012-08 | 5.24 | 7.50 | 2.00 | 6.00 | 4.58 | 8.00 | 10.31 | 5.75 | 4.57 | 4.50 | 5.95 | 8.00 | 8.88 | 5.75 |
| 2012-09 | 5.28 | 7.50 | 1.90 | 6.00 | 4.31 | 8.00 | 9.14 | 5.75 | 4.77 | 4.50 | 6.58 | 8.25 | 9.19 | 5.75 |
| 2012-10 | 5.45 | 7.25 | 1.70 | 6.00 | 4.61 | 8.00 | 9.60 | 5.75 | 4.60 | 4.50 | 6.55 | 8.25 | 7.80 | 5.75 |
| 2012-11 | 5.53 | 7.25 | 2.00 | 6.00 | 4.32 | 8.00 | 9.55 | 5.75 | 4.18 | 4.50 | 6.47 | 8.25 | 6.37 | 5.75 |
| 2012-12 | 5.84 | 7.25 | 2.50 | 6.00 | 4.30 | 8.00 | 11.17 | 5.75 | 3.57 | 4.50 | 6.58 | 8.25 | 6.16 | 5.50 |

*continues on following page*

*Table 12. Continued*

| Date | Brazil | | China | | India | | Indonesia | | Mexico | | Russia | | Turkey | |
|---|---|---|---|---|---|---|---|---|---|---|---|---|---|---|
| | Inflation | Interest | Inflation | Interest | Inflation | Interest | Inflation | Interest | Inflation | Interest | Inflation | Interest | Inflation | Interest |
| 2013-01 | 6.15 | 7.25 | 2.00 | 6.00 | 4.13 | 7.75 | 11.62 | 5.75 | 3.25 | 4.50 | 7.07 | 8.25 | 7.31 | 5.50 |
| 2013-02 | 6.31 | 7.25 | 3.20 | 6.00 | 4.81 | 7.75 | 12.06 | 5.75 | 3.55 | 4.50 | 7.28 | 8.25 | 7.03 | 5.50 |
| 2013-03 | 6.59 | 7.25 | 2.10 | 6.00 | 5.24 | 7.50 | 11.44 | 5.75 | 4.25 | 4.00 | 7.02 | 8.25 | 7.29 | 5.50 |
| 2013-04 | 6.49 | 7.50 | 2.40 | 6.00 | 5.07 | 7.50 | 10.24 | 5.75 | 4.65 | 4.00 | 7.23 | 8.25 | 6.13 | 5.00 |
| 2013-05 | 6.51 | 8.00 | 2.10 | 6.00 | 5.10 | 7.25 | 10.68 | 5.75 | 4.63 | 4.00 | 7.38 | 8.25 | 6.51 | 4.50 |
| 2013-06 | 6.70 | 8.00 | 2.70 | 6.00 | 5.51 | 7.25 | 11.06 | 6.00 | 4.09 | 4.00 | 6.88 | 8.25 | 8.30 | 4.50 |
| 2013-07 | 6.27 | 8.50 | 2.70 | 6.00 | 7.94 | 7.25 | 10.85 | 6.50 | 3.47 | 4.00 | 6.45 | 8.25 | 8.88 | 4.50 |
| 2013-08 | 6.09 | 9.00 | 2.60 | 6.00 | 7.98 | 7.25 | 10.75 | 7.00 | 3.46 | 4.00 | 6.49 | 8.25 | 8.17 | 4.50 |
| 2013-09 | 5.86 | 9.00 | 3.10 | 6.00 | 7.70 | 7.50 | 10.70 | 7.25 | 3.39 | 3.75 | 6.13 | 5.50 | 7.88 | 4.50 |
| 2013-10 | 5.84 | 9.50 | 3.20 | 6.00 | 7.72 | 7.75 | 11.06 | 7.25 | 3.36 | 3.50 | 6.25 | 5.50 | 7.71 | 4.50 |
| 2013-11 | 5.77 | 10.00 | 3.00 | 6.00 | 7.82 | 7.75 | 11.47 | 7.50 | 3.62 | 3.50 | 6.50 | 5.50 | 7.32 | 4.50 |
| 2013-12 | 5.91 | 10.00 | 2.50 | 6.00 | 7.72 | 7.75 | 9.13 | 7.50 | 3.97 | 3.50 | 6.45 | 5.50 | 7.40 | 4.50 |

*continues on following page*

Table 12. Continued

| Date | Brazil | | China | | India | | Indonesia | | Mexico | | Russia | | Turkey | |
|---|---|---|---|---|---|---|---|---|---|---|---|---|---|---|
| | Inflation | Interest | Inflation | Interest | Inflation | Interest | Inflation | Interest | Inflation | Interest | Inflation | Interest | Inflation | Interest |
| 2014-01 | 5.59 | 10.50 | 2.50 | 6.00 | 8.22 | 8.00 | 7.24 | 7.50 | 4.48 | 3.50 | 6.05 | 5.50 | 7.75 | 10.00 |
| 2014-02 | 5.68 | 10.75 | 2.00 | 6.00 | 7.75 | 8.00 | 6.73 | 7.50 | 4.23 | 3.50 | 6.19 | 5.50 | 7.89 | 10.00 |
| 2014-03 | 6.15 | 10.75 | 2.40 | 6.00 | 7.32 | 8.00 | 6.70 | 7.50 | 3.76 | 3.50 | 6.91 | 7.00 | 8.39 | 10.00 |
| 2014-04 | 6.28 | 11.00 | 1.80 | 6.00 | 7.25 | 8.00 | 7.08 | 7.50 | 3.50 | 3.50 | 7.33 | 7.50 | 9.38 | 10.00 |
| 2014-05 | 6.37 | 11.00 | 2.50 | 6.00 | 7.32 | 8.00 | 7.02 | 7.50 | 3.51 | 3.50 | 7.59 | 7.50 | 9.66 | 9.50 |
| 2014-06 | 6.52 | 11.00 | 2.30 | 6.00 | 6.70 | 8.00 | 6.49 | 7.50 | 3.75 | 3.00 | 7.80 | 7.50 | 9.16 | 8.75 |
| 2014-07 | 6.50 | 11.00 | 2.30 | 6.00 | 4.53 | 8.00 | 7.23 | 7.50 | 4.07 | 3.00 | 7.45 | 8.00 | 9.32 | 8.25 |
| 2014-08 | 6.51 | 11.00 | 2.00 | 6.00 | 3.99 | 8.00 | 6.75 | 7.50 | 4.15 | 3.00 | 7.55 | 8.00 | 9.54 | 8.25 |
| 2014-09 | 6.75 | 11.00 | 1.60 | 6.00 | 4.53 | 8.00 | 6.30 | 7.50 | 4.22 | 3.00 | 8.03 | 8.00 | 8.86 | 8.25 |
| 2014-10 | 6.59 | 11.25 | 1.60 | 6.00 | 4.83 | 8.00 | 4.98 | 7.50 | 4.30 | 3.00 | 8.29 | 8.00 | 8.96 | 8.25 |
| 2014-11 | 6.56 | 11.25 | 1.40 | 5.60 | 6.23 | 8.00 | 4.12 | 7.50 | 4.17 | 3.00 | 9.06 | 9.50 | 9.15 | 8.25 |
| 2014-12 | 6.41 | 11.75 | 1.50 | 5.60 | 8.36 | 8.00 | 5.86 | 7.75 | 4.08 | 3.00 | 11.36 | 17.00 | 8.17 | 8.25 |

continues on following page

*Table 12. Continued*

| Date | Brazil | | China | | India | | Indonesia | | Mexico | | Russia | | Turkey | |
|---|---|---|---|---|---|---|---|---|---|---|---|---|---|---|
| | Inflation | Interest | Inflation | Interest | Inflation | Interest | Inflation | Interest | Inflation | Interest | Inflation | Interest | Inflation | Interest |
| 2015-01 | 7.14 | 12.25 | 0.80 | 5.60 | 6.96 | 7.75 | 7.17 | 7.75 | 3.07 | 3.00 | 14.97 | 17.00 | 7.24 | 7.75 |
| 2015-02 | 7.70 | 12.25 | 1.40 | 5.60 | 6.29 | 7.75 | 6.30 | 7.50 | 3.00 | 3.00 | 16.71 | 15.00 | 7.55 | 7.50 |
| 2015-03 | 8.13 | 12.75 | 1.40 | 5.35 | 6.38 | 7.50 | 6.28 | 7.50 | 3.14 | 3.00 | 16.93 | 14.00 | 7.61 | 7.50 |
| 2015-04 | 8.17 | 13.25 | 1.50 | 5.35 | 6.79 | 7.50 | 5.79 | 7.50 | 3.06 | 3.00 | 16.42 | 14.00 | 7.91 | 7.50 |
| 2015-05 | 8.47 | 13.25 | 1.20 | 5.10 | 7.15 | 7.50 | 5.74 | 7.50 | 2.88 | 3.00 | 15.78 | 12.50 | 8.09 | 7.50 |
| 2015-06 | 8.89 | 13.75 | 1.40 | 4.85 | 7.26 | 7.25 | 6.10 | 7.50 | 2.87 | 3.00 | 15.29 | 11.50 | 7.20 | 7.50 |
| 2015-07 | 9.56 | 14.25 | 1.60 | 4.85 | 7.26 | 7.25 | 4.37 | 7.50 | 2.74 | 3.00 | 15.64 | 11.50 | 6.81 | 7.50 |
| 2015-08 | 9.53 | 14.25 | 2.00 | 4.60 | 7.18 | 7.25 | 4.35 | 7.50 | 2.59 | 3.00 | 15.77 | 11.00 | 7.14 | 7.50 |
| 2015-09 | 9.49 | 14.25 | 1.60 | 4.60 | 6.83 | 6.75 | 5.14 | 7.50 | 2.52 | 3.00 | 15.68 | 11.00 | 7.95 | 7.50 |
| 2015-10 | 9.93 | 14.25 | 1.30 | 4.35 | 6.25 | 6.75 | 6.32 | 7.50 | 2.48 | 3.00 | 15.59 | 11.00 | 7.58 | 7.50 |
| 2015-11 | 10.48 | 14.25 | 1.50 | 4.35 | 4.89 | 6.75 | 6.72 | 7.50 | 2.21 | 3.00 | 14.98 | 11.00 | 8.10 | 7.50 |
| 2015-12 | 10.67 | 14.25 | 1.60 | 4.35 | 3.35 | 6.75 | 6.32 | 7.50 | 2.13 | 3.25 | 12.91 | 11.00 | 8.81 | 7.50 |

*continues on following page*

*Table 12. Continued*

| Date | Brazil | | China | | India | | Indonesia | | Mexico | | Russia | | Turkey | |
|---|---|---|---|---|---|---|---|---|---|---|---|---|---|---|
| | Inflation | Interest | Inflation | Interest | Inflation | Interest | Inflation | Interest | Inflation | Interest | Inflation | Interest | Inflation | Interest |
| 2016-01 | 10.71 | 14.25 | 1.80 | 4.35 | 4.14 | 6.75 | 5.91 | 7.25 | 2.61 | 3.25 | 9.77 | 11.00 | 9.58 | 7.50 |
| 2016-02 | 10.36 | 14.25 | 2.30 | 4.35 | 4.42 | 6.75 | 5.53 | 7.00 | 2.87 | 3.75 | 8.06 | 11.00 | 8.78 | 7.50 |
| 2016-03 | 9.39 | 14.25 | 2.30 | 4.35 | 4.45 | 6.75 | 5.51 | 6.75 | 2.60 | 3.75 | 7.26 | 11.00 | 7.46 | 7.50 |
| 2016-04 | 9.28 | 14.25 | 2.30 | 4.35 | 3.60 | 6.50 | 5.86 | 6.75 | 2.54 | 3.75 | 7.24 | 11.00 | 6.57 | 7.50 |
| 2016-05 | 9.32 | 14.25 | 2.00 | 4.35 | 3.33 | 6.50 | 6.59 | 6.75 | 2.60 | 3.75 | 7.30 | 11.00 | 6.58 | 7.50 |
| 2016-06 | 8.84 | 14.25 | 1.90 | 4.35 | 3.45 | 6.50 | 6.13 | 6.50 | 2.54 | 4.25 | 7.48 | 10.50 | 7.64 | 7.50 |
| 2016-07 | 8.74 | 14.25 | 1.80 | 4.35 | 3.21 | 6.50 | 6.46 | 6.50 | 2.65 | 4.25 | 7.21 | 10.50 | 8.79 | 7.50 |
| 2016-08 | 8.97 | 14.25 | 1.30 | 4.35 | 2.79 | 6.50 | 5.30 | 5.25 | 2.73 | 4.25 | 6.84 | 10.50 | 8.05 | 7.50 |
| 2016-09 | 8.48 | 14.25 | 1.90 | 4.35 | 3.07 | 6.50 | 4.14 | 5.00 | 2.97 | 4.75 | 6.42 | 10.00 | 7.28 | 7.50 |
| 2016-10 | 7.87 | 14.00 | 2.10 | 4.35 | 3.31 | 6.25 | 3.35 | 4.75 | 3.06 | 4.75 | 6.09 | 10.00 | 7.16 | 7.50 |
| 2016-11 | 6.99 | 14.00 | 2.30 | 4.35 | 3.58 | 6.25 | 2.59 | 4.75 | 3.31 | 5.25 | 5.76 | 10.00 | 7.00 | 8.00 |
| 2016-12 | 6.29 | 13.75 | 2.10 | 4.35 | 3.02 | 6.25 | 2.23 | 4.75 | 3.36 | 5.75 | 5.38 | 10.00 | 8.53 | 8.00 |

*continues on following page*

*Table 12. Continued*

| Date | Brazil | | China | | India | | Indonesia | | Mexico | | Russia | | Turkey | |
|---|---|---|---|---|---|---|---|---|---|---|---|---|---|---|
| | Inflation | Interest | Inflation | Interest | Inflation | Interest | Inflation | Interest | Inflation | Interest | Inflation | Interest | Inflation | Interest |
| 2017-01 | 5.35 | 13.00 | 2.50 | 4.35 | 3.49 | 6.25 | 1.86 | 4.75 | 4.72 | 5.75 | 5.02 | 10.00 | 9.22 | 8.00 |
| 2017-02 | 4.76 | 12.25 | 0.80 | 4.35 | 3.83 | 6.25 | 2.62 | 4.75 | 4.86 | 6.25 | 4.59 | 10.00 | 10.13 | 8.00 |
| 2017-03 | 4.57 | 12.25 | 0.90 | 4.35 | 3.61 | 6.25 | 2.61 | 4.75 | 5.35 | 6.50 | 4.25 | 9.75 | 11.29 | 8.00 |
| 2017-04 | 4.08 | 11.25 | 1.20 | 4.35 | 4.17 | 6.25 | 2.21 | 4.75 | 5.82 | 6.50 | 4.13 | 9.75 | 11.87 | 8.00 |
| 2017-05 | 3.60 | 11.25 | 1.50 | 4.35 | 4.33 | 6.25 | 1.09 | 4.75 | 6.16 | 6.75 | 4.09 | 9.25 | 11.72 | 8.00 |
| 2017-06 | 3.00 | 10.25 | 1.50 | 4.35 | 4.37 | 6.25 | 1.08 | 4.75 | 6.31 | 7.00 | 4.35 | 9.00 | 10.90 | 8.00 |
| 2017-07 | 2.71 | 9.25 | 1.40 | 4.35 | 3.88 | 6.25 | 1.79 | 4.75 | 6.44 | 7.00 | 3.86 | 9.00 | 9.79 | 8.00 |
| 2017-08 | 2.46 | 9.25 | 1.80 | 4.35 | 3.82 | 6.00 | 2.52 | 4.50 | 6.66 | 7.00 | 3.29 | 9.00 | 10.68 | 8.00 |
| 2017-09 | 2.54 | 8.25 | 1.60 | 4.35 | 3.72 | 6.00 | 2.89 | 4.25 | 6.35 | 7.00 | 2.96 | 8.50 | 11.20 | 8.00 |
| 2017-10 | 2.70 | 7.50 | 1.90 | 4.35 | 3.58 | 6.00 | 3.24 | 4.25 | 6.37 | 7.00 | 2.73 | 8.25 | 11.90 | 8.00 |
| 2017-11 | 2.80 | 7.50 | 1.70 | 4.35 | 3.30 | 6.00 | 3.97 | 4.25 | 6.63 | 7.00 | 2.50 | 8.25 | 12.98 | 8.00 |
| 2017-12 | 2.95 | 7.00 | 1.80 | 4.35 | 3.61 | 6.00 | 4.00 | 4.25 | 6.77 | 7.25 | 2.52 | 7.75 | 11.92 | 8.00 |

*continues on following page*

*Table 12. Continued*

| Date | Brazil | | China | | India | | Indonesia | | Mexico | | Russia | | Turkey | |
|---|---|---|---|---|---|---|---|---|---|---|---|---|---|---|
| | Inflation | Interest | Inflation | Interest | Inflation | Interest | Inflation | Interest | Inflation | Interest | Inflation | Interest | Inflation | Interest |
| 2018-01 | 2.86 | 7.00 | 1.50 | 4.35 | 3.25 | 6.00 | 5.11 | 4.25 | 5.55 | 7.25 | 2.21 | 7.75 | 10.35 | 8.00 |
| 2018-02 | 2.84 | 6.75 | 2.90 | 4.35 | 3.18 | 6.00 | 4.74 | 4.25 | 5.34 | 7.50 | 2.20 | 7.50 | 10.26 | 8.00 |
| 2018-03 | 2.68 | 6.50 | 2.10 | 4.35 | 3.40 | 6.00 | 4.36 | 4.25 | 5.04 | 7.50 | 2.36 | 7.25 | 10.23 | 8.00 |
| 2018-04 | 2.76 | 6.50 | 1.80 | 4.35 | 3.41 | 6.00 | 3.97 | 4.25 | 4.55 | 7.50 | 2.41 | 7.25 | 10.85 | 8.00 |
| 2018-05 | 2.86 | 6.50 | 1.80 | 4.35 | 3.23 | 6.00 | 3.96 | 4.75 | 4.51 | 7.50 | 2.42 | 7.25 | 12.15 | 8.00 |
| 2018-06 | 4.39 | 6.50 | 1.90 | 4.35 | 3.12 | 6.25 | 3.93 | 5.25 | 4.65 | 7.75 | 2.30 | 7.25 | 15.39 | 17.75 |
| 2018-07 | 4.48 | 6.50 | 2.10 | 4.35 | 3.18 | 6.25 | 5.61 | 5.25 | 4.81 | 7.75 | 2.50 | 7.25 | 15.85 | 17.75 |
| 2018-08 | 4.19 | 6.50 | 2.30 | 4.35 | 3.20 | 6.50 | 5.61 | 5.50 | 4.90 | 7.75 | 3.07 | 7.25 | 17.90 | 17.75 |
| 2018-09 | 4.53 | 6.50 | 2.50 | 4.35 | 2.88 | 6.50 | 5.61 | 5.75 | 5.02 | 7.75 | 3.39 | 7.50 | 24.52 | 24.00 |
| 2018-10 | 4.56 | 6.50 | 2.50 | 4.35 | 3.16 | 6.50 | 5.23 | 5.75 | 4.90 | 7.75 | 3.55 | 7.50 | 25.24 | 24.00 |
| 2018-11 | 4.05 | 6.50 | 2.20 | 4.35 | 3.23 | 6.50 | 4.86 | 6.00 | 4.72 | 8.00 | 3.83 | 7.50 | 21.62 | 24.00 |
| 2018-12 | 3.75 | 6.50 | 1.90 | 4.35 | 3.13 | 6.50 | 5.24 | 6.00 | 4.83 | 8.25 | 4.27 | 7.75 | 20.30 | 24.00 |
| 2019-01 | 3.78 | 6.50 | 1.70 | 4.35 | 2.82 | 6.50 | 6.60 | 6.00 | 4.37 | 8.25 | 5.00 | 7.75 | 20.35 | 24.00 |

# Chapter 8
# Analysis Results for the Independence of the Central Banks With Fuzzy Logic


## ABSTRACT

*This chapter aims to measure the independence of the central banks of E7 economies. For this purpose, six different criteria are developed by considering similar studies in the literature. In the analysis process, fuzzy DEMATEL method is used to weight these criteria. On the other hand, both fuzzy TOPSIS and fuzzy VIKOR approaches are taken into consideration to rank E7 economies regarding the central bank independence. The findings show that preventing giving loan to the government is the most important factor while participating rate in the financial market has the weakest importance in the criteria set. It is recommended that central banks in E7 economies should not give loans to the government since this situation has a negative influence on the decisions of local and foreign investors. In addition to this issue, it is also concluded that Indonesia (A4) has the best performance in the E7 economies while Mexico (A5) has the worst performance in the central bank independency among the countries.*


## GENERAL INFORMATION ABOUT THE ANALYSIS

In this study, independence of the central banks of E7 economies is measured. For this purpose, 6 different criteria are developed by considering similar studies in the literature. With respect to the purpose and instrument independence, participating rate in the financial market (C1) and responsibility for the

DOI: 10.4018/978-1-7998-1643-0.ch008

monetary stability (C3) are chosen as criteria. In addition to them, rate of uncommitted representative in the board (C4) and applicability of legal provision (C5) represent political independence. On the other side, preventing giving loan to the government (C2) is selected as a criterion for economic independence. In the analysis process, fuzzy DEMATEL method is used to weight these criteria. After that, central banks of E7 economies are ranked according to the independence. For this purpose, both fuzzy TOPSIS and fuzzy VIKOR approaches are taken into consideration. The details of this analysis are given in the following sections.

## IDENTIFYING THE WEIGHTS OF CRITERIA

In the first step of this analysis, fuzzy DEMATEL approach is taken into consideration in order to weight the criteria. Within this framework, Tables 1 and 2 give information about the linguistic variables of the impact-relationship degrees and linguistic scales.

Table 3 explains the linguistic evaluations of decision makers.

Tables 4-8 explain triangular fuzzy numbers of the decision makers.

Table 9-16 represent the linguistic evaluations and fuzzy numbers of alternatives for the decision matrix.

Weight the criteria: The determinants of central bank independency defined as a set of criteria are weighted by using fuzzy DEMATEL. First, the averaged fuzzy values of decision makers evaluations have been computed to construct the initial direct-relation matrix by the equations (1) and (2). Table 17 defines the averaged results of the direct-relations matrix.

The normalized values of the matrix have been calculated by considering the averaged values of initial direct-relation matrix obtained from the decision makers as seen in Table 18. The results are provided by considering the formulas (3)-(5).

The crisp matrices have been constructed with the formula (6) and the results are shown in Table 19, 20, and 21 accordingly.

Identity matrix, the differences, and inverse matrix have been constructed to compute the total influence matrix. Tables 22-28 define the results respectively.

Total influence matrices have been calculated by using the formulas (7)-(12). The matrix results are seen in Tables 29-31.

*Table 1. Linguistic variables of the impact-relationship degrees*

| Influence Level | Triangular Fuzzy Numbers | | |
|---|---|---|---|
| No (N) | 0 | 0 | 0.25 |
| Low (L) | 0 | 0.25 | 0.5 |
| Medium (M) | 0.25 | 0.5 | 0.75 |
| High (H) | 0.5 | 0.75 | 1 |
| Very High (VH)) | 0.75 | 1 | 1 |

Source: Khorasaninejad et al. (2016)

*Table 2. Linguistic scales for rating of alternatives*

| Definition | Triangular Fuzzy Numbers | | |
|---|---|---|---|
| Worst (W) | 0 | 0 | 2.5 |
| Poor (P) | 0 | 2.5 | 5 |
| Fair (F) | 2.5 | 5 | 7.5 |
| Good (G) | 5 | 7.5 | 10 |
| Best (B) | 7.5 | 10 | 10 |

Source: Rostamzadeh et al. (2015)

Total-relation matrix based on triangular fuzzy numbers is represented in Table 32.

Converting fuzzy data into crisp scores deffuzzification method is applied to convert the triangular fuzzy numbers $\tilde{f}_{ij} = \left(l_{ij}, m_{ij}, u_{ij}\right)$, $j$=1,…,$J$, the crisp value of the i-th criterion is determined by the equations (13)-(21). In this process, firstly, the values of $x_{lj}$, $x_{mj}$, and $x_{uj}$ have been calculated by the equations (13)-(17) as seen in Table 33.

Secondly, the values of $x_j^{ls}$ and $x_j^{rs}$ have been computed with the formulas (18) and (19). The details are shown in Table 34.

After that, the values of $x_j^{crisp}$ have been calculated by the equation (20). Table 35 demonstrate the crisp results.

At the final step of the defuzzification process, the values of $f_{ij}$ have been employed by the formula (21) to construct the defuzzified total relation matrix. Table 36 show the defuzzified total relation matrix results.

*Table 3. Linguistic evaluations of decision makers for direct relation matrix*

| | C1 | | | | | C2 | | | | | C3 | | | | | C4 | | | | | C5 | | | | |
|---|---|---|---|---|---|---|---|---|---|---|---|---|---|---|---|---|---|---|---|---|---|---|---|---|---|
| | DM1 | DM2 | DM3 | DM4 | DM5 | DM1 | DM2 | DM3 | DM4 | DM5 | DM1 | DM2 | DM3 | DM4 | DM5 | DM1 | DM2 | DM3 | DM4 | DM5 | DM1 | DM2 | DM3 | DM4 | DM5 |
| C1 | - | - | - | - | - | H | H | M | L | M | M | M | M | M | M | L | H | L | H | M | M | M | M | H | M |
| C2 | VH | H | VH | M | H | - | - | - | - | - | H | H | VH | H | H | VH | H | M | H | H | VH | VH | VH | H | M |
| C3 | M | M | M | M | M | H | H | M | L | H | - | - | - | - | - | H | H | VH | M | H | H | H | H | H | H |
| C4 | M | H | VH | M | H | M | M | M | M | M | M | H | M | H | H | - | - | - | - | - | M | H | M | H | H |
| C5 | M | M | M | M | H | H | H | M | L | H | M | H | M | H | H | VH | H | VH | H | H | - | - | - | - | - |

*Table 4. Triangular fuzzy numbers of decision maker 1 for direct relation matrix*

| Criteria | C1 | | | C2 | | | C3 | | | C4 | | | C5 | | |
|---|---|---|---|---|---|---|---|---|---|---|---|---|---|---|---|
| C1 | 0 | 0 | 0 | 0.5 | 0.75 | 1 | 0.25 | 0.5 | 0.75 | 0 | 0.25 | 0.5 | 0.25 | 0.5 | 0.75 |
| C2 | 0.75 | 1 | 1 | 0 | 0 | 0 | 0.5 | 0.75 | 1 | 0.75 | 1 | 1 | 0.75 | 1 | 1 |
| C3 | 0.25 | 0.5 | 0.75 | 0.5 | 0.75 | 1 | 0 | 0 | 0 | 0.5 | 0.75 | 1 | 0.5 | 0.75 | 1 |
| C4 | 0.25 | 0.5 | 0.75 | 0.25 | 0.5 | 0.75 | 0.25 | 0.5 | 0.75 | 0 | 0 | 0 | 0.25 | 0.5 | 0.75 |
| C5 | 0.25 | 0.5 | 0.75 | 0.5 | 0.75 | 1 | 0.25 | 0.5 | 0.75 | 0.5 | 0.75 | 1 | 0 | 0 | 0 |

*Table 5. Triangular fuzzy numbers of decision maker 2 for direct relation matrix*

| Criteria | C1 | | | C2 | | | C3 | | | C4 | | | C5 | | |
|---|---|---|---|---|---|---|---|---|---|---|---|---|---|---|---|
| C1 | 0 | 0 | 0 | 0.5 | 0.75 | 1 | 0.25 | 0.5 | 0.75 | 0.5 | 0.75 | 1 | 0.25 | 0.5 | 0.75 |
| C2 | 0.5 | 0.75 | 1 | 0 | 0 | 0 | 0.5 | 0.75 | 1 | 0.5 | 0.75 | 1 | 0.75 | 1 | 1 |
| C3 | 0.25 | 0.5 | 0.75 | 0.5 | 0.75 | 1 | 0 | 0 | 0 | 0.5 | 0.75 | 1 | 0.5 | 0.75 | 1 |
| C4 | 0.5 | 0.75 | 1 | 0.25 | 0.5 | 0.75 | 0.5 | 0.75 | 1 | 0 | 0 | 0 | 0.5 | 0.75 | 1 |
| C5 | 0.25 | 0.5 | 0.75 | 0.5 | 0.75 | 1 | 0.5 | 0.75 | 1 | 0.5 | 0.75 | 1 | 0 | 0 | 0 |

*Table 6. Triangular fuzzy numbers of decision maker 3 for direct relation matrix*

| Criteria | C1 | | | C2 | | | C3 | | | C4 | | | C5 | | |
|---|---|---|---|---|---|---|---|---|---|---|---|---|---|---|---|
| C1 | 0 | 0 | 0 | 0.25 | 0.5 | 0.75 | 0.25 | 0.5 | 0.75 | 0 | 0.25 | 0.5 | 0.25 | 0.5 | 0.75 |
| C2 | 0.75 | 1 | 1 | 0 | 0 | 0 | 0.75 | 1 | 1 | 0.75 | 1 | 1 | 0.75 | 1 | 1 |
| C3 | 0.25 | 0.5 | 0.75 | 0.25 | 0.5 | 0.75 | 0 | 0 | 0 | 0.5 | 0.75 | 1 | 0.5 | 0.75 | 1 |
| C4 | 0.75 | 1 | 1 | 0.25 | 0.5 | 0.75 | 0.25 | 0.5 | 0.75 | 0 | 0 | 0 | 0.25 | 0.5 | 0.75 |
| C5 | 0.25 | 0.5 | 0.75 | 0.25 | 0.5 | 0.75 | 0.25 | 0.5 | 0.75 | 0.5 | 0.75 | 1 | 0 | 0 | 0 |

*Table 7. Triangular fuzzy numbers of decision maker 4 for direct relation matrix*

| Criteria | C1 | | | C2 | | | C3 | | | C4 | | | C5 | | |
|---|---|---|---|---|---|---|---|---|---|---|---|---|---|---|---|
| C1 | 0 | 0 | 0 | 0 | 0.25 | 0.5 | 0.25 | 0.5 | 0.75 | 0.5 | 0.75 | 1 | 0.5 | 0.75 | 1 |
| C2 | 0.25 | 0.5 | 0.75 | 0 | 0 | 0 | 0.5 | 0.75 | 1 | 0.5 | 0.75 | 1 | 0.5 | 0.75 | 1 |
| C3 | 0.25 | 0.5 | 0.75 | 0 | 0.25 | 0.5 | 0 | 0 | 0 | 0.25 | 0.5 | 0.75 | 0.5 | 0.75 | 1 |
| C4 | 0.25 | 0.5 | 0.75 | 0.25 | 0.5 | 0.25 | 0.5 | 0.75 | 1 | 0 | 0 | 0 | 0.5 | 0.75 | 1 |
| C5 | 0.25 | 0.5 | 0.75 | 0 | 0.25 | 0.5 | 0.5 | 0.75 | 1 | 0.5 | 0.75 | 1 | 0 | 0 | 0 |

*Table 8. Triangular fuzzy numbers of decision maker 5 for direct relation matrix*

| Criteria | C1 | | | C2 | | | C3 | | | C4 | | | C5 | | |
|---|---|---|---|---|---|---|---|---|---|---|---|---|---|---|---|
| C1 | 0 | 0 | 0 | 0.25 | 0.5 | 0.75 | 0.25 | 0.5 | 0.75 | 0.25 | 0.5 | 0.75 | 0.25 | 0.5 | 0.75 |
| C2 | 0.5 | 0.75 | 1 | 0 | 0 | 0 | 0.5 | 0.75 | 1 | 0.5 | 0.75 | 1 | 0.25 | 0.5 | 0.75 |
| C3 | 0.25 | 0.5 | 0.75 | 0.5 | 0.75 | 1 | 0 | 0 | 0 | 0.5 | 0.75 | 1 | 0.5 | 0.75 | 1 |
| C4 | 0.5 | 0.75 | 1 | 0.25 | 0.5 | 0.75 | 0.5 | 0.75 | 1 | 0 | 0 | 0 | 0.5 | 0.75 | 1 |
| C5 | 0.5 | 0.75 | 1 | 0.5 | 0.75 | 1 | 0.5 | 0.75 | 1 | 0.5 | 0.75 | 1 | 0 | 0 | 0 |

*Table 9. Linguistic evaluations of decision makers for fuzzy decision matrix*

| | C1 | | | | | C2 | | | | | C3 | | | | | C4 | | | | | C5 | | | | |
|---|---|---|---|---|---|---|---|---|---|---|---|---|---|---|---|---|---|---|---|---|---|---|---|---|---|
| | DM1 | DM2 | DM3 | DM4 | DM5 | DM1 | DM2 | DM3 | DM4 | DM5 | DM1 | DM2 | DM3 | DM4 | DM5 | DM1 | DM2 | DM3 | DM4 | DM5 | DM1 | DM2 | DM3 | DM4 | DM5 |
| A1 | F | F | P | F | P | F | F | F | F | F | F | F | F | F | F | F | F | G | G | F | G | G | F | F | F |
| A2 | F | F | F | P | F | F | F | F | F | F | F | F | F | G | F | F | F | F | F | G | F | G | G | F | F |
| A3 | F | F | F | G | F | F | F | F | G | F | F | G | G | F | F | F | F | F | G | F | F | G | G | F | F |
| A4 | G | G | F | G | G | G | F | F | F | G | F | F | G | G | F | G | F | F | F | F | F | F | F | G | G |
| A5 | F | P | F | F | F | F | F | F | F | F | F | F | G | F | F | F | F | G | F | F | F | F | G | F | F |
| A6 | F | G | F | F | P | F | F | F | F | F | F | F | F | F | G | G | F | F | F | F | F | F | G | G | G |
| A7 | F | F | P | F | F | F | F | F | F | G | F | F | F | G | G | G | F | F | F | F | F | F | G | G | F |

*Table 10. Fuzzy decision matrix of decision makers for alternative 1*

| Criteria | DM1 | | | DM2 | | | DM3 | | | DM4 | | | DM5 | | |
|---|---|---|---|---|---|---|---|---|---|---|---|---|---|---|---|
| C1 | 2.5 | 5 | 7.5 | 2.5 | 5 | 7.5 | 0 | 2.5 | 5 | 2.5 | 5 | 7.5 | 0 | 2.5 | 5 |
| C2 | 2.5 | 5 | 7.5 | 2.5 | 5 | 7.5 | 2.5 | 5 | 7.5 | 2.5 | 5 | 7.5 | 2.5 | 5 | 7.5 |
| C3 | 2.5 | 5 | 7.5 | 2.5 | 5 | 7.5 | 2.5 | 5 | 7.5 | 2.5 | 5 | 7.5 | 2.5 | 5 | 7.5 |
| C4 | 2.5 | 5 | 7.5 | 2.5 | 5 | 7.5 | 5 | 7.5 | 10 | 5 | 7.5 | 10 | 2.5 | 5 | 7.5 |
| C5 | 5 | 7.5 | 10 | 5 | 7.5 | 10 | 2.5 | 5 | 7.5 | 2.5 | 5 | 7.5 | 2.5 | 5 | 7.5 |

*Table 11. Fuzzy decision matrix of decision makers for alternative 2*

| Criteria | DM1 | | | DM2 | | | DM3 | | | DM4 | | | DM5 | | |
|---|---|---|---|---|---|---|---|---|---|---|---|---|---|---|---|
| C1 | 2.5 | 5 | 7.5 | 2.5 | 5 | 7.5 | 2.5 | 5 | 7.5 | 0 | 2.5 | 5 | 2.5 | 5 | 7.5 |
| C2 | 2.5 | 5 | 7.5 | 2.5 | 5 | 7.5 | 2.5 | 5 | 7.5 | 2.5 | 5 | 7.5 | 2.5 | 5 | 7.5 |
| C3 | 2.5 | 5 | 7.5 | 2.5 | 5 | 7.5 | 2.5 | 5 | 7.5 | 5 | 7.5 | 10 | 2.5 | 5 | 7.5 |
| C4 | 2.5 | 5 | 7.5 | 2.5 | 5 | 7.5 | 2.5 | 5 | 7.5 | 2.5 | 5 | 7.5 | 5 | 7.5 | 10 |
| C5 | 2.5 | 5 | 7.5 | 5 | 7.5 | 10 | 5 | 7.5 | 10 | 2.5 | 5 | 7.5 | 2.5 | 5 | 7.5 |

*Table 12. Fuzzy decision matrix of decision makers for alternative 3*

| Criteria | DM1 | | | DM2 | | | DM3 | | | DM4 | | | DM5 | | |
|---|---|---|---|---|---|---|---|---|---|---|---|---|---|---|---|
| C1 | 2.5 | 5 | 7.5 | 2.5 | 5 | 7.5 | 2.5 | 5 | 7.5 | 5 | 7.5 | 10 | 2.5 | 5 | 7.5 |
| C2 | 2.5 | 5 | 7.5 | 2.5 | 5 | 7.5 | 2.5 | 5 | 7.5 | 5 | 7.5 | 10 | 2.5 | 5 | 7.5 |
| C3 | 2.5 | 5 | 7.5 | 5 | 7.5 | 10 | 5 | 7.5 | 10 | 2.5 | 5 | 7.5 | 2.5 | 5 | 7.5 |
| C4 | 2.5 | 5 | 7.5 | 2.5 | 5 | 7.5 | 2.5 | 5 | 7.5 | 5 | 7.5 | 10 | 2.5 | 5 | 7.5 |
| C5 | 2.5 | 5 | 7.5 | 5 | 7.5 | 10 | 5 | 7.5 | 10 | 2.5 | 5 | 7.5 | 2.5 | 5 | 7.5 |

*Table 13. Fuzzy decision matrix of decision makers for alternative 4*

| Criteria | DM1 | | | DM2 | | | DM3 | | | DM4 | | | DM5 | | |
|---|---|---|---|---|---|---|---|---|---|---|---|---|---|---|---|
| C1 | 5 | 7.5 | 10 | 5 | 7.5 | 10 | 2.5 | 5 | 7.5 | 5 | 7.5 | 10 | 5 | 7.5 | 10 |
| C2 | 5 | 7.5 | 10 | 2.5 | 5 | 7.5 | 2.5 | 5 | 7.5 | 2.5 | 5 | 7.5 | 5 | 7.5 | 10 |
| C3 | 2.5 | 5 | 7.5 | 2.5 | 5 | 7.5 | 5 | 7.5 | 10 | 5 | 7.5 | 10 | 2.5 | 5 | 7.5 |
| C4 | 5 | 7.5 | 10 | 2.5 | 5 | 7.5 | 2.5 | 5 | 7.5 | 2.5 | 5 | 7.5 | 2.5 | 5 | 7.5 |
| C5 | 2.5 | 5 | 7.5 | 2.5 | 5 | 7.5 | 2.5 | 5 | 7.5 | 5 | 7.5 | 10 | 5 | 7.5 | 10 |

*Table 14. Fuzzy decision matrix of decision makers for alternative 5*

| Criteria | DM1 | | | DM2 | | | DM3 | | | DM4 | | | DM5 | | |
|---|---|---|---|---|---|---|---|---|---|---|---|---|---|---|---|
| C1 | 2.5 | 5 | 7.5 | 0 | 2.5 | 5 | 2.5 | 5 | 7.5 | 2.5 | 5 | 7.5 | 2.5 | 5 | 7.5 |
| C2 | 2.5 | 5 | 7.5 | 2.5 | 5 | 7.5 | 2.5 | 5 | 7.5 | 2.5 | 5 | 7.5 | 2.5 | 5 | 7.5 |
| C3 | 2.5 | 5 | 7.5 | 2.5 | 5 | 7.5 | 5 | 7.5 | 10 | 2.5 | 5 | 7.5 | 2.5 | 5 | 7.5 |
| C4 | 2.5 | 5 | 7.5 | 2.5 | 5 | 7.5 | 5 | 7.5 | 10 | 2.5 | 5 | 7.5 | 2.5 | 5 | 7.5 |
| C5 | 2.5 | 5 | 7.5 | 2.5 | 5 | 7.5 | 5 | 7.5 | 10 | 2.5 | 5 | 7.5 | 2.5 | 5 | 7.5 |

*Table 15. Fuzzy decision matrix of decision makers for alternative 6*

| Criteria | DM1 | | | DM2 | | | DM3 | | | DM4 | | | DM5 | | |
|---|---|---|---|---|---|---|---|---|---|---|---|---|---|---|---|
| C1 | 2.5 | 5 | 7.5 | 5 | 7.5 | 10 | 2.5 | 5 | 7.5 | 2.5 | 5 | 7.5 | 0 | 2.5 | 5 |
| C2 | 2.5 | 5 | 7.5 | 2.5 | 5 | 7.5 | 2.5 | 5 | 7.5 | 2.5 | 5 | 7.5 | 2.5 | 5 | 7.5 |
| C3 | 2.5 | 5 | 7.5 | 2.5 | 5 | 7.5 | 2.5 | 5 | 7.5 | 2.5 | 5 | 7.5 | 5 | 7.5 | 10 |
| C4 | 5 | 7.5 | 10 | 2.5 | 5 | 7.5 | 2.5 | 5 | 7.5 | 2.5 | 5 | 7.5 | 2.5 | 5 | 7.5 |
| C5 | 2.5 | 5 | 7.5 | 2.5 | 5 | 7.5 | 5 | 7.5 | 10 | 5 | 7.5 | 10 | 5 | 7.5 | 10 |

*Table 16. Fuzzy decision matrix of decision makers for alternative 7*

| Criteria | DM1 | | | DM2 | | | DM3 | | | DM4 | | | DM5 | | |
|---|---|---|---|---|---|---|---|---|---|---|---|---|---|---|---|
| C1 | 2.5 | 5 | 7.5 | 2.5 | 5 | 7.5 | 0 | 2.5 | 5 | 2.5 | 5 | 7.5 | 2.5 | 5 | 7.5 |
| C2 | 2.5 | 5 | 7.5 | 2.5 | 5 | 7.5 | 2.5 | 5 | 7.5 | 2.5 | 5 | 7.5 | 5 | 7.5 | 10 |
| C3 | 2.5 | 5 | 7.5 | 2.5 | 5 | 7.5 | 2.5 | 5 | 7.5 | 5 | 7.5 | 10 | 5 | 7.5 | 10 |
| C4 | 5 | 7.5 | 10 | 2.5 | 5 | 7.5 | 2.5 | 5 | 7.5 | 2.5 | 5 | 7.5 | 2.5 | 5 | 7.5 |
| C5 | 2.5 | 5 | 7.5 | 2.5 | 5 | 7.5 | 5 | 7.5 | 10 | 5 | 7.5 | 10 | 2.5 | 5 | 7.5 |

Impact and relationship map is represented by computing the values of $\left(\tilde{D}_i + \tilde{R}_i\right)^{def}$ and $\left(\tilde{D}_i - \tilde{R}_i\right)^{def}$. The values and weighting results are seen in Table 37.

According to the final results, preventing giving loan to the government (C2) is the most influencing factor while participating rate in the financial market (C1) is the most influenced criteria among the determinants of central bank independency. However, preventing giving loan to the government (C2) is the most important factor as C1 has the weakest importance in the criteria set.

Rank the alternatives: Central bank performances in the E7 economies are analyzed by considering fuzzy TOPSIS and fuzzy VIKOR comparatively.

*Table 17. Initial direct-relation fuzzy matrix*

| | C1 | | | C2 | | | C3 | | | C4 | | | C5 | | |
|---|---|---|---|---|---|---|---|---|---|---|---|---|---|---|---|
| C1 | 0.000 | 0.000 | 0.000 | 0.300 | 0.550 | 0.800 | 0.250 | 0.500 | 0.750 | 0.250 | 0.500 | 0.750 | 0.300 | 0.550 | 0.800 |
| C2 | 0.550 | 0.800 | 0.950 | 0.000 | 0.000 | 0.000 | 0.550 | 0.800 | 1.000 | 0.600 | 0.850 | 1.000 | 0.600 | 0.850 | 0.950 |
| C3 | 0.250 | 0.500 | 0.750 | 0.350 | 0.600 | 0.850 | 0.000 | 0.000 | 0.000 | 0.450 | 0.700 | 0.950 | 0.500 | 0.750 | 1.000 |
| C4 | 0.450 | 0.700 | 0.900 | 0.250 | 0.500 | 0.650 | 0.400 | 0.650 | 0.900 | 0.000 | 0.000 | 0.000 | 0.400 | 0.650 | 0.900 |
| C5 | 0.300 | 0.550 | 0.800 | 0.350 | 0.600 | 0.850 | 0.400 | 0.650 | 0.900 | 0.500 | 0.750 | 1.000 | 0.000 | 0.000 | 0.000 |

*Table 18. Normalized direct-relation fuzzy matrix*

| | C1 | | | C2 | | | C3 | | | C4 | | | C5 | | |
|---|---|---|---|---|---|---|---|---|---|---|---|---|---|---|---|
| C1 | 0.000 | 0.000 | 0.000 | 0.077 | 0.141 | 0.205 | 0.064 | 0.128 | 0.192 | 0.064 | 0.128 | 0.192 | 0.077 | 0.141 | 0.205 |
| C2 | 0.141 | 0.205 | 0.244 | 0.000 | 0.000 | 0.000 | 0.141 | 0.205 | 0.256 | 0.154 | 0.218 | 0.256 | 0.154 | 0.218 | 0.244 |
| C3 | 0.064 | 0.128 | 0.192 | 0.090 | 0.154 | 0.218 | 0.000 | 0.000 | 0.000 | 0.115 | 0.179 | 0.244 | 0.128 | 0.192 | 0.256 |
| C4 | 0.115 | 0.179 | 0.231 | 0.064 | 0.128 | 0.167 | 0.103 | 0.167 | 0.231 | 0.000 | 0.000 | 0.000 | 0.103 | 0.167 | 0.231 |
| C5 | 0.077 | 0.141 | 0.205 | 0.090 | 0.154 | 0.218 | 0.103 | 0.167 | 0.231 | 0.128 | 0.192 | 0.256 | 0.000 | 0.000 | 0.000 |

*Table 19. Normalized direct-relation fuzzy matrix (Xl)*

| | C1 | C2 | C3 | C4 | C5 |
|---|---|---|---|---|---|
| C1 | 0.000 | 0.077 | 0.064 | 0.064 | 0.077 |
| C2 | 0.141 | 0.000 | 0.141 | 0.154 | 0.154 |
| C3 | 0.064 | 0.090 | 0.000 | 0.115 | 0.128 |
| C4 | 0.115 | 0.064 | 0.103 | 0.000 | 0.103 |
| C5 | 0.077 | 0.090 | 0.103 | 0.128 | 0.000 |

*Table 20. Normalized direct-relation fuzzy matrix (Xm)*

| | C1 | C2 | C3 | C4 | C5 |
|---|---|---|---|---|---|
| C1 | 0.000 | 0.141 | 0.128 | 0.128 | 0.141 |
| C2 | 0.205 | 0.000 | 0.205 | 0.218 | 0.218 |
| C3 | 0.128 | 0.154 | 0.000 | 0.179 | 0.192 |
| C4 | 0.179 | 0.128 | 0.167 | 0.000 | 0.167 |
| C5 | 0.141 | 0.154 | 0.167 | 0.192 | 0.000 |

*Table 21. Normalized direct-relation fuzzy matrix (Xu)*

| | C1 | C2 | C3 | C4 | C5 |
|---|---|---|---|---|---|
| C1 | 0.000 | 0.205 | 0.192 | 0.192 | 0.205 |
| C2 | 0.244 | 0.000 | 0.256 | 0.256 | 0.244 |
| C3 | 0.192 | 0.218 | 0.000 | 0.244 | 0.256 |
| C4 | 0.231 | 0.167 | 0.231 | 0.000 | 0.231 |
| C5 | 0.205 | 0.218 | 0.231 | 0.256 | 0.000 |

*Table 22. Identity matrix (I)*

| | C1 | C2 | C3 | C4 | C5 |
|---|---|---|---|---|---|
| C1 | 1 | 0 | 0 | 0 | 0 |
| C2 | 0 | 1 | 0 | 0 | 0 |
| C3 | 0 | 0 | 1 | 0 | 0 |
| C4 | 0 | 0 | 0 | 1 | 0 |
| C5 | 0 | 0 | 0 | 0 | 1 |

*Table 23. Difference matrix (I-xl)*

| | C1 | C2 | C3 | C4 | C5 |
|---|---|---|---|---|---|
| C1 | 1.000 | -0.077 | -0.064 | -0.064 | -0.077 |
| C2 | -0.141 | 1.000 | -0.141 | -0.154 | -0.154 |
| C3 | -0.064 | -0.090 | 1.000 | -0.115 | -0.128 |
| C4 | -0.115 | -0.064 | -0.103 | 1.000 | -0.103 |
| C5 | -0.077 | -0.090 | -0.103 | -0.128 | 1.000 |

*Table 24. Difference matrix (I-xm)*

| | C1 | C2 | C3 | C4 | C5 |
|---|---|---|---|---|---|
| C1 | 1.000 | -0.141 | -0.128 | -0.128 | -0.141 |
| C2 | -0.205 | 1.000 | -0.205 | -0.218 | -0.218 |
| C3 | -0.128 | -0.154 | 1.000 | -0.179 | -0.192 |
| C4 | -0.179 | -0.128 | -0.167 | 1.000 | -0.167 |
| C5 | -0.141 | -0.154 | -0.167 | -0.192 | 1.000 |

*Table 25. Difference matrix (I-xu)*

| | C1 | C2 | C3 | C4 | C5 |
|---|---|---|---|---|---|
| C1 | 1.000 | -0.205 | -0.192 | -0.192 | -0.205 |
| C2 | -0.244 | 1.000 | -0.256 | -0.256 | -0.244 |
| C3 | -0.192 | -0.218 | 1.000 | -0.244 | -0.256 |
| C4 | -0.231 | -0.167 | -0.231 | 1.000 | -0.231 |
| C5 | -0.205 | -0.218 | -0.231 | -0.256 | 1.000 |

*Table 26. Inverse matrix of (I-xl)*

| | C1 | C2 | C3 | C4 | C5 |
|---|---|---|---|---|---|
| C1 | 1.044 | 0.108 | 0.106 | 0.111 | 0.122 |
| C2 | 0.209 | 1.071 | 0.212 | 0.232 | 0.232 |
| C3 | 0.121 | 0.132 | 1.063 | 0.174 | 0.184 |
| C4 | 0.160 | 0.108 | 0.151 | 1.064 | 0.157 |
| C5 | 0.132 | 0.132 | 0.156 | 0.184 | 1.069 |

*Table 27. Inverse matrix of (I-xm)*

| | C1 | C2 | C3 | C4 | C5 |
|---|---|---|---|---|---|
| C1 | 1.231 | 0.331 | 0.349 | 0.365 | 0.37365 |
| C2 | 0.509 | 1.305 | 0.515 | 0.547 | 0.547 |
| C3 | 0.387 | 0.380 | 1.279 | 0.450 | 0.458 |
| C4 | 0.417 | 0.353 | 0.412 | 1.287 | 0.429 |
| C5 | 0.397 | 0.379 | 0.421 | 0.458 | 1.296 |

*Table 28. Inverse matrix of (I-xu)*

| | C1 | C2 | C3 | C4 | C5 |
|---|---|---|---|---|---|
| C1 | 2.362 | 1.451 | 1.574 | 1.624 | 1.616 |
| C2 | 1.839 | 2.544 | 1.908 | 1.968 | 1.940 |
| C3 | 1.687 | 1.612 | 2.582 | 1.834 | 1.824 |
| C4 | 1.631 | 1.502 | 1.685 | 2.551 | 1.721 |
| C5 | 1.693 | 1.609 | 1.766 | 1.839 | 2.617 |

*Table 29. Total influence matrix for xl*

| | C1 | C2 | C3 | C4 | C5 |
|---|---|---|---|---|---|
| C1 | 0.044 | 0.108 | 0.106 | 0.111 | 0.122 |
| C2 | 0.209 | 0.071 | 0.212 | 0.232 | 0.232 |
| C3 | 0.121 | 0.132 | 0.063 | 0.174 | 0.184 |
| C4 | 0.160 | 0.108 | 0.151 | 0.064 | 0.157 |
| C5 | 0.132 | 0.132 | 0.156 | 0.184 | 0.069 |

*Table 30. Total influence matrix for xm*

| | C1 | C2 | C3 | C4 | C5 |
|---|---|---|---|---|---|
| C1 | 0.231 | 0.331 | 0.349 | 0.365 | 0.374 |
| C2 | 0.509 | 0.305 | 0.515 | 0.547 | 0.547 |
| C3 | 0.387 | 0.380 | 0.279 | 0.450 | 0.458 |
| C4 | 0.417 | 0.353 | 0.412 | 0.287 | 0.429 |
| C5 | 0.397 | 0.379 | 0.421 | 0.458 | 0.296 |

*Table 31. Total influence matrix for xu*

| | C1 | C2 | C3 | C4 | C5 |
|---|---|---|---|---|---|
| C1 | 1.362 | 1.451 | 1.574 | 1.624 | 1.616 |
| C2 | 1.839 | 1.544 | 1.908 | 1.968 | 1.940 |
| C3 | 1.687 | 1.612 | 1.582 | 1.834 | 1.824 |
| C4 | 1.631 | 1.502 | 1.685 | 1.551 | 1.721 |
| C5 | 1.693 | 1.609 | 1.766 | 1.839 | 1.617 |

For this aim, the averaged values of decision makers are used for the fuzzy decision matrix with the equation (22). Table 38 defines the averaged fuzzy decision matrix.

## RANKING THE ALTERNATIVES WITH FUZZY TOPSIS

Initially, fuzzy decision matrix has been normalized. In first step of the normalized process, the values of $c_{ij}^{*}$ have been computed by the formula (23), secondly, the values of $\tilde{r}_{ij}$ have been calculated with the formula (24) to construct the normalized values. The results are seen in Tables 39 and 40 respectively.

The weights of the criteria with fuzzy DEMATEL have been multiplied with the normalized values and weighted normalized matrix has been constructed as seen in Table 41.

The closeness coefficient values of each alternatives have been calculated by the formulas (25)-(28). Ranking results have been provided by considering the values of closeness coefficient in the decreasing order. Table 42 shows the performance results of the alternatives.

In Table 42, A4 has the best performance in the E7 economies while A5 has the worst performance in the central bank independency among the countries.

## RANKING THE ALTERNATIVES WITH FUZZY VIKOR

The fuzzy best value $\tilde{f}_j^{*}$ and fuzzy worst value $\tilde{f}_j^{-}$ of each criterion have been computed by the formula (30). The results are shown in Table 43.

*Table 32. Total-relation fuzzy matrix*

| | C1 | | | C2 | | | C3 | | | C4 | | | C5 | | |
|---|---|---|---|---|---|---|---|---|---|---|---|---|---|---|---|
| C1 | 0.044 | 0.231 | 1.362 | 0.108 | 0.331 | 1.451 | 0.106 | 0.349 | 1.574 | 0.111 | 0.365 | 1.624 | 0.122 | 0.374 | 1.616 |
| C2 | 0.209 | 0.509 | 1.839 | 0.071 | 0.305 | 1.544 | 0.212 | 0.515 | 1.908 | 0.232 | 0.547 | 1.968 | 0.232 | 0.547 | 1.940 |
| C3 | 0.121 | 0.387 | 1.687 | 0.132 | 0.380 | 1.612 | 0.063 | 0.279 | 1.582 | 0.174 | 0.450 | 1.834 | 0.184 | 0.458 | 1.824 |
| C4 | 0.160 | 0.417 | 1.631 | 0.108 | 0.353 | 1.502 | 0.151 | 0.412 | 1.685 | 0.064 | 0.287 | 1.551 | 0.157 | 0.429 | 1.721 |
| C5 | 0.132 | 0.397 | 1.693 | 0.132 | 0.379 | 1.609 | 0.156 | 0.421 | 1.766 | 0.184 | 0.458 | 1.839 | 0.069 | 0.296 | 1.617 |

*Table 33. The values of $x_{lj}$, $x_{mj}$, and $x_{uj}$*

| | $x_{lj}$ | $x_{mj}$ | $x_{uj}$ | $x_{lj}$ | $x_{mj}$ | $x_{uj}$ | $x_{lj}$ | $x_{mj}$ | $x_{uj}$ | $x_{lj}$ | $x_{mj}$ | $x_{uj}$ | $x_{lj}$ | $x_{mj}$ | $x_{uj}$ |
|---|---|---|---|---|---|---|---|---|---|---|---|---|---|---|---|
| C1 | 0.000 | 0.118 | 0.834 | 0.040 | 0.182 | 0.890 | 0.039 | 0.193 | 0.968 | 0.043 | 0.203 | 1.000 | 0.049 | 0.208 | 0.995 |
| C2 | 0.073 | 0.231 | 0.932 | 0.000 | 0.124 | 0.776 | 0.074 | 0.234 | 0.968 | 0.085 | 0.251 | 1.000 | 0.085 | 0.251 | 0.985 |
| C3 | 0.033 | 0.183 | 0.917 | 0.039 | 0.179 | 0.874 | 0.000 | 0.122 | 0.857 | 0.063 | 0.218 | 1.000 | 0.068 | 0.223 | 0.994 |
| C4 | 0.058 | 0.213 | 0.946 | 0.026 | 0.174 | 0.868 | 0.052 | 0.210 | 0.978 | 0.000 | 0.134 | 0.897 | 0.056 | 0.220 | 1.000 |
| C5 | 0.035 | 0.185 | 0.917 | 0.035 | 0.175 | 0.870 | 0.049 | 0.199 | 0.959 | 0.065 | 0.220 | 1.000 | 0.000 | 0.128 | 0.874 |

*Table 34. The values of $x_j^{ls}$ and $x_j^{rs}$*

| | $x_j^{ls}$ | $x_j^{rs}$ | $x_j^{ls}$ | $x_j^{rs}$ | $x_j^{ls}$ | $x_j^{rs}$ | $x_j^{ls}$ | $x_j^{rs}$ | $x_j^{ls}$ | $x_j^{rs}$ |
|---|---|---|---|---|---|---|---|---|---|---|
| C1 | 0.106 | 0.486 | 0.159 | 0.521 | 0.167 | 0.545 | 0.175 | 0.556 | 0.180 | 0.557 |
| C2 | 0.200 | 0.548 | 0.110 | 0.470 | 0.202 | 0.558 | 0.215 | 0.572 | 0.215 | 0.568 |
| C3 | 0.159 | 0.529 | 0.157 | 0.516 | 0.109 | 0.494 | 0.189 | 0.561 | 0.193 | 0.561 |
| C4 | 0.184 | 0.546 | 0.152 | 0.512 | 0.181 | 0.553 | 0.118 | 0.509 | 0.189 | 0.562 |
| C5 | 0.161 | 0.529 | 0.153 | 0.513 | 0.173 | 0.545 | 0.190 | 0.562 | 0.113 | 0.501 |

*Table 35. The values of $x_j^{crisp}$*

| | | | | | |
|---|---|---|---|---|---|
| **C1** | 0.240 | 0.298 | 0.317 | 0.328 | 0.332 |
| **C2** | 0.341 | 0.234 | 0.349 | 0.366 | 0.363 |
| **C3** | 0.302 | 0.293 | 0.246 | 0.341 | 0.344 |
| **C4** | 0.329 | 0.288 | 0.331 | 0.261 | 0.342 |
| **C5** | 0.304 | 0.289 | 0.320 | 0.342 | 0.253 |

*Table 36. The values of $f_{ij}$*

| | | | | | |
|---|---|---|---|---|---|
| **C1** | 0.423 | 0.515 | 0.545 | 0.563 | 0.569 |
| **C2** | 0.718 | 0.515 | 0.732 | 0.765 | 0.760 |
| **C3** | 0.598 | 0.582 | 0.499 | 0.668 | 0.673 |
| **C4** | 0.610 | 0.541 | 0.613 | 0.497 | 0.631 |
| **C5** | 0.606 | 0.581 | 0.636 | 0.675 | 0.517 |

*Table 37. Defuzzified total relation matrix and weights*

| | **C1** | **C2** | **C3** | **C4** | **C5** | $\left(\tilde{D}_i + \tilde{R}_i\right)^{def}$ | $\left(\tilde{D}_i - \tilde{R}_i\right)^{def}$ | **Weights** |
|---|---|---|---|---|---|---|---|---|
| C1 | 0.423 | 0.515 | 0.545 | 0.563 | 0.569 | 5.569 | -0.340 | 0.185 |
| C2 | 0.718 | 0.515 | 0.732 | 0.765 | 0.760 | 6.225 | 0.756 | 0.207 |
| C3 | 0.598 | 0.582 | 0.499 | 0.668 | 0.673 | 6.045 | -0.007 | 0.201 |
| C4 | 0.610 | 0.541 | 0.613 | 0.497 | 0.631 | 6.060 | -0.276 | 0.202 |
| C5 | 0.606 | 0.581 | 0.636 | 0.675 | 0.517 | 6.167 | -0.134 | 0.205 |

*Table 38. Averaged fuzzy decision matrix*

| | C1 | | | C2 | | | C3 | | | C4 | | | C5 | | |
|---|---|---|---|---|---|---|---|---|---|---|---|---|---|---|---|
| A1 | 1.50 | 4.00 | 6.50 | 2.50 | 5.00 | 7.50 | 2.50 | 5.00 | 7.50 | 3.50 | 6.00 | 8.50 | 3.50 | 6.00 | 8.50 |
| A2 | 2.00 | 4.50 | 7.00 | 2.50 | 5.00 | 7.50 | 3.00 | 5.50 | 8.00 | 3.00 | 5.50 | 8.00 | 3.50 | 6.00 | 8.50 |
| A3 | 3.00 | 5.50 | 8.00 | 3.00 | 5.50 | 8.00 | 3.50 | 6.00 | 8.50 | 3.00 | 5.50 | 8.00 | 3.50 | 6.00 | 8.50 |
| A4 | 4.50 | 7.00 | 9.50 | 3.50 | 6.00 | 8.50 | 3.50 | 6.00 | 8.50 | 3.00 | 5.50 | 8.00 | 3.50 | 6.00 | 8.50 |
| A5 | 2.00 | 4.50 | 7.00 | 2.50 | 5.00 | 7.50 | 3.00 | 5.50 | 8.00 | 3.00 | 5.50 | 8.00 | 3.00 | 5.50 | 8.00 |
| A6 | 2.50 | 5.00 | 7.50 | 2.50 | 5.00 | 7.50 | 3.00 | 5.50 | 8.00 | 3.00 | 5.50 | 8.00 | 4.00 | 6.50 | 9.00 |
| A7 | 2.00 | 4.50 | 7.00 | 3.00 | 5.50 | 8.00 | 3.50 | 6.00 | 8.50 | 3.00 | 5.50 | 8.00 | 3.50 | 6.00 | 8.50 |

*Table 39. The values of* $c_{ij}^{*}$

| | | | | | |
|---|---|---|---|---|---|
| **A1** | 42.25 | 56.25 | 56.25 | 72.25 | 72.25 |
| **A2** | 49.00 | 56.25 | 64.00 | 64.00 | 72.25 |
| **A3** | 64.00 | 64.00 | 72.25 | 64.00 | 72.25 |
| **A4** | 90.25 | 72.25 | 72.25 | 64.00 | 72.25 |
| **A5** | 49.00 | 56.25 | 64.00 | 64.00 | 64.00 |
| **A6** | 56.25 | 56.25 | 64.00 | 64.00 | 81.00 |
| **A7** | 49.00 | 64.00 | 72.25 | 64.00 | 72.25 |
| **Total** | **19.99** | **20.62** | **21.56** | **21.36** | **22.50** |

*Table 40. Normalized fuzzy decision matrix*

| | C1 | | | C2 | | | C3 | | | C4 | | | C5 | | |
|---|---|---|---|---|---|---|---|---|---|---|---|---|---|---|---|
| A1 | 0.08 | 0.20 | 0.33 | 0.12 | 0.24 | 0.36 | 0.12 | 0.23 | 0.35 | 0.16 | 0.28 | 0.40 | 0.16 | 0.27 | 0.38 |
| A2 | 0.10 | 0.23 | 0.35 | 0.12 | 0.24 | 0.36 | 0.14 | 0.26 | 0.37 | 0.14 | 0.26 | 0.37 | 0.16 | 0.27 | 0.38 |
| A3 | 0.15 | 0.28 | 0.40 | 0.15 | 0.27 | 0.39 | 0.16 | 0.28 | 0.39 | 0.14 | 0.26 | 0.37 | 0.16 | 0.27 | 0.38 |
| A4 | 0.23 | 0.35 | 0.48 | 0.17 | 0.29 | 0.41 | 0.16 | 0.28 | 0.39 | 0.14 | 0.26 | 0.37 | 0.16 | 0.27 | 0.38 |
| A5 | 0.10 | 0.23 | 0.35 | 0.12 | 0.24 | 0.36 | 0.14 | 0.26 | 0.37 | 0.14 | 0.26 | 0.37 | 0.13 | 0.24 | 0.36 |
| A6 | 0.13 | 0.25 | 0.38 | 0.12 | 0.24 | 0.36 | 0.14 | 0.26 | 0.37 | 0.14 | 0.26 | 0.37 | 0.18 | 0.29 | 0.40 |
| A7 | 0.10 | 0.23 | 0.35 | 0.15 | 0.27 | 0.39 | 0.16 | 0.28 | 0.39 | 0.14 | 0.26 | 0.37 | 0.16 | 0.27 | 0.38 |

*Table 41. Weighted normalized fuzzy decision matrix*

| | C1 | | | C2 | | | C3 | | | C4 | | | C5 | | |
|---|---|---|---|---|---|---|---|---|---|---|---|---|---|---|---|
| A1 | 0.01 | 0.04 | 0.06 | 0.03 | 0.05 | 0.08 | 0.02 | 0.05 | 0.07 | 0.03 | 0.06 | 0.08 | 0.03 | 0.05 | 0.08 |
| A2 | 0.02 | 0.04 | 0.06 | 0.03 | 0.05 | 0.08 | 0.03 | 0.05 | 0.07 | 0.03 | 0.05 | 0.08 | 0.03 | 0.05 | 0.08 |
| A3 | 0.03 | 0.05 | 0.07 | 0.03 | 0.06 | 0.08 | 0.03 | 0.06 | 0.08 | 0.03 | 0.05 | 0.08 | 0.03 | 0.05 | 0.08 |
| A4 | 0.04 | 0.06 | 0.09 | 0.04 | 0.06 | 0.09 | 0.03 | 0.06 | 0.08 | 0.03 | 0.05 | 0.08 | 0.03 | 0.05 | 0.08 |
| A5 | 0.02 | 0.04 | 0.06 | 0.03 | 0.05 | 0.08 | 0.03 | 0.05 | 0.07 | 0.03 | 0.05 | 0.08 | 0.03 | 0.05 | 0.07 |
| A6 | 0.02 | 0.05 | 0.07 | 0.03 | 0.05 | 0.08 | 0.03 | 0.05 | 0.07 | 0.03 | 0.05 | 0.08 | 0.04 | 0.06 | 0.08 |
| A7 | 0.02 | 0.04 | 0.06 | 0.03 | 0.06 | 0.08 | 0.03 | 0.06 | 0.08 | 0.03 | 0.05 | 0.08 | 0.03 | 0.05 | 0.08 |

*Table 42. The values of closeness coefficient and ranking results*

| | $D_i^*$ | $D_i^-$ | $CC_i$ | Ranking |
|---|---|---|---|---|
| A1 | 4.756 | 0.264 | 0.053 | 6 |
| A2 | 4.751 | 0.268 | 0.053 | 5 |
| A3 | 4.732 | 0.285 | 0.057 | 2 |
| A4 | 4.713 | 0.303 | 0.060 | 1 |
| A5 | 4.756 | 0.264 | 0.053 | 7 |
| A6 | 4.742 | 0.276 | 0.055 | 4 |
| A7 | 4.742 | 0.277 | 0.055 | 3 |

*Table 43. The fuzzy best and worst value*

| | $\tilde{f}_j^*$ | | | $\tilde{f}_j^-$ | | |
|---|---|---|---|---|---|---|
| C1 | 4.50 | 7.00 | 9.50 | 1.50 | 4.00 | 6.50 |
| C2 | 3.50 | 6.00 | 8.50 | 2.50 | 5.00 | 7.50 |
| C3 | 3.50 | 6.00 | 8.50 | 2.50 | 5.00 | 7.50 |
| C4 | 3.50 | 6.00 | 8.50 | 3.00 | 5.50 | 8.00 |
| C5 | 4.00 | 6.50 | 9.00 | 3.00 | 5.50 | 8.00 |

*Table 44. The values of Si, Ri, and Qi (v:0.5)*

| Alternatives | Si | Ri | Qi | Ranking |
|---|---|---|---|---|
| A1 | 0.696 | 0.207 | 0.847 | 5 |
| A2 | 0.766 | 0.207 | 0.909 | 6 |
| A3 | 0.500 | 0.202 | 0.174 | 2 |
| A4 | 0.304 | 0.202 | 0.000 | 1 |
| A5 | 0.869 | 0.207 | 1.000 | 7 |
| A6 | 0.633 | 0.207 | 0.791 | 4 |
| A7 | 0.562 | 0.202 | 0.228 | 3 |

*Table 45a. The values of Qi and ranking results by the different values of v*

| v:0 | | v:0.1 | | v:0.2 | | v:0.3 | | v:0.4 | | v:0.5 | |
|---|---|---|---|---|---|---|---|---|---|---|---|
| Qi | Ranking | Qi | Ranking | Qi | Ranking | Qi | Ranking | Qi | Ranking | Qi | Ranking |
| 1.000 | 4 | 0.969 | 5 | 0.939 | 5 | 0.908 | 5 | 0.878 | 5 | 0.847 | 5 |
| 1.000 | 4 | 0.982 | 6 | 0.964 | 6 | 0.945 | 6 | 0.927 | 6 | 0.909 | 6 |
| 0.000 | 1 | 0.035 | 2 | 0.069 | 2 | 0.104 | 2 | 0.139 | 2 | 0.174 | 2 |
| 0.000 | 1 | 0.000 | 1 | 0.000 | 1 | 0.000 | 1 | 0.000 | 1 | 0.000 | 1 |
| 1.000 | 4 | 1.000 | 7 | 1.000 | 7 | 1.000 | 7 | 1.000 | 7 | 1.000 | 7 |
| 1.000 | 4 | 0.958 | 4 | 0.916 | 4 | 0.875 | 4 | 0.833 | 4 | 0.791 | 4 |
| 0.000 | 1 | 0.046 | 3 | 0.091 | 3 | 0.137 | 3 | 0.183 | 3 | 0.228 | 3 |

*Table 45b. The values of Qi and ranking results by the different values of v*

| v:0.6 | | v:0.7 | | v:0.8 | | v:0.9 | | v:1 | |
|---|---|---|---|---|---|---|---|---|---|
| Qi | Ranking | Qi | Ranking | Qi | Ranking | Qi | Ranking | Qi | Ranking |
| 0.816 | 5 | 0.786 | 5 | 0.755 | 5 | 0.725 | 5 | 0.694 | 5 |
| 0.891 | 6 | 0.873 | 6 | 0.855 | 6 | 0.836 | 6 | 0.818 | 6 |
| 0.208 | 2 | 0.243 | 2 | 0.278 | 2 | 0.313 | 2 | 0.347 | 2 |
| 0.000 | 1 | 0.000 | 1 | 0.000 | 1 | 0.000 | 1 | 0.000 | 1 |
| 1.000 | 7 | 1.000 | 7 | 1.000 | 7 | 1.000 | 7 | 1.000 | 7 |
| 0.749 | 4 | 0.707 | 4 | 0.666 | 4 | 0.624 | 4 | 0.582 | 4 |
| 0.274 | 3 | 0.320 | 3 | 0.365 | 3 | 0.411 | 3 | 0.457 | 3 |

The values of Si, Ri, and Qi have been calculated to rank the alternatives with the equations (31)-(33). The results are demonstrated on Table 44.

Several values of v have been used between 1 and 0 for the weight of strategy of maximum group utility such as consensus, veto, and stability. Table 45 presents the results by the different values of v.

The ranking results with the all values of v provide same results except value of zero and the results of VIKOR are similar with the ranking results of fuzzy TOPSIS. This is a clear evidence that the results of comparative analysis are coherent and stable for the weight of strategy of maximum group utility.

## CONCLUSION

All countries aim to reach economic development. Therefore, take try to implement many different strategies in order to reach this purpose. The main reason is that with the help of economic development, it can be much easier to have high living standards. For example, countries try to attract the attentions of the foreign investors to make new investments. This situation has a positive contribution to the economic growth.

In order to reach this purpose, countries should also have effective financial systems. In this framework, companies can find funds easily to make new investments. In addition to this aspect, fund savers can also earn interest income by using their savings. However, financial systems should be operated effectively in order for this process to work successfully. In this context, the players in the financial system have a significant role.

Especially after the globalization, economic borders between the countries are disappeared. This situation creates many different advantages for the economies. First of all, companies get an opportunity to enter new countries. In other words, they can reach new markets. This situation has an increasing effect on the trade volume of these countries. Parallel to this aspect, it also makes contribution to the economic development of these countries.

In addition to this factor, new companies, which entered to the countries, increased the competition in these market. In such a competitive environment, these companies have to take some actions in order to deal with their competitors. Otherwise, it becomes very difficult for these companies to survive in this competition. Within this framework, these companies can prefer to decrease the price of the goods. This situation brings an advantage for the consumers in this country.

However, globalization also causes some risks for the financial players in the market. For example, many companies are under currency risks. It means that any sudden increase or decrease in currency exchange rates leads to high amount of losses for these countries. The main reason is that after the globalization, companies started to make more international trade. Therefore, they have too much foreign debts and assets so that volatility in the currency exchange rates may affect these countries negatively (Destais, 2016).

Central bank is the financial authority in the globalized financial system that can control inflation and interest rates so that it plays a very key role to increase investment amount in the country. In this framework, it is also the authority which can decrease the volatility of the currency exchange rates by purchasing or selling the foreign currencies. Central banks are the main authority to define interest rates and the amount of the money in the financial system. Moreover, assisting the development of the financial system is another responsibility of the central banks (Alfonso et al., 2016).

These responsibilities show that central banks have a crucial role so as to have an effective financial system in the country. However, governments may aim to control central banks because of some different reasons. For instance, governments may aim to take loans from the central banks when they need. In such a case, if the central banks give loans to the government without any control, it can cause inflation problem for the countries. Because of these conditions, central banks should have some specifications.

First of all, central banks should be independent in order to work effectively. For this purpose, the populist practices of political power should be prevented. Secondly, central banks should be independent in the selection of the main objectives or targets taken as basis in the policies regarding the purpose and instrument independence. In addition to them, there should not be any relationship between central bank and government with respect to the economic issues with respect to the economic independence of the central banks. As a result, it is seen that central bank independence is a crucxial factor for the sustainable economic development of the countries.

Monetary policies of the central banks also play a significant role for the effectiveness. By implementing monetary policies, central banks aim to control interest rate and money supply so that high inflation can be prevented. In order to reach this objective, central banks mainly have five different monetary policy tools which are required reserve ratio, rediscount rate, open market operations, standing facilities and asset purchase program.

In this book, it is aimed to analyze the effectiveness of the monetary policies and the independence of the central banks. In the scope of this book, E7 economies are taken into consideration which are Brazil, China, India, Indonesia, Mexico, Russia and Turkey. Hence, this book consists of four different sections in this book. In the first section, the mechanism of the financial system is defined. Also, the role of the central banks in the financial system is discussed in the second part. On the other side, the third part includes monetary policy operations of the central banks. Additionally, the final part of this book includes an application on E7 economies.

In this chapter, independence of the central banks of E7 economies is measured with the fuzzy logic. In this context, 6 different criteria are developed by considering similar studies in the literature. With respect to the purpose and instrument independence, participating rate in the financial market (C1) and responsibility for the monetary stability (C3) are chosen as criteria. In addition to them, rate of uncommitted representative in the board (C4) and applicability of legal provision (C5) represent political independence. On the other side, preventing giving loan to the government (C2) is selected as a criterion for economic independence. In the analysis process, fuzzy DEMATEL method is used to weight these criteria.

On the other side, E7 economies are selected as alternatives. Within this context, both fuzzy TOPSIS and fuzzy VIKOR approaches are taken into consideration to rank these countries with respect to the central bank independence. While considering these two different methods, it becomes possible to make comparative analysis for this issue. Therefore, it is believed that this situation has an increasing effect on the quality and appropriateness of the analysis results.

As a result of fuzzy DEMATEL approach, it is defined that preventing giving loan to the government (C2) is the most influencing factor while participating rate in the financial market (C1) is the most influenced criteria among the determinants of central bank independency. On the other side, it is also concluded that preventing giving loan to the government (C2) is the most important factor as while participating rate in the financial market (C1) has the weakest importance in the criteria set. It is understood that if central banks give loans to the government, this situation directly decreases independency of the central banks. Because this situation negatively affects the decisions of local and foreign investors, central banks in E7 economies should not give loans to the government.

Furthermore, the findings of fuzzy TOPSIS methods show that Indonesia (A4) has the best performance in the E7 economies while Mexico (A5) has the worst performance in the central bank independency among the countries. Brazil (A1) and China (A2) are other emerging economies that take place on the last ranks. On the other hand, the results of fuzzy VIKOR are similar with the ranking results of fuzzy TOPSIS. This is a clear evidence that the results of comparative analysis are coherent and stable for the weight of strategy of maximum group utility. By considering these issues, it is recommended that central banks of the emerging countries should mainly provide economic independence. With the help of this situation, it can be possible to have more effective financial system and developed economy.

It is believed that this book has some significant contribution to the literature in some aspects. Firstly, in this book three different analyses are performed in addition to the theoretical information. Another important novelty is that two analyses are made by using fuzzy logic and one analysis is performed with econometric models. Therefore, it shows that analyses are made by considering both expert opinions and quantitative information. Similarly, some important analysis results and recommendations are presented in this book to increase the effectiveness of the central banks in emerging economies. It is believed that these recommendations are very helpful for academicians and practitioners in the market.

## REFERENCES

Afonso, J. R., Araújo, E. C., & Fajardo, B. G. (2016). The role of fiscal and monetary policies in the Brazilian economy: Understanding recent institutional reforms and economic changes. *The Quarterly Review of Economics and Finance*, *62*, 41–55. doi:10.1016/j.qref.2016.07.005

Destais, C. (2016). Central bank currency swaps and the international monetary system. *Emerging Markets Finance & Trade*, *52*(10), 2253–2266. doi:10.1080/1540496X.2016.1185710

Khorasaninejad, E., Fetanat, A., & Hajabdollahi, H. (2016). Prime mover selection in thermal power plant integrated with organic Rankine cycle for waste heat recovery using a novel multi criteria decision making approach. *Applied Thermal Engineering*, *102*, 1262–1279. doi:10.1016/j.applthermaleng.2016.04.058

Rostamzadeh, R., Govindan, K., Esmaeili, A., & Sabaghi, M. (2015). Application of fuzzy VIKOR for evaluation of green supply chain management practices. *Ecological Indicators*, *49*, 188–203. doi:10.1016/j.ecolind.2014.09.045

# Conclusion

All countries aim to reach economic development. Therefore, take try to implement many different strategies in order to reach this purpose. The main reason is that with the help of economic development, it can be much easier to have high living standards. For example, countries try to attract the attentions of the foreign investors to make new investments. This situation has a positive contribution to the economic growth.

In order to reach this purpose, countries should also have effective financial systems. In this framework, companies can find funds easily to make new investments. In addition to this aspect, fund savers can also earn interest income by using their savings. However, financial systems should be operated effectively in order for this process to work successfully. In this context, the players in the financial system have a significant role.

Especially after the globalization, economic borders between the countries are disappeared. This situation creates many different advantages for the economies. First of all, companies get an opportunity to enter new countries. In other words, they can reach new markets. This situation has an increasing effect on the trade volume of these countries. Parallel to this aspect, it also makes contribution to the economic development of these countries.

In addition to this factor, new companies, which entered to the countries, increased the competition in this market. In such a competitive environment, these companies have to take some actions in order to deal with their competitors. Otherwise, it becomes very difficult for these companies to survive in this competition. Within this framework, these companies can prefer to decrease the price of the goods. This situation brings an advantage for the consumers in this country.

However, globalization also causes some risks for the financial players in the market. For example, many companies are under currency risks. It means that any sudden increase or decrease in currency exchange rates leads to high amount of losses for these countries. The main reason is that after the globalization, companies started to make more international trade. Therefore, they have too much foreign debts and assets so that volatility in the currency exchange rates may affect these countries negatively.

Central bank is the financial authority in the globalized financial system that can control inflation and interest rates so that it plays a very key role to increase investment amount in the country. In this framework, it is also the authority which can decrease the volatility of the currency exchange rates by purchasing or selling the foreign currencies. Central banks are the main authority to define interest rates and the amount of the money in the financial system. Moreover, assisting the development of the financial system is another responsibility of the central banks.

These responsibilities show that central banks have a crucial role so as to have an effective financial system in the country. However, governments may aim to control central banks because of some different reasons. For instance, governments may aim to take loans from the central banks when they need. In such a case, if the central banks give loans to the government without any control, it can cause inflation problem for the countries. Because of these conditions, central banks should have some specifications.

First of all, central banks should be independent in order to work effectively. For this purpose, the populist practices of political power should be prevented. Secondly, central banks should be independent in the selection of the main objectives or targets taken as basis in the policies regarding the purpose and instrument independence. In addition to them, there should not be any relationship between central bank and government with respect to the economic issues with respect to the economic independence of the central banks. As a result, it is seen that central bank independence is a crucial factor for the sustainable economic development of the countries.

Monetary policies of the central banks also play a significant role for the effectiveness. By implementing monetary policies, central banks aim to control interest rate and money supply so that high inflation can be prevented. In order to reach this objective, central banks mainly have five different monetary policy tools which are required reserve ratio, rediscount rate, open market operations, standing facilities and asset purchase program.

In this book, it is aimed to analyze the effectiveness of the monetary policies and the independence of the central banks. In the scope of this book, E7 economies are taken into consideration which are Brazil, China, India, Indonesia, Mexico, Russia and Turkey. Hence, this book consists of four different sections in this book. In the first section, the mechanism of the financial system is defined. Also, the role of the central banks in the financial system is discussed in the second part. On the other side, the third part includes monetary policy operations of the central banks. Additionally, the final part of this book includes an application on E7 economies.

In order to understand the effectiveness of central bank policies and independence in E7 economies, three different analysis are performed in this book. The first analysis aims to measure the effectiveness of the central banks under fuzzy logic. Within this framework, five different monetary policy instruments (required reserve ratio, rediscount rate, open market operations, standing facilities and asset purchase program) are defined as the criteria. Additionally, E7 countries are selected as the alternatives. Moreover, fuzzy DEMATEL methodology is taken into consideration to weight the criteria according to their importance. Similarly, fuzzy TOPSIS and fuzzy VIKOR approaches are used in order to rank the alternatives related to the monetary policy effectiveness.

According to the results of fuzzy DEMATEL approach, it is determined that open market operations (C3) is the most influencing factor. On the other side, it is also concluded that required reserve ratio (C1) is the most influenced criteria among the monetary policy instruments. The results explain that when central banks implement an active monetary policy, such as open market operations, it affects other monetary policies as well. On the other hand, the passive monetary policy is influenced by other monetary policy instruments.

In addition to them, it is also defiend that open market operations (C3) is the most important criterion. Nevertheless, required reserve ratio (C1) has the lowest significance. The findings show that central banks should prefer to implement active monetary policy instruments. With the help of this issue, it can be much easier to influence the market. Otherwise, changing required reserve ratio does not have any powerful impact on the market. Because emerging economies can face volatility in the market, central banks should play a very active role in order to solve the problems in the market. In this circumstance, they should prefer open market operations instead of required reserve ratio.

According to the results of fuzzy TOPSIS methods, it is defined that Indonesia (A4) has the best performance in the E7 economies. Similar to this company, Mexico (A5) is the second most successful company with respect to the effectiveness of the central bank policies. On the other side, Brazil (A1) takes place on the last rank. Parallel to this aspect, the ranking results of fuzzy VIKOR with the values of v that are higher than 0.5 are close to the ranking results of fuzzy TOPSIS. This condition gives information that the results of comparative analysis are coherent and stable for the weight of strategy of maximum group utility. While looking at these results, it is recommended that countries that takes place on the last ranks should implement more active monetary policies, such as open market operations. Therefore, it can be much easier to increase the effectiveness of monetary policies.

In the second analysis, effectiveness of the monetary policies in E7 economies is examined with the help of Kao panel cointegration analysis, Pedroni panel cointegration analysis and Dumitrescu Hurlin panel causality analysis. In the first analysis, fuzzy logic is used whereas econometric models are taken into consideration in this second analysis. For this purpose, two different variables are selected which are central bank interest rate and inflation rate. Additionally, monthly data of these variables for the periods between 1996:01-2019:02 is used in the analysis process.

According to the Kao panel cointegration analysis results, it is understood that there is a long run relationship between the variables. Similarly, as a result of Pedroni panel cointegration analysis, it is concluded that there is long term relationship between interest rate and inflation rate for E7 economies. While considering these results, it is determined that monetary policies are used effectively in these countries.

In addition to these methods, Dumitrescu Hurlin panel causality test is also considered in the analysis process. It is identified that only for lag 1, inflation does not homogeneously cause interest rate. The main reason is that probability value is greater than 0.05. In addition to this issue, for other lags, it is understood that inflation is the main cause of the interest rate. On the other side, for all three different lags, it is concluded that interest is the main cause of the inflation rate. This situation gives information that interest rate decisions of the central banks in E7 economies are very successful to control the inflation rate.

On the other hand, in the third analysis, independence of the central banks of E7 economies is measured with the fuzzy logic. In this context, 6 different criteria are developed by considering similar studies in the literature. With respect to the purpose and instrument independence, participating rate in the financial market (C1) and responsibility for the monetary stability (C3) are chosen as criteria. In addition to them, rate of uncommitted representative in the board (C4) and applicability of legal provision (C5) represent political independence. On the other side, preventing giving loan to the government (C2) is selected as a criterion for economic independence. In the analysis process, fuzzy DEMATEL method is used to weight these criteria.

On the other side, E7 economies are selected as alternatives. Within this context, both fuzzy TOPSIS and fuzzy VIKOR approaches are taken into consideration to rank these countries with respect to the central bank independence. While considering these two different methods, it becomes possible to make comparative analysis for this issue. Therefore, it is believed that this situation has an increasing effect on the quality and appropriateness of the analysis results.

As a result of fuzzy DEMATEL approach, it is defined that preventing giving loan to the government (C2) is the most influencing factor while participating rate in the financial market (C1) is the most influenced criteria among the determinants of central bank independency. On the other side, it is also concluded that preventing giving loan to the government (C2) is the most important factor as while participating rate in the financial market (C1) has the weakest importance in the criteria set. It is understood that if central banks give loans to the government, this situation directly decreases independency of the central banks. Because this situation negatively affects the decisions of local and foreign investors, central banks in E7 economies should not give loans to the government.

Furthermore, the findings of fuzzy TOPSIS methods show that Indonesia (A4) has the best performance in the E7 economies while Mexico (A5) has the worst performance in the central bank independency among the countries. Brazil (A1) and China (A2) are other emerging economies that take place on the last ranks. On the other hand, the results of fuzzy VIKOR are similar with the ranking results of fuzzy TOPSIS. This is a clear evidence that the results of comparative analysis are coherent and stable for the weight of strategy of maximum group utility. By considering these issues, it is recommended that central banks of the emerging countries should mainly provide economic independence. With the help of this situation, it can be possible to have more effective financial system and developed economy.

It is believed that this book has some significant contribution to the literature in some aspects. Firstly, in this book three different analyses are performed in addition to the theoretical information. Another important novelty is that two analyses are made by using fuzzy logic and one analysis is performed with econometric models. Therefore, it shows that analyses are made by considering both expert opinions and quantitative information. Similarly, some important analysis results and recommendations are presented in this book to increase the effectiveness of the central banks in emerging economies. It is believed that these recommendations are very helpful for academicians and practitioners in the market.

# Compilation of References

Abdel-Basset, M., Manogaran, G., Gamal, A., & Smarandache, F. (2018). A hybrid approach of neutrosophic sets and DEMATEL method for developing supplier selection criteria. *Design Automation for Embedded Systems*, 1–22.

Abdel-Basset, M., Manogaran, G., Gamal, A., & Smarandache, F. (2019). A Group Decision Making Framework Based on Neutrosophic TOPSIS Approach for Smart Medical Device Selection. *Journal of Medical Systems*, *43*(2), 38. doi:10.100710916-019-1156-1 PMID:30627801

Abdel-Basset, M., Mohamed, M., & Smarandache, F. (2018). A hybrid neutrosophic group ANP-TOPSIS framework for supplier selection problems. *Symmetry*, *10*(6), 226. doi:10.3390ym10060226

Abdel-Basset, M., Saleh, M., Gamal, A., & Smarandache, F. (2019). An approach of TOPSIS technique for developing supplier selection with group decision making under type-2 neutrosophic number. *Applied Soft Computing*, *77*, 438–452. doi:10.1016/j.asoc.2019.01.035

Abdel-Basset, M., Zhou, Y., Mohamed, M., & Chang, V. (2018). A group decision making framework based on neutrosophic VIKOR approach for e-government website evaluation. *Journal of Intelligent & Fuzzy Systems*, *34*(6), 4213–4224. doi:10.3233/JIFS-171952

Abdlaziz, R. A., Naseem, N. A. M., & Slesman, L. (2018). Dutch Disease effect of Oil Price on Agriculture Sector: Evidence from Panel Cointegration of Oil Exporting Countries. *International Journal of Energy Economics and Policy*, *8*(5), 241–250.

Abdullah, L., & Zulkifli, N. (2018). A new DEMATEL method based on interval type-2 fuzzy sets for developing causal relationship of knowledge management criteria. *Neural Computing & Applications*, 1–17.

Abdullah, S. M., Siddiqua, S., & Huque, R. (2017). Is health care a necessary or luxury product for Asian countries? An answer using panel approach. *Health Economics Review*, *7*(1), 4. doi:10.118613561-017-0144-8 PMID:28124312

Abidin, I. S. Z., Bakar, N. A., & Haseeb, M. (2015). Exploring trade relationship between Malaysia and the OIC member countries: A panel cointegration approach (1995-2012). *Asian Journal of Scientific Research*, *8*(1), 107–121. doi:10.3923/ajsr.2015.107.121

Abimelech Paye Gbatu, Z. W., Wesseh Jr, P. K., & Sesay, V. A. (2018). *What precipitates growth in CO2 emissions?: New evidence from a panel of economic community of West African states (ECOWAS). International Journal of Energy Sector Management*. doi:10.1108/IJESM-09-2017-0001

Ab-Rahim, R., & Chiang, S. N. (2016). Market structure and performance of Malaysian banking industry. *Journal of Financial Reporting and Accounting*, *14*(2), 158–177. doi:10.1108/JFRA-11-2014-0086

Acuña-Carvajal, F., Pinto-Tarazona, L., López-Ospina, H., Barros-Castro, R., Quezada, L., & Palacio, K. (2019). An integrated method to plan, structure and validate a business strategy using fuzzy DEMATEL and the balanced scorecard. *Expert Systems with Applications*, *122*, 351–368. doi:10.1016/j.eswa.2019.01.030

Acuña-Soto, C. M., Liern, V., & Pérez-Gladish, B. (2018). A VIKOR-based approach for the ranking of mathematical instructional videos. *Management Decision*.

Adalı, Z., & Yüksel, S. (2017). *Causality relationship between foreign direct investments and economic improvement for developing economies*. Academic Press.

Addae, B. A., Zhang, L., Zhou, P., & Wang, F. (2019). Analyzing barriers of Smart Energy City in Accra with two-step fuzzy DEMATEL. *Cities (London, England)*, *89*, 218–227. doi:10.1016/j.cities.2019.01.043

Aderemi, T. A., Adebayo, A. G., Jolayemi, A. L., & Kalejaiye, G. T. (2018). Panel Cointegration and Granger Causality Approach to Foreign Direct Investment and Economic Growth in BRICS Countries. *Acta Universitatis Danubius. Œconomica, 15*(2).

Adhikary, B., & Kutsuna, K. (2016). Small Business Finance in Bangladesh: Can'Crowdfunding'Be an Alternative? *Review of Integrative Business and Economics Research*, *4*, 1–21.

Adler, G., Castro, P., & Tovar, C. E. (2016). Does central bank capital matter for monetary policy? *Open Economies Review*, *27*(1), 183–205. doi:10.100711079-015-9360-1

Afolabi, L. O., Abu, B. N., & Azman, A. M. (2016). Openness and ECOWAS regional trade: a panel cointegration analysis using a gravity model. *Актуальні проблеми економіки*, (3), 319-328.

Afolabi, L. O., Aznin, A. B., & Izraf, A. A. (2017). ECOWAS Regional Integration and Trade Effect: A Dynamic Panel Cointegration Method Using the Gravity Model. *International Journal of Economic Perspectives*, *11*(1).

Afonso, J. R., Araújo, E. C., & Fajardo, B. G. (2016). The role of fiscal and monetary policies in the Brazilian economy: Understanding recent institutional reforms and economic changes. *The Quarterly Review of Economics and Finance*, *62*, 41–55. doi:10.1016/j.qref.2016.07.005

Agbo, E. I., & Nwankwo, S. N. P. (2018). Effect of Financial Sector Development on Economic Growth: A Case of Nigeria. *Journal of Economics and Sustainable Development*, *9*(20), 80–91.

Agur, I. (2019). Revisiting the institutional determinants of central bank independence. *Applied Economics Letters*, 1–6.

Ahmad, M. O., Lwakatare, L. E., Kuvaja, P., Oivo, M., & Markkula, J. (2017). An empirical study of portfolio management and Kanban in agile and lean software companies. *Journal of Software: Evolution and Process*, *29*(6), e1834.

Akhtar, M. H., Sheikh, M. R., & Anam, A. (2016). Financial Development, Energy Consumption and Trade Openness Nexus: Empirical Evidence from Selected South Asian Countries. *Pakistan Journal of Social Sciences*, *36*(1).

Akram, V., & Rath, B. N. (2019). Is there any evidence of tax-and-spend, spend-and-tax or fiscal synchronization from panel of Indian state? *Applied Economics Letters*, 1–4.

Albaity, M., & Mustafa, H. (2018). International and Macroeconomic Determinants of Oil Price: Evidence from Gulf Cooperation Council Countries. *International Journal of Energy Economics and Policy*, *8*(1), 69–81.

Alberici, A., & Querci, F. (2016). The quality of disclosures on environmental policy: The profile of financial intermediaries. *Corporate Social Responsibility and Environmental Management*, *23*(5), 283–296. doi:10.1002/csr.1375

Alcaraz, C., Claessens, S., Cuadra, G., Marques-Ibanez, D., & Sapriza, H. (2018). *Whatever it takes. What's the impact of a major nonconventional monetary policy intervention?* Academic Press.

Aldan, A., & Çulha, O. Y. (2016). The role of the extensive margin in export of Turkey: A comparative analysis. *Central Bank Review*, *16*(2), 59–64. doi:10.1016/j.cbrev.2016.05.002

Ali, H. S., Adaa, A. H. M. A., Lin, W. L., & Youssouf, M. A. (2018). Biomass energy consumption and economic growth: Panel data evidence from ASEAN member countries. *GeoJournal*, *83*(6), 1339–1348. doi:10.100710708-017-9839-y

Ali, K., Moktadir, M. A., Shaikh, A. A., Deb, A. K., & Rashed-Ul-Islam, M. (2018). Challenges Evaluation for Adoption of SCP Practices in Footwear Industry of Bangladesh: A DEMATEL Approach. *Journal of Operations and Strategic Planning*, *1*(2), 168–184. doi:10.1177/2516600X18812984

Alikar, N., Mousavi, S. M., Ghazilla, R. A. R., Tavana, M., & Olugu, E. U. (2017). A bi-objective multi-period series-parallel inventory-redundancy allocation problem with time value of money and inflation considerations. *Computers & Industrial Engineering*, *104*, 51–67. doi:10.1016/j.cie.2016.12.006

Ali, Q., Yaseen, M. R., & Khan, M. T. I. (2019). The causality of road traffic fatalities with its determinants in upper middle income countries: A continent-wide comparison. *Transportation Research Part A, Policy and Practice*, *119*, 301–312. doi:10.1016/j.tra.2018.12.002

Ali, S., Bashir, T., Ahmed, T., Ishaq, A., & Shahzad, S. J. H. (2018). The Determinants of Bank Stock Prices: A Panel Approach. *South Asian Journal of Management Sciences*, *12*(2), 116–129. doi:10.21621ajms.2018122.01

Al-Mulali, U., Ozturk, I., & Lean, H. H. (2015). The influence of economic growth, urbanization, trade openness, financial development, and renewable energy on pollution in Europe. *Natural Hazards*, *79*(1), 621–644. doi:10.100711069-015-1865-9

Aloini, D., Dulmin, R., Mininno, V., Pellegrini, L., & Farina, G. (2018). Technology assessment with IF-TOPSIS: An application in the advanced underwater system sector. *Technological Forecasting and Social Change*, *131*, 38–48. doi:10.1016/j.techfore.2017.07.010

Alper, K., Binici, M., Demiralp, S., Kara, H., & Özlü, P. (2018). Reserve requirements, liquidity risk, and bank lending behavior. *Journal of Money, Credit and Banking*, *50*(4), 817–827. doi:10.1111/jmcb.12475

Alsaleh, M., & Abdul-Rahim, A. S. (2018). Bioenergy industry and the growth of the energy sector in the EU-28 region: Evidence from panel cointegration analysis. *Journal of Renewable and Sustainable Energy*, *10*(5), 053103. doi:10.1063/1.5032323

Alzahrani, A. I., Al-Samarraie, H., Eldenfria, A., & Alalwan, N. (2018). A DEMATEL method in identifying design requirements for mobile environments: Students' perspectives. *Journal of Computing in Higher Education*, *30*(3), 466–488. doi:10.100712528-018-9176-2

Ameri, A. A., Pourghasemi, H. R., & Cerda, A. (2018). Erodibility prioritization of sub-watersheds using morphometric parameters analysis and its mapping: A comparison among TOPSIS, VIKOR, SAW, and CF multi-criteria decision making models. *The Science of the Total Environment*, *613*, 1385–1400. doi:10.1016/j.scitotenv.2017.09.210 PMID:29898506

Amiri, A. J. G., & Gong, Z. (2018). The Impact of liquidity on Economic Growth in America's Economy Using a New Approach TVP-FAVAR. *Revista Publicando*, *5*(14), 370–385.

Amiri, M., Pourghasemi, H. R., Arabameri, A., Vazirzadeh, A., Yousefi, H., & Kafaei, S. (2019). Prioritization of Flood Inundation of Maharloo Watershed in Iran Using Morphometric Parameters Analysis and TOPSIS MCDM Model. In *Spatial Modeling in GIS and R for Earth and Environmental Sciences* (pp. 371–390). Elsevier. doi:10.1016/B978-0-12-815226-3.00016-8

Ananthakumar, K., Rajamani, D., Balasubramanian, E., & Davim, J. P. (2019). Measurement and optimization of multi-response characteristics in plasma arc cutting of Monel 400™ using RSM and TOPSIS. *Measurement*, *135*, 725–737. doi:10.1016/j.measurement.2018.12.010

Anastasiou, D., Louri, H., & Tsionas, M. (2019). Nonperforming loans in the euro area: A re core–periphery banking markets fragmented? *International Journal of Finance & Economics*, *24*(1), 97–112. doi:10.1002/ijfe.1651

Andaleeb, S., Abbasi, M. A., Naqvi, S. I. H., & Ali, S. (2018). Determinants Of Capital Structure Of Leasing Companies In Pakistan. *Archives of Business Research*, *6*(3). doi:10.14738/abr.63.4145

Andrea, S. (2015). Testing Monetary Exchange Rate Models With Panel Cointegration Tests. *Annals of the University of Oradea: Economic Science*, *25*(1), 643–651.

Andrei, J. V., Mieila, M., & Panait, M. (2017). The impact and determinants of the energy paradigm on economic growth in European Union. *PLoS One*, *12*(3), e0173282. doi:10.1371/journal.pone.0173282 PMID:28301505

Anginer, D., Demirguc-Kunt, A., Huizinga, H., & Ma, K. (2018). Corporate governance of banks and financial stability. *Journal of Financial Economics*, *130*(2), 327–346. doi:10.1016/j.jfineco.2018.06.011

Angrist, J. D., Jordà, Ò., & Kuersteiner, G. M. (2018). Semiparametric estimates of monetary policy effects: String theory revisited. *Journal of Business & Economic Statistics*, *36*(3), 371–387. doi:10.1080/07350015.2016.1204919

Appiah, K., Du, J., Yeboah, M., & Appiah, R. (2019). Causal correlation between energy use and carbon emissions in selected emerging economies—panel model approach. *Environmental Science and Pollution Research International*, 1–17. PMID:30684181

Araujo, C. A. S., Wanke, P., & Siqueira, M. M. (2018). A performance analysis of Brazilian public health: TOPSIS and neural networks application. *International Journal of Productivity and Performance Management*, *67*(9), 1526–1549. doi:10.1108/IJPPM-11-2017-0319

Arce, Ó., Nuño, G., & Thomas, C. (2019). *A large central bank balance sheet? Floor vs corridor systems in a new Keynesian environment*. Academic Press.

Arshad, N., Ismail, M. T., & Rahman, R. A. (2018, June). Macroeconomic determinants of selected Asia housing market. In. AIP Conference Proceedings: Vol. 1974. *No. 1* (p. 040001). AIP Publishing. doi:10.1063/1.5041675

Arun, K., & Yıldırım, D. Ç. (2017). Effects of foreign direct investment on intellectual property, patents and R&D. *Queen Mary Journal of Intellectual Property*, *7*(2), 226–241. doi:10.4337/qmjip.2017.02.05

Atanasov, V., Davies, R. J., & Merrick, J. J. Jr. (2015). Financial intermediaries in the midst of market manipulation: Did they protect the fool or help the knave? *Journal of Corporate Finance*, *34*, 210–234. doi:10.1016/j.jcorpfin.2015.07.011

Atthirawong, W., Panprung, W., & Leerojanaprapa, K. (2018). Using DEMATEL To Explore The Relationship Of Factors Affecting Consumers' Behaviors In Buying Green Products. In ECMS (pp. 317-322). Academic Press.

Aviso, K. B., Lucas, R. I. G., Tapia, J. F. D., Promentilla, M. A. B., & Tan, R. R. (2018). Identifying Key Factors to Learning Process Systems Engineering and Process Integration through DEMATEL. *Chemical Engineering Transactions*, *70*, 265–270.

Awasthi, A., Govindan, K., & Gold, S. (2018). Multi-tier sustainable global supplier selection using a fuzzy AHP-VIKOR based approach. *International Journal of Production Economics*, *195*, 106–117. doi:10.1016/j.ijpe.2017.10.013

Ayad, H. (2019). The effect of terms of trade on current account balance: Harberger-Laursen-Metzler effect in Arabic countries. *Journal of Smart Economic Growth*, *4*(1).

Aydin, M. (2019). Renewable and non-renewable electricity consumption–economic growth nexus: Evidence from OECD countries. *Renewable Energy*, *136*, 599–606. doi:10.1016/j.renene.2019.01.008

Aydin, M., & Malcioglu, G. (2016). Financial development and economic growth relationship: The case of OECD countries. *Journal of Applied Research in Finance and Economics*, *2*(1), 1–7.

Aye, G. C., & Edoja, P. E. (2017). Effect of economic growth on CO2 emission in developing countries: Evidence from a dynamic panel threshold model. *Cogent Economics & Finance*, *5*(1), 1379239. doi:10.1080/23322039.2017.1379239

Aytaç, I. A., Rankin, B. H., & İbikoğlu, A. (2015). The social impact of the 2008 global economic crisis on neighborhoods, households, and individuals in Turkey. *Social Indicators Research*, *124*(1), 1–19. doi:10.100711205-014-0769-5

Azevedo, L. F. P., & Pereira, P. L. V. (2018). *Effects of official and unofficial central bank communication on the Brazilian interest rate curve*. Academic Press.

Azimifard, A., Moosavirad, S. H., & Ariafar, S. (2018). Designing steel supply chain and assessing the embedded CO2 emission based on the input-output table by using DEMATEL method. *Management Decision*, *56*(4), 757–776. doi:10.1108/MD-05-2017-0478

Azimifard, A., Moosavirad, S. H., & Ariafar, S. (2018). Selecting sustainable supplier countries for Iran's steel industry at three levels by using AHP and TOPSIS methods. *Resources Policy*, *57*, 30–44. doi:10.1016/j.resourpol.2018.01.002

Babajide, A., Isola, L., & Somoye, R. O. (2016). Stock market response to economic growth and interest rate volatility: Evidence from Nigeria. *International Journal of Economics and Financial Issues*, *6*(1), 354–360.

Baccour, L. (2018). Amended fused TOPSIS-VIKOR for classification (ATOVIC) applied to some UCI data sets. *Expert Systems with Applications*, *99*, 115–125. doi:10.1016/j.eswa.2018.01.025

Baiardi, D., Bianchi, C., & Lorenzini, E. (2015). The price and income elasticities of the top clothing exporters: Evidence from a panel data analysis. *Journal of Asian Economics*, *38*, 14–30. doi:10.1016/j.asieco.2015.03.003

Bai, C., & Sarkis, J. (2018). Integrating sustainability into supplier selection: A grey-based TOPSIS analysis. *Technological and Economic Development of Economy*, *24*(6), 2202–2224. doi:10.3846/tede.2018.5582

Bakir, S., Khan, S., Ahsan, K., & Rahman, S. (2018). Exploring the critical determinants of environmentally oriented public procurement using the DEMATEL method. *Journal of Environmental Management*, *225*, 325–335. doi:10.1016/j.jenvman.2018.07.081 PMID:30099147

Balcioglu, H. (2016). Foreign Aid and Economic Growth: A Panel Cointegration for Selected Turkic Republics. *International Journal of Business and Social Research*, *6*(6), 17–23. doi:10.18533/ijbsr.v6i6.947

Bayramoğlu, A. T., & Öztürk, Z. (2018). Assessing the Twin and Triple Deficit Hypotheses in Developing Economies: A Panel Causality Analysis. In *Global Approaches in Financial Economics, Banking, and Finance* (pp. 209–225). Cham: Springer. doi:10.1007/978-3-319-78494-6_10

Bech, M. L., & Garratt, R. (2017, September). *Central bank cryptocurrencies. BIS Quarterly Review.*

Belošević, I., Kosijer, M., Ivić, M., & Pavlović, N. (2018). Group decision making process for early stage evaluations of infrastructure projects using extended VIKOR method under fuzzy environment. *European Transport Research Review, 10*(2), 43. doi:10.118612544-018-0318-4

Berger, A. N., Roman, R. A., & Sedunov, J. (2019). Did TARP reduce or increase systemic risk? The effects of government aid on financial system stability. *Journal of Financial Intermediation*, 100810. doi:10.1016/j.jfi.2019.01.002

Berggren, N., Daunfeldt, S. O., & Hellström, J. (2016). Does social trust speed up reforms? The case of central-bank independence. *Journal of Institutional Economics, 12*(2), 395–415. doi:10.1017/S1744137415000284

Bergsten, C. F. (2017). *Dilemmas of the Dollar: Economics and Politics of United States International Monetary Policy: Economics and Politics of United States International Monetary Policy*. Routledge.

Berriel, T. C., & Bhattarai, S. (2009). Monetary policy and central bank balance sheet concerns. *The B.E. Journal of Macroeconomics, 9*(1). doi:10.2202/1935-1690.1770

Bhagawati, M. T., Manavalan, E., Jayakrishna, K., & Venkumar, P. (2019). Identifying Key Success Factors of Sustainability in Supply Chain Management for Industry 4.0 Using DEMATEL Method. In *Proceedings of International Conference on Intelligent Manufacturing and Automation* (pp. 583-591). Springer. 10.1007/978-981-13-2490-1_54

Bhatia, M. S., & Srivastava, R. K. (2018). Analysis of external barriers to remanufacturing using grey-DEMATEL approach: An Indian perspective. *Resources, Conservation and Recycling, 136*, 79–87. doi:10.1016/j.resconrec.2018.03.021

Bhat, S. A., Ganaie, A. A., Khan, N. A., & Kamaiah, B. (2018). Grants-in-Aid and State Domestic Product: An Empirical Analysis in India. In *Challenges and Issues in Indian Fiscal Federalism* (pp. 107–120). Singapore: Springer. doi:10.1007/978-981-10-6217-9_9

Bianchi, F., & Civelli, A. (2015). Globalization and inflation: Evidence from a time-varying VAR. *Review of Economic Dynamics, 18*(2), 406–433. doi:10.1016/j.red.2014.07.004

Bianchini, A. (2018). 3PL provider selection by AHP and TOPSIS methodology. *Benchmarking: An International Journal, 25*(1), 235–252. doi:10.1108/BIJ-08-2016-0125

Bian, T., Zheng, H., Yin, L., & Deng, Y. (2018). Failure mode and effects analysis based on D numbers and TOPSIS. *Quality and Reliability Engineering International, 34*(4), 501–515. doi:10.1002/qre.2268

Bildirici, M. (2018). Impact of military on biofuels consumption and GHG emissions: The evidence from G7 countries. *Environmental Science and Pollution Research International*, *25*(14), 13560–13568. doi:10.100711356-018-1545-x PMID:29492823

Blancheton, B. (2016). Central bank independence in a historical perspective. Myth, lessons and a new model. *Economic Modelling*, *52*, 101–107. doi:10.1016/j.econmod.2015.02.027

Blanco, I., & Wehrheim, D. (2017). The bright side of financial derivatives: Options trading and firm innovation. *Journal of Financial Economics*, *125*(1), 99–119. doi:10.1016/j.jfineco.2017.04.004

Block, J. H., Cumming, D. J., & Vismara, S. (2017). International perspectives on venture capital and bank finance for entrepreneurial firms. *Economia e Politica Industriale*, *44*(1), 3–22. doi:10.100740812-017-0069-6

Bodea, C., & Hicks, R. (2015). Price stability and central bank independence: Discipline, credibility, and democratic institutions. *International Organization*, *69*(1), 35–61. doi:10.1017/S0020818314000277

Brahmana, R., Kontesa, M., & Gilbert, R. E. (2018). Income diversification and bank performance: Evidence from malaysian banks. *Economic Bulletin*, *38*(2), 799–809.

Braun, B. (2015). Governing the future: The European Central Bank's expectation management during the Great Moderation. *Economy and Society*, *44*(3), 367–391. doi:10.1080/03085147.2015.1049447

Braun, B. (2016). Speaking to the people? Money, trust, and central bank legitimacy in the age of quantitative easing. *Review of International Political Economy*, *23*(6), 1064–1092. doi:10.1080/09692290.2016.1252415

Brogi, M., & Lagasio, V. (2018). Environmental, social, and governance and company profitability: Are financial intermediaries different? *Corporate Social Responsibility and Environmental Management*.

Bruno, V., & Shin, H. S. (2015). Capital flows and the risk-taking channel of monetary policy. *Journal of Monetary Economics*, *71*, 119–132. doi:10.1016/j.jmoneco.2014.11.011

Bu, Y., Guo, M., & Cheng, P. (2018). Optimization of Enhanced Geothermal System Power Generation Investment Scheme Based on Fuzzy VIKOR Model. In *E3S Web of Conferences* (Vol. 57, p. 01001). EDP Sciences. doi:10.1051/e3sconf/20185701001

Büyüközkan, G., Göçer, F., & Karabulut, Y. (2019). A new group decision making approach with IF AHP and IF VIKOR for selecting hazardous waste carriers. *Measurement*, *134*, 66–82. doi:10.1016/j.measurement.2018.10.041

Çalı, S., & Balaman, Ş. Y. (2019). A novel outranking based multi criteria group decision making methodology integrating ELECTRE and VIKOR under intuitionistic fuzzy environment. *Expert Systems with Applications*, *119*, 36–50. doi:10.1016/j.eswa.2018.10.039

Can, M., & Gozgor, G. (2018). Revisiting the tourism-growth nexus: Evidence from a new index for the market diversification of tourist arrivals. *Current Issues in Tourism, 21*(10), 1157–1170. doi:10.1080/13683500.2016.1268103

Carlson, W. H., & Lackman, C. L. (2018). Raising Interest Rates: IOER vs. OMO: Interest on Excess Reserves vs Open Market Operations. *International Journal of Financial Research, 9*(1), 142–146. doi:10.5430/ijfr.v9n1p142

Carreras, O., Davis, E. P., & Piggott, R. (2018). Assessing macroprudential tools in OECD countries within a cointegration framework. *Journal of Financial Stability, 37*, 112–130. doi:10.1016/j.jfs.2018.04.004

Carriere-Swallow, M. Y., Faruqee, M. H., & Srinivasan, M. K. (2016). *Challenges for Central Banking: Perspectives from Latin America*. International Monetary Fund.

Cassola, N., & Koulischer, F. (2019). The collateral channel of open market operations. *Journal of Financial Stability, 41*, 73–90. doi:10.1016/j.jfs.2019.03.002

Cavallaro, F., Zavadskas, E. K., Streimikiene, D., & Mardani, A. (2019). Assessment of concentrated solar power (CSP) technologies based on a modified intuitionistic fuzzy topsis and trigonometric entropy weights. *Technological Forecasting and Social Change, 140*, 258–270. doi:10.1016/j.techfore.2018.12.009

Ceballos, B., Pelta, D. A., & Lamata, M. T. (2018). Rank reversal and the VIKOR method: An empirical evaluation. *International Journal of Information Technology & Decision Making, 17*(02), 513–525. doi:10.1142/S0219622017500237

Certa, A., Enea, M., Galante, G. M., Izquierdo, J., & Fata, C. M. L. (2018). Food safety risk analysis from the producers' perspective: Prioritisation of production process stages by HACCP and TOPSIS. *International Journal of Management and Decision Making, 17*(4), 396–414. doi:10.1504/IJMDM.2018.095720

Chakraborty, T., Majumder, M., & Khare, A. (2019). Application of AHP-VIKOR and GMDH framework to develop an indicator to identify utilisation potential of wave energy converter with respect to location. *International Journal of Spatio-Temporal Data Science, 1*(1), 98–113. doi:10.1504/IJSTDS.2019.097603

Chamon, M., & Garcia, M. (2016). Capital controls in Brazil: Effective? *Journal of International Money and Finance, 61*, 163–187. doi:10.1016/j.jimonfin.2015.08.008

Chang, C. C., & Chen, P. Y. (2018). Analysis of critical factors for social games based on extended technology acceptance model: A DEMATEL approach. *Behaviour & Information Technology, 37*(8), 774–785. doi:10.1080/0144929X.2018.1480654

Chang, C., Liu, Z., Spiegel, M. M., & Zhang, J. (2018). Reserve requirements and optimal chinese stabilization policy. *Journal of Monetary Economics*.

Chauhan, A., Singh, A., & Jharkharia, S. (2018). An interpretive structural modeling (ISM) and decision-making trail and evaluation laboratory (DEMATEL) method approach for the analysis of barriers of waste recycling in India. *Journal of the Air & Waste Management Association, 68*(2), 100–110. doi:10.1080/10962247.2016.1249441 PMID:28278038

Chen, W., Shen, Y., & Wang, Y. (2018). Evaluation of economic transformation and upgrading of resource-based cities in Shaanxi province based on an improved TOPSIS method. *Sustainable Cities and Society, 37*, 232-240.

Chen, C. T., Huang, S. F., & Hung, W. Z. (2018). Linguistic VIKOR method for project evaluation of ambient intelligence product. *Journal of Ambient Intelligence and Humanized Computing*, 1–11.

Chen, D., Guan, Y., Zhang, T., & Zhao, G. (2017). Political connection of financial intermediaries: Evidence from China's IPO market. *Journal of Banking & Finance, 76*, 15–31. doi:10.1016/j.jbankfin.2016.11.023

Chen, T. Y. (2018). Remoteness index-based Pythagorean fuzzy VIKOR methods with a generalized distance measure for multiple criteria decision analysis. *Information Fusion, 41*, 129–150. doi:10.1016/j.inffus.2017.09.003

Chen, Y. H., Wang, S. W., Lee, C., & Lin, C. T. (2018). Using the DEMATEL Method to Explore the Critical Factors That Influence Visitors to Purchase Museum Cultural Products. *Journal of Testing and Evaluation, 46*(5).

Chong, T. T. L., & Liu, W. (2017). The roadmap of interest rate liberalisation in China. *Economic and Political Studies, 5*(4), 421–440. doi:10.1080/20954816.2017.1384614

Chou, T. K., & Buchdadi, A. D. (2016). Bank performance and its underlying factors: A study of rural banks in Indonesia. *Accounting and Finance Research, 5*(3), 55–63. doi:10.5430/afr.v5n3p55

Chou, Y. C., Yen, H. Y., Dang, V. T., & Sun, C. C. (2019). Assessing the Human Resource in Science and Technology for Asian Countries: Application of Fuzzy AHP and Fuzzy TOPSIS. *Symmetry, 11*(2), 251. doi:10.3390ym11020251

Claessens, S., & Van Horen, N. (2015). The impact of the global financial crisis on banking globalization. *IMF Economic Review, 63*(4), 868–918. doi:10.1057/imfer.2015.38

Codato, A., Cavalieri, M., Perissinotto, R., & Dantas, E. G. (2016). Economic mainstream and power: A profile analysis of Central Bank directors during PSDB and PT governments in Brazil. *Nova Economia, 26*(3), 687–720. doi:10.1590/0103-6351/2845

Coibion, O., Gorodnichenko, Y., Kueng, L., & Silvia, J. (2017). Innocent Bystanders? Monetary policy and inequality. *Journal of Monetary Economics, 88*, 70–89. doi:10.1016/j.jmoneco.2017.05.005

Conrad, C., & Hartmann, M. (2019). On the determinants of long-run inflation uncertainty: Evidence from a panel of 17 developed economies. *European Journal of Political Economy, 56*, 233–250. doi:10.1016/j.ejpoleco.2018.09.002

Conti-Brown, P. (2018). Central banking and institutional change in the United States: punctuated equilibrium in the development of money, finance and banking. *Research Handbook on Central Banking*, 6.

Coombs, N. (2017). Macroprudential versus monetary blueprints for financial reform. *Journal of Cultural Economics, 10*(2), 207–216. doi:10.1080/17530350.2016.1234404

Corsetti, G., Dedola, L., Jarociński, M., Maćkowiak, B., & Schmidt, S. (2018). Macroeconomic stabilization, monetary-fiscal interactions, and Europe's monetary union. *European Journal of Political Economy*.

Corwin, S. A., Larocque, S. A., & Stegemoller, M. A. (2017). Investment banking relationships and analyst affiliation bias: The impact of the global settlement on sanctioned and non-sanctioned banks. *Journal of Financial Economics, 124*(3), 614–631. doi:10.1016/j.jfineco.2017.03.005

Costa, F., Denis Granja, A., Fregola, A., Picchi, F., & Portioli Staudacher, A. (2019). Understanding Relative Importance of Barriers to Improving the Customer–Supplier Relationship within Construction Supply Chains Using DEMATEL Technique. *Journal of Management Engineering, 35*(3), 04019002. doi:10.1061/(ASCE)ME.1943-5479.0000680

Cui, F. B., You, X. Y., Shi, H., & Liu, H. C. (2018). Optimal siting of electric vehicle charging stations using pythagorean fuzzy vikor approach. *Mathematical Problems in Engineering*, 2018.

Cui, L., Chan, H. K., Zhou, Y., Dai, J., & Lim, J. J. (2018). Exploring critical factors of green business failure based on grey-decision making trial and evaluation laboratory (DEMATEL). *Journal of Business Research*.

Cúrdia, V., & Woodford, M. (2011). The central-bank balance sheet as an instrument of monetarypolicy. *JournalofMonetaryEconomics, 58*(1), 54–79. doi:10.1016/j.jmoneco.2010.09.011

Dalapati, S., & Pramanik, S. (2018). A revisit to NC-VIKOR based MAGDM strategy in neutrosophic cubic set environment. *Neutrosophic Sets and Systems, 21*, 131–141.

Daneshvar Rouyendegh, B., Yildizbasi, A., & Arikan, Ü. Z. (2018). Using intuitionistic fuzzy TOPSIS in site selection of wind power plants in Turkey. *Advances in Fuzzy Systems*.

de Haan, J., Bodea, C., Hicks, R., & Eijffinger, S. C. (2018). Central bank independence before and after the crisis. *Comparative Economic Studies, 60*(2), 183–202. doi:10.105741294-017-0050-4

de Medeiros, G. B., Portugal, M. S., & Aragón, E. K. D. S. B. (2016). Robust monetary policy, structural breaks, and nonlinearities in the reaction function of the Central Bank of Brazil. *Economía, 17*(1), 96–113. doi:10.1016/j.econ.2016.01.001

de Vilaca Burgos, A., de Oliveira Filho, J. D., Suares, M. V. C., & de Almeida, R. S. (2017). *Distributed ledger technical research in Central Bank of Brazil*. Working Paper.

Del Negro, M., & Sims, C. A. (2015). When does a central bank' s balance sheet require fiscal support? *Journal of Monetary Economics, 73*, 1–19. doi:10.1016/j.jmoneco.2015.05.001

Dellepiane-Avellaneda, S. (2015). The Political Power of Economic Ideas: The Case of 'Expansionary Fiscal Contractions'. *British Journal of Politics and International Relations, 17*(3), 391–418. doi:10.1111/1467-856X.12038

Demiralp, S., & Demiralp, S. (2019). Erosion of Central Bank independence in Turkey. *Turkish Studies, 20*(1), 49–68. doi:10.1080/14683849.2018.1505512

Dempster, M. (2018). *The End of Alchemy: Money*. Banking and the Future of the Global Economy.

Desai, H., Rajgopal, S., & Yu, J. J. (2016). Were information intermediaries sensitive to the financial statement-based leading indicators of bank distress prior to the financial crisis? *Contemporary Accounting Research, 33*(2), 576–606. doi:10.1111/1911-3846.12161

Destais, C. (2016). Central bank currency swaps and the international monetary system. *Emerging Markets Finance & Trade, 52*(10), 2253–2266. doi:10.1080/1540496X.2016.1185710

Dev, S., Aherwar, A., & Patnaik, A. (2019). Material Selection for Automotive Piston Component Using Entropy-VIKOR Method. *Silicon*, 1-15.

Devadoss, A. V., Prabakaran, R., & Felix, A. (2018). A Hybrid Scenario FCM with VIKOR Technique for Ranking the Factors. *International Journal of Pure and Applied Mathematics, 119*(9), 233–244.

Dincer, H., & Hacioglu, U. (2017). Investigating the Economic Vulnerability Factors of Emerging Markets After the Global Financial Crisis of 2008 With a Hybrid Multi-Criteria Decision-Making Approach. In Handbook of Research on Economic, Financial, and Industrial Impacts on Infrastructure Development (pp. 313-333). IGI Global.

Dincer, H., & Yuksel, S. (2019). IT2-based Fuzzy Hybrid Decision Making Approach to Soft Computing. *IEEE Access*.

Dincer, H., Hacioglu, U., & Yilmaz, R. (2013). *The effect of integrated marketing communication competencies on banking performance: analysis with fuzzy VIKOR method*. Academic Press.

Dinçer, H., Hacıoğlu, Ü., & Yüksel, S. (2018). Evaluating the Effects of Economic Imbalances on Gold Price in Turkey With MARS Method and Discussions on Microfinance. In Microfinance and Its Impact on Entrepreneurial Development, Sustainability, and Inclusive Growth (pp. 115-137). IGI Global.

Dinçer, H., Yüksel, S., & Adalı, Z. (2019). Economic Effects in Islamic Stock Development of the European Countries: Policy Recommendations for Ethical Behaviors. In Handbook of Research on Managerial Thinking in Global Business Economics (pp. 58-78). IGI Global.

Dinçer, H., Yüksel, S., & Kartal, M. T. (2016). Evaluating the Corporate Governance Based Performance of Participation Banks in Turkey with the House of Quality Using an Integrated Hesitant Fuzzy MCDM [Türkiye'de Katılım Bankalarının Kurumsal Yönetiminin Çok Değişkenli Entegre Bulanık Karar Verme Yaklaşımı Kullanılarak Kalite Evi ile Değerlendirilmesi]. *BDDK Bankacılık ve Finansal Piyasalar Dergisi, 10*(1).

Dinçer, H., Yüksel, S., & Kartal, M. T. (2019). The Role of Bank Interest Rate in the Competitive Emerging Markets to Provide Financial and Economic Stability. *Ekonomi, İşletme ve Maliye Araştırmaları Dergisi, 1*(2).

Dinçer, H., Yüksel, S., & Pınarbaşı, F. (2019). SERVQUAL-Based Evaluation of Service Quality of Energy Companies in Turkey: Strategic Policies for Sustainable Economic Development. In The Circular Economy and Its Implications on Sustainability and the Green Supply Chain (pp. 142-167). IGI Global.

Dinçer, H., Yüksel, S., Adalı, Z., & Aydın, R. (2019). Evaluating the Role of Research and Development and Technology Investments on Economic Development of E7 Countries. In Organizational Transformation and Managing Innovation in the Fourth Industrial Revolution (pp. 245-263). IGI Global.

Dinçer, H., Yüksel, S., Yazici, M., & Pınarbaşı, F. (2019). Assessing Corporate Social Responsibilities in the Banking Sector: As a Tool of Strategic Communication During the Global Financial Crisis. In Handbook of Research on Global Issues in Financial Communication and Investment Decision Making (pp. 1-27). IGI Global.

Dincer, H. (2015). Profit-based stock selection approach in banking sector using Fuzzy AHP and MOORA method. *Global Business and Economics Research Journal, 4*(2), 1–26.

Dincer, H. (2018). HHI-based evaluation of the European banking sector using an integrated fuzzy approach. *Kybernetes*.

Dinçer, H., Akdeniz, O. O., & Hacioglu, U. (2018). Competitive strategy selection in the European banking sector using a hybrid decision-making approach. *Zbornik Radova Ekonomski Fakultet u Rijeka, 36*(1), 211–240.

Dinçer, H., Bozaykut-Buk, T., Emir, Ş., Yuksel, S., & Ashill, N. (2019). Using the fuzzy multicriteria decision making approach to evaluate brand equity: A study of privatized firms. *Journal of Product and Brand Management*.

Dinçer, H., & Görener, A. (2011). Performans değerlendirmesinde AHP-VIKOR ve AHP-TOPSIS yaklaşımları: Hizmet sektöründe bir uygulama. *Sigma: Mühendislik ve Fen Bilimleri Dergisi, 29*, 244–260.

Dincer, H., & Hacioglu, U. (2013). Performance evaluation with fuzzy VIKOR and AHP method based on customer satisfaction in Turkish banking sector. *Kybernetes, 42*(7), 1072–1085. doi:10.1108/K-02-2013-0021

Dincer, H., & Hacioglu, U. (2015). A comparative performance evaluation on bipolar risks in emerging capital markets using fuzzy AHP-TOPSIS and VIKOR approaches. *The Engineering Economist, 26*(2), 118–129.

Dincer, H., Hacioglu, U., Tatoglu, E., & Delen, D. (2016). A fuzzy-hybrid analytic model to assess investors' perceptions for industry selection. *Decision Support Systems, 86*, 24–34. doi:10.1016/j.dss.2016.03.005

Dinçer, H., Hacıoğlu, Ü., & Yüksel, S. (2016). Managerial and Market-Based Appraisal of Agriculture Banking Using ANP and ELECTRE Method. *Management & Organizational Studies*, *3*(3), 29–40. doi:10.5430/mos.v3n3p29

Dinçer, H., Hacıoğlu, Ü., & Yüksel, S. (2016). The Impacts of Financial Variables on Employment Planning in Turkish Banking Sector. *International Journal of Sustainable Entrepreneurship and Corporate Social Responsibility*, *1*(2), 1–20. doi:10.4018/IJSECSR.2016070101

Dincer, H., Hacioglu, U., & Yuksel, S. (2016a). Balanced scorecard-based performance assessment of Turkish banking sector with analytic network process. *International Journal of Decision Sciences & Applications-IJDSA*, *1*(1), 1–21.

Dincer, H., Hacioglu, U., & Yuksel, S. (2016b). Performance assessment of deposit banks with CAMELS analysis using fuzzy ANP-moora approaches and an application on Turkish banking sector. *Asian Journal of Research in Business Economics and Management*, *6*(2), 32–56. doi:10.5958/2249-7307.2016.00009.8

Dinçer, H., Hacıoğlu, Ü., & Yüksel, S. (2017). A Strategic Approach to Global Financial Crisis in Banking Sector: A Critical Appraisal of Banking Strategies Using Fuzzy ANP and Fuzzy Topsis Methods. *International Journal of Sustainable Economies Management*, *6*(1), 1–21. doi:10.4018/ijsem.2017010101

Dinçer, H., Hacıoğlu, Ü., & Yüksel, S. (2017). Balanced scorecard based performance measurement of European airlines using a hybrid multicriteria decision making approach under the fuzzy environment. *Journal of Air Transport Management*, *63*, 17–33. doi:10.1016/j.jairtraman.2017.05.005

Dinçer, H., Hacıoğlu, Ü., & Yüksel, S. (2018). Conflict Risk and Defense Expenses and Their Impact on the Economic Growth. In *Handbook of Research on Military Expenditure on Economic and Political Resources* (pp. 1–23). IGI Global. doi:10.4018/978-1-5225-4778-5.ch001

Dinçer, H., Hacıoğlu, Ü., & Yüksel, S. (2018). Determining Influencing Factors of Currency Exchange Rate for Decision Making in Global Economy Using MARS Method. In *Geopolitics and Strategic Management in the Global Economy* (pp. 261–273). IGI Global. doi:10.4018/978-1-5225-2673-5.ch013

Dincer, H., Uzunkaya, S. S., & Yüksel, S. (2019). An IT2-Based Hybrid Decision-Making Model Using Hesitant Fuzzy Linguistic Term Sets for Selecting the Development Plan of Financial Economics. *International Journal of Computational Intelligence Systems*, *12*(2), 460–473. doi:10.2991/ijcis.d.190312.001

Dinçer, H., & Yüksel, S. (2018). Comparative Evaluation of BSC-Based New Service Development Competencies in Turkish Banking Sector with the Integrated Fuzzy Hybrid MCDM Using Content Analysis. *International Journal of Fuzzy Systems*, *20*(8), 2497–2516. doi:10.100740815-018-0519-y

Dinçer, H., & Yüksel, S. (2018). Financial Sector-Based Analysis of the G20 Economies Using the Integrated Decision-Making Approach with DEMATEL and TOPSIS. In *Emerging Trends in Banking and Finance* (pp. 210–223). Cham: Springer. doi:10.1007/978-3-030-01784-2_13

Dinçer, H., & Yüksel, S. (2019). Identifying the Causality Relationship between Health Expenditure and Economic Growth: An Application on E7 Countries. *Journal of Health Systems And Policies*, *1*, 5.

Dincer, H., & Yuksel, S. (2019). IT2-Based Fuzzy Hybrid Decision Making Approach to Soft Computing. *IEEE Access: Practical Innovations, Open Solutions*, *7*, 15932–15944. doi:10.1109/ACCESS.2019.2895359

Dinçer, H., & Yüksel, S. (2019). Multidimensional evaluation of global investments on the renewable energy with the integrated fuzzy decision-making model under the hesitancy. *International Journal of Energy Research.*

Dinçer, H., Yüksel, S., & Adalı, Z. (2017). Identifying Causality Relationship between Energy Consumption and Economic Growth in Developed Countries. *International Business and Accounting Research Journal*, *1*(2), 71–81. doi:10.15294/ibarj.v1i2.9

Dinçer, H., Yuksel, S., & Adalı, Z. (2018). Relationship Between Non-Performing Loans, Industry, and Economic Growth of the African Economies and Policy Recommendations for Global Growth. In *Globalization and Trade Integration in Developing Countries* (pp. 203–228). IGI Global. doi:10.4018/978-1-5225-4032-8.ch009

Dinçer, H., Yuksel, S., & Bozaykut-Buk, T. (2018). Evaluation of Financial and Economic Effects on Green Supply Chain Management With Multi-Criteria Decision-Making Approach: Evidence From Companies Listed in BIST. In *Handbook of Research on Supply Chain Management for Sustainable Development* (pp. 144–175). IGI Global. doi:10.4018/978-1-5225-5757-9.ch009

Dinçer, H., Yüksel, S., & Çetiner, İ. T. (2019). Strategy Selection for Organizational Performance of Turkish Banking Sector With the Integrated Multi-Dimensional Decision-Making Approach. In *Handbook of Research on Contemporary Approaches in Management and Organizational Strategy* (pp. 273–291). IGI Global. doi:10.4018/978-1-5225-6301-3.ch014

Dinçer, H., Yüksel, S., Eti, S., & Tula, A. (2019). Effects of Demographic Characteristics on Business Success: An Evidence From Turkish Banking Sector. In *Handbook of Research on Business Models in Modern Competitive Scenarios* (pp. 304–324). IGI Global. doi:10.4018/978-1-5225-7265-7.ch016

Dinçer, H., Yüksel, S., Korsakienė, R., Raišienė, A. G., & Bilan, Y. (2019). IT2 Hybrid Decision-Making Approach to Performance Measurement of Internationalized Firms in the Baltic States. *Sustainability*, *11*(1), 296. doi:10.3390u11010296

Dinçer, H., Yüksel, S., & Martínez, L. (2019). Balanced scorecard-based Analysis about European Energy Investment Policies: A hybrid hesitant fuzzy decision-making approach with Quality Function Deployment. *Expert Systems with Applications*, *115*, 152–171. doi:10.1016/j.eswa.2018.07.072

Dinçer, H., Yüksel, S., & Martínez, L. (2019). Interval type 2-based hybrid fuzzy evaluation of financial services in E7 economies with DEMATEL-ANP and MOORA methods. *Applied Soft Computing*.

Dinçer, H., Yüksel, S., Pınarbaşı, F., & Çetiner, İ. T. (2019). Measurement of Economic and Banking Stability in Emerging Markets by Considering Income Inequality and Nonperforming Loans. In *Maintaining Financial Stability in Times of Risk and Uncertainty* (pp. 49–68). IGI Global. doi:10.4018/978-1-5225-7208-4.ch003

Dinçer, H., Yüksel, S., & Şenel, S. (2018). Analyzing the global risks for the financial crisis after the great depression using comparative hybrid hesitant fuzzy decision-making models: Policy recommendations for sustainable economic growth. *Sustainability*, *10*(9), 3126. doi:10.3390u10093126

Ding, X. F., & Liu, H. C. (2018). A 2-dimension uncertain linguistic DEMATEL method for identifying critical success factors in emergency management. *Applied Soft Computing*, *71*, 386–395. doi:10.1016/j.asoc.2018.07.018

Dobuzinskis, L. (2019). Financial Regulation and Monetary Policy: The Spectre of Government Failure. In *The Failure of Financial Regulation* (pp. 37–69). Cham: Palgrave Macmillan. doi:10.1007/978-3-030-05680-3_2

Dogan, E., & Aslan, A. (2017). Exploring the relationship among CO2 emissions, real GDP, energy consumption and tourism in the EU and candidate countries: Evidence from panel models robust to heterogeneity and cross-sectional dependence. *Renewable & Sustainable Energy Reviews*, *77*, 239–245. doi:10.1016/j.rser.2017.03.111

Dogan, E., & Inglesi-Lotz, R. (2017). Analyzing the effects of real income and biomass energy consumption on carbon dioxide (CO2) emissions: Empirical evidence from the panel of biomass-consuming countries. *Energy*, *138*, 721–727. doi:10.1016/j.energy.2017.07.136

Dogan, E., Sebri, M., & Turkekul, B. (2016). Exploring the relationship between agricultural electricity consumption and output: New evidence from Turkish regional data. *Energy Policy*, *95*, 370–377. doi:10.1016/j.enpol.2016.05.018

Dogan, E., & Seker, F. (2016). The influence of real output, renewable and non-renewable energy, trade and financial development on carbon emissions in the top renewable energy countries. *Renewable & Sustainable Energy Reviews*, *60*, 1074–1085. doi:10.1016/j.rser.2016.02.006

Dogan, E., Seker, F., & Bulbul, S. (2017). Investigating the impacts of energy consumption, real GDP, tourism and trade on CO2 emissions by accounting for cross-sectional dependence: A panel study of OECD countries. *Current Issues in Tourism*, *20*(16), 1701–1719. doi:10.1080/13683500.2015.1119103

Dong, K., Sun, R., Hochman, G., Zeng, X., Li, H., & Jiang, H. (2017). Impact of natural gas consumption on CO2 emissions: Panel data evidence from China's provinces. *Journal of Cleaner Production*, *162*, 400–410. doi:10.1016/j.jclepro.2017.06.100

Dong, W., & Bao, X. (2018, August). Application of Improved Interval Numbers TOPSIS Method Based on Mahalanobis Distance in the Evaluation of SME Public Service Platform. In *2018 International Conference on Information Technology and Management Engineering (ICITME 2018)*. Atlantis Press. 10.2991/icitme-18.2018.47

Donohoe, M. P. (2015). The economic effects of financial derivatives on corporate tax avoidance. *Journal of Accounting and Economics*, *59*(1), 1–24. doi:10.1016/j.jacceco.2014.11.001

dos Santos, B. M., Godoy, L. P., & Campos, L. M. (2019). Performance evaluation of green suppliers using entropy-TOPSIS-F. *Journal of Cleaner Production*, *207*, 498–509. doi:10.1016/j.jclepro.2018.09.235

Doumpos, M., Gaganis, C., & Pasiouras, F. (2015). Central bank independence, financial supervision structure and bank soundness: An empirical analysis around the crisis. *Journal of Banking & Finance*, *61*, S69–S83. doi:10.1016/j.jbankfin.2015.04.017

Dowd, K. (2015). Central bank stress tests: Mad, bad, and dangerous. *The Cato Journal*, *35*, 507.

Duarte, R., Pinilla, V., & Serrano, A. (2016). Globalization and natural resources: The expansion of the Spanish agrifood trade and its impact on water consumption, 1965–2010. *Regional Environmental Change*, *16*(1), 259–272. doi:10.100710113-014-0752-3

Dumitrescu, E. I., & Hurlin, C. (2012). Testing for Granger non-causality in heterogeneous panels. *Economic Modelling*, *29*(4), 1450–1460. doi:10.1016/j.econmod.2012.02.014

Dwivedi, G., Srivastava, R. K., & Srivastava, S. K. (2018). A generalised fuzzy TOPSIS with improved closeness coefficient. *Expert Systems with Applications*, *96*, 185–195. doi:10.1016/j.eswa.2017.11.051

Edward, N. (2017). *Corruption, Bank Access and Distribution of Social Benefits: The Case for Central Bank Digital Currency as an Alternative to Cash in Indonesia*. Available at SSRN 3095805

Egbetunde, T., & Akinlo, A. E. (2015). Financial globalization and economic growth in Sub-Saharan Africa: Evidence from panel cointegration tests. *African Development Review*, *27*(3), 187–198. doi:10.1111/1467-8268.12140

Eggertsson, G. B., & Proulx, K. (2016). *Bernanke's No-arbitrage Argument Revisited: Can Open Market Operations in Real Assets Eliminate the Liquidity Trap? (No. w22243)*. National Bureau of Economic Research.

Eken, A., Ozek, A., Cakmak, B., & Serdengecti, S. (2019). New electronic data delivery system of Central Bank of the Republic of Turkey. *IFC Bulletins Chapters, 49*.

Emeç, Ş., & Akkaya, G. (2018). Stochastic AHP and fuzzy VIKOR approach for warehouse location selection problem. *Journal of Enterprise Information Management*, *31*(6), 950–962. doi:10.1108/JEIM-12-2016-0195

Emir, S., Dincer, H., Hacioglu, U., & Yuksel, S. (2015). Comparative Study of Outlier Detection Algorithms via Fundamental Analysis Variables. *International Journal of Research in Business and Social Science, 4*(4), 45-60.

Erdogdu, A. P. A. (2017). Functioning and Effectiveness of Monetary Transmission Mechanisms: Turkey Applications. *The Journal of Finance*, *5*(1), 29–41.

Ergeç, E. H., & Ersin, İ. (2019). The Relationships between Public Expenditure and Sectorial Employment in Turkey. *BİLTÜRK Ekonomi ve İlişkili Çalışmalar Dergisi*, *1*(2), 150–168.

Ersin, İ., & Duran, S. (2017). Faizsiz Finans Döngüsünü Oluşturma Açisindan Adil Ekonomik Düzen Söyleminin Kredileşme İlkeleri Ve Uygulanabilirliğinin Değerlendirilmesi. *Electronic Turkish Studies*, *12*(8).

Ersin, İ., & Ergeç, E. H. (2018). Harcama Bileşenleri Ve Sektörel İstihdam Arasindaki Nedensellik İlişkisi. *Yönetim ve Ekonomi Araştırmaları Dergisi*, *16*(Özel Sayı 1), 161-180.

Ersin, İ. (2018). İhracata Dayalı Büyüme Hipotezinin Test Edilmesi: MINT Ülkeleri Örneği. *Ekonomi, İşletme ve Maliye Araştırmaları Dergisi*, *1*(1), 26–38.

Ersin, İ., & Eti, S. (2017). Measuring the Waste-Conscious and Saving Habits of the Youth in Turkey: The Sample of Istanbul Medipol University. *International Journal of Islamic Economics and Finance Studies*, *3*(3).

Ervural, B. C., Zaim, S., Demirel, O. F., Aydin, Z., & Delen, D. (2018). An ANP and fuzzy TOPSIS-based SWOT analysis for Turkey's energy planning. *Renewable & Sustainable Energy Reviews*, *82*, 1538–1550. doi:10.1016/j.rser.2017.06.095

Eti, S. (2019). The Use of Quantitative Methods in Investment Decisions: A Literature Review. In *Handbook of Research on Global Issues in Financial Communication and Investment Decision Making* (pp. 256–275). IGI Global. doi:10.4018/978-1-5225-9265-5.ch013

Eti, S., & İnel, M. N. (2016). A research on comparison of regression models explaining the profitability base on financial data. *International Journal of Business and Management*, *4*(10), 470–475.

Evans, O. (2019). Digital politics: Internet and democracy in Africa. *Journal of Economic Studies (Glasgow, Scotland)*, *46*(1), 169–191. doi:10.1108/JES-08-2017-0234

Everett, R. (2017). *Russia's Crisis Modernisation Fallacy: An analysis of the 1998 and 2008 economic crises and their effects on the development of the Central Bank of Russia* (Doctoral dissertation). University of Kent.

Fei, L., Deng, Y., & Hu, Y. (2018). DS-VIKOR: A new multi-criteria decision-making method for supplier selection. *International Journal of Fuzzy Systems*, 1–19.

Feng, Y., Hong, Z., Tian, G., Li, Z., Tan, J., & Hu, H. (2018). Environmentally friendly MCDM of reliability-based product optimisation combining DEMATEL-based ANP, interval uncertainty and Vlse Kriterijumska Optimizacija Kompromisno Resenje (VIKOR). *Information Sciences*, *442*, 128–144. doi:10.1016/j.ins.2018.02.038

Fernández-Albertos, J. (2015). The politics of central bank independence. *Annual Review of Political Science*, *18*(1), 217–237. doi:10.1146/annurev-polisci-071112-221121

Fiedler, S., Jannsen, N., Reitz, S., & Wolters, M. (2016). Is Globalization Reducing the Ability of Central Banks to Control Inflation? A Literature Review with an Application to the Euro Area. *Review of Economics, 67*(3), 231–253. doi:10.1515/roe-2016-0007

Figueiredo, A., & Parhizgari, A. M. (2017). Currency volatility and bid-ask spreads of ADRs and local shares. *Global Finance Journal, 34*, 54–71. doi:10.1016/j.gfj.2016.07.002

Fontana, A., & Scheicher, M. (2016). An analysis of euro area sovereign CDS and their relation with government bonds. *Journal of Banking & Finance, 62*, 126–140. doi:10.1016/j.jbankfin.2015.10.010

Fratzscher, M., Duca, M. L., & Straub, R. (2016). ECB unconventional monetary policy: Market impact and international spillovers. *IMF Economic Review, 64*(1), 36–74. doi:10.1057/imfer.2016.5

Fries, C. P., & Kohl-Landgraf, P. (2018). *Smart Derivative Contracts (Detaching Transactions from Counterparty Credit Risk: Specification, Parametrisation, Valuation).* Available at SSRN 3163074

Furuoka, F. (2017). Renewable electricity consumption and economic development: New findings from the Baltic countries. *Renewable & Sustainable Energy Reviews, 71*, 450–463. doi:10.1016/j.rser.2016.12.074

Galaz, V., Gars, J., Moberg, F., Nykvist, B., & Repinski, C. (2015). Why ecologists should care about financial markets. *Trends in Ecology & Evolution, 30*(10), 571–580. doi:10.1016/j.tree.2015.06.015 PMID:26411614

Galí, J. (2015). *Monetary policy, inflation, and the business cycle: an introduction to the new Keynesian framework and its applications.* Princeton University Press.

Gallemore, J., Gipper, B., & Maydew, E. (2019). Banks as tax planning intermediaries. *Journal of Accounting Research.*

Ganesh Kumar, P., Meikandan, M., Sakthivadivel, D., & Vigneswaran, V. S. (2018). Selection of optimum glazing material for solar thermal applications using TOPSIS methodology. *International Journal of Ambient Energy*, 1-5.

Ganji, S. S., Rassafi, A. A., & Kordani, A. A. (2018). Vehicle safety analysis based on a hybrid approach integrating DEMATEL, ANP and ER. *KSCE Journal of Civil Engineering, 22*(11), 4580–4592. doi:10.100712205-018-1720-0

Garcia Osma, B., Mora, A., & Porcuna-Enguix, L. (2019). *Prudential Supervisors' Independence and Income Smoothing in European Banks.* Available at SSRN 3172753

Gardas, B. B., Raut, R. D., & Narkhede, B. (2018). Evaluating critical causal factors for post-harvest losses (PHL) in the fruit and vegetables supply chain in India using the DEMATEL approach. *Journal of Cleaner Production, 199*, 47–61. doi:10.1016/j.jclepro.2018.07.153

Gardas, B. B., Raut, R. D., & Narkhede, B. (2018). Modelling the challenges to sustainability in the textile and apparel (T&A) sector: A Delphi-DEMATEL approach. *Sustainable Production and Consumption*, *15*, 96–108. doi:10.1016/j.spc.2018.05.001

Garriga, A. C. (2016). Central bank independence in the world: A new data set. *International Interactions*, *42*(5), 849–868. doi:10.1080/03050629.2016.1188813

Gbatu, A. P., Wang, Z., Wesseh Jr, P. K., & Sesay, V. A. (2018). What precipitates growth in CO2 emissions? New evidence from a panel of economic community of West African states (ECOWAS). *International Journal of Energy Sector Management*.

Gertler, M., & Karadi, P. (2015). Monetary policy surprises, credit costs, and economic activity. *American Economic Journal. Macroeconomics*, *7*(1), 44–76. doi:10.1257/mac.20130329

Ghadikolaei, A. S., Madhoushi, M., & Divsalar, M. (2018). Extension of the VIKOR method for group decision making with extended hesitant fuzzy linguistic information. *Neural Computing & Applications*, *30*(12), 3589–3602. doi:10.100700521-017-2944-5

Ghate, C., Gupta, S., & Mallick, D. (2017). The inflationary impact of the grain procurement policy in India. *International Growth Centre Blog*.

Gibson, H. D., Hall, S. G., & Tavlas, G. S. (2016). The effectiveness of the ECB's asset purchase programs of 2009 to 2012. *Journal of Macroeconomics*, *47*, 45–57. doi:10.1016/j.jmacro.2015.09.006

Goncharov, I., Novotny-Farkas, Z., & Wu, X. (2019). *Disclosure Choice When Market-Wide Externalities Matter: Evidence from IFRS Adoptions by Central Banks*. Available at SSRN 3330830

Goodhart, C., & Lastra, R. (2018). Populism and central bank independence. *Open Economies Review*, *29*(1), 49–68. doi:10.100711079-017-9447-y

Gopal, J., Sangaiah, A. K., Basu, A., & Gao, X. Z. (2018). Integration of fuzzy DEMATEL and FMCDM approach for evaluating knowledge transfer effectiveness with reference to GSD project outcome. *International Journal of Machine Learning and Cybernetics*, *9*(2), 225–241. doi:10.100713042-015-0370-5

Gorener, A., Dincer, H., & Hacioglu, U. (2013). *Application of multi-objective optimization on the basis of ratio analysis (MOORA) method for bank branch location selection*. Academic Press.

Görgen, H. İ. (2018). *Turkey and Argentina: a comparative study on industrial policies in the post–2001 financial crisis period* (Doctoral dissertation). Bilkent University.

Gorus, M. S., & Aslan, M. (2019). Impacts of economic indicators on environmental degradation: Evidence from MENA countries. *Renewable & Sustainable Energy Reviews*, *103*, 259–268. doi:10.1016/j.rser.2018.12.042

Goyal, S., Routroy, S., & Singhal, A. (2018). Analyzing environment sustainability enablers using fuzzy DEMATEL for an Indian steel manufacturing company. *Journal of Engineering, Design and Technology*.

Greer, I., & Hauptmeier, M. (2016). Management whipsawing: The staging of labor competition under globalization. *Industrial & Labor Relations Review*, *69*(1), 29–52. doi:10.1177/0019793915602254

Guerra, M. (2017). Monetary Policy and the Propagation of Shocks Under Imperfect Exchange-Rate Pass-Through. *Sobre México. Revista de Economía*, *3*(3), 46–65.

Gupta, P. K., & Kaur, S. (2015, October). Credit Rating Framework for Financing of SMEs in India and role of central bank. In *Proceedings of Business and Management Conferences* (No. 3005373). International Institute of Social and Economic Sciences.

Gupta, H. (2018). Evaluating service quality of airline industry using hybrid best worst method and VIKOR. *Journal of Air Transport Management*, *68*, 35–47. doi:10.1016/j.jairtraman.2017.06.001

Gupta, H., & Barua, M. K. (2018). A grey DEMATEL-based approach for modeling enablers of green innovation in manufacturing organizations. *Environmental Science and Pollution Research International*, 1–23. PMID:29357076

Guy, D. B. (2018). Empirical Analysis and Forecast of Electricity Demand in West African Economic and Monetary Zone: Evidence from Panel ADRL Modelling. *Asian Journal of Economic Modelling*, *6*(3), 257–273. doi:10.18488/journal.8.2018.63.257.273

Hadi-Vencheh, A., Mohammadghasemi, A., Hosseinzadeh Lotfi, F., & Khalil Zadeh, M. (2018). Group multiple criteria ABC inventory classification using TOPSIS approach extended by Gaussian interval type-2 fuzzy sets and optimization programs. *Scientia Iranica*, *0*(0), 0. doi:10.24200ci.2018.5539.1332

Haga, M. (2015). On central bank independence and political cycles. *Journal of Applied Econometrics*, *18*(2), 267–295.

Hall, R. E., & Reis, R. (2015). *Maintaining central-bank financial stability under new-style central banking (No. w21173)*. National Bureau of Economic Research. doi:10.3386/w21173

Hammad, S. A. K. (2019). The size of the legal reserve and the stability of the rate of inflation: The case of Iraq study for the period 2004-2016. *Tikrit Journal Of Administrative and Economic Sciences*, *2*(42), 277.

Han, M. (2015). *A comparative study of central bank regulation and financial stability: lessons for the People's Republic of China* (Doctoral dissertation). Durham University.

Han, C., Zhao, Y., Lin, Z., Ding, Y., Yang, L., Lin, G., ... Ye, X. (2018). Critical lines identification for skeleton-network of power systems under extreme weather conditions based on the modified VIKOR method. *Energies*, *11*(6), 1355. doi:10.3390/en11061355

Hanes, C. (2018). Explaining the appearance of open-mouth operations in the 1990s US. *The North American Journal of Economics and Finance*.

Han, H., & Trimi, S. (2018). A fuzzy TOPSIS method for performance evaluation of reverse logistics in social commerce platforms. *Expert Systems with Applications*, *103*, 133–145. doi:10.1016/j.eswa.2018.03.003

Hansen, S., & McMahon, M. (2016). Shocking language: Understanding the macroeconomic effects of central bank communication. *Journal of International Economics*, *99*, S114–S133. doi:10.1016/j.jinteco.2015.12.008

Hartani, N. H., Bakar, N. A. A., & Haseeb, M. (2015). The nexus between female labor force participation and female total fertility rate in selected ASEAN countries: Panel cointegration approach. *Modern Applied Science*, *9*(8), 29.

Haryanto, S. (2016). Profitability Identification of National Banking through Credit, Capital, Capital Structure, Efficiency, and Risk Level. *Jurnal Dinamika Manajemen*, *7*(1), 11–21. doi:10.15294/jdm.v7i1.5749

Haseeb, A., Xia, E., Saud, S., Ahmad, A., & Khurshid, H. (2019). Does information and communication technologies improve environmental quality in the era of globalization? An empirical analysis. *Environmental Science and Pollution Research International*, 1–15. PMID:30710332

Hashemi, H., Mousavi, S., Zavadskas, E., Chalekaee, A., & Turskis, Z. (2018). A new group decision model based on grey-intuitionistic fuzzy-ELECTRE and VIKOR for contractor assessment problem. *Sustainability*, *10*(5), 1635. doi:10.3390u10051635

Haslem, J. A. (2015). Mutual fund heterogeneity and fee dispersion. *The Journal of Wealth Management*, *18*(1), 41–48. doi:10.3905/jwm.2015.18.1.041

Hassan, S. (2018). Long Run Energy Demand and Its Determinants: A Panel Cointegration Analysis of the Association of Southeast Asian Nations-5. *International Journal of Energy Economics and Policy*, *8*(4), 270–279.

Hassler, U., & Hosseinkouchack, M. (2016). Panel cointegration testing in the presence of linear time trends. *Econometrics*, *4*(4), 45. doi:10.3390/econometrics4040045

Hatefi, S. M., & Tamošaitienė, J. (2019). An integrated fuzzy DEMATEL-fuzzy ANP model for evaluating construction projects by considering interrelationships among risk factors. *Journal of Civil Engineering and Management*, *25*(2), 114–131. doi:10.3846/jcem.2019.8280

Hayo, B., & Neumeier, F. (2018). *Central Bank Independence in New Zealand: Public Knowledge About and Attitude Towards the Policy Target Agreement.* Available at SSRN 3318545

Heinemann, T. (2016). Relational geographies of emerging market finance: The rise of Turkey and the global financial crisis 2007. *European Urban and Regional Studies*, *23*(4), 645–661. doi:10.1177/0969776414531970

Henning, C. R. (2015). The ECB as a strategic actor: Central banking in a politically fragmented monetary union. In J. A. Caporaso & M. Rhodes (Eds.), *The ECB as a Strategic Actor: Central Banking in a Politically Fragmented Monetary Union*. New York: Oxford University Press.

He, R. (2017). The Study on the Problem of the Relationship between the "Heterogeneity" of the Neighbor Enterprise and the Financing Efficiency of SMEs in China—Empirical Data from China Industrial Enterprises Database. *Open Journal of Applied Sciences*, *7*(04), 171–183. doi:10.4236/ojapps.2017.74015

Hess, P. (2017). The Ongoing Evolution of Payment Instruments in China: A Case Study in Financial Innovation, and on the Role of the Central Bank. In *Cash in East Asia* (pp. 117–131). Cham: Springer. doi:10.1007/978-3-319-59846-8_8

Holland, J. (2019). A new approach to research and theory development for financial firms-building a "house with windows". *Journal of Financial Regulation and Compliance.*

Hosseini, M., & Owlia, M. S. (2016). Designing a model for measuring and analyzing the relational capital using factor analysis: Case study, Ansar bank. *Journal of Intellectual Capital*, *17*(4), 734–757. doi:10.1108/JIC-04-2016-0042

Hou, X., Li, S., & Wang, Q. (2018). Financial structure and income inequality: Evidence from China. *Emerging Markets Finance & Trade*, *54*(2), 359–376. doi:10.1080/1540496X.2017.1347780

Hu, R., Wei, Q., & Zhang, Q. (2015, February). The Timing of Central Bank Communication: Evidence from China. *Asian Finance Association (AsianFA) 2015 Conference Paper.*

Huang, X., Silva, E., & Hassani, H. (2018). Causality between Oil Prices and Tourist Arrivals. *Stats*, *1*(1), 134–154. doi:10.3390tats1010010

Hudson, A. (2017). *The law on financial derivatives (No. 6)*. Sweet and Maxwell Ltd.

Hu, J., Zhang, X., Yang, Y., Liu, Y., & Chen, X. (2018). New doctors ranking system based on VIKOR method. *International Transactions in Operational Research.* doi:10.1111/itor.12569

Hulagu, T., & Yalcin, C. (2016). Micro evidence on foreign exchange liabilities and the exchange rate risk in non-financial firms in Turkey: a descriptive analysis. *IFC Bulletin*, (41).

Hussein, K. (2016). Bank-Level Stability Factors and Consumer Confidence—A Comparative Study of Islamic and Conventional Banks' Product Mix. In *Islamic Finance* (pp. 86–104). Cham: Palgrave Macmillan. doi:10.1007/978-3-319-30918-7_6

Hwang, C. L., & Yoon, K. S. (1981). *Multiple attribute decision making: Methods and applications*. Berlin: Springer-Verlag. doi:10.1007/978-3-642-48318-9

Ibhagui, O. W. (2019). Does the long-run monetary model hold for Sub-Saharan Africa? A time series and panel-cointegration study. *Research in International Business and Finance*, *47*, 279–303. doi:10.1016/j.ribaf.2018.08.004

Iglesias, J., Ortiz, A., & Rodrigo, T. (2017). *How do the EM Central Bank talk? A Big Data approach to the Central Bank of Turkey* (No. 17/24). Academic Press.

Ilgin, M. A. (2019). A DEMATEL-Based Disassembly Line Balancing Heuristic. *Journal of Manufacturing Science and Engineering*, *141*(2), 021002. doi:10.1115/1.4041925

Indahingwati, A., Barid, M., Wajdi, N., Susilo, D. E., Kurniasih, N., & Rahim, R. (2018). Comparison Analysis of TOPSIS and Fuzzy Logic Methods On Fertilizer Selection. *Int. J. Eng. Technol, 7*(2.3), 109-114.

Inglesi-Lotz, R., & Dogan, E. (2018). The role of renewable versus non-renewable energy to the level of CO2 emissions a panel analysis of sub-Saharan Africa's Big 10 electricity generators. *Renewable Energy, 123*, 36–43. doi:10.1016/j.renene.2018.02.041

Işık, C., & Shahbaz, M. (2015). Energy consumption and economic growth: A panel data aproach to OECD countries. *International Journal of Energy Science, 5*(1), 1–5. doi:10.12783/ijes.2015.0501.01

Ismail, A. G., Nik Abdul Ghani, N. A. R., & Mat Zain, M. N. (2016). Tawarruq time deposit with wakalah principle: An option that triggers new issues. *International Journal of Islamic and Middle Eastern Finance and Management, 9*(3), 388–396. doi:10.1108/IMEFM-05-2014-0048

Iwata, K., & Takagi, S. (2012). Central bank balance sheet expansion: Japan's experience. *BIS Paper*, (66g).

Jäger, P., & Schmidt, T. (2016). The political economy of public investment when population is aging: A panel cointegration analysis. *European Journal of Political Economy, 43*, 145–158. doi:10.1016/j.ejpoleco.2016.04.004

Jain, V., Sangaiah, A. K., Sakhuja, S., Thoduka, N., & Aggarwal, R. (2018). Supplier selection using fuzzy AHP and TOPSIS: A case study in the Indian automotive industry. *Neural Computing & Applications, 29*(7), 555–564. doi:10.100700521-016-2533-z

Janaki, D., Izadbakhsh, H., & Hatefi, S. (2018). The evaluation of supply chain performance in the Oil Products Distribution Company, using information technology indicators and fuzzy TOPSIS technique. *Management Science Letters, 8*(8), 835–848. doi:10.5267/j.msl.2018.6.004

Jasmine, M. F., Mona, E. F., & Talla, A. E. H. (2019). A New Insight into the Measurement of Central Bank Independence. *Journal of Central Banking Theory and Practice, 8*(1), 67–96. doi:10.2478/jcbtp-2019-0004

Jayaraman, T. K., Lau, L. S., & Ng, C. F. (2018). Role of Financial Sector Development as a Contingent Factor in the Remittances and Growth Nexus: A Panel Study of Pacific Island Countries. *Remittances Review, 3*(1), 51–74. doi:10.33182/rr.v3i1.426

Jeanne, O., & Svensson, L. E. (2007). Credible commitment to optimal escape from a liquidity trap: The role of the balance sheet of an independent central bank. *The American Economic Review, 97*(1), 474–490. doi:10.1257/aer.97.1.474

Jianjun, L., & Xun, H. (2016). The Macroeconomic Effect of Shadow Credit Market Financing. *Applied Economics and Finance, 3*(3), 158–171. doi:10.11114/aef.v3i3.1587

Ji, M. (2018, September). Analysis of Machine Failure Sorting Based on Directed Graph and DEMATEL. In *International Workshop of Advanced Manufacturing and Automation* (pp. 377-382). Springer.

Jin, T., & Kim, J. (2018). What is better for mitigating carbon emissions–Renewable energy or nuclear energy? A panel data analysis. *Renewable & Sustainable Energy Reviews, 91*, 464–471. doi:10.1016/j.rser.2018.04.022

Jitmaneeroj, B., Lamla, M. J., & Wood, A. (2019). The implications of central bank transparency for uncertainty and disagreement. *Journal of International Money and Finance, 90*, 222–240. doi:10.1016/j.jimonfin.2018.10.002

Johnson, J. (2018). The Bank of Russia: from central planning to inflation targeting. In Research Handbook on Central Banking. Edward Elgar Publishing. doi:10.4337/9781784719227.00012

Jordan, J. L., & Luther, W. J. (2019). *Central Bank Independence and the Federal Reserve's New Operating Regime.* Available at SSRN 3313068

Juhro, S. M. (2015). The role of the central bank in promoting sustainable growth: perspectives on the implementation of flexible ITF in Indonesia. *Afro Eurasian Studies Journal, 4*(1).

Kahalé, N. (2017). Superreplication of financial derivatives via convex programming. *Management Science, 63*(7), 2323–2339. doi:10.1287/mnsc.2017.2786

Kais, S., & Mounir, B. M. (2017). Causal interactions between environmental degradation, renewable energy, nuclear energy and real GDP: A dynamic panel data approach. *Environment Systems & Decisions, 37*(1), 51–67. doi:10.100710669-016-9619-0

Kalkavan, H., & Ersin, I. (2019). Determination of Factors Affecting the South East Asian Crisis of 1997 Probit-Logit Panel Regression: The South East Asian Crisis. In Handbook of Research on Global Issues in Financial Communication and Investment Decision Making (pp. 148-167). IGI Global.

Kamińska, A., Parkitna, A., Rutkowska, M., Górski, A., & Wilimowska, Z. (2018, September). Economic Determinants of the Effectiveness of Polish Enterprises. In *International Conference on Information Systems Architecture and Technology* (pp. 36-48). Springer, Cham.

Kao, C., & Chiang, M. H. (2001). On the estimation and inference of a cointegrated regression in panel data. In *Nonstationary panels, panel cointegration, and dynamic panels* (pp. 179–222). Emerald Group Publishing Limited.

Kapingura, F. M. (2018). Relationship between foreign capital flows, domestic investment and savings in the SADC region. *Development Southern Africa, 35*(4), 554–568. doi:10.1080/0376835X.2018.1487279

Karanfil, F., & Li, Y. (2015). Electricity consumption and economic growth: Exploring panel-specific differences. *Energy Policy, 82*, 264–277. doi:10.1016/j.enpol.2014.12.001

Kartal, M. T., Yüksel, S., & Zengin, S. (2017). Türk Bankacılık Sektöründeki Kar Dağıtım Kısıtlamalarının Yatırımcıların Kararları Üzerindeki Etkileri. *Bankacılık ve Sermaye Piyasası Araştırmaları Dergisi, 1*(1), 38–51.

Kaur, H., & Dhaliwal, N. K. (2016). Operational performance of factoring companies in India: A study of SBI Global factors and Canbank factors. *Abhigyan*, *33*(4), 12–23.

Kaur, J., Sidhu, R., Awasthi, A., Chauhan, S., & Goyal, S. (2018). A DEMATEL based approach for investigating barriers in green supply chain management in Canadian manufacturing firms. *International Journal of Production Research*, *56*(1-2), 312–332. doi:10.1080/00207543.2017.1395522

Kazancoglu, Y., Kazancoglu, I., & Sagnak, M. (2018). Fuzzy DEMATEL-based green supply chain management performance: Application in cement industry. *Industrial Management & Data Systems*, *118*(2), 412–431. doi:10.1108/IMDS-03-2017-0121

Kenward, L. R. (2016). The Macro Forecasting Record of the Indonesian Financial Authorities, 2004–15. *Bulletin of Indonesian Economic Studies*, *52*(3), 321–342. doi:10.1080/00074918.2016.1198466

Kern, A., Rau-Göhring, M., & Reinsberg, B. (2019). IMF conditionality and central bank independence. *European Journal of Political Economy*, *59*, 212–229. doi:10.1016/j.ejpoleco.2019.03.002

Ketenci, N. (2016). The Feldstein–Horioka Puzzle and structural breaks: Evidence from the largest countries of Asia. *Margin - the Journal of Applied Economic Research*, *10*(3), 337–354. doi:10.1177/0973801016645216

Khadan, J., & Ruprah, I. J. (2019). The Economic and Political Costs of Diversification as a Way Out of a Recession: The Case of Trinidad and Tobago. In *Development, Political, and Economic Difficulties in the Caribbean* (pp. 117–148). Cham: Palgrave Macmillan. doi:10.1007/978-3-030-02994-4_7

Khan, M. S. A., Abdullah, S., Ali, A., & Amin, F. (2018). An extension of VIKOR method for multi-attribute decision-making under Pythagorean hesitant fuzzy setting. *Granular Computing*, 1-14.

Khan, M. A., & Abbas, F. (2016). The dynamics of electricity demand in Pakistan: A panel cointegration analysis. *Renewable & Sustainable Energy Reviews*, *65*, 1159–1178. doi:10.1016/j.rser.2016.06.054

Khedrigharibvand, H., Azadi, H., Bahrami, H., Tesfamariam, Z., Bazzazi, A. A., De Maeyer, P., & Witlox, F. (2018). Sustainable rangeland management in southwest Iran: Application of the AHP-TOPSIS approach in ranking livelihood alternatives. *The Rangeland Journal*, *40*(6), 603–614. doi:10.1071/RJ17038

Khorasaninejad, E., Fetanat, A., & Hajabdollahi, H. (2016). Prime mover selection in thermal power plant integrated with organic Rankine cycle for waste heat recovery using a novel multi criteria decision making approach. *Applied Thermal Engineering*, *102*, 1262–1279. doi:10.1016/j.applthermaleng.2016.04.058

Kiani, B., Liang, R. Y., & Gross, J. (2018). Material selection for repair of structural concrete using VIKOR method. *Case Studies in Construction Materials, 8*, 489-497.

Kilic, C. (2015). Effects of Globalization on Economic Growth: Panel Data Analysis for Developing Countries. *Petroleum-Gas University of Ploiesti Bulletin, Technical Series, 67*(1).

Kimatu, J. N. (2016). Evolution of strategic interactions from the triple to quad helix innovation models for sustainable development in the era of globalization. *Journal of Innovation and Entrepreneurship, 5*(1), 16. doi:10.118613731-016-0044-x

Kim, J. H., & Ahn, B. S. (2019). Extended VIKOR method using incomplete criteria weights. *Expert Systems with Applications, 126*, 124–132. doi:10.1016/j.eswa.2019.02.019

Kirikkaleli, D., Sokri, A., Candemir, M., & Ertugrul, H. M. (2018). Panel cointegration: Long-run relationship between internet, electricity consumption and economic growth. Evidence from oecd countries. *Investigacion Economica, 77*(303), 161–176. doi:10.22201/fe.01851667p.2018.303.64158

Kisman, Z. (2017). Model For Overcoming Decline in Credit Growth (Case Study of Indonesia with Time Series Data 2012M1-2016M12). *Journal of Internet Banking and Commerce, 22*(3), 1–11.

Kizilkaya, O., Ay, A., & Akar, G. (2016). Dynamic relationship among foreign direct investments, human capital, economic freedom and economic growth: Evidence from panel cointegration and panel causality analysis. *Theoretical & Applied Economics, 23*(3).

Kollmann, R. (2016). Discussion of "Financial Intermediation in a Global Environment". *International Journal of Central Banking*.

Komal, R., & Abbas, F. (2015). Linking financial development, economic growth and energy consumption in Pakistan. *Renewable & Sustainable Energy Reviews, 44*, 211–220. doi:10.1016/j.rser.2014.12.015

Kononenko, O. V., & Chudinovskikh, M. V. (2018). Comparative Analysis of the Depositor Rights' Protection Systems in the Russian Federation and the Republic of Belarus. *Journal of the Ural State University of Economics, 19*(5), 32–43. doi:10.29141/2073-1019-2018-19-5-3

Koulinas, G. K., Demesouka, O. E., Marhavilas, P. K., Vavatsikos, A. P., & Koulouriotis, D. E. (2019). Risk Assessment Using Fuzzy TOPSIS and PRAT for Sustainable Engineering Projects. *Sustainability, 11*(3), 615. doi:10.3390u11030615

Kumar, A., & Dixit, G. (2018). Evaluating critical barriers to implementation of WEEE management using DEMATEL approach. *Resources, Conservation and Recycling, 131*, 101–121. doi:10.1016/j.resconrec.2017.12.024

Kumar, A., Kaviani, M. A., Bottani, E., Dash, M. K., & Zavadskas, E. K. (2018). Investigating the role of social media in polio prevention in India: A Delphi-DEMATEL approach. *Kybernetes, 47*(5), 1053–1072. doi:10.1108/K-06-2017-0210

Kumar, A., Pal, A., Vohra, A., Gupta, S., Manchanda, S., & Dash, M. K. (2018). Construction of capital procurement decision making model to optimize supplier selection using Fuzzy Delphi and AHP-DEMATEL. *Benchmarking: An International Journal*, *25*(5), 1528–1547. doi:10.1108/BIJ-01-2017-0005

Kumar, K., & Garg, H. (2018). TOPSIS method based on the connection number of set pair analysis under interval-valued intuitionistic fuzzy set environment. *Computational & Applied Mathematics*, *37*(2), 1319–1329. doi:10.100740314-016-0402-0

Kumar, N. R. (2017). Intelligenece Report for Female Players & Non Players. *Indian Journal of Forensic Medicine & Toxicology*, *11*(2), 387–389. doi:10.5958/0973-9130.2017.00150.5

Kwok, P. K., & Lau, H. Y. (2019). Hotel selection using a modified TOPSIS-based decision support algorithm. *Decision Support Systems*, *120*, 95–105. doi:10.1016/j.dss.2019.02.004

Ladu, M. G., & Meleddu, M. (2016). Productivity, Wage and Inflation Relationship for a Sample of Developed Countries: New Evidence from Panel Cointegration Tests with Multiple Structural Breaks. *International Journal of Applied Economics*, *13*, 15–31.

Lakshmi, T. V., & Reddy, M. S. (2017). Impact of NPAs on Indian Schedule Commercial Banking Sector and Instruments Initiated by the Central Bank of India. *Asian Journal of Research in Banking and Finance*, *7*(3), 18–37. doi:10.5958/2249-7323.2017.00011.6

Lan, L. S., & Nugroho, J. L. E. (2019, March). Management commitment to service quality and service recovery performance of customer service officer at PT. Bank Central Asia, Tbk. Surabaya-Indonesia. In *16th International Symposium on Management (INSYMA 2019)*. Atlantis Press. 10.2991/insyma-19.2019.49

Lastra, R. M. (2018). 15. The institutional path of central bank independence. *Research Handbook on Central Banking*, 296.

Lau, L. S., Choong, C. K., Ng, C. F., Liew, F. M., & Ching, S. L. (2018). Is nuclear energy clean? Revisit of Environmental Kuznets Curve hypothesis in OECD countries. *Economic Modelling*.

Law, C. H., Tee, C. L., & Lau, W. T. (2019). The Impacts of Financial Integration on the Linkages Between Monetary Independence and Foreign Exchange Reserves. *International Economic Journal*, 1–24.

Lazzarini, S. G., Musacchio, A., Bandeira-de-Mello, R., & Marcon, R. (2015). What do state-owned development banks do? Evidence from BNDES, 2002–09. *World Development*, *66*, 237–253. doi:10.1016/j.worlddev.2014.08.016

Lee, C. C., & Tseng, H. C. (2018, January). Integrating fuzzy membership function, entropy method and VIKOR to select qualified and stable employee. In *2018 International Conference on Information Management and Processing (ICIMP)* (pp. 26-31). IEEE. 10.1109/ICIMP1.2018.8325836

Leksono, E. B., Suparno, S., & Vanany, I. (2018). Development of Performance Indicators Relationships on Sustainable Healthcare Supply Chain Performance Measurement Using Balanced Scorecard and DEMATEL. *International Journal on Advanced Science Engineering Information Technology, 8*(1), 115-122.

Lentner, C., Szegedi, K., & Tatay, T. (2017). Social Responsibility in the Operation of Central Banks. *Financial and Economic Review, 16*(2), 64–85.

Levieuge, G., Lucotte, Y., & Ringuedé, S. (2018). Central bank credibility and the expectations channel: Evidence based on a new credibility index. *Review of World Economics, 154*(3), 493–535. doi:10.100710290-018-0308-6

Liang, D., Xu, Z., Liu, D., & Wu, Y. (2018). Method for three-way decisions using ideal TOPSIS solutions at Pythagorean fuzzy information. *Information Sciences, 435*, 282–295. doi:10.1016/j.ins.2018.01.015

Liang, D., Zhang, Y., Xu, Z., & Jamaldeen, A. (2019). Pythagorean fuzzy VIKOR approaches based on TODIM for evaluating internet banking website quality of Ghanaian banking industry. *Applied Soft Computing, 78*, 583–594. doi:10.1016/j.asoc.2019.03.006

Liang, W. Z., Zhao, G. Y., & Hong, C. S. (2018). Performance assessment of circular economy for phosphorus chemical firms based on VIKOR-QUALIFLEX method. *Journal of Cleaner Production, 196*, 1365–1378. doi:10.1016/j.jclepro.2018.06.147

Li, B., Xiong, W., Chen, L., & Wang, Y. (2017). The impact of the liquidity coverage ratio on money creation: A stock-flow based dynamic approach. *Economic Modelling, 67*, 193–202. doi:10.1016/j.econmod.2016.12.016

Li, H., Li, F., Shi, D., Yu, X., & Shen, J. (2018). Carbon Emission Intensity, Economic Development and Energy Factors in 19 G20 Countries: Empirical Analysis Based on a Heterogeneous Panel from 1990 to 2015. *Sustainability, 10*(7), 2330. doi:10.3390u10072330

Li, J., Fang, H., & Song, W. (2019). Sustainable supplier selection based on SSCM practices: A rough cloud TOPSIS approach. *Journal of Cleaner Production.*

Lin, K. P., Tseng, M. L., & Pai, P. F. (2018). Sustainable supply chain management using approximate fuzzy DEMATEL method. *Resources, Conservation and Recycling, 128*, 134–142. doi:10.1016/j.resconrec.2016.11.017

Linnerooth-Bayer, J., & Hochrainer-Stigler, S. (2015). Financial instruments for disaster risk management and climate change adaptation. *Climatic Change, 133*(1), 85–100. doi:10.100710584-013-1035-6

Lin, S., Li, C., Xu, F., Liu, D., & Liu, J. (2018). Risk identification and analysis for new energy power system in China based on D numbers and decision-making trial and evaluation laboratory (DEMATEL). *Journal of Cleaner Production, 180*, 81–96. doi:10.1016/j.jclepro.2018.01.153

Li, S., & Zhou, C. (2019). What are the impacts of demographic structure on CO2 emissions? A regional analysis in China via heterogeneous panel estimates. *The Science of the Total Environment*, *650*, 2021–2031. doi:10.1016/j.scitotenv.2018.09.304 PMID:30290345

Liu, C. (2019). FinTech and Its Disruption to Financial Institutions. In *Organizational Transformation and Managing Innovation in the Fourth Industrial Revolution* (pp. 104–124). IGI Global. doi:10.4018/978-1-5225-7074-5.ch006

Liu, F., Aiwu, G., Lukovac, V., & Vukic, M. (2018). A multicriteria model for the selection of the transport service provider: A single valued neutrosophic DEMATEL multicriteria model. *Decision Making: Applications in Management and Engineering*, *1*(2), 121–130.

Liu, H. C. (2019). FMEA Using Combination Weighting and Fuzzy VIKOR and Its Application to General Anesthesia. In *Improved FMEA Methods for Proactive Healthcare Risk Analysis* (pp. 151–172). Singapore: Springer. doi:10.1007/978-981-13-6366-5_7

Liu, H. C., Wang, L. E., Li, Z., & Hu, Y. P. (2019). Improving Risk Evaluation in FMEA With Cloud Model and Hierarchical TOPSIS Method. *IEEE Transactions on Fuzzy Systems*, *27*(1), 84–95. doi:10.1109/TFUZZ.2018.2861719

Liu, J., & Wei, Q. (2018). Risk evaluation of electric vehicle charging infrastructure public-private partnership projects in China using fuzzy TOPSIS. *Journal of Cleaner Production*, *189*, 211–222. doi:10.1016/j.jclepro.2018.04.103

Liu, K., Liu, Y., & Qin, J. (2018). An integrated ANP-VIKOR methodology for sustainable supplier selection with interval type-2 fuzzy sets. *Granular Computing*, *3*(3), 193–208. doi:10.100741066-017-0071-4

Liu, R., Sun, H., Zhang, L., Zhuang, Q., Zhang, L., Zhang, X., & Chen, Y. (2018). Low-Carbon Energy Planning: A Hybrid MCDM Method Combining DANP and VIKOR Approach. *Energies*, *11*(12), 3401. doi:10.3390/en11123401

Liu, T., Deng, Y., & Chan, F. (2018). Evidential supplier selection based on DEMATEL and game theory. *International Journal of Fuzzy Systems*, *20*(4), 1321–1333. doi:10.100740815-017-0400-4

Liu, W. S., Agbola, F. W., & Dzator, J. A. (2016). The impact of FDI spillover effects on total factor productivity in the Chinese electronic industry: A panel data analysis. *Journal of the Asia Pacific Economy*, *21*(2), 217–234. doi:10.1080/13547860.2015.1137473

Liu, Y., Yan, B., & Zhou, Y. (2016). Urbanization, economic growth, and carbon dioxide emissions in China: A panel cointegration and causality analysis. *Journal of Geographical Sciences*, *26*(2), 131–152. doi:10.100711442-016-1259-2

Liu, Z., Ming, X., & Song, W. (2019). A framework integrating interval-valued hesitant fuzzy DEMATEL method to capture and evaluate co-creative value propositions for smart PSS. *Journal of Cleaner Production*.

Liu, Z., & Spiegel, M. M. (2017). Reserve Requirements as a Chinese Macro Policy Tool. *FRBSF Economic Letter*, *2017*, 15.

Li, Y., Chiu, Y. H., Lin, T. Y., & Huang, Y. Y. (2019). Market share and performance in Taiwanese banks: Min/max SBM DEA. *Top (Madrid)*, 1–20.

Li, Y., & Mathiyazhagan, K. (2018). Application of DEMATEL approach to identify the influential indicators towards sustainable supply chain adoption in the auto components manufacturing sector. *Journal of Cleaner Production*, *172*, 2931–2941. doi:10.1016/j.jclepro.2017.11.120

Loganathan, N., Taha, R., Ahmad, N., & Subramaniam, T. (2017). Taxation, growth and the stock traded nexus in emerging Asian countries: Heterogeneous and semi-parametric panel estimates. *Economic research-. Ekonomska Istrazivanja*, *30*(1), 566–580. doi:10.1080/1331677X.2017.1305789

López-Balderas, N., Hernández-Romano, J., Cámara-Contreras, M., Bravo-Sarmiento, E., & Hernández-Romano, P. A. (2019). Trends in prevalence of HIV and syphilis in a central blood bank of Veracruz, Mexico. *Transfusion and Apheresis Science*, *58*(1), 94–99. doi:10.1016/j.transci.2018.12.001 PMID:30554960

Lopez, L., & Weber, S. (2018). Testing for Granger causality in panel data. *The Stata Journal*, *17*(4), 972–984. doi:10.1177/1536867X1801700412

Lord, C. (2019). No epistocracy without representation? The case of the European Central Bank. *European Political Science*, *20*(1), 1–15.

Luan, B., Yin, R., Xu, P., Wang, X., Yang, X., Zhang, L., & Tang, X. (2019). Evaluating Green Stormwater Infrastructure strategies efficiencies in a rapidly urbanizing catchment using SWMM-based TOPSIS. *Journal of Cleaner Production*.

Luburić, R. (2017). Strengthening the Three Lines of Defence in Terms of More Efficient Operational Risk Management in Central Banks. *Journal of Central Banking Theory and Practice*, *6*(1), 29–53. doi:10.1515/jcbtp-2017-0003

Luthra, S., Mangla, S. K., Shankar, R., Prakash Garg, C., & Jakhar, S. (2018). Modelling critical success factors for sustainability initiatives in supply chains in Indian context using Grey-DEMATEL. *Production Planning and Control*, *29*(9), 705–728. doi:10.1080/09537287.2018.1448126

Lu, W. C. (2017). Greenhouse gas emissions, energy consumption and economic growth: A panel cointegration analysis for 16 Asian countries. *International Journal of Environmental Research and Public Health*, *14*(11), 1436. doi:10.3390/ijerph14111436 PMID:29165399

Lv, Z. (2019). Deepening or lessening? The effects of tourism on regional inequality. *Tourism Management*, *72*, 23–26. doi:10.1016/j.tourman.2018.11.009

Ma, F., Shi, W., Yuen, K. F., Sun, Q., & Guo, Y. (2019). Multi-stakeholders' assessment of bike sharing service quality based on DEMATEL–VIKOR method. *International Journal of Logistics Research and Applications*, 1-24.

Magazzino, C. (2018). Fiscal Sustainability in the EU. *Atlantic Economic Journal*, *46*(3), 297–311. doi:10.100711293-018-9588-4

Mahmoodi, M. (2017). The Relationship between economic growth, renewable energy, and CO2 emissions: Evidence from panel data approach. *International Journal of Energy Economics and Policy*, *7*(6), 96–102.

Mahmoodi, M., & Mahmoodi, E. (2018). Environmental quality, renewable energy, trade openness and economic growth: Evidence from two groups of developing countries. *Asian Journal of Water, Environment and Pollution*, *15*(2), 177–185. doi:10.3233/AJW-180030

Majumdar, R., Kapur, P. K., & Khatri, S. K. (2019). Assessing software upgradation attributes and optimal release planning using DEMATEL and MAUT. *International Journal of Industrial and Systems Engineering*, *31*(1), 70–94. doi:10.1504/IJISE.2019.096886

Mangla, S. K., Luthra, S., Jakhar, S. K., Tyagi, M., & Narkhede, B. E. (2018). Benchmarking the logistics management implementation using Delphi and fuzzy DEMATEL. *Benchmarking: An International Journal*, *25*(6), 1795–1828. doi:10.1108/BIJ-01-2017-0006

Manova, K. (2015). *Global value chains and multinational activity with financial frictions. The Age of Global Value Chains: Maps and Policy Issues* (pp. 187–200). London: CEPR.

Mansour, A., Musaad, H., Zhang Ya, B., & Ameer, W. (2017). The Long-Run Effect of Outward Foreign Direct Investment and Macroeconomic Variables on Domestic Investment: Evidence from World Major Economies Using Panel ARDL Approach. *JL Pol'y & Globalization*, *63*, 39.

Mao, N., Song, M., Pan, D., & Deng, S. (2018). Comparative studies on using RSM and TOPSIS methods to optimize residential air conditioning systems. *Energy*, *144*, 98–109. doi:10.1016/j.energy.2017.11.160

Maroof, Z., Hussain, S., Jawad, M., & Naz, M. (2018). Determinants of industrial development: A panel analysis of South Asian economies. *Quality & Quantity*, 1–29.

Marthinsen, J. E. (2018). *Risk takers: uses and abuses of financial derivatives*. Walter de Gruyter GmbH & Co KG. doi:10.1515/9781547400034

Martin, F. M. (2015). Debt, inflation and central bank independence. *European Economic Review*, *79*, 129–150. doi:10.1016/j.euroecorev.2015.07.009

Masciandaro, D., & Romelli, D. (2019). *Peaks and troughs: Economics and political economy of central bank independence cycles*. Academic Press.

Maskell, B. H., Baggaley, B., & Grasso, L. (2016). *Practical lean accounting: a proven system for measuring and managing the lean enterprise*. Productivity Press. doi:10.1201/b11454

Mavi, R. K., & Standing, C. (2018). Critical success factors of sustainable project management in construction: A fuzzy DEMATEL-ANP approach. *Journal of Cleaner Production*, *194*, 751–765. doi:10.1016/j.jclepro.2018.05.120

McCauley, R., & Ma, G. (2015). Transforming central bank liabilities into government debt: The case of China. *China & World Economy*, *23*(4), 1–18. doi:10.1111/cwe.12118

McLeod, M. S., Moore, C. B., Payne, G. T., Sexton, J. C., & Evert, R. E. (2018). Organizational virtue and stakeholder interdependence: An empirical examination of financial intermediaries and IPO firms. *Journal of Business Ethics, 149*(4), 785–798. doi:10.100710551-016-3021-1

McRae, K., Durr, S., & Manzo, D. (2017). an initial assessment of changes to the Bank of canada's Framework for market Operations. *Bank of Canada Review, 2017*(Autumn), 42–52.

McVea, H. (2017). Central counterparties and sale and repurchase agreements: Regulating financial markets in the light of yet another false dawn. *Journal of Corporate Law Studies, 17*(1), 111–135. doi:10.1080/14735970.2016.1254451

Miljkovic, T., Miljkovic, D., & Maurer, K. (2018). Examining the impact on mortality arising from climate change: Important findings for the insurance industry. *European Actuarial Journal, 8*(2), 363–381. doi:10.100713385-018-0178-2

Miron, R. J., Sculean, A., Cochran, D. L., Froum, S., Zucchelli, G., Nemcovsky, C., ... Stavropoulos, A. (2016). Twenty years of enamel matrix derivative: The past, the present and the future. *Journal of Clinical Periodontology, 43*(8), 668–683. doi:10.1111/jcpe.12546 PMID:26987551

Mirzaei, A., & Moore, T. (2016). Banking performance and industry growth in an oil-rich economy: Evidence from Qatar. *The Quarterly Review of Economics and Finance, 60*, 58–69. doi:10.1016/j.qref.2015.06.001

Mohammed, A., Harris, I., Soroka, A., Naim, M. M., & Ramjaun, T. (2018). Evaluating Green and Resilient Supplier Performance: AHP-Fuzzy Topsis Decision-Making Approach. In ICORES (pp. 209-216). Academic Press.

Moreira, R. (2019). Inflation and real exchange rate and macroeconomic gaps: Causality for 50 emerging and developing countries. *Economic Bulletin, 39*(1), 142–158.

Mosikari, T. J., Senosi, M. C., & Eita, J. H. (2016). Manufactured exports and economic growth in Southern African Development Community (SADC) region: A panel cointegration approach. *Acta Universitatis Danubius: Oeconomica, 12*(5).

Mousavizade, F., & Shakibazad, M. (2019). Identifying and ranking CSFs for KM implementation in urban water and sewage companies using ISM-DEMATEL technique. *Journal of Knowledge Management, 23*(1), 200–218. doi:10.1108/JKM-05-2018-0321

Moutinho, V., Varum, C., & Mota, J. (2018). The environment–growth dilemma: New evidence using a panel cointegration approach. *Journal of Environmental Economics and Policy, 7*(2), 166–183. doi:10.1080/21606544.2017.1383312

Muda, I. (2017). User Impact of Literacy on Treatment Outcomes Quality Regional Financial Information System. *Management Dynamics in the Knowledge Economy, 5*(2), 307–326. doi:10.25019/MDKE/5.2.08

Mukhtarov, S., Yüksel, S., & Mammadov, E. (2018). *Factors that increase credit risk of Azerbaijani banks*. Academic Press.

Naczyk, M., & Hassel, A. (2019). Insuring individuals… and politicians: Financial services providers, stock market risk and the politics of private pension guarantees in Germany. *Journal of European Public Policy*, 1–20.

Nagahisarchoghaei, M., Nagahi, M., & Soleimani, N. (2018). Impact of Exchange Rate Movements on Indian Firm Performance. *International Journal of Finance and Accounting*, *7*(4), 108–121.

Nahar, A., Subadriyah, S., & Sofwan, A. (2018). The Analysis of Human Resources Policies and Regional Financial Accounting System on Regional Government Financial Statements' Quality. *Srıwıjaya Internatıonal Journal Of Dynamıc Economıcs And Busıness*, *1*(4), 387–404. doi:10.29259ijdeb.v1i4.387-404

Narayan, S. W., & Rehman, M. U. (2018). Portfolio Diversification Opportunities Within Emerging and Frontier Stock Markets: Evidence from Ten Asian Countries. *Buletin Ekonomi Moneter dan Perbankan, 21*(1), 1-22.

Narayanamoorthy, S., Geetha, S., Rakkiyappan, R., & Joo, Y. H. (2019). Interval-valued intuitionistic hesitant fuzzy entropy based VIKOR method for industrial robots selection. *Expert Systems with Applications*, *121*, 28–37. doi:10.1016/j.eswa.2018.12.015

Nasre Esfahani, M., & Rasoulinezhad, E. (2015). Will be there new CO2 emitters in the future? Evidence of long-run panel co-integration for N-11 countries. *International Journal of Energy Economics and Policy*, *6*(3), 463–470.

Nasreen, S., & Anwar, S. (2018). How Financial Stability Affects Economic Development in South Asia: A Panel data Analysis. *European Online Journal of Natural and Social Sciences, 7*(1), 54.

Näther, M. (2018). The effect of the central bank's standing facilities on interbank lending and bank liquidity holding. *Economic Theory*, 1–41.

Nazari, M. A., Aslani, A., & Ghasempour, R. (2018). Analysis of solar farm site selection based on TOPSIS approach. *International Journal of Social Ecology and Sustainable Development*, *9*(1), 12–25. doi:10.4018/IJSESD.2018010102

Ndlovu, B., Faisa, F., Resatoglu, N. G., & Türsoy, T. (2018). The Impact Macroeconomic Variables on Stock Returns: A Case of the Johannesburg Stock Exchange. *Romanian Statistical Review*, (2).

Neely, C. J. (2015). Unconventional monetary policy had large international effects. *Journal of Banking & Finance*, *52*, 101–111. doi:10.1016/j.jbankfin.2014.11.019

Nelson, B., Pinter, G., & Theodoridis, K. (2018). Do contractionary monetary policy shocks expand shadow banking? *Journal of Applied Econometrics*, *33*(2), 198–211. doi:10.1002/jae.2594

Neuts, B. (2019). Tourism and urban economic growth: A panel analysis of German cities. *Tourism Economics*.

Ng, C. F., Choong, C. K., Ching, S. L., & Lau, L. S. (2019). The Impact of Electricity Production From Renewable And Non-Renewable Sources On Co2 Emissions: Evidence From OECD Countries. *International Journal Of Business And Society*, *20*(1), 365–382.

Nguyen, K. H., & Kakinaka, M. (2019). Renewable energy consumption, carbon emissions, and development stages: Some evidence from panel cointegration analysis. *Renewable Energy, 132*, 1049–1057. doi:10.1016/j.renene.2018.08.069

Nguyen, P., Banh, L., Bui, V., & Hoang, D. (2018). Multi-response optimization of process parameters for powder mixed electro-discharge machining according to the surface roughness and surface micro-hardness using Taguchi-TOPSIS. *International Journal of Data and Network Science*, *2*(4), 109–119. doi:10.5267/j.ijdns.2018.9.001

Nica, E., Manole, C., & Potcovaru, A. M. (2016). Competition in the worldwide workplace: Economic globalization and labor rights. *Journal of Self-Governance and Management Economics*, *4*(3), 73. doi:10.22381/JSME4320165

Nica, E., & Potcovaru, A. M. (2015). Effective m-government services and increased citizen participation: Flexible and personalized ways of interacting with public administrations. *Journal of Self-Governance and Management Economics*, *3*(2), 92–97.

Nicolay, R., & de Oliveira, A. J. (2019). Inflation volatility, monetary policy signaling and clarity of the central bank communication: Evidence from an inflation targeting emerging economy. *Journal of Economic Studies*. (accepted for publication)

Nikolova, L. V., Rodionov, D. G., & Afanasyeva, N. V. (2017). Impact of globalization on innovation project risks estimation. *European Research Studies*, *20*(2), 396.

Nishiyama, Y. (2017). Open market operations and associated movements of the federal funds rate during the week prior to target changes. *Journal of Economics and Finance*, *41*(4), 806–828. doi:10.100712197-016-9380-8

Nwandu, E. (2016). Impact of Rising Interest Rate on the Performances of the Nigerian Manufacturing Sector. *European Journal of Business and Management*.

Obstfeld, M., & Duval, R. (2018). *Tight monetary policy is not the answer to weak productivity growth*. Retrieved from http://voxeu. org/article/tight-monetary-policy-not-answer-weak-productivity-growth

Ocampo, L. A., Tan, T. A. G., & Sia, L. A. (2018). Using fuzzy DEMATEL in modeling the causal relationships of the antecedents of organizational citizenship behavior (OCB) in the hospitality industry: A case study in the Philippines. *Journal of Hospitality and Tourism Management*, *34*, 11–29. doi:10.1016/j.jhtm.2017.11.002

Oktar, S., & Yüksel, S. (2015). 1998 Yılında Rusya'da Yaşanan Bankacılık Krizi Ve Öncü Göstergeleri. *Marmara University Journal of Economic & Administrative Sciences, 37*(2).

Oktar, S., & Yüksel, S. (2015). *Bankacılık krizlerinin erken uyarı sinyalleri: Türkiye üzerine bir uygulama*. Academic Press.

Oktar, S., & Yüksel, S. (2016). Bankalarin Türev Ürün Kullanimini Etkileyen Faktörler: Mars Yöntemi ile Bir Inceleme/Determinants of the Use Derivatives in Banking: An Analysis with MARS Model. *Finans Politik & Ekonomik Yorumlar*, *53*(620), 31.

Omer, M. (2016). *Should Central Bank Forget Reserve Requirements? Assessment of Reserve Requirements in Transmitting SBP's Policy Shocks to Retail Interest Rates and Exchange Rate (No. 81)*. State Bank of Pakistan, Research Department.

Ortega, R. G., Vázquez, M. L., Figueiredo, J. A., & Guijarro-Rodríguez, A. (2018). Sinos River basin social-environmental prospective assessment of water quality management using fuzzy cognitive maps and neutrosophic AHP-TOPSIS. *Neutrosophic Sets & Systems, 23*.

Osman, M., Gachino, G., & Hoque, A. (2016). Electricity consumption and economic growth in the GCC countries: Panel data analysis. *Energy Policy*, *98*, 318–327. doi:10.1016/j.enpol.2016.07.050

Ouenniche, J., Pérez-Gladish, B., & Bouslah, K. (2018). An out-of-sample framework for TOPSIS-based classifiers with application in bankruptcy prediction. *Technological Forecasting and Social Change*, *131*, 111–116. doi:10.1016/j.techfore.2017.05.034

Ozcan, B., & Ozturk, I. (2019). Renewable energy consumption-economic growth nexus in emerging countries: A bootstrap panel causality test. *Renewable & Sustainable Energy Reviews*, *104*, 30–37. doi:10.1016/j.rser.2019.01.020

Park, H., & Van Horn, P. (2015). Did the Reserve Requirement Increases of 1936–37 Reduce Bank Lending? Evidence from a Quasi-Experiment. *Journal of Money, Credit and Banking*, *47*(5), 791–818. doi:10.1111/jmcb.12235

Pedroni, P. (2004). Panel cointegration: Asymptotic and finite sample properties of pooled time series tests with an application to the PPP hypothesis. *Econometric Theory*, *20*(3), 597–625. doi:10.1017/S0266466604203073

Peng, X., & Dai, J. (2018). Approaches to single-valued neutrosophic MADM based on MABAC, TOPSIS and new similarity measure with score function. *Neural Computing & Applications*, *29*(10), 939–954. doi:10.100700521-016-2607-y

Perissinotto, R. M., Cavalieri, M. A. R., Dantas, E. G., & Dias, R. P. (2017). Social networks and the recruitment of directorates and presidents of the Central Bank of Brazil (1994-2016). *Tempo Social*, *29*(3), 61–82. doi:10.11606/0103-2070.ts.2017.125881

Piskorski, T., Seru, A., & Witkin, J. (2015). Asset quality misrepresentation by financial intermediaries: Evidence from the RMBS market. *The Journal of Finance*, *70*(6), 2635–2678. doi:10.1111/jofi.12271

Ponticelli, J., & Alencar, L. S. (2016). Court enforcement, bank loans, and firm investment: Evidence from a bankruptcy reform in Brazil. *The Quarterly Journal of Economics*, *131*(3), 1365–1413. doi:10.1093/qje/qjw015

Popescu, G. H., Mieila, M., Nica, E., & Andrei, J. V. (2018). The emergence of the effects and determinants of the energy paradigm changes on European Union economy. *Renewable & Sustainable Energy Reviews*, *81*, 768–774. doi:10.1016/j.rser.2017.08.055

Pourjavad, E., & Shahin, A. (2018). Hybrid performance evaluation of sustainable service and manufacturing supply chain management: An integrated approach of fuzzy dematel and fuzzy inference system. *Intelligent Systems in Accounting, Finance & Management*, *25*(3), 134–147. doi:10.1002/isaf.1431

Pradhan, R. P., Arvin, M. B., & Bahmani, S. (2018). Are innovation and financial development causative factors in economic growth? Evidence from a panel granger causality test. *Technological Forecasting and Social Change*, *132*, 130–142. doi:10.1016/j.techfore.2018.01.024

Pradhan, R. P., Mallik, G., & Bagchi, T. P. (2018). Information communication technology (ICT) infrastructure and economic growth: A causality evinced by cross-country panel data. *IIMB Management Review*, *30*(1), 91–103. doi:10.1016/j.iimb.2018.01.001

Pramanik, S., & Mallick, R. (2018). VIKOR based MAGDM Strategy with Trapezoidal Neutrosophic Numbers. *Neutrosophic Sets and Systems*, 118.

Pramanik, S., Dalapati, S., Alam, S., & Roy, T. K. (2018). NC-VIKOR Based MAGDM Strategy under Neutrosophic Cubic Set Environment. *Neutrosophic Sets and Systems*, *20*(1), 95–108.

Puffer, S. M., McCarthy, D. J., & Jaeger, A. M. (2016). Institution building and institutional voids: Can Poland's experience inform Russia and Brazil? *International Journal of Emerging Markets*, *11*(1), 18–41. doi:10.1108/IJoEM-02-2015-0027

Quezada, L. E., López-Ospina, H. A., Palominos, P. I., & Oddershede, A. M. (2018). Identifying causal relationships in strategy maps using ANP and DEMATEL. *Computers & Industrial Engineering*, *118*, 170–179. doi:10.1016/j.cie.2018.02.020

Rad, T. G., Sadeghi-Niaraki, A., Abbasi, A., & Choi, S. M. (2018). A methodological framework for assessment of ubiquitous cities using ANP and DEMATEL methods. *Sustainable Cities and Society, 37*, 608-618.

Rahimi, M., & Rad, A. A. (2017). Internet usage, electricity consumption and economic growth: Evidence from a panel of developing-8 countries. *International Journal of Energy Economics and Policy*, *7*(3), 152–156.

Rahim, M., Adam, P., Saenong, Z., Atmodjo, E., Rumbia, W. A., & Tamburaka, I. P. (2018). Causal Relationship between Electric Consumption and Economic Growth in South East Sulawesi. *International Journal of Energy Economics and Policy*, *8*(6), 29–34.

Rahim, R., Supiyandi, S., Siahaan, A. P. U., Listyorini, T., Utomo, A. P., Triyanto, W. A., ... Khairunnisa, K. (2018, June). TOPSIS Method Application for Decision Support System in Internal Control for Selecting Best Employees. *Journal of Physics: Conference Series*, *1028*(1), 012052. doi:10.1088/1742-6596/1028/1/012052

Rahman, M. N., & Grewal, H. S. (2017). Foreign direct investment and international trade in BIMSTEC: Panel causality analysis. *Transnational Corporations Review*, *9*(2), 112–121. doi:1 0.1080/19186444.2017.1326720

Rahman, M., & Mustafa, M. (2017). Financial deepening and stock market returns: Panel data analyses for selected developed and developing economies. *International Journal of Monetary Economics and Finance*, *10*(1), 96–109. doi:10.1504/IJMEF.2017.081287

Rahnama, A., Astaneh, H., & Hajian, M. (2019). The relationship between tourism and equality in income distribution in developed and developing countries: An application of Panel VAR model. *European Journal of Tourism Research*, *21*(21), 124–131.

Rajesh, R. (2018). Measuring the barriers to resilience in manufacturing supply chains using Grey Clustering and VIKOR approaches. *Measurement*, *126*, 259–273. doi:10.1016/j.measurement.2018.05.043

Rani, P., Jain, D., & Hooda, D. S. (2018). Shapley function based interval-valued intuitionistic fuzzy VIKOR technique for correlative multi-criteria decision making problems. *Iranian Journal of Fuzzy Systems*, *15*(1), 25–54.

Rao, M., Prasad, R. V., & Subbaiah, K. V. (2018). Experimental Investigation of Process Parameters While Milling of AA8011 Using MCDM/MADM Method-TOPSIS. *Journal of Production Research & Management*, *8*(2), 1–7.

Rasoulinezhad, E., & Kang, G. S. (2016). A panel data analysis of South Korea's trade with OPEC member countries: The gravity model approach. *Indian Economic Review*, *20*(2), 203–224.

Rasoulinezhad, E., & Saboori, B. (2018). Panel estimation for renewable and non-renewable energy consumption, economic growth, CO 2 emissions, the composite trade intensity, and financial openness of the commonwealth of independent states. *Environmental Science and Pollution Research International*, *25*(18), 17354–17370. doi:10.100711356-018-1827-3 PMID:29654460

Razak, M. I. M., Ridzuan, A. R., Masdek, N. R. N. M., Rasid, M. F. R. M., Ibrahim, Z., & Talib, A. H. (2017). Determinants of Environmental Quality in Selected Asia Pacific Countries Based on Panel Estimation. *Advanced Science Letters*, *23*(9), 9215–9219. doi:10.1166/asl.2017.10057

Rehman, M. U., Shah, S. M. A., & Hussain, J. G. (2019). Commonalities of Equity Market Fundamentals and Return Comovements: An Emerging and Frontier Market Perspective. *Revista Evidenciação Contábil & Finanças*, *7*(1), 133–151. doi:10.22478/ufpb.2318-1001.2019v7n1.37062

Reis, J. (2016). The Emergence of Central Banks and Banking Supervision in Comparative Perspective. In *State and Financial Systems in Europe and the USA* (pp. 139–154). Routledge. doi:10.4324/9781315610603

Revelli, C., & Viviani, J. L. (2015). Financial performance of socially responsible investing (SRI): What have we learned? A meta-analysis. *Business Ethics (Oxford, England)*, *24*(2), 158–185. doi:10.1111/beer.12076

Rey, H. (2016). International channels of transmission of monetary policy and the Mundellian trilemma. *IMF Economic Review*, *64*(1), 6–35. doi:10.1057/imfer.2016.4

Rocheteau, G., Wright, R., & Xiao, S. X. (2018). Open market operations. *Journal of Monetary Economics*, *98*, 114–128. doi:10.1016/j.jmoneco.2018.04.012

Rockoff, H. (2018). Milton Friedman and Anna J. Schwartz on the Inherent Instability of Fractional Reserve Banking. In *Coping with Financial Crises* (pp. 107–129). Singapore: Springer. doi:10.1007/978-981-10-6196-7_5

Rodriguez Garcia, V., Meyfroidt, P., & Gaspart, F. (2018). *Agricultural intensification and land use change: A panel cointegration approach to test induced intensification, land sparing and rebound-effect*. Academic Press.

Rodriguez-Fernandez, M. (2016). Social responsibility and financial performance: The role of good corporate governance. *BRQ Business Research Quarterly*, *19*(2), 137–151. doi:10.1016/j.brq.2015.08.001

Ross, C., Wiggins, R., & Metrick, A. (2015). European Central Bank Tools and Policy Actions A: Open Market Operations, Collateral Expansion and Standing Facilities. *Yale Program on Financial Stability Case Study*.

Rostamkalaei, A., & Freel, M. (2016). The cost of growth: Small firms and the pricing of bank loans. *Small Business Economics*, *46*(2), 255–272. doi:10.100711187-015-9681-x

Rostamzadeh, R., Ghorabaee, M. K., Govindan, K., Esmaeili, A., & Nobar, H. B. K. (2018). Evaluation of sustainable supply chain risk management using an integrated fuzzy TOPSIS-CRITIC approach. *Journal of Cleaner Production*, *175*, 651–669. doi:10.1016/j.jclepro.2017.12.071

Rostamzadeh, R., Govindan, K., Esmaeili, A., & Sabaghi, M. (2015). Application of fuzzy VIKOR for evaluation of green supply chain management practices. *Ecological Indicators*, *49*, 188–203. doi:10.1016/j.ecolind.2014.09.045

Roy, J., Adhikary, K., Kar, S., & Pamucar, D. (2018). A rough strength relational DEMATEL model for analysing the key success factors of hospital service quality. *Decision Making: Applications in Management and Engineering*, *1*(1), 121–142.

Rule, G. (2015). *Understanding the central bank balance sheet*. Handbooks.

Saeed, S., & Hassan, A. (2018). Inter-linkages between liquidity and stock returns: An empirical investigation through panel cointegration. *Pakistan Journal of Commerce and Social Sciences*, *12*(2), 617–637.

Sahuc, J. G. (2016). The ECB's asset purchase programme: A model-based evaluation. *Economics Letters*, *145*, 136–140. doi:10.1016/j.econlet.2016.06.009

Saidi, K., & Mbarek, M. B. (2016). Nuclear energy, renewable energy, CO2 emissions, and economic growth for nine developed countries: Evidence from panel Granger causality tests. *Progress in Nuclear Energy*, *88*, 364–374. doi:10.1016/j.pnucene.2016.01.018

Sajjad Ali Khan, M., Abdullah, S., Yousaf Ali, M., Hussain, I., & Farooq, M. (2018). Extension of TOPSIS method base on Choquet integral under interval-valued Pythagorean fuzzy environment. *Journal of Intelligent & Fuzzy Systems*, *34*(1), 267–282. doi:10.3233/JIFS-171164

Salahesh, T., Kazerooni, A., & Asgharpur, H. (2017). The Role of Interest Coverage Ratio in Monetary Transmission Mechanism: Evidence from Iran. *Journal of Economic & Management Perspectives, 11*(4), 409–420.

Salahuddin, M., Alam, K., & Ozturk, I. (2016). The effects of Internet usage and economic growth on CO2 emissions in OECD countries: A panel investigation. *Renewable & Sustainable Energy Reviews, 62*, 1226–1235. doi:10.1016/j.rser.2016.04.018

Saleh, A. S., Assaf, A. G., Ihalanayake, R., & Lung, S. (2015). A panel cointegration analysis of the impact of tourism on economic growth: Evidence from the Middle East region. *International Journal of Tourism Research, 17*(3), 209–220. doi:10.1002/jtr.1976

Salisu, A. A., & Ayinde, T. O. (2016). Testing the martingale difference hypothesis (MDH) with structural breaks: Evidence from foreign exchanges of Nigeria and South Africa. *Journal of African Business, 17*(3), 342–359. doi:10.1080/15228916.2016.1183274

Sapova, A., Porshakov, A., Andreev, A., & Shatilo, E. (2018). *Review of Methodological Specifics of Consumer Price Index Seasonal Adjustment in the Bank of Russia Under the inflation targeting regime, the main goal of the Bank of Russia is to maintain price stability. In order to analyse the options that the central bank can use to implement its monetary policy aimed at bringing inflation down to sustainable low levels it is necessary to understand, considering the available short-term statistical data, the dynamics of consumer prices and individual components of ... (No. wps33).* Bank of Russia.

Saraç, M., & Zeren, F. (2015). The dependency of Islamic bank rates on conventional bank interest rates: Further evidence from Turkey. *Applied Economics, 47*(7), 669–679. doi:10.1080/00036846.2014.978076

Saridakis, G., Mendoza, M. A., Muñoz Torres, R. I., & Glover, J. (2016). The relationship between self-employment and unemployment in the long-run: A panel cointegration approach allowing for breaks. *Journal of Economic Studies (Glasgow, Scotland), 43*(3), 358–379. doi:10.1108/JES-11-2013-0169

Sasikumar, P., & Vimal, K. E. K. (2019). Evaluation and Selection of Green Suppliers Using Fuzzy VIKOR and Fuzzy TOPSIS. In *Emerging Applications in Supply Chains for Sustainable Business Development* (pp. 202–218). IGI Global. doi:10.4018/978-1-5225-5424-0.ch012

Sayari, N., Sari, R., & Hammoudeh, S. (2018). The impact of value added components of GDP and FDI on economic freedom in Europe. *Economic Systems, 42*(2), 282–294. doi:10.1016/j.ecosys.2017.03.003

Sekmen, F., & Gokirmak, H. (2018). Causal relationship between internet use and economic development for selected Central Asian economies. *Theoretical and Applied Economics, 22*(616), 145-152.

Selim, H., Galal, A., Elbadawi, I., & Nugent, J. (2018, September). Does Central Bank Independence Matter in Arab Oil Exporters. *Economic Research Forum Working Papers* (No. 1223).

Şen, A. Y., Semiz, N., Güneş, B., Algül, D., Gergin, Z., & Dönmez, N. D. (2018, August). The Selection of a Process Management Software with Fuzzy Topsis Multiple Criteria Decision Making Method. In *The International Symposium for Production Research* (pp. 150-167). Springer.

Şengül, Ü., Eren, M., Shiraz, S. E., Gezder, V., & Şengül, A. B. (2015). Fuzzy TOPSIS method for ranking renewable energy supply systems in Turkey. *Renewable Energy, 75*, 617–625. doi:10.1016/j.renene.2014.10.045

Sennaroglu, B., Yilmazer, K. B., Tuzkaya, G., & Tuzkaya, U. R. (2018). A DEMATEL Integrated Interval Valued Intuitionistic Fuzzy PROMETHEE Approach for Parking Lots Evaluation. *Journal of Multiple-Valued Logic & Soft Computing, 30.*

Sennaroglu, B., & Celebi, G. V. (2018). A military airport location selection by AHP integrated PROMETHEE and VIKOR methods. *Transportation Research Part D, Transport and Environment, 59*, 160–173. doi:10.1016/j.trd.2017.12.022

Sepehri-Rad, A., Sadjadi, S., & Sadi-Nezhad, S. (2019). An application of DEMATEL for transaction authentication in online banking. *International Journal of Data and Network Science, 3*(2), 71–76. doi:10.5267/j.ijdns.2019.1.002

Setiawan, M. I., Surjokusumo, S., Ma'soem, D. M., Johan, J., Hasyim, C., Kurniasih, N., ... Nasihien, R. D. (2018, January). Business Centre Development Model of Airport Area in Supporting Airport Sustainability in Indonesia. *Journal of Physics: Conference Series, 954*(1), 012024. doi:10.1088/1742-6596/954/1/012024

Setyawati, I., Suroso, S., Suryanto, T., & Nurjannah, D. S. (2017). Does financial performance of Islamic banking is better? Panel Data Estimation. *European Research Studies, 20*(2), 592.

Seyedmohammadi, J., Sarmadian, F., Jafarzadeh, A. A., Ghorbani, M. A., & Shahbazi, F. (2018). Application of SAW, TOPSIS and fuzzy TOPSIS models in cultivation priority planning for maize, rapeseed and soybean crops. *Geoderma, 310*, 178–190. doi:10.1016/j.geoderma.2017.09.012

Sezer, S., & Abasiz, T. (2016). The Effect Of Information And Communication Technologies On Economic Growth In Oecd Countries. *Annals-Economy Series, 6*, 31–36.

Shafighi, N., Shaari, A. H., Gharleghi, B., Sarmidi, T., & Omar, K. (2016). Financial integration via panel cointegration approaches in ASEAN+ 5. *Journal of Economic Studies (Glasgow, Scotland), 43*(1), 2–15. doi:10.1108/JES-08-2014-0141

Shah, A., & Bahri, A. (2017). *Asymmetric and Symmetric Volatility Models for Exchange Rates in India–The Impact of the Net Purchase of US Dollars by the Central Bank and Net Inflows by Foreign Institutional Investors*. Academic Press.

Shahi, E., Alavipoor, F. S., & Karimi, S. (2018). The development of nuclear power plants by means of modified model of Fuzzy DEMATEL and GIS in Bushehr, Iran. *Renewable & Sustainable Energy Reviews, 83*, 33–49. doi:10.1016/j.rser.2017.10.073

Sharif, A., Raza, S. A., Ozturk, I., & Afshan, S. (2019). The dynamic relationship of renewable and nonrenewable energy consumption with carbon emission: A global study with the application of heterogeneous panel estimations. *Renewable Energy, 133*, 685–691. doi:10.1016/j.renene.2018.10.052

Sharma, M. P. (2016). Comprehensive study of Kisan Credit Card at Central Bank of India-A useful credit tool for rural development. *IBMRD's Journal of Management Research, 5*(1), 21–29.

Sharma, R., Sibal, R., & Sabharwal, S. (2019). Software Vulnerability Prioritization: A Comparative Study Using TOPSIS and VIKOR Techniques. In *System Performance and Management Analytics* (pp. 405–418). Singapore: Springer. doi:10.1007/978-981-10-7323-6_32

Sharma, Y. K., Mangla, S. K., Patil, P. P., & Uniyal, S. (2018). Sustainable Food Supply Chain Management Implementation Using DEMATEL Approach. In *Advances in Health and Environment Safety* (pp. 115–125). Singapore: Springer. doi:10.1007/978-981-10-7122-5_13

Shcherbakov, V., & Larsson, E. (2016). Radial basis function partition of unity methods for pricing vanilla basket options. *Computers & Mathematics with Applications (Oxford, England), 71*(1), 185–200. doi:10.1016/j.camwa.2015.11.007

Shen, F., Ma, X., Li, Z., Xu, Z., & Cai, D. (2018). An extended intuitionistic fuzzy TOPSIS method based on a new distance measure with an application to credit risk evaluation. *Information Sciences, 428*, 105–119. doi:10.1016/j.ins.2017.10.045

Shen, K. W., & Wang, J. Q. (2018). Z-VIKOR method based on a new comprehensive weighted distance measure of Z-number and its application. *IEEE Transactions on Fuzzy Systems, 26*(6), 3232–3245. doi:10.1109/TFUZZ.2018.2816581

Shiratsuka, S. (2010). Size and composition of the central bank balance sheet: Revisiting Japan's experience of the quantitative easing policy. *Monetary and Economic Studies, 28*(3), 79–105.

Shi, X., Li, J., Wang, F., Dinçer, H., & Yüksel, S. (2019). A Hybrid Decision-Making Approach for the Service and Financial-Based Measurement of Universal Health Coverage for the E7 Economies. *International Journal of Environmental Research and Public Health, 16*(18), 3295. doi:10.3390/ijerph16183295 PMID:31500288

Shojaei, P., Haeri, S. A. S., & Mohammadi, S. (2018). Airports evaluation and ranking model using Taguchi loss function, best-worst method and VIKOR technique. *Journal of Air Transport Management, 68*, 4–13. doi:10.1016/j.jairtraman.2017.05.006

Sianturi, M., Wulan, S., Suginam, S., Rohminatin, R., & Mesran, M. (2018). Implementasi Metode VIKOR Untuk Menentukan Bahan Kulit Terbaik Dalam Pembuatan Ikat Pinggang. *JURIKOM, 5*(1), 56–60.

Siddiqui, A., & Rehman, A. U. (2017). The human capital and economic growth nexus: In East and South Asia. *Applied Economics, 49*(28), 2697–2710. doi:10.1080/00036846.2016.1245841

Simab, M., Javadi, M. S., & Nezhad, A. E. (2018). Multi-objective programming of pumped-hydro-thermal scheduling problem using normal boundary intersection and VIKOR. *Energy*, *143*, 854–866. doi:10.1016/j.energy.2017.09.144

Sims, C. A. (2016, August). Fiscal policy, monetary policy and central bank independence. *Kansas Citi Fed Jackson Hole Conference*.

Siregar, D., Nurdiyanto, H., Sriadhi, S., Suita, D., Khair, U., Rahim, R., ... Siahaan, A. P. U. (2018, June). Multi-Attribute Decision Making with VIKOR Method for Any Purpose Decision. *Journal of Physics: Conference Series*, *1019*(1), 012034. doi:10.1088/1742-6596/1019/1/012034

Si, S. L., You, X. Y., Liu, H. C., & Zhang, P. (2018). DEMATEL technique: A systematic review of the state-of-the-art literature on methodologies and applications. *Mathematical Problems in Engineering*.

Song, L., & Mi, J. (2016). Port infrastructure and regional economic growth in China: A Granger causality analysis. *Maritime Policy & Management*, *43*(4), 456–468. doi:10.1080/03088839.2015.1134831

Ssali, M. W., Du, J., Mensah, I. A., & Hongo, D. O. (2019). Investigating the nexus among environmental pollution, economic growth, energy use, and foreign direct investment in 6 selected sub-Saharan African countries. *Environmental Science and Pollution Research International*, 1–16. PMID:30796658

Suganthi, L. (2018). Multi expert and multi criteria evaluation of sectoral investments for sustainable development: An integrated fuzzy AHP, VIKOR/DEA methodology. *Sustainable Cities and Society*, *43*, 144-156.

Sunder, J., Sunder, S. V., & Zhang, J. (2018). Balance sheet conservatism and debt contracting. *Contemporary Accounting Research*, *35*(1), 494–524. doi:10.1111/1911-3846.12356

Sun, G., Guan, X., Yi, X., & Zhou, Z. (2018). An innovative TOPSIS approach based on hesitant fuzzy correlation coefficient and its applications. *Applied Soft Computing*, *68*, 249–267. doi:10.1016/j.asoc.2018.04.004

Surovneva, K. A., & Sukhorukova, N. V. (2017). The role of the central bank of Russia in ensuring stability of the banking system. *Russian Journal of Agricultural and Socio-Economic Sciences*, *61*(1), 4–9. doi:10.18551/rjoas.2017-01.01

Sutrikanti, N., Situmorang, H., Fachrurrazi, F., Nurdiyanto, H., & Mesran, M. (2018). Implementasi Pendukung Keputusan Dalam Pemilihan Calon Peserta Cerdas Cermat Tingkat SMA Menerapkan Metode VIKOR. *JURIKOM*, *5*(2), 109–113.

Suzuki, Y., & Miah, M. D. (2017). China's non-performing bank loan crisis: The role of economic rents 1. In *Banking and Economic Rent in Asia* (pp. 71–85). Routledge. doi:10.4324/9781315558677-6

Tabassum, U., & Alam, S. (2018). Two way Panel Causality Analysis for Degree of Trade Openness and Size of City. *Journal of Basic and Applied Sciences*, *14*, 32–44. doi:10.6000/1927-5129.2018.14.06

Tagoe, N. A. (2016). The Emerging Role of Financial Intermediaries in the Financial Market of Ghana. *Bus Eco J*, *7*(253), 2.

Taleai, M., Safarpour, M., & Javadi, G. (2019). Potential Evaluation for Establishment of Solar Power Plants Using Multi-Criteria Decision Making Methods: OWA and TOPSIS (case study: Qazvin-Iran). *The Journal of Spatial Planning*, *22*(4), 1–27.

Tallman, E., & White, E. N. (2017, May). Monetary Policy When One Size Does Not Fit All: the Federal Reserve Banks and the Recession of 1920–1921. *Workshop on Monetary and Financial History Federal Reserve Bank of Atlanta and Emory University*.

Tang, H., Shi, Y., & Dong, P. (2019). Public blockchain evaluation using entropy and TOPSIS. *Expert Systems with Applications*, *117*, 204–210. doi:10.1016/j.eswa.2018.09.048

Tavana, M., Di Caprio, D., & Santos-Arteaga, F. J. (2018). An extended stochastic VIKOR model with decision maker's attitude towards risk. *Information Sciences*, *432*, 301–318. doi:10.1016/j.ins.2017.12.019

Taylor, M. W., Arner, D. W., & Gibson, E. C. (2019). Central Banks' New Macroprudential Consensus. The Oxford Handbook of the Economics of Central Banking, 482.

Thornton, D. L. (2019). The Fed and Short-Term Rates: Is It Open Market Operations, Open Mouth Operations or Interest Rate Smoothing? *Federal Reserve Bank of St. Louis Working Paper Series*, (1999-022).

Tian, G., Liu, X., Zhang, M., Yang, Y., Zhang, H., Lin, Y., ... Li, Z. (2019). Selection of take-back pattern of vehicle reverse logistics in China via Grey-DEMATEL and Fuzzy-VIKOR combined method. *Journal of Cleaner Production*, *220*, 1088–1100. doi:10.1016/j.jclepro.2019.01.086

Tian, G., Zhang, H., Zhou, M., & Li, Z. (2018). AHP, gray correlation, and TOPSIS combined approach to green performance evaluation of design alternatives. *IEEE Transactions on Systems, Man, and Cybernetics. Systems*, *48*(7), 1093–1105. doi:10.1109/TSMC.2016.2640179

Tian, Z. P., Wang, J. Q., & Zhang, H. Y. (2018). An integrated approach for failure mode and effects analysis based on fuzzy best-worst, relative entropy, and VIKOR methods. *Applied Soft Computing*, *72*, 636–646. doi:10.1016/j.asoc.2018.03.037

Tiba, S., & Frikha, M. (2018). Africa Is Rich, Africans Are Poor! A Blessing or Curse: An Application of Cointegration Techniques. *Journal of the Knowledge Economy*, 1-26.

Titiyal, R., Bhattacharya, S., & Thakkar, J. J. (2019). The distribution strategy selection for an e-tailer using a hybrid DANP VIKOR MCDM model. *Benchmarking. International Journal (Toronto, Ont.)*.

Titzck, S., & van den End, J. W. (2019). *The impact of size, composition and duration of the central bank balance sheet on inflation expectations and market prices*. Academic Press.

Toporowski, J. (2019). Open market operations. The Oxford Handbook of the Economics of Central Banking, 436.

Torğul, B., & Paksoy, T. (2019). A New Multi Objective Linear Programming Model for Lean and Green Supplier Selection with Fuzzy TOPSIS. In *Lean and Green Supply Chain Management* (pp. 101–141). Cham: Springer. doi:10.1007/978-3-319-97511-5_4

Trivedi, S. R., & Srinivasan, B. (2016). Impact of Central Bank Intervention in the Foreign Exchange Market: Evidence from India Using an Event Study Approach. *Economic Papers: A Journal of Applied Economics and Policy, 35*(4), 389-402.

Tsai, S. B. (2018). Using the DEMATEL model to explore the job satisfaction of research and development professionals in china's photovoltaic cell industry. *Renewable & Sustainable Energy Reviews*, *81*, 62–68. doi:10.1016/j.rser.2017.07.014

Tugcu, C. T. (2018). Panel Data Analysis in the Energy-Growth Nexus (EGN). In The Economics and Econometrics of the Energy-Growth Nexus (pp. 255-271). Academic Press.

Tuna, G., Göleç, N., & Tuna, V. E. (2017). The relationship between oil and stock prices: The case of developing and developed countries. *Theoretical & Applied Economics, 24*(4).

Tunay, K. B., Tunay, N., & Akhisar, İ. (2015). Interaction between Internet banking and bank performance: The case of Europe. *Procedia: Social and Behavioral Sciences*, *195*, 363–368. doi:10.1016/j.sbspro.2015.06.335

Tunay, K. B., & Yüksel, S. (2017). The relationship between corporate governance and foreign ownership of the banks in developing countries. *Contaduría y Administración*, *62*(5), 1627–1642. doi:10.1016/j.cya.2017.05.007

Tunay, N., Tunay, K. B., & Özataç, N. (2018). International Insurance Industry and Systemic Risk. In *Emerging Trends in Banking and Finance* (pp. 241–249). Cham: Springer. doi:10.1007/978-3-030-01784-2_15

Tunay, N., Yüksel, S., & Tunay, K. B. (2019). The Effects of Technology on Bank Performance in Advanced and Emerging Economies: An Empirical Analysis. In *Handbook of Research on Managerial Thinking in Global Business Economics* (pp. 263–280). IGI Global. doi:10.4018/978-1-5225-7180-3.ch015

Ture, H., Dogan, S., & Kocak, D. (2018). Assessing Euro 2020 Strategy Using Multi-criteria Decision Making Methods: VIKOR and TOPSIS. *Social Indicators Research*, 1–21.

Udude, C. C., & Nwachukwu, U. G. (2016). An Empirical Study of the Relationship between Interest Rate and Investment in Nigeria (1980-2013). *NG-Journal of Social Development*, *417*(3948), 1–17.

Umam, K., Sulastri, V. E., Andini, T., Sutiksno, D. U., & Mesran, M. (2018). Perancangan Sistem Pendukung Keputusan Penentuan Prioritas Produk Unggulan Daerah Menggunakan Metode VIKOR. *JURIKOM*, *5*(1), 43–49.

Upper, C., Patel, N., Villar, A., Arslan, Y., Jašová, M., Takáts, E., ... Yetman, J. (2016). *Why is inflation so high and volatile in Brazil? A primer*. Academic Press.

Uztürk, D., Büyüközkan, G., Negüs, A. F., & Öztek, M. Y. (2018). 2-Tuple Based VIKOR Methodology for Green Building Certification Selection. In *Proceedings of the World Congress on Engineering* (*Vol. 2*). Academic Press.

Valickova, P., Havranek, T., & Horvath, R. (2015). Financial development and economic growth: A meta-analysis. *Journal of Economic Surveys*, *29*(3), 506–526. doi:10.1111/joes.12068

Vidyarthi, H. (2015). Energy consumption and growth in South Asia: Evidence from a panel error correction model. *International Journal of Energy Sector Management*, *9*(3), 295–310. doi:10.1108/IJESM-10-2013-0002

Vinodh, S., Balagi, T. S., & Patil, A. (2016). A hybrid MCDM approach for agile concept selection using fuzzy DEMATEL, fuzzy ANP and fuzzy TOPSIS. *International Journal of Advanced Manufacturing Technology*, *83*(9-12), 1979–1987. doi:10.100700170-015-7718-6

Vollmer, U., & Wiese, H. (2016). Central bank standing facilities, counterparty risk, and OTC-interbank lending. *The North American Journal of Economics and Finance*, *36*, 101–122. doi:10.1016/j.najef.2015.12.003

Walter, S. (2017). Globalization and the demand-side of politics: How globalization shapes labor market risk perceptions and policy preferences. *Political Science Research and Methods*, *5*(1), 55–80. doi:10.1017/psrm.2015.64

Wang, B., Song, J., Ren, J., Li, K., Duan, H., & Wang, X. E. (2019). Selecting sustainable energy conversion technologies for agricultural residues: A fuzzy AHP-VIKOR based prioritization from life cycle perspective. *Resources, Conservation and Recycling*, *142*, 78–87. doi:10.1016/j.resconrec.2018.11.011

Wang, J. G., & Yang, J. (2016). Enjoy "Free Rides" with the "Core Firms"—Supply Chain Financing. In *Financing without Bank Loans* (pp. 85–95). Singapore: Springer. doi:10.1007/978-981-10-0901-3_7

Wang, J., Wei, G., & Lu, M. (2018). An extended VIKOR method for multiple criteria group decision making with triangular fuzzy neutrosophic numbers. *Symmetry*, *10*(10), 497. doi:10.3390ym10100497

Wang, L. (2018). Monetary-fiscal policy interactions under asset purchase programs: Some comparative evidence. *Economic Modelling*, *73*, 208–221. doi:10.1016/j.econmod.2018.03.019

Wang, L., Cao, Q., & Zhou, L. (2018). Research on the influencing factors in coal mine production safety based on the combination of DEMATEL and ISM. *Safety Science*, *103*, 51–61. doi:10.1016/j.ssci.2017.11.007

Wang, L., Zhang, H. Y., Wang, J. Q., & Li, L. (2018). Picture fuzzy normalized projection-based VIKOR method for the risk evaluation of construction project. *Applied Soft Computing*, *64*, 216–226. doi:10.1016/j.asoc.2017.12.014

Wang, S., Fang, C., Wang, Y., Huang, Y., & Ma, H. (2015). Quantifying the relationship between urban development intensity and carbon dioxide emissions using a panel data analysis. *Ecological Indicators*, *49*, 121–131. doi:10.1016/j.ecolind.2014.10.004

Wang, S., Liu, Q., Yuksel, S., & Dincer, H. (2019). Hesitant Linguistic Term Sets-Based Hybrid Analysis for Renewable Energy Investments. *IEEE Access: Practical Innovations, Open Solutions*, *7*, 114223–114235. doi:10.1109/ACCESS.2019.2935427

Wang, Y., Chen, L., & Kubota, J. (2016). The relationship between urbanization, energy use and carbon emissions: Evidence from a panel of Association of Southeast Asian Nations (ASEAN) countries. *Journal of Cleaner Production*, *112*, 1368–1374. doi:10.1016/j.jclepro.2015.06.041

Wang, Y., Chen, W., Zhao, M., & Wang, B. (2019). Analysis of the influencing factors on CO 2 emissions at different urbanization levels: Regional difference in China based on panel estimation. *Natural Hazards*, 1–19.

Wang, Y., Kang, Y., Wang, J., & Xu, L. (2017). Panel estimation for the impacts of population-related factors on CO2 emissions: A regional analysis in China. *Ecological Indicators*, *78*, 322–330. doi:10.1016/j.ecolind.2017.03.032

Wang, Z., Gao, J. M., Wang, R. X., Chen, K., Gao, Z. Y., & Zheng, W. (2018). Failure mode and effects analysis by using the house of reliability-based rough VIKOR approach. *IEEE Transactions on Reliability*, *67*(1), 230–248. doi:10.1109/TR.2017.2778316

Wang, Z., Xu, G., Wang, H., & Ren, J. (2019). Distributed energy system for sustainability transition: A comprehensive assessment under uncertainties based on interval multi-criteria decision making method by coupling interval DEMATEL and interval VIKOR. *Energy*, *169*, 750–761. doi:10.1016/j.energy.2018.12.105

Wanke, P., Azad, M. A. K., Barros, C. P., & Hassan, M. K. (2016). Predicting efficiency in Islamic banks: An integrated multicriteria decision making (MCDM) approach. *Journal of International Financial Markets, Institutions and Money*, *45*, 126–141. doi:10.1016/j.intfin.2016.07.004

Wijesiri, M., Martínez-Campillo, A., & Wanke, P. (2019). Is there a trade-off between social and financial performance of public commercial banks in India? A multi-activity DEA model with shared inputs and undesirable outputs. *Review of Managerial Science*, *13*(2), 417–442. doi:10.100711846-017-0255-y

Wildau, G. (2017). China Central Bank Chief Warns of 'Minsky Moment': Risk of Excessive Optimism as China Reports Strong Headline GDP Growth. *The Financial Times*.

Williams, J. C. (2018). *Moving toward'normal'US monetary policy: remarks at the Joint Bank Indonesia-Federal Reserve Bank of New York Central Banking Forum, Nusa Dua, Indonesia* (No. 296). Academic Press.

Wu, Y., Zhang, B., Xu, C., & Li, L. (2018). Site selection decision framework using fuzzy ANP-VIKOR for large commercial rooftop PV system based on sustainability perspective. *Sustainable Cities and Society, 40*, 454-470.

Wu, J. C., & Xia, F. D. (2016). Measuring the macroeconomic impact of monetary policy at the zero lower bound. *Journal of Money, Credit and Banking*, *48*(2-3), 253–291. doi:10.1111/jmcb.12300

Wu, M., Li, C., Fan, J., Wang, X., & Wu, Z. (2018). Assessing the global productive efficiency of Chinese banks using the cross-efficiency interval and VIKOR. *Emerging Markets Review*, *34*, 77–86. doi:10.1016/j.ememar.2017.10.005

Wuryandani, G., & Mardiani, I. (2015). Surveys as leading information to support central bank policy formulation: the case of Indonesia. *IFC Bulletins Chapters, 39*.

Wu, T., Liu, X., & Liu, F. (2018). An interval type-2 fuzzy TOPSIS model for large scale group decision making problems with social network information. *Information Sciences*, *432*, 392–410. doi:10.1016/j.ins.2017.12.006

Wu, Z., Xu, J., Jiang, X., & Zhong, L. (2019). Two MAGDM models based on hesitant fuzzy linguistic term sets with possibility distributions: VIKOR and TOPSIS. *Information Sciences*, *473*, 101–120. doi:10.1016/j.ins.2018.09.038

Wyplosz, C. (2019). Limits to the independence of the ECB. *Review of World Economics*, 1–7.

Xi, N., Ding, N., & Wang, Y. (2005). How required reserve ratio affects distribution and velocity of money. *Physica A*, *357*(3-4), 543–555. doi:10.1016/j.physa.2005.04.014

Xu, D., Tang, S., & Guttman, D. (2019). China's campaign-style Internet finance governance: Causes, effects, and lessons learned for new information-based approaches to governance. *Computer Law & Security Review*, *35*(1), 3–14. doi:10.1016/j.clsr.2018.11.002

Yadav, D. K., & Barve, A. (2018). Segmenting critical success factors of humanitarian supply chains using fuzzy DEMATEL. *Benchmarking: An International Journal*, *25*(2), 400–425. doi:10.1108/BIJ-10-2016-0154

Yadav, G., Seth, D., & Desai, T. N. (2018). Prioritising solutions for Lean Six Sigma adoption barriers through fuzzy AHP-modified TOPSIS framework. *International Journal of Lean Six Sigma*, *9*(3), 270–300. doi:10.1108/IJLSS-06-2016-0023

Yadegaridehkordi, E., Hourmand, M., Nilashi, M., Shuib, L., Ahani, A., & Ibrahim, O. (2018). Influence of big data adoption on manufacturing companies' performance: An integrated DEMATEL-ANFIS approach. *Technological Forecasting and Social Change*, *137*, 199–210. doi:10.1016/j.techfore.2018.07.043

Yang, C., Lan, S., & Tseng, M. L. (2019). Coordinated development path of metropolitan logistics and economy in Belt and Road using DEMATEL–Bayesian analysis. *International Journal of Logistics Research and Applications*, *22*(1), 1–24. doi:10.1080/13675567.2018.1439907

Yang, W., Pang, Y., Shi, J., & Wang, C. (2018). Linguistic hesitant intuitionistic fuzzy decision-making method based on VIKOR. *Neural Computing & Applications*, *29*(7), 613–626. doi:10.100700521-016-2526-y

Yang, W., Xu, K., Lian, J., Ma, C., & Bin, L. (2018). Integrated flood vulnerability assessment approach based on TOPSIS and Shannon entropy methods. *Ecological Indicators*, *89*, 269–280. doi:10.1016/j.ecolind.2018.02.015

Yazdi, M. (2018). Risk assessment based on novel intuitionistic fuzzy-hybrid-modified TOPSIS approach. *Safety Science*, *110*, 438–448. doi:10.1016/j.ssci.2018.03.005

Yildiz, A., & Uğur, L. (2018). Evaluation of 3D printers used in additive manufacturing by using interval type-2 fuzzy TOPSIS method. *Journal of Engineering Research and Applied Science*, *7*(2), 984–993.

Yılmaz, E., & Aslan, T. (2016). Usage Derivatives In Management Financial Risks: A Study On Firms In Borsa Istanbul (Bist) 100 Stock Index. *Journal of Business Research*, *8*(1), 663–678.

Yimer, M. M. (2018). Lending and Cash Required Reserve: Empirical Evidence from Ethiopian Commercial Bank. *European Scientific Journal, ESJ*, *14*(13), 179. doi:10.19044/esj.2018.v14n13p179

Yu, C. P. (2016). Why are there always inconsistent answers to the relation between the PPI and CPI? Re-examination using Panel Data Analysis. *International Review of Accounting, Banking & Finance, 8*(1).

Yüksel, S. (2015). *Bankacılık krizlerinin erken uyarı sinyalleri: Türkiye üzerine bir uygulama*. Academic Press.

Yüksel, S. (2016a). Bankacılık Krizlerinin Erken Uyarı Sinyalleri: Türkiye Üzerine Bir Uygulama. *Akademisyen Kitabevi, 1*.

Yüksel, S., & Adalı, Z. (2017). *Determining influencing factors of unemployment in Turkey with MARS method*. Academic Press.

Yüksel, S., & Kavak, P. T. (2019). Do Financial Investment Decisions Affect Economic Development?: An Analysis on Mortgage Loans in Turkey. In Handbook of Research on Global Issues in Financial Communication and Investment Decision Making (pp. 168-191). IGI Global.

Yüksel, S., & Oktar, S. (2017). *Okun yasasının farklı gelişme düzeyindeki ülkelere ilişkin ekonometrik analizi*. Academic Press.

Yüksel, S., & Zengin, S. (2016b). *Causality relationship between import, export and growth rate in developing countries*. Academic Press.

Yüksel, S., Canöz, İ., & Adalı, Z. (2017). Türkiye'deki Mevduat Bankalarının Fiyat-Kazanç Oranını Etkileyen Değişkenlerin Mars Yöntemi İle Belirlenmesi. *Fiscaoeconomia*, (3).

Yüksel, S., Özsarı, M., & Canöz, İ. (2016). *Influencing factors of currency risk of deposit banks in Turkey by using probit method*. Academic Press.

Yüksel, S., Zengin, S., & Kartal, M. T. (2016). Banka Personelinin Teftiş Kuruluna Bakış Açısının Değerlendirilmesi [An Evaluation of the Perspectives of Bank Personnel Regarding Internal Audit Department]. *Finans Politik & Ekonomik Yorumlar, 53*(622).

Yüksel, S. (2016). Bankaların Takipteki Krediler Oranını Belirleyen Faktörler: Türkiye İçin Bir Model Önerisi. *Bankacılar Dergisi, 98*, 41–56.

Yüksel, S. (2016). Rusya Ekonomisinde Büyüme, Issizlik ve Enflasyon Arasindaki Nedensellik Iliskileri/The Causality Relationship Between Growth, Unemployment and Inflation in Russian Economy. *Finans Politik & Ekonomik Yorumlar, 53*(614), 43.

Yüksel, S. (2016). Türkiye'de Cari İşlemler Açığının Belirleyicileri: Mars Yöntemi ile Bir İnceleme. *Bankacılar Dergisi, 96*(27), 102–121.

Yüksel, S. (2017). Determinants of the credit risk in developing countries after economic crisis: A case of Turkish banking sector. In *Global financial crisis and its ramifications on capital markets* (pp. 401–415). Cham: Springer. doi:10.1007/978-3-319-47021-4_28

Yüksel, S. (2017). Strategies Out of Global Recession in Emerging Markets: An Application for 2008 Global Crisis. In *Global Business Strategies in Crisis* (pp. 57–75). Cham: Springer. doi:10.1007/978-3-319-44591-5_5

Yüksel, S. (2017). The impacts of research and development expenses on export and economic growth. *International Business and Accounting Research Journal, 1*(1), 1–8. doi:10.15294/ibarj.v1i1.1

Yüksel, S., & Adalı, Z. (2017). Farklı kredi türleri ve ekonomik büyüme arasındaki nedensellik ilişkisinin belirlenmesi: Türkiye üzerine bir uygulama. *Politik Ekonomik Kuram, 1*(1), 1–21. doi:10.30586/pek.319282

Yüksel, S., & Canöz, İ. (2017). Does Islamic Banking Contribute to Economic Growth and Industrial Development in Turkey. *Ikonomika, 2*(1), 93–102. doi:10.24042/febi.v2i1.945

Yüksel, S., Canöz, İ., & Özsarı, M. (2017). Causality relationship between interest rate of deposit banks and profit share rate of islamic banks in turkey. *IKONOMIKA, 2*(2), 131–148. doi:10.24042/febi.v2i2.1894

Yüksel, S., Dinçer, H., & Emir, Ş. (2017). Comparing the performance of Turkish deposit banks by using DEMATEL, Grey Relational Analysis (GRA) and MOORA approaches. *World Journal of Applied Economics, 3*(2), 26–47. doi:10.22440/wjae.3.2.2

Yüksel, S., Dincer, H., & Hacioglu, U. (2015). CAMELS-based Determinants for the Credit Rating of Turkish Deposit Banks. *International Journal of Finance & Banking Studies, 4*(4), 1.

Yüksel, S., Dinçer, H., & Meral, Y. (2019). Financial Analysis of International Energy Trade: A Strategic Outlook for EU-15. *Energies, 12*(3), 431. doi:10.3390/en12030431

Yüksel, S., Mukhtarov, S., & Mammadov, E. (2016). Comparing the efficiency of Turkish and Azerbaijani banks: An application with data envelopment analysis. *International Journal of Economics and Financial Issues*, *6*(3).

Yüksel, S., Mukhtarov, S., Mammadov, E., & Özsarı, M. (2018). Determinants of Profitability in the Banking Sector: An Analysis of Post-Soviet Countries. *Economies*, *6*(3), 41. doi:10.3390/economies6030041

Yüksel, S., & Özsarı, M. (2016). *Türkiye'deki Bireysel Krediler ile Enflasyon ve Cari İşlemler Açığı Arasındaki Nedensellik İlişkisinin İncelenmesi*. Roma: Econworld Konferansı.

Yüksel, S., & Özsarı, M. (2017). Türkiye'nin Kredi Notunu Etkileyen Faktörlerin MARS Yöntemi İle Belirlenmesi. *Politik Ekonomik Kuram*, *1*(2), 16–31. doi:10.30586/pek.356929

Yüksel, S., & Özsari, M. (2017a). Türkiye Cumhuriyet Merkez Bankası'nın Döviz Rezervlerine Etki Eden Makroekonomik Faktörlerin Belirlenmesi. *Finans Politik & Ekonomik Yorumlar*, *54*(631), 41–53.

Yüksel, S., & Özsari, M. (2017b). Identifying the Factors Influence Turkish Deposit Banks to Join Corporate Social Responsibility Activities by Using Panel Probit Method. *International Journal of Finance & Banking Studies*, *6*(1), 39.

Yüksel, S., & Zengin, S. (2016a). leading indicators of 2008 global crisis: An analysis with logit and mars methods. *Finansal Araştırmalar ve Çalışmalar Dergisi*, *8*(15), 495–518.

Yuksel, S., & Zengin, S. (2017). Influencing factors of net interest margin in Turkish banking sector. *International Journal of Economics and Financial Issues*, *7*(1).

Yüksel, S., Zengin, S., & Kartal, M. T. (2016). Identifying the macroeconomic factors influencing credit card usage in Turkey by using MARS method. *China-USA Business Review*, *15*(12), 611–615.

Yurdakul, M., & İç, Y. T. (2018). Development of a multi-level performance measurement model for manufacturing companies using a modified version of the fuzzy TOPSIS approach. *Soft Computing*, *22*(22), 7491–7503. doi:10.100700500-018-3449-6

Zaghdoudi, T. (2017). Internet usage, renewable energy, electricity consumption and economic growth: Evidence from developed countries. *Economics Bulletin Access Econ*, *37*(3), 1612–1619.

Zaman, K., Abdullah, A., Khan, A., Nasir, M. R. M., Hamzah, T. A. A. T., & Hussain, S. (2016). Dynamic linkages among energy consumption, environment, health and wealth in BRICS countries: Green growth key to sustainable development. *Renewable & Sustainable Energy Reviews*, *56*, 1263–1271. doi:10.1016/j.rser.2015.12.010

Zaman, K., Moemen, M. A. E., & Islam, T. (2017). Dynamic linkages between tourism transportation expenditures, carbon dioxide emission, energy consumption and growth factors: Evidence from the transition economies. *Current Issues in Tourism*, *20*(16), 1720–1735. doi:10.1080/13683500.2015.1135107

Zaman, K., Shahbaz, M., Loganathan, N., & Raza, S. A. (2016). Tourism development, energy consumption and Environmental Kuznets Curve: Trivariate analysis in the panel of developed and developing countries. *Tourism Management*, *54*, 275–283. doi:10.1016/j.tourman.2015.12.001

Zare, A., Feylizadeh, M., Mahmoudi, A., & Liu, S. (2018). Suitable computerized maintenance management system selection using grey group TOPSIS and fuzzy group VIKOR: A case study. *Decision Science Letters*, *7*(4), 341–358. doi:10.5267/j.dsl.2018.3.002

Zareie, A., Sheikhahmadi, A., & Khamforoosh, K. (2018). Influence maximization in social networks based on TOPSIS. *Expert Systems with Applications*, *108*, 96–107. doi:10.1016/j.eswa.2018.05.001

Zengin, S., & Yüksel, S. (2016). *Likidite riskini etkileyen faktörler: Türk bankacılık sektörü üzerine bir inceleme*. Academic Press.

Zengin, S., & Yüksel, S. (2016). A comparison of the views of internal controllers/auditors and branch/call center personnel of the banks for operational risk: A case for Turkish banking sector. *International Journal of Finance & Banking Studies*, *5*(4), 10.

Zengin, S., Yüksel, S., & Kartal, M. T. (2018). Understanding the Factors that aFFect Foreign direct investment in Turkey by Using mars method. *Finansal Araştırmalar ve Çalışmalar Dergisi*, *10*(18), 1309–1123.

Zeng, S., Chen, S. M., & Kuo, L. W. (2019). Multiattribute decision making based on novel score function of intuitionistic fuzzy values and modified VIKOR method. *Information Sciences*.

Zhang, C., & Zhou, X. (2016). Does foreign direct investment lead to lower CO2 emissions? Evidence from a regional analysis in China. *Renewable & Sustainable Energy Reviews*, *58*, 943–951. doi:10.1016/j.rser.2015.12.226

Zhao, J., & Gong, Y. (2018, April). Data Driven Topsis Method and Its Application in E-commerce APP. In *Proceedings of the 2018 International Conference on Big Data and Computing*(pp. 49-52). ACM. 10.1145/3220199.3220214

Zhou, F., Wang, X., & Goh, M. (2018). Fuzzy extended VIKOR-based mobile robot selection model for hospital pharmacy. *International Journal of Advanced Robotic Systems*, *15*(4), 1729881418787315. doi:10.1177/1729881418787315

Zhou, F., Wang, X., Lim, M. K., He, Y., & Li, L. (2018). Sustainable recycling partner selection using fuzzy DEMATEL-AEW-FVIKOR: A case study in small-and-medium enterprises (SMEs). *Journal of Cleaner Production*, *196*, 489–504. doi:10.1016/j.jclepro.2018.05.247

Zhou, W., Yin, W., Peng, X., Liu, F., & Yang, F. (2018). Comprehensive evaluation of land reclamation and utilisation schemes based on a modified VIKOR method for surface mines. *International Journal of Mining, Reclamation and Environment*, *32*(2), 93–108. doi:10.1080/17480930.2016.1228031

# About the Authors

**Hasan Dinçer** is an Associate Professor of finance at Istanbul Medipol University, Faculty of Economics and Administrative Sciences, Istanbul-Turkey. Dr. Dincer has BAs in Financial Markets and Investment Management at Marmara University. He received PhD in Finance and Banking with his thesis entitled "The Effect of Changes on the Competitive Strategies of New Service Development in the Banking Sector". He has work experience in the finance sector as a portfolio specialist and his major academic studies focuses on financial instruments, performance evaluation, and economics. He is the executive editor of the International Journal of Finance and Banking Studies (IJFBS) and the founder member of the Society for the Study of Business and Finance (SSBF). His research interests lie in banking, finance and financial crisis. He has more than 150 scientific articles and some of them are indexed in SSCI, Scopus and Econlit. Also, he is the editor of some books that were published by Springer and IGI Global.

**Serhat Yüksel** is Associate Professor of finance in İstanbul Medipol University. Before this position, he worked as a senior internal auditor for seven years in Finansbank, Istanbul-Turkey and 1 year in Konya Food and Agriculture University as an assistant professor. Dr. Yüksel has a BS in Business Administration (in English) from Yeditepe University (2006) with full scholarship. He got his master degree from the economics in Boğaziçi University (2008). He also has a PhD in Banking from Marmara University (2015). His research interests lie in banking, finance and financial crisis. He has more than 120 scientific articles and some of them are indexed in SSCI, Scopus and Econlit. Also, he is the editor of some books that were published by Springer and IGI Global.

# Index

www.ingramcontent.com/pod-product-compliance
Lightning Source LLC
LaVergne TN
LVHW061539290926
849162LV00004B/850